W.E.B. DuBois, Race, and the City

W.E.B. DuBois, Race, and the City

The Philadelphia Negro and Its Legacy

EDITED BY

Michael B. Katz
and Thomas J. Sugrue

PENN

University of Pennsylvania Press

Philadelphia

10 9 8 7 6 5 4 3 2 1

Published by
University of Pennsylvania Press
Philadelphia, Pennsylvania 19104-4011

Library of Congress Cataloging-in-Publication Data

W.E.B. DuBois, race, and the city : the Philadelphia Negro and its
legacy / edited by Michael B. Katz and Thomas J. Sugrue.
    p.   cm.
  Includes bibliographical references and index.
  ISBN 0-8122-3362-X (alk. paper). —
ISBN 0-8122-1593-1 (pbk. : alk. paper)
  1. Du Bois, W. E. B. (William Edward Burghardt), 1868–1963
Philadelphia Negro — Congresses. 2. Afro-Americans — Pennsylvania —
Philadelphia — Congresses. 3. Domestics — Pennsylvania —
Philadelphia — Congresses. 4. Philadelphia (Pa.) — Social
conditions. — Congresses. I. Katz, Michael B., 1939– .
II. Sugrue, Thomas J., 1962– . III. Title: WEB DuBois, race, and
the city.
F158.9.N4W16   1998
305.896′073074811 — DC21   97-47731
                             CIP

Contents

Preface   vii

Note on the Editions   xi

Introduction: The Context of *The Philadelphia Negro*   1
MICHAEL B. KATZ AND THOMAS J. SUGRUE

Part I: DuBois and the Color Line   39

1. "The World Was Thinking Wrong About Race":
The Philadelphia Negro and Nineteenth-Century Science   41
MIA BAY

2. W.E.B. DuBois's Archaeology of Race: Re-Reading
"The Conservation of Races"   61
THOMAS C. HOLT

3. Giant Steps: W.E.B. DuBois and the Historical Enterprise   77
ROBERT GREGG

Part II: DuBois's Philadelphia   101

4. "Lifework" and Its Limits: The Problem of Labor in
The Philadelphia Negro   103
JACQUELINE JONES

5. "The 'Brotherly Love' for Which This City Is Proverbial
Should Extend to All": The Everyday Lives of Working-Class
Women in Philadelphia and Atlanta in the 1890s   127
TERA W. HUNTER

Part III: The Problem of the Twentieth Century   153

6. The "Philadelphia Negro" Then and Now: Implications
for Empirical Research   155
ANTONIO MCDANIEL

7. Operation Street Corner: The Wharton Centre and the
Juvenile Gang Problem in Philadelphia, 1945–1958   195
V. P. FRANKLIN

8. The Global Inner City: Toward a Historical Analysis   217
CARL HUSEMOLLER NIGHTINGALE

9. Drugs and Violence in the Inner City   259
ELIJAH ANDERSON

Contributors   279
Index   281

Preface

In 1896 W.E.B. DuBois arrived at the University of Pennsylvania to begin the research that resulted in his great book, *The Philadelphia Negro*. This volume celebrates the centenary of his project. With the assistance of a grant from the National Endowment for the Humanities, the editors invited a number of scholars to place *The Philadelphia Negro* in its intellectual and social contexts and to reflect on the book's meaning for interpreting the intersections of race and the city today. The scholars presented their essays at a lively two-day seminar at the University of Pennsylvania in May 1995; they subsequently revised them for this volume. The editors have added an interpretive introduction.

In his methodologically innovative and empirically rich study, DuBois carefully mapped every black residence, church, and business in the city's Seventh Ward; pored through censuses to paint a detailed portrait of black Philadelphia's occupational and family structure; interviewed employers and black workers; and chronicled extensive workplace discrimination. From personal observations and city records he also unblinkingly told the story of crime and violence among the city's poorest residents. Whereas many subsequent commentators have pointed to these achievements, they have neglected DuBois's close attention to history. For DuBois, an unbroken chain linked the contemporary experience of African Americans to a past of slavery and racial oppression. DuBois stressed an important point re-emphasized by the authors of each of the following essays: the role of history understood both as a legacy and as continuous change — as a story of both structure and agency — in shaping the fate of African Americans. The essays situate DuBois and his pioneering study in the intellectual milieu of the late nineteenth century. They consider his contributions to subsequent social scientific and historical studies of the city. Motivated by DuBois's deeply humane vision of racial equality, they build on *The Philadelphia Negro*, reexamining DuBois's city, past and present, bringing together ethnography, historical research, and statistical analysis. In the end, *The Philadelphia Negro* does not tell a story about timelessness, of the depressing sameness of past and present. For just as DuBois looked out onto a dramatically changing world, restructured by global capitalism and powerfully resurgent forces of race, so too do we.

The following essays are divided into three sections. In the first section, Mia Bay, Thomas Holt, and Robert Gregg situate *The Philadelphia Negro* in the development of W.E.B. DuBois's thought, particularly regarding the vexing issue of race. DuBois's Philadelphia research, they show, was pivotal in his reformulation of the concept of race, one of his most important contributions to twentieth-century social thought. In the second section, Jacqueline Jones and Tera Hunter revisit DuBois's Philadelphia. Their essays consider the operation of the city's labor market, which DuBois called the "centre and kernel" of the "Negro problem." And they move beyond the limitations of DuBois's work to consider the everyday agency of poor African Americans in resisting the oppression of race and class. In the third section, Antonio McDaniel, V. P. Franklin, Carl Nightingale, and Elijah Anderson take up many of the central themes DuBois researched, drawing important links between DuBois's city and ours, and highlighting the profound transformations that have affected the lives of inner-city blacks since the turn of the century. Together, we hope these essays lead to a further reappraisal of DuBois's seminal work and to renewed interest in the problems of urban African Americans past and present.

A number of individuals and institutions made the publication of this book possible. Mary Frances Berry of the University of Pennsylvania and Robin D. G. Kelley of New York University helped develop the ideas for the conference, commented on essays, and provided invaluable support. In addition, Farah Griffin, Kenneth Kusmer, Barbara Savage, and Eric Schneider offered searching critiques of draft chapters. Mark Frazier Lloyd tracked down documents in the University of Pennsylvania Archives. A number of essays benefited from the careful editing of Russ Kazal and Frances Kohler. Finally, Cindy Crumrine expertly copyedited the entire manuscript.

The conference on W.E.B. DuBois and *The Philadelphia Negro* that led to this volume was supported by National Endowment for the Humanities Grant RX-21550-94. Special thanks to David Coder of the NEH for his assistance. We received additional funding from the Social Science Research Council's Committee for Research on the Urban Underclass, through the support of the Rockefeller Foundation, and from the Dean of the Faculty of Arts and Sciences of the University of Pennsylvania. Penn's History Department and Urban Studies Program graciously provided facilities and staff. Debra Shutika energetically coordinated the conference and Deborah Broadnax, Sheila Dickson, Hannah Poole, and Erin Steigler offered administrative support. Larry Goldsmith, Elaine Simon, Dana Barron, Kirby Randolph, Katie Rode, Charles Stewart, and Lorrin Thomas also helped greatly along the way.

All royalties from the sale of this volume will be donated to the Social Studies Department at West Philadelphia High School, whose teachers carry forth in endeavors W.E.B. DuBois certainly would have admired. They persevere against formidable odds in an era when cities, and especially their African American children, have been pushed to the economic and political margins.

Note on the Editions of *The Philadelphia Negro*

DuBois's book has appeared in numerous editions since its first publication in 1899. Almost all have been facsimile reprints of the first edition, and the page citations in this volume are to those page numbers. Introductory material to the editions listed below is cited as needed.

W.E. Burghardt DuBois. *The Philadelphia Negro: A Social Study.* Together with a Special Report on Domestic Service, by Isabel Eaton. Publication of the University of Pennsylvania, Series in Political Economy and Public Law, no. 14. Philadelphia: Published for the University, 1899.

W.E.B. DuBois. *The Philadelphia Negro: A Social Study.* Together with a Special Report on Domestic Service, by Isabel Eaton. Publications of the University of Pennsylvania, Series in Political Economy and Public Law, no. 14. New York: B. Blom, 1967.

W.E.B. DuBois. *The Philadelphia Negro: A Social Study.* Together with a Special Report on Domestic Service, by Isabel Eaton. Introduction by E. Digby Baltzell. New York: Schocken Books, 1967.

W.E.B. DuBois. *The Philadelphia Negro: A Social Study.* New Introduction by Herbert Aptheker. Millwood, N.Y.: Kraus-Thomson, 1973.

W.E.B. DuBois. *The Philadelphia Negro: A Social Study.* With a New Introduction by Elijah Anderson. Together with a Special Report on Domestic Service, by Isabel Eaton. Philadelphia: University of Pennsylvania Press, 1996.

Figure 1. Saint Mary Street, 1875. Blacks and whites lived together in poverty in the crowded alleyways and courtyards of Philadelphia's Seventh Ward. Places like Saint Mary Street attracted the attention of reformers concerned about overcrowding, crime, liquor, and vice, all depicted here. Courtesy of The Library Company of Philadelphia.

Introduction

The Context of *The Philadelphia Negro*

*The City, the Settlement House Movement, and
the Rise of the Social Sciences*

Michael B. Katz and Thomas J. Sugrue

In June 1896, W.E.B. DuBois, then twenty-eight years old and married three weeks, received a telegram from Charles C. Harrison, acting provost of the University of Pennsylvania: "Are ready to appoint you for one year at nine hundred dollars maximum payable monthly from date of service. If you wish appointment will write definitely." Harrison had piqued the interest of one of nineteenth-century America's most promising young intellectuals. DuBois had risen rapidly from humble origins in Great Barrington, Massachusetts. Educated at Fisk and in Berlin, he became the first African American to be awarded a doctorate by Harvard. Eager to escape his first job at parochial Wilberforce University in Ohio, where he had been teaching classics for two years, DuBois moved with his wife Nina into an apartment in the Philadelphia Settlement at Seventh and Lombard Streets, near the heart of one of the city's largest African American neighborhoods.[1]

Arriving in Philadelphia in August of 1896, the DuBoises found themselves in a city that was the antithesis of Wilberforce. Late nineteenth-century Philadelphia was an industrial giant, the second largest city in the United States. Traveling from the train station to the Philadelphia Settlement House, DuBois undoubtedly sensed the dynamism, the promise, and the deep-rooted problems of a city undergoing wrenching economic changes. For most of the nineteenth century, Philadelphia had been a premier shipping and trading center, an outlet for the rich agricultural land of New Jersey, Lancaster County (Pennsylvania), and points to the west. Ships plied the Delaware River, loaded with southern cotton bound for the city; filled with corn, cloth, and shoes as they headed down the coast to Newport, Charleston, and Savannah. The region's transportation hub, by the 1850s

Philadelphia had also become the heart of the nation's burgeoning railroad industry. Rail lines connected Philadelphia to Pennsylvania's rich veins of anthracite coal, only ninety miles to the northwest. And they connected the city to the steel and iron manufacturers of Pittsburgh and Wheeling, several hundred miles to the west. As the headquarters of the massive Pennsylvania Railroad empire, Philadelphia nurtured a business elite whose influence spread across the nation.

By the 1890s Philadelphia had achieved prominence as a center of industrial innovation and specialization. A national center of textile and clothing manufacturing, the city was home to one of the country's largest agglomerations of lace makers, carpet weavers, and fabric manufacturers. But no one industry predominated. The city housed a remarkably diverse range of manufacturers, including machine tool and hardware production, publishing, and tanning. Heavier industries also employed thousands of Philadelphians: steelmaking and forging, shipbuilding, and railroad engine assembly. Countless other specialty firms clustered in the city: Philadelphia was an important center of the American cigar industry, a major producer of dental instruments and cutlery, home to the world-famous Stetson hat makers, and a major producer of fairground carousels. Dozens of food processing plants, breweries, and dairies catered to the needs of the city's burgeoning population of laborers.[2]

When he wrote *The Philadelphia Negro* DuBois had grounds for optimism as Philadelphia rebounded from the depression of 1893–96. He marveled at the rapid growth the city had enjoyed in the decades following the Civil War, writing that "new methods of conducting business and industry are now rife. . . . Manufacturing of all kinds has increased by leaps and bounds in the city, and to-day employs three times as many men as in 1860, paying three hundred millions annually in wages; hacks and expressmen have turned into vast inter-urban businesses: restaurants have become palatial hotels — the whole face of business is being gradually transformed" (p. 45). The industrial city of the 1890s was, for DuBois and many Americans, a strange and exciting world, one of extraordinary, if unfulfilled, promise.

As DuBois entered the city for the first time, passing from the train depot through Center City toward the Philadelphia Settlement, he saw before him the entire industrial metropolis in microcosm. The ostentation of the city's new wealth was visible in the elaborate facade of the nearly finished Second Empire-style City Hall. Along Market Street stretched the cast-iron facades of the city's grand department stores, Lit Brothers and Wanamaker's. Around Rittenhouse Square and along Spruce and Locust Streets stood elaborate four-story Italianate row houses and posh clubs. The stately Georgian-revival mansions of Delancey Place and Pine Street housed many bankers, executives, entrepreneurs, and lawyers who had prospered from the city's economic boom. To the west, near the University of Pennsylvania, a new class of corporate managers who sought the area's quasi-suburban

Figure 2. W.E.B. DuBois, Nina Gomer DuBois, and Burghardt DuBois, 1897. Courtesy of Special Collections and Archives, W.E.B. DuBois Library, University of Massachusetts, Amherst.

amenities and could afford the short trolley ride to the offices of Center City built substantial Queen Anne homes. A walk through the innumerable blue-collar neighborhoods that ringed Center City revealed neat blocks of small, impeccably maintained "Philadelphia-style" row houses that gave the city the highest rate of single-family homeownership of the nation's ten largest cities.

Yet for the vast majority of black Philadelphians the promise of the postwar city remained unmet. "After the war and emancipation," lamented DuBois, "great hopes were entertained by the Negroes for rapid advancement, and nowhere did they seem better founded than Philadelphia" (p. 39). But those hopes, particularly in the economy and in housing, were dashed. Nearly 50 percent of Philadelphians, but only 8.2 percent of black residents of the Seventh Ward, the largely black section of the city that was the basis of DuBois's research, found industrial employment. Although highly dangerous and often insecure, industrial work provided wages and opportunities for advancement unparalleled in the domestic and service sector where most blacks found work. One of the ironies of turn-of-the-century Philadelphia was that blacks lived in the closest proximity to the city's best industrial jobs, yet remained almost entirely closed out of them.[3] Other ethnic groups established residential neighborhoods that allowed easy access to industrial employment. White working-class Philadelphians tended to live close to the city's mills, machine shops, and manufactories, and the factories served as the hubs of dozens of thriving neighborhoods. In the shadow of the mills, workers used their hard-earned savings to purchase modest row homes. A majority of white Philadelphians were homeowners.

The privilege of homeownership did not come as readily to black working families in the city. Housing conditions graphically highlighted the contrast between blacks and whites. Nearly a third of black Philadelphians lived in the Seventh Ward, a district that extended from the Delaware to the Schuylkill River in a narrow band across Lombard, Pine, and South Streets. The more substantial houses, home to the city's black elite, lined the major streets, particularly Lombard west of Ninth Street and Rodman Street. But most of the ward's blacks crowded into decrepit brick row homes huddled along the narrow alleys, courtyards, and back streets that broke through the city's relentless grid. Numerous "blind alleys and dark holes" subdivided the neat grid of Philadelphia. Many alley dwellers lived in "trinities," tiny houses with "three rooms one above the other, small, poorly lighted, and poorly ventilated" that often shared a common outhouse (p. 294). Because nearly one-third of black Philadelphians depended on subtenants and boarders, their houses were often densely packed.[4] The narrow streets ran as open sewers and waste disposal areas for the residents of the nearby houses. "Penetrate into one of these houses and beyond into the back yard, if there is one," wrote a city inspector quoted by DuBois, "and there will be found a pile of ashes, garbage and filth, the accumulation of the winter, perhaps of the whole year" (p. 307).[5]

DuBois, the Seventh Ward, and the Settlement Movement

In the midst of this maze of courts and alleys, tucked into a bleak and inauspicious courtyard called Saint Mary Street on the border of the Fifth and Seventh Wards, was the Philadelphia Settlement. The Settlement, which cosponsored DuBois's research with the University of Pennsylvania, originated in 1857 as the Saint Mary Street Colored Mission Sabbath School, founded by wealthy merchant George Stewart. The school later added a nursery, kindergarten, and playground. In 1884, under the leadership of Quaker philanthropist Susan Wharton, it became the Saint Mary Street Library and began classes and vocational training in carpentry and cooking.[6] On April 1, 1892, Susan Wharton and her cousins Hannah Fox and Helen Parrish transformed the library into the Philadelphia College Settlement, which served the entire neighborhood, not just blacks.[7] Fox and Parrish, influenced by the English housing reformer Octavia Hill, made

Figure 3. Typical street scene of deteriorating row houses in the Seventh Ward, 1890s. Courtesy of Temple University, Urban Archives.

housing their special interest. Fox donated a house for the Settlement. The Saint Mary Street Library Association also pledged $1,000 per year for two years and secured the use of the Stuart Memorial Church with a hall and three classrooms linked to the Settlement by Starr Garden.[8]

From its inception, the Philadelphia Settlement was part of the College Settlement Association, which had encouraged its creation and, starting with $600 in 1892, made annual contributions toward its maintenance. Susan Wharton sat on the executive committee of the College Settlement Association, which formed in the spring of 1890 to promote settlement work among college women and to find money for settlements. "A College Settlement," pointed out Vida Scudder, secretary of its electoral board, "has a two-fold value." Its "primary and highest ambition" remained to concentrate "its power on the definite effort to bring brightness and help to a limited neighborhood." Less obvious, but of great importance, the "education of our college women is one great mission of College Settlements." The settlement movement, which had spread from Toynbee Hall in England first to Chicago and then to New York in the United States, rested on the assumption that "in the awakened intelligence and consecration of the cultured class lies, after all, the most serious promise for the success of that great movement toward social reconstruction in the midst of which we live."[9]

As Scudder described their mission, settlements stressed the role of knowledge and of class in social improvement. Knowledge came through two activities: personal experience and social investigation. By bringing well-to-do young women and men to live among the poor and undertaking research, settlements fused the advantages of class and education in the formation of the new leadership cadre they believed essential to social reform. Although settlement workers lived among the poor, they did not expect social change to flow from the bottom of the social structure upward. Not grass-roots democrats, they resembled nineteenth-century missionaries to the heathen more than community organizers of the 1960s. Working in the settlement milieu, DuBois not unexpectedly also stressed the importance of knowledge and class — within the black community and among whites. He looked to enlightened white leadership to lead the work of racial reconstruction, and he concluded that Philadelphia's black elite had abdicated its role in racial leadership. He hoped his massive study of black Philadelphia would light a fire under both. The road from the settlement house to the "talented tenth" was neither very long nor indirect.

The first of the college settlements originated in a gathering of four Smith College alumnae in the autumn of 1887. Conversation had turned to "the new economics, the new awakening of practical philanthropy in England, Toynbee Hall and the principles for which it stood." The women agreed on the need for parallel action in America and set to work. Their model differed from the British in two important ways: it rested on a secular rather than a religious foundation, and the leaders were women, not men. "In the autumn of 1888 an appeal was sent out from Boston that met with a ready and generous response. A house was taken at 95 Rivington street, New York, and the first College Settlement for Women was opened in October, 1889." The next year a group of college women organized the College Settlements Association with "electors" from Wellesley, Smith, Vassar, Bryn Mawr, and "the non-collegiate element." In the next two years alumnae from the Annex (Radcliffe), Packer and Wells, Cornell, Swarthmore, Mount Holyoke, and Elmira joined in the work.[10]

By 1893 the Association had helped found two new settlements in Philadelphia and Boston. Philadelphia proved challenging and instructive because "all of the circumstances were so different . . . that it was seen the work would be, to a large extent, without precedent." Unlike those in New York, the settlement was "on a side street in a shiftless neighborhood among a less provident class of people, many of them being colored."[11] As such, the Philadelphia Settlement opened a new area for research and social action.

Because DuBois's *Philadelphia Negro* dominates images of the city's Seventh Ward in the late nineteenth century, it is easy to forget that blacks constituted a minority of the residents of the Fifth and Seventh Ward neighborhoods the Philadelphia Settlement served. Within the Seventh Ward, wrote Mrs. Eliza Butler Kirkbride, sometime candidate for ward school director, were both "unnumbered municipal problems" and "all the forces that perpetuate, as well as those that tend to destroy, a city's life. Although, of course not in every sense representative, it would yet be hard to find a more complete type in miniature of the American city in our time."[12]

In 1892, Hannah Fox, then secretary to the Settlement residents, described Saint Mary Street, home of the Settlement, as "two blocks in length; on one side of it is the shopping street of the poor people; on the other, lodging houses and small stores of the negro population, while the intersecting streets are populated by German Jews and the representatives of many peoples who form a mixed population with no prevailing elements." Crossing and recrossing these streets was a "net-work of alleys, the houses in which are small and occupied by negroes."[13] Helena S. Dudley, who became head resident, embellished Fox's description of the neighborhood. The street was

not attractive. The houses are small, many of them wooden and look as if they were rotting away; the street is only two blocks long, with several courts leading from it, giving access to an astonishing number of small houses. . . . The grimy irregularity of the houses gives relief to the glimpses of sky behind; a tiny shop, with lattice window, has surely strayed hither from the London of Dickens; the park next the Settlement brings a pathetic memory of distant country spaces, and anyone who cares for the drama actualized can watch all day, without wearying, the shifting groups of half-clad children, with their varying nationalities—the dark Hebrew women, or patient negroes, or stout Germans, who live out their story day after day before the eyes of the street. The population of St. Mary's Street itself is made up chiefly of the most shiftless element of the colored people, with a plentiful and ever-increasing sprinkling of Russian and German Jews. The Italian quarter is a few streets to the south, but some stray Italians are in this district.[14]

Even an observer on the left wing of the settlement movement, like Helena Dudley, saw ethnic diversity through the lens of conventional stereotypes as she described neighborhood life. "The children were very friendly, and the door never opened without a horde of curly-headed Jews or little 'pickaninnies' pouring into the hall. . . . The race characteristics are shown in picturesque contrast from our windows. The Jews work very hard. Opposite us is a house where you can see a lamp burning all night. Near it are men's fingers bending over a machine. . . . On the other side of the house is a court where the negroes live. Here work does not go on, or but very little of it, either by day or night. . . . During the summer nights there is scarcely an hour of quiet between the noise of the late revelers and that of the early workmen."[15]

At least one activity sponsored by the Settlement, a military drill for black boys, remained segregated at the time, and white boys had a club of their own. Only "one club for little girls, it being a sewing class," had been formed by 1892–93. Dudley also noticed differences in the reading preferences of Jews and blacks who borrowed books from the Settlement's library. "The Jewish boys and girls read a good deal; they enjoy books of adventures, of travel and of history, whereas the colored boys are enthusiastic for Alger's thrilling romances."[16] Even in the late nineteenth century, black youngsters, trapped by poverty, barred from jobs, and bruised by racism, turned for vicarious rewards to fantasy.[17]

Through the lens of late nineteenth-century racial stereotypes, Dudley saw a typically heterogeneous urban neighborhood. As in other northern industrial cities, extensive ethnic diversity characterized late nineteenth-century Philadelphia. Although poor blacks were likely to live in close proximity to other blacks, the dispersion of Philadelphia's black population throughout the city meant that almost all blacks lived in close proximity to whites. About half the city's black population lived in the Seventh Ward and the adjoining Fourth, Fifth, and Eighth. But none of these wards was majority black. As a result, poor blacks and whites came into contact to a degree unimaginable in the late twentieth-century city. They shared the same dank alleys and crude outdoor facilities. They interacted in countless small ways—cooperative and hostile. Black and white children together played and fought in the same streets.[18]

What united the district's population, "whatever their nationality," were poverty and the "pressure of great numbers." Families often lived "in one, or, at most two, rooms, and sometimes take boarders. The rooms are mostly bare. A large bed, straw mattress, with but few bed clothes, a stove, a few broken chairs, and children—these are the regular articles of furniture for St. Mary Street." The Philadelphia Settlement became an oasis amid the poverty of Saint Mary Street. The eleven-room house was "very cozy and compact. Down stairs there is a square hall, dining room, parlor, and kitchen, opening into one another. The fittings of the house are very simple but very pretty, and the effect on entering the hall with its open staircase and coal grate and archway leading to the little parlor, in which is a pretty flower window, is most pleasing."[19] A reader of the Philadelphia Settlement's reports would not learn of the vibrant organizational infrastructure of black

Philadelphia — the many churches, mutual benefit societies, branches of the Odd Fellows, and clubs. Although a reader would not know it from its reports, the Philadelphia Settlement moved into a community with an indigenous civil society, not into an institutional desert.

Unlike his Settlement associates, DuBois did not fail to enumerate and interpret the many institutions that preceded the Settlement — and remained after it had left.[20] First in importance were the churches. The "social life of the Negro centres in his church — baptism, wedding and burial, gossip and courtship, friendship and intrigue — all lie in these walls," wrote DuBois (p. 205).[21] DuBois counted 55 "Negro churches with 12,845 members owning $907,729 worth of property with an annual income of at least $94,968" (p. 221). All the major denominations located churches in or near the Seventh Ward and engaged in missionary work and charity. The Episcopal church at Eighth and Bainbridge ran two missions, helped with the Fresh Air Fund, operated an ice mission and a vacation school for thirty-five children, and employed a parish visitor. As well, it was the site of University Extension lectures and good music, and had organized an insurance society and Home for the Homeless on Lombard Street (p. 217). Aside from churches, the most important organizations among blacks included "secret societies, beneficial societies, insurance societies, cemeteries, building and loan associations, labor unions, homes of various sorts and political clubs." The largest and most powerful of these was the Odd Fellows with 19 lodges and 1,188 members in Philadelphia (p. 222). Black Philadelphia also produced seven newspapers and journals. The *Tribune* was the "chief news sheet . . . filled generally with social notes of all kinds, and news of movements among Negroes over the country" (p. 229). Black Philadelphians had founded their own institutions, besides organizations: the Home for Aged and Infirm Colored Persons, Douglass Hospital and Training School, Woman's Exchange and Girls' Home, three cemeteries, Home for the Homeless, and special schools — the Institute for Colored Youth, House of Industry, Raspberry Street Schools and Jones' School for Girls, YMCA, and University Extension Center (p. 230).[22] To be sure, observed DuBois, black Philadelphia lacked the organizational density and maturity of the white city. Nonetheless, he found its accomplishments remarkable. "All this world of co-operation and subordination into which the white child is in most cases born is, we must not forget, new to the slave's sons" (p. 234). Like today's theorists of civil society or social capital, DuBois stressed the importance of these voluntary associations; "it is apparent that the largest hope for the ultimate rise of the Negro lies in this mastery of the art of social organized life" (p. 233).[23] While the leaders of the Philadelphia Settlement might agree, their reports remained blind to the associational life that flourished around them.

A remarkable variety of living conditions characterized the Seventh Ward. On its eastern side, around the Settlement, was "a district composed largely of Italians and Russians, recently arrived in this country and living under unfavorable conditions." At the western border of the Seventh Ward, on the Schuylkill River, was "a district which has all that a semi-commercial river bank in a large city displays," while "larger and more valuable residences" clustered along its northern edge. Its "southern boundary" was "devoted to small retail shops, supplying a large population of small householders."[24] Whether rich or poor, most families in the Seventh Ward — 4,083 of 5,722 in the early 1890s — lived in separate houses. Only 1,002 families lived in houses with two families each and 639 with three or more. In the whole ward but seventeen dwellings housed six or more families.[25]

In the nineteenth-century "walking city" rich and poor lived in close proximity. On the bustling streets of Philadelphia, it was nearly impossible for the well-to-do to avoid the less fortunate, for whites to avoid blacks. The Seventh Ward included the handsome four-story brick town houses on the 900 block of Clinton Street, where Susan Wharton and Charles C. Harrison lived, and the block of South Broad Street, home to Hannah Fox. Proud stone and brick row homes, many with ten or twelve rooms, which housed Philadelphia's elite, lined Spruce and Pine streets, the grandest in the fashionable Rittenhouse Square area west of Broad Street. Gracious marble steps and cornices, tall windows, and ornate ironwork signaled to passersby the wealth of the residents within.

This world of wealth was not foreign to Philadelphia's African Americans, even if it was unattainable to them. As DuBois noted, "the mass of Negroes are in the economic world purveyors to the rich — working in private houses, in hotels, large stores, etc." (p. 296). In the Seventh Ward, DuBois and his assistant Isabel Eaton found that over 61 percent of black men worked as domestics and over 88 percent of black women found work in the service sector. Employment as domestics, housekeepers, cooks, and janitors barely provided a subsistence-level living, for as DuBois acerbically noted, "from long custom and from competition, their wages for this work are not high" (p. 296, n. 6).[26] A sizable segment of the black population lived with wealthy white families; in 1880, 19 percent of Philadelphia's black women and 8 percent of black men lived in white-headed households. In her canvass of domestic workers, Eaton found 109 butlers, 76 coachmen, 4 valets, and 4 lady's maids in the ward (p. 445). Even more blacks lived literally in the shadow of the Seventh Ward's rich, in thousands of small houses only a few hundred yards away from the city's most prestigious addresses. Far more than the modern city, Philadelphia remained a jumble of ethnicity, race, and class, of small clusters scattered in complicated patterns rather than in large, homogeneous areas.[27]

The Seventh Ward, in fact, was experiencing transition. Blacks constituted about 30 percent of its residents, immigrants between 20 and 25 percent. About half of the native born had foreign-born parents. DuBois pointed to the excess of women to men as a source of social problems among the ward's blacks; unbalanced sex ratios also marked the ward's whites and were largest among the foreign born. (In 1900, for instance, among the foreign born with foreign-born parents, women outnumbered men 3,221 to 1,899; among blacks, the numbers were 5,436 and 5,026.) Here, perhaps, lay another source of the ward's unsavory reputation. Although in the 1890s the city of Philadelphia grew from 1,046,964 to 1,293,697, the population of the Seventh Ward dropped from 30,179 to 28,137. Whites were leaving as blacks moved in: the white population declined from 21,177 to 17,496, while the black population increased from 8,861 to 10,462. During the DuBoises' residence, this demographic shift challenged the diversity of the Philadelphia Settlement and forced it to decide how black an institution it would become.[28]

The DuBoises arrived a year after the Settlement had moved into larger quarters at 617 Carver (later Rodman) Street. Hannah Fox had purchased the new house along with the four adjoining houses, which she intended to use as model tenements. The Settlement also occupied property on Lombard Street. "The demolition of the old rookeries at Seventh and Lombard, and the erection of the building to be used as the Kitchen and Coffee House with a fine tenement house adjoining it in Lombard Street has done away with a most unsightly and unsanitary corner," observed the head resident— with no mention of the fate of the tenants displaced. In fact, many of the area's displaced (predominantly black) residents moved just a few blocks to the west, changing the complexion of the Seventh Ward. The new property reflected the Settlement's expanded activities. It took delight in the creation of Theodore Starr Park, built on the site of houses demolished on Sixth Street, and it announced the publication of a monthly newsletter, the *College Settlement News.*[29]

The Settlement cooperated closely with public agencies that served the poor. The board of education appointed one of its residents as a second teacher in the kindergarten branch of the James Forten School at Sixth and Lombard. Another resident, Dr. Frances C. VanGasken, served as medical inspector for the Board of Health; the Free Library of Philadelphia appointed a resident as assistant librarian for the library's College Settlement branch. The daily program of regular work in the winter of 1894 and 1895 included the kindergarten, a doctor's office, a savings bank, and the library. Other activities were scattered throughout the week: carpenter shop, freehand drawing, reading club, mechanical drawing, English classes, Clover Club, women's sewing class, Little Helpers, Area Club, Whittier Club, Dudley Pioneer Corps, Holy Club, games, gymnastic club, Tynall Club, Davis Cadets, Daisy Chain, Citizenship Club, choir drill, and lectures. The Settlement also organized special activities for its residents, including classes in social science,[30] and sent representatives to speak at conferences of the College Settlement Association and elsewhere in the city. In 1894–95, for instance, the Settlement's delegates spoke at a conference of the Child Saving

Agencies of Philadelphia, at three conferences of the Women's Union in the Interest of Labor, and at the Civic Club.[31]

The Settlement also cooperated with the Society for Organizing Charity (SOC) and shared its belief in the importance of reducing indiscriminate relief through the application of work tests. One resident even became a visitor for the Fifth Ward branch of the SOC. The superintendent of the SOC, noted the Settlement's head resident, Katherine B. Davis, did as much as he could with limited funds, "but with no efficient corps of visitors and little money it is impossible to expect him, single handed, to cope with the situation. If we can do no more we shall at least offer the services of one or two residents as visitors for the coming winter."[32] Whatever the situation in other cities and despite historians' claims about hostility between them, in Philadelphia no tension seemed to strain relations between the Settlement and the "scientific charity" movement.[33]

Although residence lay at the heart of the original settlement idea, many women found difficulty in remaining in residence for relatively long times. In 1892–93, for instance, the average resident in the Philadelphia Settlement stayed only five months. The privilege of settlement residence, moreover, was not free; the cost was five dollars per week for residents and one dollar per day for visitors.[34] Head resident Katherine B. Davis wrote of the problems settlements experienced "from a constantly changing family of residents." A permanent head worker by herself was "not sufficient to secure and fix" an "accurate knowledge of the neighborhood and its needs," and short-term residents could not take advantage of "large and important opportunities for helpfulness in connection with other agencies." The problem lay in familial expectations for unmarried, unemployed daughters. With "some justice" a father supporting a daughter believed her home should be beneath his roof. "He may be willing to spare her for a winter, even a year, but there are few fathers who, unless she marries or necessity compels, think it right for his daughter to be permanently away from home." With "self-supporting women" the situation differed. A growing number of young women, "whatever the financial condition of their parents," wanted "to take care of themselves," and parents increasingly respected this "natural desire" of "trained and educated women." For the Settlement the answer was clear: find income for residents by placing them in neighborhood jobs, which was a plan the Philadelphia Settlement followed with some success. In 1894–95, Davis reported, eight of eleven residents had remained six months or more, the "best showing since the Settlement opened."[35]

To leaders of the settlement movement, the importance of residence could not be overemphasized. Living in a settlement house fostered the empathy essential to bridging the gap between classes through residents' identification with the problems of the poor and constructive working relationships with the neighborhood. Newspapers, commented Helena Dudley, had accustomed readers to lurid descriptions of misery; "ardent educators" brought "squads" of students to "penetrate with shocking curiosity into the most harrowing and hidden secrets of the miserable life of the poor." Reading about the poor, even inspecting their housing, however, did not substitute for living among them. No alternative could take the place of the need to "identify oneself" with the awful conditions described by the press, "to be as a neighbor among neighbors; to hear day by day the stolid, terrible gossip of the street; to take, as one insensibly comes to take, the point of view on matters moral and physical of people sleeping seven in a room. It is no longer the 'problem of the masses' that confronts one, but the suffering of the individual man or woman of like passions with ourselves."[36] There were, then, good reasons beyond the need of an underpaid researcher to find cheap housing for the DuBoises to live at the Settlement.

Residence added lived experience to bare statistical facts. It also proved the commitment of the researcher to the use of knowledge for social improvement. Only high social purpose justified the intrusion into individual lives represented by research. Writing the introductory comments to *Hull-House Maps and Papers*, which, along with Charles Booth's monumental *Life and Labours of the People of London*, was the model for DuBois's research in Philadelphia, Agnes Sinclair Holbrook observed, "Insistent probing into the lives of the poor would come with bad grace even from government officials, were the statistics so inconsiderable as to afford no working basis for further improvement. . . . All spasmodic and sensational throbs of curious interest are ineffectual as well as unjustifiable. The painful nature of minute investigation, and the personal impertinence of many of the questions asked, would be unendurable and unpardonable were it not for the conviction that the public conscience when roused must demand better surroundings for the most inert and long-suffering citizens of the commonwealth."[37] Still, although the DuBoises lived at the Settlement, its annual reports did not list them as residents. (Isabel Eaton, by contrast, was listed among the residents as CSA fellow.) Whether this was because of their race or relation to the work of the Settlement remains unknown.[38]

The idea that brought DuBois to Philadelphia had originated with Susan Wharton, who first proposed a study of the Seventh Ward's black population. Wharton at the time served as a member of the Executive Committee of the Philadelphia College Settlement. In 1895 she assembled an interracial conference at her home of "persons interested in the welfare of this race." She also wrote to her neighbor, acting provost of the University of Pennsylvania, Charles C. Harrison, a retired sugar magnate, asking "the cooperation of the University in a plan for the better understanding of the colored people, especially of their position in this city. . . . The College Settlement wishes to co-operate in the movement and will probably engage a woman who can reside in St. Mary Street." Late in the fall of 1896, Harrison presided at a "parlor meeting" in her house. With his support added to that of others at the meeting, who included "representative colored leaders," Wharton asked the university's young sociology professor, Samuel McCune Lindsay, then active in the CSA, to organize the study; Lindsay chose DuBois.[39]

DuBois believed that Philadelphia's reform-minded elite had brought him to the city with a hidden agenda. In the midst of one of its "periodic spasms of reform," he remembered, reformers wanted to document the cause of political corruption in "one of the worst governed of America's badly governed cities." They looked to an investigation with the "imprimatur of the University" to give "scientific sanction" to the already known source of corruption. The "underlying cause was evident to most white Philadelphians: the corrupt, semi-criminal vote of the Negro Seventh Ward."[40] Settlement residents had mounted their own attack on corruption by repeatedly campaigning for the election of a woman from the Seventh Ward as a ward school director, but the ward's black voters helped defeat their increasingly vigorous campaigns, which enlisted the Settlement's entire staff.[41]

Blacks remained loyal to the Republican political machine, which helped them with jobs. Excluded from nearly all desirable white occupations, blacks found a small opening in public offices and public works. Their votes seemed a fair price. Settlement workers might offer them better government, but they could not supply jobs. To the contrary, reform would "throw many worthy Negroes out of employment." The "very reformers who want votes for specific reforms," observed DuBois, who saw the situation clearly, "will not themselves work beside Negroes, or admit them to positions in their stores or offices, or lend them friendly aid when in trouble." Even more, reformers missed the pride blacks took in their councilmen and policemen, who filled their positions honorably, even if they first obtained them through "shady 'politics.'" Should blacks, DuBois asked, "surrender these tangible evidences of the rise of their race to forward the good-hearted but hardly imperative demands of a crowd of women?" (pp. 383–84).[42]

Many forces other than insensitivity to the importance of jobs, the machine, or the black vote, contributed to the defeat of the women candidates for ward school director. They met antagonism from the ward's schoolteachers, apathy from the affluent, and hostility to their gender. Canvassing "the various classes of votes," women reformers found themselves "impressed by the marked contrast in the attitude of the richer, better, and more educated classes toward municipal politics, as distinguished from that of the so-called ignorant people in the small streets." On the grand streets — Spruce, Pine, Delancey, Trinity Place — they met striking ignorance of the electoral process and the issues, not to mention apathy. There they encountered "citizens whose bosom swelled with pride as they declared: 'I never vote.'" In the "small streets," however, "the voter appeared to know these facts as well as the canvasers." Indeed, in these streets, "in the midst of all the wretchedness, dirt, and ignorance, there was scarcely a single instance of indifference to questions of government." In part, neglect of the election reflected disinterest in the public schools. The wealthy sent their children to private, the Catholics to parochial schools. "The only class of which the religious and moral portion" showed interest in public schools were "the colored population, because they send their children to them, and are obliged to do so, or keep them at home, none of the private schools admitting them." Realizing the importance and sorry state of the public schools, a number of black leaders, including the eminent educator Fannie Coppin, had supported the women reformers' bid for election.[43]

DuBois and some subsequent historians awarded at least some reformers too little credit for understanding political realities, and they read motives too singly. As she reflected on the defeat, one campaign organizer observed that in every division of the ward the machine kept "two or three men who all the year around are keeping up relations with the voters, obtaining, for instance, through the ward bosses, for men out of work, places on the traction lines and on railroads, helping to get their children transferred from school to school, and organizing political clubs whose rent and expenses are paid by the office holders." Even more, these men knew "every voter, at least by sight." Although their homes backed onto the houses of voters in the small streets, alleys, and lanes, wealthy reformers hardly knew their poor and working-class neighbors. Not surprisingly, ordinary voters had preferred the machine politicians who "had taken the trouble" to know them "before they asked for their vote" rather than the women who had ignored them until the campaign. The moral was clear: "each of us should . . . take the division in which she lives, and make it a point before the next election to know all about it. . . . If there is trouble, sickness or death in the little row of houses which are at the back of almost every one of our dwellings, it ought to be understood that the Civic Club [a reform organization of women founded in 1894] representative is the best person in the division to go to." Women reformers also should join with the Charity Organization Society to "investigate cases in the division, and distribute its relief."[44] While they should not stoop to corruption, argued this now veteran campaigner, Philadelphia's elite women reformers needed to emulate the machine if reform hoped to win office.

If settlement workers failed to advance reform through politics, they could still deploy another potent weapon: research. Philadelphia's settlement house leaders participated in an international network of reformers committed to the power of social investigation. Indeed, research constituted a crucial component of settlement work. The "great movement toward social reconstruction," believed the college women, required hard facts. Documenting conditions among the urban poor would awaken the conscience of the rich and powerful and provide data for social and political reform. "A Settlement," wrote Helena S. Dudley, the head resident at Philadelphia, "can do little to solve the questions which perplex our philanthropic specialists. It may be that the cause of the evils we seek to remedy is too deep for our palliatives. But whatever the cause of the poverty, whatever the remedy, we all agree that we must have knowledge of facts."[45]

From its early years, the College Settlement Association raised fellowship money for women college graduates to undertake applied social research while living as settlement residents. In 1893–94, for instance, the CSA sponsored three fellowships. Ada S. Woolfold, Wellesley, investigated "The Obstacles to Sanitary Living Among the Poor" in New York and Boston; Katherine Pearson Woods, "non-collegiate," studied "Diseases and Accidents Incident to Occupations" in Boston and Philadelphia; and Isabel Eaton, Smith, documented "Receipts and Expenses of Wage Earners in the Garment Trades" in Chicago and New York.[46]

Eaton would hold another fellowship to work with DuBois and investigate domestic service in Philadelphia. A contributor to *Hull-House Maps and Papers*, she probably had been recommended for the job by Jane Addams. (In October 1895 Susan Wharton had written to Addams: "Do you know of anyone capable of being an investigator of the Negro problem? Such a person would live at the Phil. Settlement and receive $300. for about ten months work. The University of Penna. to have entire direction of the investigation.") Wharton also invited Addams to lecture at the Philadelphia Settlement. Convinced of the role of research in social reform, Wharton almost certainly saw DuBois's role as replicating the *Hull-House Maps and Papers* in Philadelphia. DuBois, for his part, paid high praise to Florence Kelley and Addams. "Save Jane Addams," he observed at the time of Kelley's death in 1932, "there is not another social worker in the United States who has had either her insight or her daring, so far as the American Negro is concerned."[47]

DuBois's remarks referred obliquely to the settlements' shabby record with blacks. "The majority of settlement houses," reports historian Elisabeth Lasch-Quinn in *Black Neighbors*, "either excluded blacks, conducted segregated activities, closed down completely, or followed their former white neighbors out of black neighborhoods."[48] Even Hull House compiled a far less than exemplary record on race. In its early years the Philadelphia Settlement's record appeared better than most. It chose to open in a partially black neighborhood; although some clubs were segregated, most activities attempted to bring together blacks and white immigrants. And, of course, it initiated and cosponsored DuBois's great study of black Philadelphia.

Nonetheless, in 1897–98 the Settlement decided to move. It had been cooperating with other agencies to persuade the city to extend Starr Park, and it occupied space on which the park would stand. At first, "it was thought that a change not of a few squares only, but of some miles, might be advisable." Public opinion, however, forced the Settlement to retract. "To the minds of our friends we became birds of passage." Thus, in January 1898, the executive committee decided to remain "down-town," within a mile of the existing location. "We believe we have struck root deeply enough to make transplanting unwise." The new move, although short in distance, would bring a welcome change in the Settlement's demography. "A location something less than a mile distant, and further to the southeast, will bring us into touch with a more varied population, Jewish, Italian, German and English-speaking population of foreign birth, as well as a considerable ad-mixture of Americans."[49] Never intended as a wholly black institution, the Settlement found its demography almost certainly had been altered by the movement of whites out of the Seventh Ward and the increasing migration of blacks. Faced with the prospect of the identification of the Settlement as a black institution, the executive committee voted to move to an area with a far smaller black population. At their new location at Third and Christian Streets, the social workers found that they were "nearer the centre of our old constituency; we have a more varied population, racially and indus-trially." By 1899, the Settlement's new head resident reported that "the whole number of cases . . . are fairly balanced in number." Achieving that "balance" meant a dramatic decline in the proportion of blacks to other groups served by the Settlement. In 1898, about 15 percent of all patients visited by the Settlement's nurses were black; in 1900, only about 4 percent were black.[50]

DuBois and the Origins of Sociology at the University of Pennsylvania

The Settlement was not the only institution responding to demographic shifts. Two decades earlier the other sponsor of DuBois's research, the Uni-versity of Pennsylvania, had left center city altogether for forty-eight and one-half acres in the city's then-suburban western edge. Its first dormitories, "arranged on the 'cottage' plan of contiguous houses," opened in 1896–97; in all, the University occupied twenty-two buildings. Taught by 258 "officers of instruction," 1,984 of the 2,834 students came from Pennsylvania.[51] None of the faculty and an indeterminate, but tiny, number of students were black. (The first black student graduated from the College in 1883 and from the Wharton School in 1887.)[52] Undergraduate instruction in sociology took place in the Wharton School, founded in 1881, which, at the time, remained "the Course in Finance and Economy" of the College; the Depart-ment of Philosophy, in effect the University's graduate school, remained home to graduate instruction in sociology.[53]

With a strictly research appointment, DuBois did no teaching. As "assis-tant in sociology," he had been appointed by the trustees "as investigator of the social conditions of the Colored race in this City, in connection with the work of the Wharton School." Almost certainly as a concession to Professor Samuel McCune Lindsay, who had hired DuBois, his presence merited one brief mention in the University's *Catalogue* during the second year of his appointment. In 1897, Lindsay had complained to the secretary of the Uni-

versity, Jesse Y. Burk, about the omission of DuBois from the *Catalogue*. Burk
responded lamely that he had not reported DuBois's appointment to the
editor of the catalogue because it "was not considered one which placed
him on the staff. . . . Indeed I should not have known where to place or what
to call him for the purposes of a circular of information."[54] Although his
name appeared the next year as assistant in sociology, a 1930–31 history of
the sociology department at Penn by one of its professors, James H. S.
Brossard, made no mention of DuBois's presence or work.[55] The most significant research in the history of the department still remained invisible.[56]

In the 1890s, however, the university did not try to camouflage its support
of DuBois's research. To the contrary, Provost Charles C. Harrison, who had
helped raise the money for DuBois's appointment, described the purposes
of DuBois's study and asked for public cooperation. His letter of introduction for DuBois not only supplied DuBois with credentials; it revealed that
the University found Philadelphia's black population at once a mystery and
a problem in need of solution. Clearly, he did not expect DuBois to find
internal sources of strength or a population that could improve itself without the intervention of philanthropic white Philadelphians.

In connection with the College Settlement, the Trustees of the University of Pennsylvania have undertaken the study of the social condition of the Colored People of the
Seventh Ward of Philadelphia. The University has entered upon this work as a part of
its duty and wishes to make the investigation as thorough and exact as possible. We
want to know precisely how this class of people lives; what occupations they follow;
from what occupations they are excluded; how many of their children go to school;
and to ascertain every fact which will throw light upon this social problem; and then
having this information and these accurate statistics before us, to see to what extent
and in what way, proper remedies may be applied. Dr. W.E.B. DuBois is the investigator on behalf of the University, and I write to bespeak for him your cordial reception
and earnest cooperation.[57]

Although sociology was new to Penn and its staff small, DuBois found
himself in an intellectual environment congenial to his research. How much
interchange with his colleagues DuBois enjoyed remains unknown. Nonetheless, an empirical account of the black residents of the city's Seventh
Ward fit nicely with the thrust of sociological interests at Penn. According to
Brossard, in Penn's sociology department the emphasis had been placed
"overwhelmingly . . . upon good teaching," and the "problem type of
course" had "predominated. The material presented to the students is concrete and factual. There has been among the members of the group little
indulgence in philosophizing and a general reticence to theorize prematurely. There has been no overzealous bidding for professional recognition."[58] Brossard accurately captured the department's emphasis on teaching and its practical, problem-oriented direction, which, certainly, reflected
its placement in the Wharton School. However, he misrepresented the pro-

fessional aspirations and accomplishments of its early members, who pioneered in the building of academic disciplines, organizations, and journals.

Robert Ellis Thompson, who became the initial dean of the Wharton School in 1881, had first taught a course in "social science" at Penn in 1869–70, but the first course identified as sociology, "The Elements of Sociology," was taught in 1891–92 by Dr. Frederick W. Moore, temporarily appointed instructor in sociology as a leave replacement for Professor Roland Falkner, who had joined the faculty in 1888–89 and taught statistics.[59] Falkner and Davis R. Dewey of the Massachusetts Institute of Technology were the first two American professors with the word "statistics" in their professorial title. A graduate of Philadelphia's Central High School and, at age nineteen, of the University of Pennsylvania, Falkner became the first to teach statistics full-time; he described his undergraduate course, "Statistics," required for Wharton seniors, as "A study of population in Europe and America," which included "Structure of the population, numbers, density, races and nationalities, sex, age, conjugal condition and occupation" as well as several other economic, demographic, and social topics that paralleled the organization of DuBois's research schedules.[60] As statistician for the U.S. Committee on Finance, Falkner "directed the most exhaustive investigation of prices and wages in the United States up to that time." Falkner left Penn in 1900 to become chief of the Division of Documents at the Library of Congress.[61]

Eminent as Falkner became, Penn's most famous social scientist remained Simon N. Patten. Patten had been recruited by the chairman of the Department of Economics, Edmund James. Appointed in 1883 after two years of graduate study in Germany, James became a leading player in the creation of economics as a discipline and in shaping the Wharton School. In class, James substituted the German professorial lecture for recitations and drills, and in 1885 he introduced the University's first research seminar. James wanted to turn Wharton into a "School of Political and Social Science." Although he failed to realize his grand design, his "vision of the practical university," according to the school's historian, "would remain the foundation of the Wharton School program." James attracted many of the serious sons of Philadelphia's elite. Although most entered business, several, including Falkner, went on to careers in academics or reform, or in journalism and letters. James hoped to influence public affairs not, as had his predecessors, through journalism but through research and the practical application of scholarship. Thus, for example, he wrote a long analysis of modern municipalities, the gas supply, and the "Gas Question" in Philadelphia and in 1889 transformed the Philadelphia Social Science Association into the American Academy of Political and Social Science. He was also instrumental in founding the American Economic Association. Nonetheless, despite James's accomplishments, Charles C. Harrison, a wealthy member of the trustees, long had disliked him, and when Harrison became provost he promptly forced James's resignation. James moved to the University of Chicago.[62]

Among James's most enduring accomplishments had been hiring Simon N. Patten, a friend also trained in Germany and, according to Sass, "perhaps the greatest mind in the history of the institution." "For almost a third of a century," writes Brossard in his history of sociology at Penn, Patten, who came to Penn in 1888, "was a sort of spiritual father to the Wharton School." Although often identified as a sociologist, Patten remained primarily an economist noted for the originality and importance of his ideas (seen, for instance, in *The Economic Basis of Protection, The Development of English Thought, The Social Basis of Religion,* and *The New Basis of Civilization*), his inspirational teaching, and his involvement with the practical work of reform. Patten, according to his junior colleague Samuel McCune Lindsay, played "a much greater part than can ever be known in initiating and actually guiding the university extension movement, the ... labor movement, housing reform, prevention of tuberculosis, education and training of social workers and other allied and similar activities. He was a big factor in the *Survey* and the periodicals that preceded it. He took an immense interest in the feminist movement. His mind was always at work on problems of practical, elementary, and secondary education."[63] Patten's teaching reflected his interests in the intersection of politics and economics, the practical application of scholarship, and training in research. In the college, Patten taught "Political Economy"; in the graduate program, "History of Political Economy," "Practical Applications of Economic Theory," "The Problems of Sociology," and "Investigation of Special Topics," another research course.

In the 1890s, Patten shared the sociology-related teaching with Falkner and Samuel McCune Lindsay, his former student in Wharton. After his graduation from Penn in 1889, Lindsay had continued his education in Germany at Halle, where he received his doctorate in 1892. He joined the faculty of Penn in 1894 as the first full-time professor of sociology and began a distinguished career noted more for its contributions to public service than for original scholarship.[64] Among his appointments were as commissioner of education for Puerto Rico, 1902–4; first secretary, later chairman of the National Child Labor Committee; president of the American Academy of Political and Social Science; director, New York School of Philanthropy; president of the Academy of Political Science; and president of the American Association for Labor Legislation. In 1907, he left Penn to become professor of social legislation at Columbia. Even more than Patten, Lindsay directed his teaching toward the application of social science to social problems and reform. Lindsay's "Descriptive Sociology," required of Wharton sophomores, included not only theory, represented by Spencer's *Study of Sociology,* but more practical texts as well, notably Amos Warner's

American Charities. His course "Social Pathology" was an "advanced" study of "Pauperism and Treatment of the Defective and Delinquent Classes," compulsory for juniors. Also compulsory for juniors was his course "Sociological Field Work." In the first part of the course, Lindsay took students to "mills, factories and business establishments" and, in the latter, to "charitable and correctional institutions." It was, perhaps, as part of this course, or his elective "Charity Organization," that DuBois shepherded a group of undergraduates around the Seventh Ward.[65] ("I did no instructing save once to pilot a pack of idiots through the Negro slums.")[66] Lindsay's courses revealed his interest in social problems, involvement with social reform, and association with philanthropic agencies outside the university. They also pointed to his embrace of "scientific charity," with its emphasis on investigating and classifying the poor using moral criteria; on centralizing charity; and on gathering empirical data about poverty and its concomitants, such as poor housing, disease, and the conditions of employment. In these years, DuBois shared these conventional views about poverty, which began to lose favor only later in the 1890s.[67] Lindsay's graduate courses also stressed the interplay between theory and practice: "Sociological Field Work" (which included "Study by individual investigation of the pathological phenomena of the slums"); "History and Organization of Philadelphia Charities"; "Modern Socialism"; and "Sociological Theory."[68]

The titles of Lindsay's courses changed slightly in subsequent years; the course in charity organization was dropped; but the mix of theory and practice, with a strong fieldwork component and a concentration on social issues remained. (Lindsay may have dropped the course on Philadelphia charities because he had finished his research on the subject, published in 1895 as a directory of the city's "educational institutions and societies.")[69] The single published notice of DuBois's presence at Penn in a University catalogue appeared as a "Note" following the description of Lindsay's fieldwork course for 1897–98.

Note: The special sociological investigation of the condition of the Negroes in the Seventh Ward of Philadelphia, begun in September 1896, under the direction of William E. Burkhardt Du Bois, Ph. D., will be concluded by January 1, 1898. The results will be published by Dr. Du Bois, who was appointed Assistant in Sociology for the year 1896–97 to conduct the investigation.[70]

Among the faculty at Penn, DuBois remembered only Lindsay with any warmth. Lindsay had chosen him for the task. "If Lindsay had been a smaller man and had been induced to follow the usual American pattern of treating Negroes, he would have asked me to assist him as his clerk in this study. Probably I would have accepted having nothing better in sight for work in sociology. But Lindsay regarded me as a scholar in my own right and probably proposed to make me an instructor."[71] How Lindsay first learned of DuBois remains unknown. Nonetheless, by the time of his arrival, DuBois would be well known in Philadelphia's social science circles. In 1897 the *Annals of the American Academy of Political and Social Science*, edited by Falkner and published in Philadelphia, carried a highly favorable review of DuBois's 1896 book, *The Suppression of the African Slave Trade*, by Bernard C. Steiner of Johns Hopkins, who called it "a thoroughly good piece of work. His research has been exhaustive and accurate and he has so incorporated the results of that research that the reader has a true book and not an ill-digested collection of facts."[72] At the time of his appointment to Penn, his book on the slave trade was in press. Both DuBois's "training and personal qualifications for the projected work," wrote Lindsay in his introduction to the first edition of *The Philadelphia Negro*, "proved to be far greater than our highest expectations, and his signal services in the educational uplift of his people, both before and since his term of service at the University of Pennsylvania, have won for him a public recognition that renders any introduction of Dr. DuBois quite unnecessary."[73]

Also in 1896 in the *Annals*, DuBois published a devastating review of Frederick L. Hoffman, *Race Traits and Tendencies of the American Negro*. DuBois's critique foreshadowed key methods and themes he would use in *The Philadelphia Negro*. Hoffman projected the eventual disappearance of the Negro through a higher death rate influenced by " 'race traits and tendencies' rather than . . . conditions of life." DuBois concentrated his attack on Hoffman's methods and sources. Despite his many tables, Hoffman had failed to omit the "fallacies of the statistical method," which was "nothing but the application of logic to counting, and no amount of counting will justify a departure from the severe rules of correct reasoning." DuBois showed how Hoffman relied on incomparable sets of statistics; incorrectly extrapolated from the small urban black population to the much larger rural population of the South; ignored trends prior to the 1880–90 decade; and omitted comparisons to a number of foreign cities with rates of mortality and population growth less favorable than those prevailing among American blacks. Hoffman had misidentified the phenomenon requiring explanation. Not the threat of population extinction but the contradictions in the data required analysis, wrote DuBois in a passage that foreshadowed the major themes of his new research project: the coexistence of contradictory trends among blacks; the social and moral differentiation of black communities; crime as one outcome of dashed aspirations; and the pervasive force of white racial prejudice.

The proper interpretation of apparently contradictory social facts is a matter requiring careful study and deep insight. If, for instance, we find among American Negroes to-day, at the very same time, increasing intelligence and increasing crime, increasing wealth and disproportionate poverty, increasing religious and moral activity and high rate of illegitimacy in births, we can no more fasten upon the bad as typifying the general tendency than we can upon the good. . . . Such contradictory facts are not facts pertaining to the "race" but to its various classes, which development since emancipation has differentiated. As is natural with all races, material and mental development has, in the course of a single generation, progressed farther than the moral. . . . On the other hand, when the younger generation came on the stage with exaggerated but laudable hopes of "rising," and found that a dogged Anglo-Saxon prejudice had shut nearly every avenue of advancement in their faces, the energies of many undoubtedly found an outlet in crime.[74]

One might write the recent history of African Americans, albeit in less moralistic language, with the same themes.

In his autobiography, DuBois claimed he started his study with "no 're-search methods' " and "asked little advice as to procedure."[75] The situation, however, was a little more complicated. Lindsay sent drafts of DuBois's proposed questionnaire to many individuals and institutions for comment. (One survives in the DuBois archives at the University of Massachusetts and one in the Booker T. Washington papers in Washington, D.C.) His letter read:

Enclosed please find the proof-sheets of the schedules which have been adopted for the Investigation into the Condition of the Negroes in Ward Seven of the City of Philadelphia. We desire to make this investigation as thorough as possible and to have the results in such shape as to be comparable with similar work undertaken in other cities. The work is being done by Mr. W.E.B. Du Bois, Ph. D. (Harvard) and Miss Isabel Easton, B.L. (Smith), under the direction of this department of the University, which will print all results worthy of publication.

Will you kindly examine the enclosed proofs and return them at once with any corrections or suggestions which in your judgment will add to the value of the investigation?

One surviving response from an unknown writer at Cornell suggested following an existing model, either the U.S. Census of 1890 or the Massachusetts state census of 1895. Some of the instructions on the schedules, claimed the writer, should be fuller. "Are all persons having any trace of African blood negroes and will you not find objection raised to your using the term negro? Why not . . . the census word 'colored' or the word their journals prefer afro-american?" The writer also suggested a "less objectionable method of framing" item 11, "Wanting or defective in mind, sight, hearing or speech; maimed or deformed?" "The similar question on 11th Census aroused a storm of public indignation."[76] The final version of the schedule incorporated the writer's suggested revision: "Sound and healthy in mind, sight, hearing, speech, limbs and body?" Indeed, changes between the draft schedule and the final version suggest that DuBois received many recommendations from reviewers.

DuBois did not sample. He personally "visited and talked with 5,000 persons." Where possible, he recorded on schedules. "Other information I stored in my memory or wrote out as memoranda. I went through the Philadelphia libraries for data, gained access in many instances to private libraries of colored folk and got individual information. I mapped the district, classifying it by conditions; I compiled two centuries of the Negro in Philadelphia and in the Seventh Ward." The result of this work on which DuBois "labored morning, noon, and night" was "that fat volume" which "few persons ever read . . . but that they treat . . . with respect, and that consoles me."[77]

DuBois's method, common to Progressive Era social scientists and reformers, was based on the belief in the importance of gathering information as the first step toward improving society. But DuBois defined the task of research with even greater precision. "The social problem is ever a relation between conditions and action," he wrote, shortly after completing the research for *The Philadelphia Negro*, "as conditions and actions vary and change from group to group from time to time and from place to place, so social problems change, develop, and grow." The key was to realize that the Negro problem, "like others, has had a long historical development, has changed with the growth and evolution of the nation; moreover it is not *one* problem, but rather a plexus of social problems, some new, some old, some simple, some complex." As complex and historically grounded as the Negro problem was, research on the topic remained, in DuBois's view, "lamentably unsystematic and fragmentary." Moreover, "much of the work done on the Negro question is notoriously uncritical; uncritical in choosing the proper point of view from which to study those problems, and, finally, uncritical from the distinct bias in the minds of so many writers."[78] At the historical moment that black historian Rayford Logan later called the "nadir" of race relations in American history, DuBois's call for the thorough study of black America was not merely academic. Researchers, DuBois argued, should not simply gather information, but amass and interpret data with the greatest care so that "we might *know* instead of *think* about the Negro problems." Research represented the first step in the dispelling of ignorance.[79]

By conceiving of the Negro problem as a historical problem, contingent and ever changing, DuBois planted the seeds of a powerful critique of racial essentialism. The wretched conditions that faced the Philadelphia Negro did not spring from innate racial deficiencies, as conventional wisdom held. The impoverishment of urban blacks did not reveal hereditary inferiority, nor did alarmingly high mortality rates prove that the race, left to fend for itself in a Darwinian world, was gradually disappearing. Blacks' limited opportunities in the workplace were a historically specific manifestation of prejudice and discrimination, not of their inherent limitations. DuBois rooted his study in a fundamental critique of biological notions of race. He rejected both the lingering monogenetic views that prevailed in black religious circles and the statistical Anglo-Saxonism that moved to the fore of the human sciences in the 1890s.[80]

DuBois's racial thinking was, however, far advanced from his ethnographic strategy. Philadelphia's blacks had not welcomed DuBois with open arms. Encountering a "natural dislike of being studied like a strange species," DuBois repeatedly "met again and in different guise those curious cross-currents and inner social whirlings. They set me to groping. I concluded that I did not know so much as I might about my own people." In the end, "I had learned far more from Philadelphia Negroes than I had taught them concerning the Negro Problem."[81]

The tensions that run through *The Philadelphia Negro* were in part the result of the clash between DuBois's assumptions and the reality of black Philadelphia. DuBois's research agenda started with the conventional wisdom of charity organization and late nineteenth-century social thought. DuBois, like many observers, focused on the pathologies of the family and on criminality, moving uncertainly between explanations that emphasized individual moral and behavioral deficiencies and those that focused on the forces of racial inequality, prejudice, and discrimination. Likewise, DuBois argued for the redemptive nature of work for its own sake. But his experience led him to challenge, albeit tentatively, some of the central verities of late nineteenth-century charity. Whereas many reformers held that charity sapped the work ethic of the poor, DuBois gave lip service to the ideal of self-help but offered a far more radical analysis of the causes of poverty than did many of his sponsors. The "centre and kernel of the Negro problem," wrote DuBois, "is the narrow opportunities afforded Negroes for earning a decent living" (p. 394). Systematically excluded from most of the city's well-paying industrial jobs, Philadelphia's blacks were concentrated disproportionately in the service sector. As DuBois wrote, in one of his best documented and passionate passages, "No matter how well trained a Negro may be, or how fitted for work of any kind, he cannot in the ordinary course of competition hope to be much more than a menial servant" (p. 323). Offering moving examples of black professionals who could not find employment, of artisans excluded from their trades, of high school graduates relegated to jobs as scrubwomen, DuBois bristled particularly at the summary exclusion of blacks from the ranks of "foremen, managers and clerks — the lieutenants of industry who direct its progress." Perhaps referring obliquely to his own second-tier status at the University of Pennsylvania, DuBois bitingly asked "what university would appoint a promising young Negro as a tutor?" (p. 327).[82]

DuBois certainly learned some hard truths about American academic life. "It would have been a fine thing," he recalled in his autobiography, "if after this difficult, successful piece of work, the University of Pennsylvania had at least offered me a temporary instructorship in the college of the Wharton School." Certainly, Harvard "had never dreamed of such a thing." DuBois was not looking for a permanent appointment, but "an academic accolade from a great American university would have given impetus to my life work which I was already determined to make in a Negro institution in the South." What "galled was that such an idea never even occurred to this institution whose head was a high official in the Sugar Trust."[83] Still, in 1898 he remained publicly supportive of Penn. There was "no better way" that the American university could "repay the unusual munificence of its bene-factors than by placing before the nation a body of scientific truth in the light of which they could solve some of their most vexing social problems." Therefore, the University of Pennsylvania deserved "credit." For "she has been the first to recognize her duty in this respect, and in so far as restricted means and opportunity allowed, has attempted to study the Negro prob-lems in a single definite locality."[84]

The *American Sociological Review* showed its racism by not reviewing *The Philadelphia Negro*. However, reviews appeared in several other journals and magazines. Some reflected their author's position or prejudice: the pride of blacks (from *AME Church Review*: "At last we have a volume of the highest scientific value on a sociological subject and written by a Negro");[85] the casual racism common among historians (from the *American Historical Re-view*: "what Dr. DuBois does not give, more knowledge of the effects of the mixing of blood of very different races, and of the possibilities of absorp-tion of inferior into superior groups of mankind. He speaks of the 'na-tural repugnance to close intermingling with unfortunate ex-slaves,' but we believe that the separation is due to differences of race more than of status.");[86] the patronizing pro-southern views of the *Nation* ("the lesson taught by this investigation is one of patience and sympathy toward the South, whose difficulties have been far greater than those of the North").[87]

Three themes run through most of the reviews: praise for DuBois's re-search and analysis, recognition of the obstacles to black employment, and commentary on race prejudice. Reviewers welcomed the empirical study of blacks and praised DuBois's thoroughness and fair-minded presentation of the "facts." The reviewer for *Yale Review* called *The Philadelphia Negro* "not merely a credit to its author and to the race of which he is a member; it is a credit to American scholarship, and a distinct and valuable addition to the world's stock of knowledge concerning an important and obscure theme. It is the sort of book of which we have too few, and of which it is impossible that one should have too many."[88] The *Charities Review* called it a "careful, pains-taking, and intelligent study. . . . the book can be relied on as giving a true picture of the condition of the Philadelphia Negro."[89] *City and State* en-thused, "While the book abounds in statistics and is devoted to facts, it is as interesting as a novel, thanks to the skill with which the author has worked up his material."[90] The review in the *Sunday School Times* singled out the barriers to employment described by DuBois. "Even in Philadelphia it is almost useless for negro men and women to fit themselves for any higher work than household service or waiting in a hotel. Case after case is cited in which educated negroes have been debarred from any employment for which their education fits them."[91] Employment barriers formed the major theme of the longest and most acute review, written for the *Journal of Political Economy* by social scientist and settlement worker Katherine Bement Davis.

"Dr. DuBois," she writes, "recognizes the economic side of the problem as that which presents at the same time the greatest importance and the greatest difficulties." "The causes which limit the occupations of the negro," Davis observed, "are twofold—first the inefficiency which comes from lack of experience and training, and second, the prejudice of the whites."[92]

The reviewer for the *Outlook* argued that DuBois's fair-minded restraint lent great weight to his account of discrimination. "In no respect does Dr. DuBois attempt to bend the facts so as to plead the case of his race. . . . For this restraint he is well repaid in the greater effectiveness it gives to his chapter on the discriminations still in force against the employment of negroes. It is this chapter that especially appeals to the conscience of the Nation."[93] Even the *Nation* acknowledged the force of racism revealed by DuBois. "Turning from legal restriction to social repression, we find that race hatred has prevailed down to a very recent period."[94]

"Many readers of this report," predicted Lindsay in his introduction, "will look most eagerly for what is said on the subject of race-prejudice and the so-called 'color-line.' I feel sure that no one can read Chapter XVI without being impressed with the impartiality and self-control of the writer. Dr. DuBois has treated the facts he obtained with the delicacy of an artist." DuBois had revealed that "the better-educated classes among the Philadelphia Negroes feel very keenly the injustice of the class antagonism that comes from the indiscriminate classing of all Negroes together, and the imputing to all of the shortcoming of the ignorant, vicious, and criminal. This fact, and the proof that such is the habit among the bulk of the white population, comes out frequently in the following pages." Like other readers, Lindsay found DuBois's restraint admirable. By amassing facts and masking his outrage, DuBois escaped the charge of bias. Echoing the retreat from "advocacy to objectivity" in American social science, Lindsay observed that DuBois had "wisely refrained for the most part from drawing conclusions or introducing anything that savors of personal judgment."[95]

In January 1898, before *The Philadelphia Negro* appeared in print, DuBois summarized his conclusions about "Negro Problems" in a lead article for the *Annals of the American Academy of Political and Social Science* and foreshadowed the "fair-mindedness" and restraint that would so impress reviewers. "Fair-mindedness," in practice, meant pointing out failings among the black population. "Negro problems," according to DuBois, "can be divided into two distinct but correlated parts, depending on two facts: First—Negroes do not share the full national life because as a mass they have not reached a sufficiently high grade of culture. Secondly—They do not share the full national life because there has always existed in America a conviction—varying in intensity, but always widespread—that people of Negro blood should not be admitted into the group life of the nation no matter what their condition might be." Of all the important parts of the nation, "the Negro is by far the most ignorant. . . . The great deficiency of the Negro . . . is his small knowledge of the art of organized social life — the last expression of human culture. . . . This is shown in the grosser forms of sexual immorality, disease and crime, and also in the difficulty of race organization for common ends or in intellectual lines." Racial prejudice, the "second class of Negro problems," lay at the root of blacks' "poverty, ignorance, and social degradation." Racism "makes it more difficult for black men to earn a living or spend their earnings as they will; it gives them poorer school facilities and restricted contact with cultured classes; and it becomes, throughout the land, a cause and excuse for discontent, lawlessness, laziness, and injustice."[96]

Given DuBois's restraint and candor, Lindsay found all the more compelling — "a serious charge, and worthy of reflection" — DuBois's conclusion about the consequences of a racism that failed to draw social and moral distinctions among the city's black population. "Thus the class of Negroes which the prejudices of the city have distinctly encouraged is that of the criminal, the lazy and the shiftless; for them the city teems with institutions and charities; for them there is succor and sympathy; for them Philadelphians are thinking and planning; but for the educated and industrious young colored man who wants work and not platitudes, wages and not alms, just rewards and not sermons — for such colored men Philadelphia apparently has no use," DuBois had written (p. 352).

For Lindsay, racism, as limned by DuBois, not only unjustly tarnished the reputation of respectable blacks and denied them the opportunity to earn a decent living; it also blocked the operations of scientific charity. Institutionalized in Charity Organization Societies, scientific charity, according to Lindsay, rested on three principles: "*Co-operation* and mutual helpfulness among existing charities; *Investigation* as a basis for the elimination of fraud and for the securing of suitable and adequate relief; *Restoration* of the pauper to normal working-power — the only rational end in relief work."[97] Scientific charity assumed a connection between respectability and reward. Upright behavior led if not to wealth, at least to independence. It interpreted the great impediments to independence as twofold: indiscriminate charity that perversely encouraged dependence and immoral behavior that bred poverty. Through the reorganization of charity, the manipulation of sanctions (basing relief on work and good behavior), and individual counseling, scientific charity proposed simultaneously to reduce the cost of relief (or, in our modern terms, welfare) and raise individuals from dependence. Scientific charity also emphasized the distinction between public and private charity. Public charity shouldered the "more or less perfunctory tasks . . . too heavy for private shoulders to bear" and dealt "with a hopeless element in the social wreckage which must be provided for in a humane way, and prevented, if possible, from accumulating too rapidly or contaminating the closely allied product just outside the almshouse door." Private charity, by contrast, formed the "more conspicuous form of charity" and its "thousand little variations" served as the "measure" of the "real charitable activity of a city." Although founded in 1878, the Philadelphia Society for Organizing Charity, the primary vehicle for rationalizing private charity, remained hobbled, less effective than its counterparts in other major cities, according to Lindsay. The SOC, for one thing, had failed to streamline the city's private charitable apparatus. As late as 1895, 300 organizations handed out relief in the city, and 250 "educational ones" did "charitable work." The city's 675 churches also supplied both relief and education. Even this list remained incomplete. The SOC's financial administration remained decentralized in ward committees, leading to "much duplication in the appeals for money"; petty jealousies among existing charities discouraged cooperation; and the SOC's practice of handing out relief in emergencies contradicted the fundamental rules of good charity organization society practice, which restricted the umbrella organization to coordination, investigation, and referral. Anything else excited the "jealousy and opposition of other relief-giving agencies" and, ultimately, reduced charitable giving.[98] With these impediments, charity organization in Philadelphia faced a difficult enough struggle, but what if artificial impediments intervened between the mechanisms of scientific charity and its expected outcomes? All would be in vain. This, for Lindsay, was the consequence of the racism so convincingly portrayed by DuBois. "If the Negroes themselves, that is their upper ranks, cannot command these privileges and secure them, or, if competent to possess them, they are denied the possession by the organized prejudices of the stronger race around them, and these prejudices cannot be broken down, then scientific philanthropy is helpless to point the way to their improvement, and the present haphazard efforts of unthinking charity would better cease altogether."[99] DuBois had shown how racism fueled the "social wreckage" that threatened the contamination of respectable Philadelphia.

In her review, Katherine Bement Davis showed less concern with unleashing scientific charity than with exposing the roots of black poverty, as described by DuBois. Together, Lindsay's introduction and Davis's review point to the uneasy coexistence of scientific charity and progressivism — of nineteenth- and twentieth-century approaches to poverty — in *The Philadelphia Negro*. Davis highlighted DuBois's finding of a higher rate of employment among blacks than among whites: 78 percent of Seventh Ward blacks compared to 55.1 percent of the whole population of Philadelphia were reported in "gainful occupations." This result, which "was to be anticipated," indicated "an absence of accumulated wealth, arising from poverty and low wages."[100] In three articles written for the *New York Times* in 1901, DuBois continued to emphasize the economic consequences of employment discrimination by comparing the situation of blacks in Boston, Philadelphia, and New York. Blacks, he pointed out, as "a race are not lazy. The canvass of the Federation of Churches in typical New York tenement districts has shown that while nearly 99 per cent. of the black men were wage earners, only 92 per cent. of the Americans and 90 per cent. of the Germans were at work."[101] Low wages, confinement to menial jobs, and exclusion from opportunities for advancement — not the lack of jobs — confronted black men. Despite the haunting parallels between DuBois's urban North and our own, nothing more sharply distinguishes the present from the past than the addition of chronic joblessness to the insults associated with race in America.

DuBois's Philadelphia and Ours

At first glance, the continuity between DuBois's Philadelphia and ours leaps from the pages of his great book. Then, as now, African Americans experienced disproportionate poverty, clustered in the worst jobs, lived in segregated neighborhoods, watched their children die young, and suffered the insults of racism. The roots of current black poverty, marginalization, and the multiple crises of the inner cities appear in embryo in Philadelphia at the end of the nineteenth century.

First glances, however, can deceive. To tell the story of African Americans in Philadelphia in terms of continuity over a century would be facile. The context of black experience has altered so fundamentally that comparisons mislead and threaten to obscure the sources and dimensions of current circumstances and to inhibit the development of constructive and realistic responses.[102]

Think, for instance, of the public and private assistance available to African Americans in need in DuBois's time and ours. In the 1890s, black Philadelphians could call on no form of public assistance as a right. The city had abolished outdoor relief (what today we would call welfare); there was no comparable state or federal program. Whether out of work, single parents, or elderly, blacks had to turn to private charity, notably the Society for Organizing Charity, which doled out miserable amounts of assistance following minute investigations of applicants' need and merit. Settlement houses offered very little help with food, shelter, fuel, or clothing. Churches and private charities provided a little more; some hospitals admitted charity patients; when all else failed, the poorhouse beckoned. For all its weaknesses, the welfare state of the 1990s — Temporary Assistance for Needy Families, Supplemental Social Security, Social Security, Food Stamps, Unemployment Insurance, Medicare, Medicaid — offers an array and level of benefits unimaginable in the 1890s.[103]

In the 1890s, Philadelphia's African Americans, a majority migrants from the South, composed only about 5 percent of the city's population. A century later, for the most part natives of Philadelphia, they constituted about 40 percent. Their numerical presence translated into political power undreamed of a century earlier: high political office in city, state, and federal governments and a large presence among appointed officials. Their ascendance in government, the professions, and business, abetted by affirmative action, reflected the growth of a black middle class, seen as well in a great increase in homeownership and a radical decline in the percentage in poverty.[104]

The growth of a black middle class fueled increased residential differentiation, as more affluent African Americans moved to the city's Oak Lane, Mount Airy, or Overbrook sections or to the near suburbs, such as Cheltenham and Yeadon. Although segregation remained high, even among affluent blacks, their dispersion helped increase the concentration of poverty in inner city neighborhoods, whose social structure became less diverse over time. Indeed, studies of language underscored the growing isolation of poor African American communities in inner cities.[105]

In the late nineteenth century, American blacks lived mainly in the South. As sharecroppers and tenant farmers at the height of Jim Crow, they suffered from extraordinary poverty, exploitation, lack of opportunity, a repressive political regime, the constant threat of violence, and the denial of basic human freedoms. Northern cities represented lands of hope. African Americans migrated northward at a time of expanding work opportunity. Even if menial, jobs existed along with schools for children and a less proscriptive racial order. Looking back, the situation of blacks in turn-of-the-century Philadelphia looks bleak; from the view of a tenant farm in rural Virginia, it almost certainly appeared a world better. Despite deprivation and discrimination, African Americans in late nineteenth-century Philadelphia, even DuBois, could look to the future with some hope and optimism.

The great irony is that the material improvement during the late twentieth century, the extension of civil rights, and the accession to political office accompanied lowered expectations of progress and the decline of Philadelphia and other once-great cities as arenas for mobility and generators of jobs. New sources of disadvantage and marginalization added to or modified preexisting roots of inequity. Some resulted from global economic changes that undermined manufacturing and sucked jobs out of older cities; others emerged from public policies: New Deal agricultural policies that drove blacks from the land; transportation policies that balkanized cities with freeways; subsidized suburbanization that lured whites from cities; government-encouraged redlining that denied mortgage money to African Americans; urban renewal that destroyed homes and warehoused poor families in cheap, segregated towers.

Within inner cities, especially among the young, observers talk of worsening race relations and a mood of nihilism and hopelessness acted out through drugs and violence. Institutional collapse fuels cynicism and hopelessness among the young in the ghettos of Philadelphia and other cities: not only do the police fail to protect; their corruption poses a threat to safety.[106]

The failure of schools disadvantages youngsters in the job market in the global city. Cuts in social benefits — in Philadelphia, for instance, the state's decimation of General Assistance and the city's reduction in funds for social services — have shredded the safety net, with more tears coming. Even the infrastructure that makes daily life tolerable crumbles, especially in poor neighborhoods: street surfaces, pockmarked by potholes, decay; garbage and abandoned houses disfigure the landscape; water mains burst; bridges rust away; and cuts in public transportation appear likely.

African American disadvantage in Philadelphia has persisted throughout the twentieth century. But changes in its sources, shape, and contexts have resulted in a configuration of experience without historical precedent. The blend of interracial cooperation, self-help, and elite engagement recommended by DuBois in the 1890s, as he later realized, could not attack the structural sources of the inequities he documented. They read as even more anticlimactic and inadequate today. The issue is not whether the circumstances of Philadelphia's African Americans are better or worse today than a hundred years ago. The point is to use history not to offer a perverse nostalgia, a facile lament for persistent immiseration. Rather, it is to use history to explain the very different world that DuBois would find in Philadelphia today. Without a clear-eyed understanding of the new world of Philadelphia's African Americans and its sources, we are unlikely to see a more hopeful conclusion to the next century than to the one that marks the distance between DuBois's Philadelphia and ours.

Notes

1. David Levering Lewis, *W.E.B. Du Bois: Biography of a Race, 1869–1919* (New York: Henry Holt, 1993), p. 178.

2. Bruce Laurie and Mark Schmitz, "Manufacture and Productivity: The Making of an Industrial Base, Philadelphia, 1850–1880," in *Philadelphia: Work, Space, Family, and Group Experience in the Nineteenth Century*, ed. Theodore Hershberg (New York: Oxford University Press, 1981), pp. 43–92; Walter Licht, *Getting Work: Philadelphia, 1840–1950* (Cambridge, Mass.: Harvard University Press, 1992), pp. 1–16; and Philip Scranton and Walter Licht, *Work Sights: Industrial Philadelphia, 1890–1950* (Philadelphia: Temple University Press, 1986).

3. Stephanie Greenberg, "Industrial Location and Ethnic Residential Patterns in an Industrializing City: Philadelphia, 1880," in Hershberg, *Philadelphia*, pp. 215–16, 220–22.

4. Claudia Goldin, "Family Strategies and the Family Economy in the Late Nineteenth Century: The Role of Secondary Workers," in Hershberg, *Philadelphia*, pp. 282, 296–98, notes that nearly one-third of black-headed households had boarders or subtenants, compared to about 16 percent of those headed by Germans, Irish, and native-born whites. The figure compares roughly with DuBois's finding that 38 percent of families in the Seventh Ward took in boarders or subtenants. See *Philadelphia Negro*, p. 290.

5. John Sutherland, "Housing the Poor in the City of Homes: Philadelphia at the Turn of the Century," in *The Peoples of Philadelphia: A History of Ethnic Groups and Lower-Class Life, 1790–1940* ed. Allen F. Davis and Mark H. Haller (Philadelphia: Temple University Press, 1973), pp. 175–77, 184–85.

6. Herbert Aptheker, "Introduction" to the 1973 edition of *Philadelphia Negro*, p. 8.

7. Report of the Philadelphia Settlement in College Settlements Association, *Third Annual Report From September 1, 1891, to September 1, 1892* (Philadelphia: Avil Printing and Lithographing Co., 1892), p. 46. (College Settlements Association hereafter referred to as CSA.)

8. Aptheker, "Introduction," p. 18.

9. CSA, *Second Annual Report of the College Settlements Association for the Year 1891* (New York: Brown and Wilson, 1892), p. 7.

10. CSA, *Second Annual Report*, p. 6. On the settlement movement more generally, see Allen Davis, *Spearheads for Reform: The Social Settlements and the Progressive Movement, 1890–1914* (New York: Oxford University Press, 1967).

11. Philadelphia Settlement Report, in CSA, *Second Annual Report*, p. 46.

12. Eliza Butler Kirkbride, "Personal Aspects of the Canvass," in *The Story of a Woman's Municipal Campaign by the Civic Club for School Reform in the Seventh Ward of Philadelphia*, ed. Mrs. Talcott Williams (Philadelphia: American Academy of Political and Social Science, 1895), p. 39.

13. CSA, *Second Annual Report*, p. 46.

14. Philadelphia Settlement Report, in CSA, *Fourth Annual Report of the College Settlements Association, From September 1, 1892, to September 1, 1893* (Philadelphia: Avil Printing and Lithographing, 1894), pp. 22–23.

15. CSA, *Fourth Annual Report*, pp. 22–23.

16. CSA, *Fourth Annual Report*, p. 24.

17. Carl Husemoller Nightingale, *On the Edge: A History of Poor Black Children and Their American Dreams* (New York: Basic Books, 1993).

18. Theodore Hershberg et al., "A Tale of Three Cities: Blacks, Immigrants, and Opportunity in Philadelphia, 1850–1880, 1930, 1970," in Hershberg, *Philadelphia*, pp. 469–70. The index of dissimilarity, a measurement of the degree of segregation for blacks, was 53 in 1880 and 62 in 1930. For a further discussion of segregation, see McDaniel essay, this volume.

19. CSA, *Second Annual Report*, p. 47.

20. Roger Lane, *William Dorsey's Philadelphia and Ours: On the Past and Future of the Black City in America* (New York: Oxford University Press, 1991), pp. 231–336, offers an excellent description of black organizations.

21. For further discussion of churches in black Philadelphia, see Robert Gregg, *Sparks from the Anvil of Oppression: Philadelphia's African Methodists and Southern Migrants, 1890–1940* (Philadelphia: Temple University Press, 1993).

22. On black schools more generally, see Vincent P. Franklin, *The Education of Black Philadelphia: The Social and Educational History of a Minority Community* (Philadelphia: University of Pennsylvania Press, 1979).

23. Robert Putnam, "The Prosperous Community: Social Capital and Public Life," *American Prospect* (Spring 1993): 35–42.

24. Sophia Wells Royce Williams, "The Work of Organization," in Williams, *Woman's Municipal Campaign*, p. 19.

25. Williams, "Work of Organization," p. 17.

26. Goldin, "Family Strategies and the Family Economy"; see also chapter by Hunter, this volume.

27. For an evocative description of Philadelphia as a walking city, see Sam Bass Warner, Jr., *The Private City: Philadelphia in Three Periods of Its Growth*, rev. ed. (Philadelphia: University of Pennsylvania Press, 1987). On urban spatial patterns more generally, see Thomas J. Sugrue, "The Structures of Urban Poverty: The Reorganization of Space and Work in Three Periods of American History," in *The "Underclass" Debate: Views from History*, ed. Michael B. Katz (Princeton, N.J.: Princeton University Press, 1993), pp. 92–95.

28. U.S. Bureau of the Census, *Eleventh Census of Population, 1890*, pt. 1 (Washington, D.C.: U.S. Government Printing Office, 1893); *Twelfth Census of Population, 1900*, pt. 1 (Washington, D.C.: U.S. Government Printing Office, 1903).

29. On the effects of slum clearance efforts in the Fifth Ward, see *Philadelphia Negro*, pp. 61–62, esp. n. 11.

30. Philadelphia Settlement Report, in CSA, *Sixth Annual Report of the College Settlements Association, From September 1, 1894, to September 1, 1895* (Philadelphia: Dunlap Printing, 1895), pp. 24–28.

31. CSA, *Sixth Annual Report*, p. 25.

32. CSA, *Sixth Annual Report*, p. 26.

33. For an earlier emphasis on the distinction between the Charity Organization Society and the settlement houses, see Michael B. Katz, *In the Shadow of the Poorhouse: A Social History of Welfare in America* (New York: Basic Books, 1986), p. 159.

34. CSA, *Fourth Annual Report*, p. 30.

35. CSA, *Sixth Annual Report*, pp. 25, 32.

36. CSA, *Fourth Annual Report*, pp. 22–23.

37. Agnes Sinclair Holbrook, "Map Notes and Comments," in Residents of Hull-House, *Hull-House Maps and Papers* (Boston: Thomas Y. Crowell, 1895), pp. 13–14; Booth's multivolume *Life and Labour of the People of London* was published between 1889 and 1891.

38. Philadelphia Settlement Report, in CSA, *Eighth Annual Report of the College Settlements Association, From October 1, 1896 to October 1, 1897* (Cambridge, Mass.: Cooperative Press, 1897), p. 31.

39. Samuel McCune Lindsay, "Introduction" to the 1899 edition of *The Philadelphia Negro*, pp. ix–x; Aptheker, "Introduction," pp. 12–13; Lewis, *DuBois*, pp. 187–88.

40. *The Autobiography of W.E.B. DuBois: A Soliloquy on Viewing My Life from the Last Decade of Its First Century* (New York: International Publishers, 1968), pp. 194–95.

41. Philadelphia Settlement Report, in CSA, *Seventh Annual Report of the College Settlements Association, From September 1, 1895, to October 1, 1896* (Chicago: Harman, Geng and Co., 1896), p. 31; *Eighth Annual Report*, pp. 28–29.

42. Lane, *Dorsey*, pp. 197–230, has an excellent discussion of black politics and its relation to the Republican machine.

43. Williams, "The Work of Organization," pp. 24–25, 61, 36–37.

44. Williams, "The Work of Organization," p. 38.

45. CSA, *Third Annual Report*, p. 27. On national reform efforts, see Robyn Muncy, *Creating a Female Dominion in American Reform, 1890–1935* (New York: Oxford University Press, 1991); Ellen Fitzpatrick, *Endless Crusade: Women Social Scientists and Progressive Reform* (New York: Oxford University Press, 1990).

46. Report of the Committee on Fellowships in CSA, *Fifth Annual Report of the College Settlements Association, From September 1, 1893, to September 1, 1894* (Philadelphia: Avil Printing and Lithographing, 1894), p. 10.

47. Quoted in Mary Jo Deegan, "W.E.B. Du Bois and the Women of Hull-House, 1895–1899," *American Sociologist* 19 (Winter 1988): 305, 309.

48. Elisabeth Lasch-Quinn, *Black Neighbors: Race and the Limits of Reform in the American Settlement House Movement, 1890–1945* (Chapel Hill: University of North Carolina Press, 1993), p. 3; Thomas Lee Philpott, *The Slum and the Ghetto: Neighborhood Deterioration and Middle Class Reform, Chicago, 1880–1930* (New York: Oxford University Press, 1978), pp. 274–75, 341.

49. Philadelphia Settlement Report, in CSA, *Ninth Annual Report of the College Settlements Association, From October 1, 1897, to October 1, 1898* (New York: Wm. P. Atkin and Co., 1898), pp. 25–26.

50. Philadelphia Settlement Report, in CSA, *Tenth Annual Report, From October 1,*

1898 to October 1, 1899 (Boston: Press of A. T. Bliss and Co., 1899), pp. 35, 37; Philadelphia Settlement Report, in CSA, *Eleventh Annual Report, From October 1, 1899, to October 1, 1900* (Boston: Press of A. T. Bliss and Co., 1900), 52.

51. *Catalogue of the University of Pennsylvania, 1895–1896* (Philadelphia: Printed for the University, 1895), p. 7; *Catalogue, 1896–97*, p. 478.

52. "Blacks at Penn" (special collection, University Archives and Records Center, University of Pennsylvania).

53. See the various editions of the *Catalogue* for the organization of instruction.

54. Jesse Y. Burk to Samuel McCune Lindsay, February 11, 1897, W.E.B. DuBois Papers, University Archives and Records Center, University of Pennsylvania. Lewis, *DuBois*, p. 180, attributes the sentiments in the letter to Harrison; by our reading, they belong clearly to Burk.

55. James H. S. Brossard, "A History of Sociology at the University of Pennsylvania," *General Magazine and Historical Chronicle*, 33, 1 (October 1930): 406–22; 33, 3 (July 1931): 505–17.

56. *Catalogue, 1897–1898*, p. 218.

57. Charles C. Harrison "To whom it may concern," August 15, 1896, original University of Massachusetts Library, Amherst, Massachusetts; copy, DuBois Papers, University Archives and Records Center, University of Pennsylvania.

58. Brossard, "A History of Sociology," pp. 510–11.

59. Brossard, "A History of Sociology," pp. 407, 411.

60. *Catalogue, 1896–1897*, p. 153.

61. "American Statisticians of the Nineteenth Century," *American Statistical Association Journal* (September 1958): 697–99.

62. Steven A. Sass, *The Pragmatic Imagination: A History of the Wharton School, 1881–1981* (Philadelphia: University of Pennsylvania Press, 1982), pp. 59–85.

63. Brossard, "A History of Sociology," pp. 413–15, quote p. 415. On Patten at Wharton, see Sass, *Pragmatic Imagination*, pp. 91–126. For a biography of Patten, see Daniel M. Fox, *The Discovery of Abundance: Simon N. Patten and the Transformation of Social Theory* (Ithaca, N.Y.: Cornell University Press, 1967).

64. Sass, *Pragmatic Imagination*, p. 106; Samuel McCune Lindsay, *A Bibliography of the Faculty of Political Science, Columbia University, 1880–1930* (New York: Columbia University Press, 1931), p. 153.

65. *Catalogue, 1896–1897*.

66. *Autobiography of W.E.B. Du Bois*, p. 197. On DuBois at Penn, see also Lewis, *DuBois*, pp. 179–210.

67. On scientific charity and charity organization, see Katz, *In the Shadow of the Poorhouse*, pp. 58–84.

68. *Catalogue, 1896–1897*, p. 206.

69. Samuel McCune Lindsay, *Civic Club Digest of the Educational and Charitable Institutions and Societies of Philadelphia*, compiled by a Committee of the Social Science Section of the Civic Club, with an introduction, "Social Aspects of Philadelphia Relief Work" (Philadelphia: Civic Club, 1895).

70. *Catalogue, 1897–1898*, p. 218.

71. *Autobiography of W.E.B. DuBois*, p. 194.

72. Bernard C. Steiner, review of *The Suppression of the African Slave Trade to the United States of America, 1638–1870*, by W. E. Burghardt DuBois, *Annals of the American Academy of Political and Social Science* 9 (January–June 1897): 116–19.

73. Lindsay, "Introduction," p. xi.

74. W. E. Burghardt DuBois, review of *Race Traits and Tendencies of the American Negro*, by Frederick L. Hoffman, *Annals of the American Academy of Political and Social Science* (1897): 127–33.

75. *Autobiography of W.E.B. DuBois*, p. 198.

76. Letter, November 28, 1896, addressed "Dear Sir" and signed by Samuel McCune Lindsay, University Archives and Records Center, University of Pennsylvania; original, DuBois Archives, University of Massachusetts, Amherst; personal communication from Mark Lloyd, archivist, University of Pennsylvania, February 7, 1996.

77. *Autobiography of W.E.B. DuBois*, p. 198.

78. W. E. Burghardt DuBois, "The Study of the Negro Problems," *Annals of the American Academy of Political and Social Science*, 11 (January 1898): 11.

79. W.E.B. DuBois, "The Twelfth Census and the Negro Problems," *Southern Workman* 29 (May 1900): 309; Rayford Logan, *The Negro in American Life and Thought: The Nadir, 1877–1901* (New York: Harper, 1954). For a lengthier discussion of the ways *The Philadelphia Negro* shaped DuBois's research agenda, see David Turley, "Black Social Science and Black Politics in the Understanding of the South: DuBois, the Atlanta University Studies, and the Crisis, 1897–1920," in *Race and Class in the American South Since 1890*, ed. Melvyn Stokes and Rick Halpern (Oxford: Berg, 1994), pp. 139–57.

80. See chapters by Bay, Holt, and Gregg, this volume; see also Kevin K. Gaines, *Uplifting the Race: Black Leadership, Politics, and Culture in the Twentieth Century* (Chapel Hill: University of North Carolina Press, 1996), pp. 152–78.

81. *Autobiography of W.E.B. DuBois*, pp. 198–99.

82. For further discussion of these issues, see chapter by Jones, this volume.

83. *Autobiography of W.E.B. DuBois*, pp. 198–99.

84. DuBois, "The Study of the Negro Problems," p. 22.

85. Baltimore *Ledger*, December 23, 1899, p. 1; *AME Church Review* 16 (January 1900): 395–95 (April 1900): 502.

86. Anonymous review, *American Historical Review* 6 (October 1900): 162–64.

87. "The Negro Problem in the North," *Nation* 69, 179 (October 26, 1899): 310.

88. W.E.B., review, *Yale Review* 8 (May 1900): 110–11.

89. Henry L. Phillips, review of *The Philadelphia Negro*, *Charities Review* 9, 12 (February 1900): 575–78.

90. C. R. Woodruff, review of *The Philadelphia Negro*, *City and State* (January 4, 1900).

91. Review of *The Philadelphia Negro*, *Sunday School Times* (January 6, 1900).

92. Katherine Bement Davis, "The Condition of the Negro in Philadelphia," *Journal of Political Economy* 8 (December 1899–September 1900): 248–60.

93. *Outlook* (November 11, 1899): 647–48.

94. "The Negro Problem in the North," p. 310.

95. Mary Furner, *Advocacy and Objectivity: A Crisis in the Professionalization of American Social Science, 1865–1905* (Lexington: University of Kentucky Press, 1975); Peter Novick, *That Noble Dream: The "Objectivity Question" and the American Historical Profession* (New York: Cambridge University Press, 1988).

96. DuBois, "The Study of the Negro Problem," pp. 7–8.

97. Samuel McCune Lindsay, "The Charity Problem in Philadelphia," *Citizen* (October 1896): 263; italics in original.

98. Lindsay, "The Charity Problem," pp. 263–66.

99. Lindsay, "Introduction," pp. xiv–xv.

100. Davis, "The Condition of the Negro," p. 251.

101. W. E. Burghardt DuBois, *The Black North in 1901: A Social Study*, a series of articles originally appearing in the *New York Times*, November–December 1901 (reprint, New York: Arno Press and New York Times, 1969), p. 6.

102. For a discussion of these issues, see the essays in Katz, *"Underclass" Debate*.

103. For overviews, see Katz, *In the Shadow of the Poorhouse*; James T. Patterson,

America's Struggle Against Poverty, 1900–1994 (Cambridge, Mass.: Harvard University Press, 1995).

104. Carolyn Adams, David Bartelt, David Elesh, Ira Goldstein, Nancy Kleniewski, and William Yancey, *Philadelphia: Neighborhoods, Division, and Conflict in a Postindustrial City* (Philadelphia: Temple University Press, 1991).

105. Leonard Blumberg and Michael Lalli, "Little Ghettoes: A Study of Negroes in the Suburbs," *Phylon* 27 (1966): 117–31; William Labov, *Language in the Inner City: Studies in the Black English Vernacular* (Philadelphia: University of Pennsylvania Press, 1972). More generally, see Douglas S. Massey and Nancy A. Denton, *American Apartheid: Segregation and the Making of the Underclass* (Cambridge, Mass.: Harvard University Press, 1993).

106. See chapters by V. P. Franklin, Carl Husemoller Nightingale, and Elijah Anderson, this volume.

Part I
DuBois and the Color Line

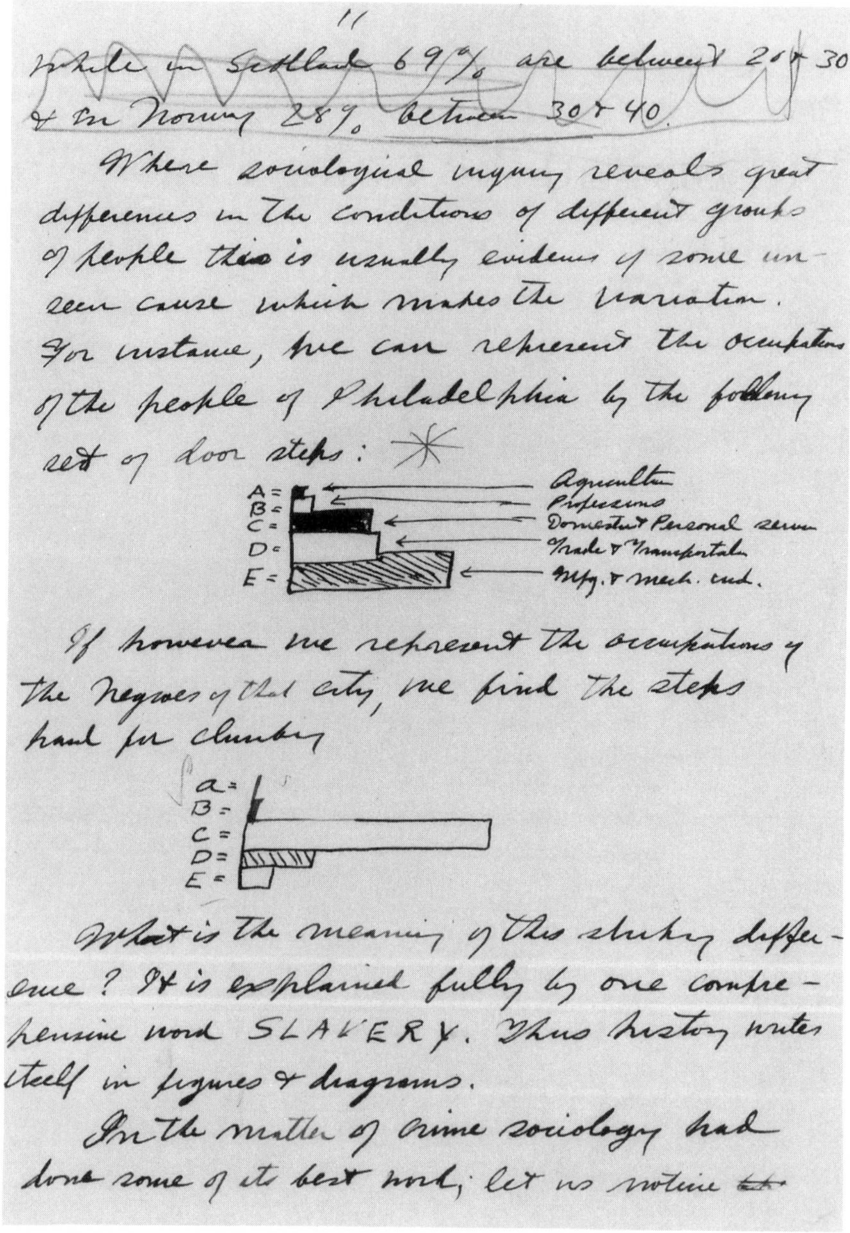

while in Scotland 69% are between 20 & 30
& in Norway 28% between 30 & 40.

Where sociological inquiry reveals great differences in the conditions of different groups of people this is usually evidence of some unseen cause which makes the variation. For instance, we can represent the occupations of the people of Philadelphia by the following set of door steps: *

A = ——————— Agriculture
B = ——————— Professions
C = ——————— Domestic & Personal service
D = ——————— Trade & Transportation
E = ——————— Mfg. & mech. ind.

If however we represent the occupations of the Negroes of that city, we find the steps hard for climbing

a =
B =
C =
D =
E =

What is the meaning of this striking difference? It is explained fully by one comprehensive word SLAVERY. Thus history writes itself in figures & diagrams.

In the matter of crime sociology had done some of its best work; let us notice th

Figure 4. Page from DuBois, "A Program for a Sociological Society." Courtesy of Special Collections and Archives, W.E.B. DuBois Library, University of Massachusetts, Amherst.

Chapter 1
"The World Was Thinking Wrong About Race"
The Philadelphia Negro *and Nineteenth-Century Science*

Mia Bay

"Nobody ever reads that fat volume on 'The Philadelphia Negro,'" W.E.B. DuBois wrote in 1920, recalling his second book two decades after it was published, "but they treat it with respect, and that consoles me."[1] Since then DuBois's massive 1899 survey of black Philadelphia has picked up many readers, although its reappraisal came too late to provide any further consolation to DuBois. Republished by two publishing houses in 1967 — four years after DuBois's death — *The Philadelphia Negro* has been revisited over the last thirty years by scholars in a variety of disciplines, and pronounced a seminal work in an impressive number of fields. On the basis of *The Philadelphia Negro* and his subsequent sociological studies at Atlanta University, DuBois has been widely celebrated as one of the founding fathers of American sociology.[2] Likewise, *The Philadelphia Negro* has won DuBois the title of "pioneer anthropologist" from scholars in that field who argue that DuBois's study initiated "black urban anthropology."[3] In addition, his study has also been cited as an early contribution to urban history, and as a neglected classic in the historical school of economics.[4]

DuBois's study of the Philadelphia Negro has emerged as a classic across the disciplines precisely because it was written before the modern disciplines of sociology, anthropology, history, and economics were fully formed. Although justly celebrated for its contributions to all these fields, *The Philadelphia Negro*'s relationship to the more amorphous social science of its own day has been overshadowed by the retrospective appreciations it has received from scholars intent on establishing it as a pioneering work within their various nascent disciplines. Its intellectual achievement has been assessed, above all, in terms of its innovative use of social science practices that became commonplace long after it was published, such as participant observation, census taking, the interview, and the historical and economic analysis of government data. Yet such appreciations tend to measure mostly the symbolic significance — as a "black first" — of a book so neglected in its own day that most of its innovations were not so much picked up as rediscovered by later social scientists. Moreover, what is lost in these retrospective celebrations of *The Philadelphia Negro* is a clear sense of what the study meant in its own day, in DuBois's thought especially.

To understand *The Philadelphia Negro* in its own context we must consider DuBois's study in relationship to nineteenth-century intellectual traditions, rather than focus on the way it contributed to and foreshadowed later developments in American science. It must be considered with reference to DuBois's educational and scientific training, the racial thought of his intellectual milieu, and the investigative goals he pursued. As we shall see, considered in context, *The Philadelphia Negro* emerges less as a project of any of one of the still-forming social science disciplines than as an iconoclastic study of what was known in the 1890s as "the Negro problem" — which was the subject that DuBois sought to illuminate when he accepted the University of Pennsylvania's invitation to study the Negroes of Philadelphia's Seventh Ward.

As such, *The Philadelphia Negro* must be understood as an important example of what Nancy Leys Stepan and Sander L. Gilman have called the "critical tradition" of challenges to scientific racism by minority authors — a tradition that was particularly rich and vital among nineteenth-century African American intellectuals.[5] The first empirical study of social problems among American blacks, DuBois's *Philadelphia Negro* was a radical and deliberate departure from the research methods employed by his white colleagues to study the same subjects. By starting with the presumption "that Negro problems are the problems of human beings; that they cannot be explained away by fantastic theories, ungrounded assumptions, or metaphysical subtleties" (pp. iii–v), DuBois broke ranks with the white social scientists of the 1890s, who almost invariably assumed that deficiencies characteristic of the race made Negro problems quite different from other people's problems.[6]

Accordingly, his methodological innovations reflected a conceptual advance that is all too easily overlooked by modern readers. Today, DuBois's presumptions seem commonsensical, and it is difficult to see the rather dry collection of facts and figures DuBois presents in *The Philadelphia Negro* as any kind of advance in racial thought. Yet the empirical method DuBois can be seen developing in this study broke away from the theoretical orientation of the mainstream social science of his day, and also heralded an important shift within the critical tradition of African American challenges to scientific racism. Published at the turn of the century, *The Philadelphia Negro* appeared just as DuBois and other black thinkers were beginning to abandon the nineteenth-century science of the races — ethnology — for social science.

Whereas traditional defenses of black equality had drawn on the Bible, citing as a scriptural principle "of one blood God created all the nations of men" (Acts 17:26), DuBois and a few other academically trained black intellectuals of this period began to attempt to marshal empirical evidence to controvert white racial theories.

Their efforts converged and coincided with Franz Boas's insistence, first articulated in the 1890s, that science had established no fixed equation between race and human capacities.[7] And in years to come black intellectuals would be the first to welcome the "culture concept" Boas developed over the next couple of decades. In the first decades of the twentieth century, black thinkers and leaders eagerly embraced and promoted Boas's idea that differences in culture rather than innate racial traits of any kind were all that divided the races.

In the 1890s, however, with the culture concept still a few years ahead, black racial thought was in flux. Always complex and contradictory, Du-Bois's ideas about race were particularly fluid during this period, for the young scholar began his scientific career struggling to establish the secular, scientific meaning of race, to combat racism, and to divine the scientific laws that would foster the advancement of the black race. Considered in context, *The Philadelphia Negro* can illuminate both this personal struggle and the neglected history of the black critical tradition of challenges to scientific racism.

"To Find Out What Was the Matter": The Black and White Scientific Traditions and *The Philadelphia Negro*

Certainly, it was the Negro problem, rather than any more narrow scientific question, that the University of Pennsylvania sought to highlight when it commissioned the study. According to DuBois's rather cynical recollection of his dealings with the University of Pennsylvania, the study was conceived when Philadelphia, always "one of the worst governed of American's badly governed cities, was having one of its periodic spasms of reform." So in 1896, fresh out of graduate school, the young DuBois was offered a one-year appointment to perform a study designed to illuminate the causes of political corruption in Philadelphia, which was also expected to document the reformers' foregone conclusions on the matter. "A thorough study of the causes was called for," DuBois recollected. "Not but what the underlying cause was evident to most white Philadelphians: the corrupt semi-criminal vote of the Negro seventh ward. Everyone agreed that here laid the cancer; but would it not be well to elucidate the known causes by a scientific investigation, with the imprimatur of the university?"[8]

When they appointed DuBois, however, the University of Pennsylvania got a researcher with his own hidden agenda. DuBois came to the study of the Negro problem in Philadelphia with his own ambitions, and they were quite different from those of his white sponsors. Trained at Fisk and Harvard and in Berlin, DuBois had begun his academic career teaching at Wilberforce the previous year, "ready and eager to begin a life-work leading to the emancipation of the American Negro." "History and the other social sciences were to be weapons," he recalled in 1944, looking back on that period of his life, "to be sharpened and applied by research and writing." Teaching at Wilberforce had not forwarded his ambitions—"I was doing nothing directly in the social science and saw no immediate prospect." But with his invitation from the University of Pennsylvania, "the door of opportunity opened: just a crack to be sure, but a distinct opening."[9]

DuBois squeezed through this opening with large ambitions. Selected by the University "as an expendable black person brought there to do a predictable job,"[10] DuBois ignored his sponsors' presumptions about problems of the Seventh Ward and set out to "find out what was the matter in this area and why." Philadelphia offered him the perfect laboratory in which to develop and refine the goals he had held since he applied to graduate school six years earlier, to study social science "with a view of the ultimate application of its principles to the social and economic advancement of the Negro people."[11] What remained was for DuBois to find a way to harness social science to black advancement. The intellectual challenge he faced was daunting, for there were no precedents for what he was trying to do.

In its analysis of race relations, especially, 1890s sociology was based on theoretical speculations rather than on empirical research. Bent on creating "grand theories" of society that could be employed to analyze and solve the social problems of Gilded Age America, the founding fathers of American sociology invariably explained racial inequities with reference to natural laws. These natural laws offered little support to DuBois's search for the scientific principles that would foster black progress. Although northern sociologists held out more hope than southern sociologists that natural law did not forever bar the advancement and assimilation of the Negro, even the most liberal northern sociologists held low opinions of the capabilities of nonwhites and "were unable to envision an egalitarian society in the foreseeable future."[12] In the South and North, alike, sociological inferences about black capacities owed a great deal to ideas of Herbert Spencer and other American evolutionists, who popularized a Social Darwinism that "placed blacks at the primitive end of the evolutionary scale."[13] Gloomily interpreted, as they frequently were in the 1890s, the Darwinian laws governing race development heralded nothing short of the extinction of American blacks, a prediction not uncommon in 1890s social science.

Indeed, Booker T. Washington felt as if he had "just finished reading his own funeral sermon" after reading one example of the era's white social science: Frederick L. Hoffman's *Race Traits and Tendencies* (1896). Hoffman, like a number of other white sociologists, contended that blacks were "doomed to extinction unless somehow made to face the struggle for existence without paternalism."[14] Of course, Darwinism did not have to be seen as the death knell for the black race, and DuBois railed against interpretations such as Hoffman's in *The Philadelphia Negro*. He and other African Americans of his day were certainly able to come up with more sanguine interpretations of Social Darwinism — the most obvious example being the implicit Social Darwinism featured in Washington's doctrine of industrial education, which promised to provide black laborers with the skills and discipline needed to compete more successfully in the Darwinian struggle. For DuBois's purposes as he began *The Philadelphia Negro*, nonetheless, the understanding of natural laws of race development enshrined in white social science posed an obstacle. It ensured that the work of his colleagues could provide little guidance to a young black scholar bent on advancing the prospects of his race.

Moreover, since white sociology's natural laws and negative assessments of black capacity tended to be based on evolutionary theory rather than any sort of empirical evidence, American social science offered no research models for DuBois as he set up his study of Philadelphia's black population. White social scientists, as DuBois caustically informed one of them, were content to base their analyses of Negro problems on information gathered from "the car window & associated press dispatches."[15] In breaking with the slipshod and speculative research techniques his white colleagues brought to the study of Negroes, DuBois was forced to develop his research strategy as he went along. "I started out with no 'research methods,'" DuBois later recalled, "and asked for little advice as to procedure."[16]

DuBois's intellectual isolation was compounded by the fact that his scholarly training and scientific ambition set him apart from most of the other black critics of scientific racism in his generation. In an era when the professionalization of science had begun to "separate science from both 'high' literary culture and popular culture," DuBois's impressive educational credentials made him one of the few black intellectuals qualified to engage with the increasingly racist social science of the day on its own terms.[17] In order to do so, however, DuBois would have to break an earlier ethnological critical tradition of black racial thought, which had begun to sound increasingly outmoded as science and religion split in the late nineteenth century.

From the 1830s onward black thinkers had defended the character and capabilities of their race against the attacks of pro-slavery apologists and the anti-black dogma with arguments that evoked Christian monogenism as the ultimate line of defense against arguments for black inferiority. In efforts that aimed, above all, to counter the arguments for polygenesis — the separate origins of the races — made by white scientists in the American school of ethnology, African American intellectuals crafted their own version of ethnology. Like white ethnology, black ethnology blended science with scriptural interpretation in the manner common to American science up until the late nineteenth century. Drawing on the environmentalist tradition of nineteenth-century science, African American thinkers argued that different climates, not different creations, had distinguished the races. On the key issue of the origins of the races, their arguments for human unity always rested on the Scriptures, reminding those who might succumb to white ethnological doctrine that God had created all men of one blood.[18] Even secular-minded nineteenth-century black intellectuals such as Frederick Douglass countered the arguments for polygenesis with reference to the Scriptures. "The credit of the Bible is at stake," Douglass thundered in an 1854 lecture, "The Claims of the Negro Ethnologically Considered," which critiqued the polygenetic theories of black inferiority developed by white scientists such as Josiah Nott, Louis Aggasiz, and Samuel Morton.[19]

Christian monogenism was, of course, a perfectly creditable defense against polygenesis, since polygenesis centered around the wholly unsecular premise that white people descended from Adam and Eve. In the late nineteenth century, however, when black thinkers continued to evoke virtually identical monogenetic arguments to counter the new racist ideas arising out of the fledging science of biological evolution, the black ethnological tradition began to sound out of step with the increasingly secular scientific thought of the late nineteenth century. More than anything else, the increasing scientific irrelevance of the black ethnological tradition of Christian monogenism reflected the gulf that began to divide scientific discourse from religious and popular thought as the century ended. African Americans were far from the only Americans still supporting the biblical account of creation in the late nineteenth century. And in an era when Darwin's ideas about the impermanence of the species were often invoked to support the polygenist tenet that black people were a separate species, Christian monogenism remained a relevant account of the origins of the races. Nonetheless, by the 1890s, theological accounts of the descent of man were increasingly uncommon in scientific discourse.

In the 1890s, therefore, when the scientifically minded DuBois set out to make a study of his people, he could draw little from the racial thought of his fellow black intellectuals, who with a few exceptions still tended to put a great deal of emphasis on Christian monogenism in their discussions of the past and future of the black race. Many of the black thinkers of the 1890s were ministers, whose attacks on scientific racism quite naturally featured a good bit of theology. They included men such as Benjamin Tucker Tanner, Joseph Hayne, and Harvey Johnson, who all published monographs on ethnology charting the biblical descent of the Negro race from Noah's son Ham — which often also emphasized that his progeny were not afflicted by Noah's curse.[20] But even turn-of-the-century textbooks on black history and development ranging from George Washington Williams's 1885 classic, *The History of the Negro Race in America*, to H. F. Kletzing and William Crogman's much later work *The Progress of a Race*, began with biblically based chapters titled "Unity of the Races."[21]

More to the point, ethnology appears even in studies quite similar in scope and subject to DuBois's Philadelphia project, which often began with statements on the ethnological status of the Negro. For instance, E. R. Carter's *The Black Side: A Partial History of the Business, Religious, and Educational Side of the Negro in Atlanta*, which was published in 1894, opened with an ethnological review of the achievements of the race by Bishop Henry MacNeal Turner. In his introduction to the book, Turner, whose other publications included a pamphlet on ethnology, celebrated "the adventure and enterprise of the Hamitic Races," and rebuked those who suggested that the Negro had "been created an inferior race by that God who was no respecter of persons."[22]

With his training, DuBois could not help but be aware that such arguments had, as Stepan and Gilman put it, "lost ground as an acceptable style of scientific argumentation in mainstream science." Accordingly, a little noted feature of DuBois's early intellectual development is the self-conscious distance he put between scientific inquiry and Christian monogenism as he began his scientific career. This distancing can be observed in "The Conservation of the Races," a speech he made before the American Negro Academy in 1897. Prepared when DuBois was at Pennsylvania working on *The Philadelphia Negro*, "The Conservation of the Races" is now mostly remembered for its unvarnished racial essentialism, but it also shows him working out his scientific approach to studying Negro problems. It begins with a pointed disavowal of the usefulness of invoking monogenism in discussions of race. American Negroes, DuBois told the members of the Academy, were not studying the laws of race development because they opposed the negative assumptions about capacities and status of their race that undergirded most discussions of race. Consequently, African Americans had "been led to deprecate and minimize race distinctions, to believe intensely that of one blood God created all nations, and to speak of human brotherhood as though it were a possibility already dawning tomorrow."[23]

"In our calmer moments," DuBois went on to counter "we must acknowledge that human beings are divided into races; that in this country the two most extreme types of the world's races have met." Rather than reject race by holding on to biblical notions of man, DuBois was arguing, Afro-Americans must study race and harness its power for their own development. In doing so, as a number of modern day commentators have observed, DuBois assigned race an essential reality — invoking history and sociology as the constitutive elements of race, but never quite escaping biology.[24] Yet underlying his essentialist message was a call for empirical data so open-ended that it made his call for "the conservation of the races" a tentative hypothesis at best.

"What is the real meaning of race," DuBois asked, "what has, in the past, been the law of race development, and what lessons has the past history of race development to teach the rising Negro people?" Even as he tried to define what races were, DuBois got lost in a string of questions. "Unfortunately for scientists," DuBois complained, "the criteria for race are most exasperatingly intermingled." He continued:

Color does not agree with texture of hair, for many of the dark races have straight hair; nor does color agree with breadth of head, for the yellow Tartar has a broader head than the German; nor again has the science of language succeeded so far in clearing up the relative authority of these various and contradictory criteria. The final word of science, so far is that we have at least two, perhaps three great families of human beings — the whites the Negroes, possibly the yellow race.

Unable even to name the races with any certainty, DuBois admitted that they might "transcend scientific definition."[25]

Thus, DuBois's essentialism in "The Conservation of the Races" went hand in hand with a call for the kind of empirical data that would ultimately undercut his belief in the existence of "subtle, delicate and elusive" differences "which have silently but definitely separated men into groups."[26] Indeed, his willingness to accept the possibility of racial differences — to *investigate* that possibility — along with his willingness to abandon the traditionally biblical defenses of black equality seem to have been crucial features of his attack on the racial science of his day. An aggressively secular spirit of inquiry, which eschewed any presumption of racial unity, infuses his scientific work of the late 1890s. "That there are differences between the white and black races is certain," he told the American Academy of Political and Social Science in 1898, "but just what those differences are is known to none with any approach to certainty."[27] Likewise, in 1903 he began yet another appeal to the Academy's members for scientific data on Negro problems with a dismissal of scripturally based ethnological arguments about race. Complaining that Americans were far too ignorant of "social facts and processes," he relegated ethnology to the nursery school, lamenting, "We print in the opening paragraphs of our children's histories theories of the origin and destiny of the races that make the gravest of us smile."[28]

"We Simply Collect the Facts": DuBois's Scientific Method in *The Philadelphia Negro*

DuBois's empiricism in *The Philadelphia Negro* shows him opposing both the biblically based ethnology of his African American contemporaries and the "fantastic theories" of his white colleagues. Born out of DuBois's intellectual isolation, the study illustrates the immense challenges faced by black intellectuals who sought to deconstruct scientific racism at the turn of the century. Accordingly, it is only with reference to these challenges that the scientific method employed by DuBois in *The Philadelphia Negro* can be fully understood; while not entirely successful, DuBois's struggle to depart from both the white American and African American approaches to Negro problems of his era shaped the parameters of this work in important ways.

His scientific ambitions for *The Philadelphia Negro* unsupported by American models, white or black, DuBois based his study on European social theory and practice. He drew much of the structure and methodology for his study from Charles Booth's *Life and Labour of the People in London* (1889–1902), a massive 17-volume work of empirical sociology. Not yet complete even after DuBois finished work on *The Philadelphia Negro*, Booth's study surveyed the occupations, incomes, lodgings, and lifestyles of London's population. A businessman as well as a reformer and amateur social scientist, Charles Booth was an English shipping and leather magnate who "carried over to his research habits of inquiry he had cultivated in his business." His study sought "facts and figures" for philanthropists to use to assess the well-being of London's populations, and relied on extensive interviews with informants, as well as census returns and municipal records, to amass this data.[29]

DuBois's choice of Booth's *Life and Labour of the People of London* as a model for his research in Philadelphia was an inspired one, for much of Booth's study explored the nature and causes of poverty among Londoners. For obvious reasons, Booth's study of nineteenth-century London's relatively homogeneous population considered this question without regard to race, and therefore had much to offer a scholar interested in emphasizing that "the problems of Negroes are the problems of human beings." DuBois drew much of his research design from Booth, logging "some 835 hours interviewing approximately 2,500 households," using research schedules patterned after Booth's.[30] Like Booth, he eschewed sampling, tabulating approximately fifteen thousand household schedules himself.

In addition, Booth's study may have offered DuBois conceptual insights as well. According to Gertrude Himmelfarb, Booth's most innovative contribution to the study of poverty was his "delineation of classes of the poor." As a reformer, Booth was particularly interested in distinguishing between the "poor," "very poor," and "the lowest class of occasional loafers, and semi-criminals," to better establish how poverty could be remedied—he proposed making the lowest of the poor "servants of the state."[31] Although less drawn to Draconian remedies than Booth was, DuBois was also interested in delineating classes. Just as Booth found it necessary to dissuade late nineteenth-century Londoners from seeing all of the poor as indigent paupers, DuBois realized that he had to discourage white Americans from seeing "the Negroes as composing one practically homogeneous mass." "[W]ell meaning people continually do this," DuBois wrote, speaking with an ire borne of personal experience. "They regale the thugs and whore-mongers and gamblers of Seventh and Lombard streets with congratulations on what the Negroes have done in a quarter century, and pity for their disabilities; and they scold the caterers of Addison street for the pickpockets and paupers of the race" (pp. 309–10).

Not content to dismiss the white community's blindness to class distinctions among Negroes with ridicule only, DuBois went on to sketch out the class structure of black Philadelphia, dividing its population into four grades, ranging from an elite grade of families who earned "sufficient income to live well" to the "submerged tenth," a fourth grade made up of "criminals, prostitutes and loafers." Prosaic though it may seem today, DuBois's brief outline of the social classes among American Negroes was an innovative observation that also laid the groundwork for an argument he would later develop when he spoke of "the talented tenth" in *The Souls of Black Folk*. Properly understood, *The Philadelphia Negro* suggested, black society contained a responsible elite who could be hoped to guide its less fortunate masses. The novelty of DuBois's class argument in the study is emphasized by David Levering Lewis, who points out: "Before it was identified and described in *The Philadelphia Negro*, the class structure of Afro-America was mostly unknown, utterly mysterious, and widely considered nonexistent. Most white people supposed that the periodic appearance of exceptional or 'representative black people' was due to providence, 'mixed blood,' or some mysterious current passing through the dark, undifferentiated mass. Otherwise, there were only good Negroes and bad ones."[32]

Great though DuBois's debt to Booth was, he took a still crucial inspiration for his empirical method from Gustav Schmoller, a German political economist whose seminars he had attended in Berlin. Breaking with the deductive methods of earlier economists, Schmoller and other members of a new German school of economics that emerged at the end of the nineteenth century maintained that historical studies should provide the empirical base for all economic theory. Schmoller, in particular, thought that empirical study should be employed to regulate human affairs, believing "that innumerable small accurate studies of all phases of man's social life would accumulate a body of information on which social policy could be based."[33] Both *The Philadelphia Negro* and DuBois's subsequent Atlanta University studies illustrate the profound impression Schmoller had on DuBois, for they represent his attempts to realize Schmoller's vision.

Whereas DuBois drew on the research design of Booth's *Life and Labour of the People of London* for his research methods, schedules, and grades, Schmoller's ideas provided him with the conceptual key for *The Philadelphia Negro* and his other turn-of-the-century scientific work. The German scientist's call for a scientific method based on the "accumulation of facts" provided DuBois with an approach that could bypass both the racist assumptions buried in white sociology's natural laws, and black thought's reliance on the Scriptures for its antiracist tenets.[34] Moreover, Schmoller's emphasis on historical information held a deep appeal for DuBois, whose doctoral work had been in history. Accordingly, he presented black Philadelphia's social problems in a two-hundred-year time frame to trace the development of the Seventh Ward. "One cannot study the Negro in freedom," he pointed out, "and come to general conclusions about his destiny without knowing his history in slavery."[35]

For DuBois, Schmoller's vision of science was more than just an intellectual solution; it formed a framework for the positivist faith that had propelled the young black academic's social science career. Schmoller's idea of science called for the most disinterested empiricism. He insisted that research never be compromised by recommendations for reform — a mandate DuBois embraced wholeheartedly, despite his hopes for linking science and black advancement. "We simply collect the facts; others may use them as they will," DuBois said of his Philadelphia work in 1897.[36] Elsewhere he warned, "Students must be careful to insist that science as such — be it physics, chemistry, psychology, or sociology — has but one aim: the discovery of truth. . . . Any attempt to give it a double aim, to make social reform the immediate instead of the mediate object of a search for truth, will inevitably tend to defeat both objects."[37]

DuBois's confidence in the ultimate convergence between science and justice is a striking act of faith within the context of the racial nadir of the 1890s. Black Americans had once "hoped for much from science," as a writer in the *Colored American* mourned in 1839, only to find science lending its authority to one racist theory after another.[38] By the 1890s, the idea of hierarchy among the races was woven in the very fabric of American science. Yet it was the very pervasiveness of racist assumptions in American science that made empiricism take on such a special salience for DuBois. As he saw it, an information-based science should serve to counter the manifestly irrational ideas about black people many whites held. Moreover, only through a shift toward empirical research could these ideas be pushed out of science. DuBois made this point eloquently at the American Academy of Political and Social Science in 1897:

The most baneful cause of uncritical study of the Negro is the manifest and far-reaching bias of its writers. Americans are born in many cases with deep, fierce convictions on the Negro question, and in other cases imbibe them from their environment. When such men come to write on the subject, without technical training, without breadth of view, and in some cases without a deep sense of the sanctity of scientific truth, their testimony, however interesting, as opinion, must of necessity be worthless as science.[39]

The Philadelphia Negro in Considered Context

The methodological and conceptual challenges that DuBois faced as he designed his Philadelphia study were then exceeded by the challenges he faced in writing up his study. The empirical results that DuBois had collected did not support white conventional wisdom about black social problems. The facts and figures he gathered in Philadelphia suggested that an interwoven combination of racism, poverty, and the lingering aftereffects of slavery—such as disadvantages in employment—were at the root of black Philadelphia's social ills. Yet such an argument could not be stated baldly by DuBois, whose own Victorian sensibility would not have supported a purely environmental explanation for all of the Seventh Ward's social problems, in any case. Elitist by temperament, and very much given to moralizing about lower-class manners and behavior, DuBois was inclined to blame at least some area's problems on the failings of its "bottom class" denizens—an outlook that made him capable of discussing life in the Seventh Ward with enough disapproval to seem credible to his white contemporaries. But the book would nonetheless require a high-wire act. Writing *The Philadelphia Negro* demanded that DuBois find a way to speak to both white and black audiences without seeming partisan and at the same time wrestle with conflicts between his own presumptions and his empiricist method. Little wonder that the result was, as David Levering Lewis notes, a "great, schizoid monograph."[40] As such, *The Philadelphia Negro* dramatizes the tensions in turn-of-the-century black racial thought.

As Lewis so shrewdly observes, since DuBois was determined "to gain the widest and most respectful hearing possible" for *The Philadelphia Negro*

he obviously must have calculated that it would be necessary to write what amounted almost to two books in one—one that would not be immediately denounced or ridiculed by the arbiters of mainstream knowledge, influence, and order for its transparent heterodoxy; and a second one that would, over time, deeply penetrate the social sciences and gradually improve race-relations policy through its not immediately apparent interpretive radicalism. He set about writing a study affirming and modifying, yet also significantly subverting, the received sociological wisdom of his day.[41]

DuBois was aided in this complex task by his own lingering adherence to certain Victorian verities. In addition to showcasing DuBois's elitist temperament, for instance, *The Philadelphia Negro* displays DuBois's penchant for racial stereotypes. Like most black thinkers of his era, he was not immune to racialist conceptions of black temperament, and above all favored the few positive stereotypes associated with Afro-Americans.[42] Probably because its author was quite sincerely impressed by the cooperation he received from his subjects, *The Philadelphia Negro* is larded with references to the "proverbial candor and good nature of the Negro" (pp. 63, 91 n. 7, 97). A product of its time in other respects as well, DuBois's portrait of black Philadelphia is colored through by social Darwinism. With dispassionate detachment, DuBois refers to his subjects as a "half-developed race" (p. 351) and "a people comparatively low in the scale of civilization" (p. 66). He is not at all surprised to find evidence of drunkenness and disorder among the slaves in colonial Pennsylvania, describing such behavior as "the low condition of morals which we should expect in a barbarous people forced to labor in a strange land" (p. 15). These and other Darwinian references are then elaborated in his conclusion when he suggests that Negroes in cities such as Philadelphia have reached a "mediaeval stage" of "social evolution" (p. 392).

The Philadelphia Negro's Darwinist references and racial stereotypes are worth noting. Usually glossed over by scholars intent on establishing DuBois as social science pioneer — Werner J. Lange, for example, writes that the young DuBois "needless to say, . . . had little use for social Darwinism" — they are one source of this pathbreaking book's schizoid character.[43] More important, they illustrate how the scientific logic DuBois brought to *The Philadelphia Negro* forced him to debate his own assumptions as well as those of others. Some of the book's most striking internal contradictions arise from its author's unsuccessful struggle to blend his study's empirical results with his own Victorian outlook and elitism.

Without ever reconciling its arguments, for example, *The Philadelphia Negro* simultaneously attributes the lack of advancement among the city's African American laborers to their own failings and to the poor opportunities offered by a highly discriminatory and segregated labor market. Black labor's problems, of course, did not have to be limited to one cause or the other. Nevertheless, *The Philadelphia Negro* juxtaposed unsubstantiated paternalist generalities about the deficiencies of Negro labor with overwhelming evidence that black laborers were shut out of many professions without elaboration. "The Negro is as a rule," DuBois observes at one point, "willing, honest and good-natured; but he also is as a rule, careless, unreliable and unsteady" (p. 97). Elsewhere he adds that typical Negroes are "hardworking people, proverbially good-natured; lacking a little in foresight and forehandedness, and in 'push'" (p. 315). Referring to no particular evidence, the observations appear amid reams of data showing that black employment in Philadelphia had been severely restricted for the last fifty years, at least, by "competition, industrial change, [and] color prejudice" (p. 145). Such juxtapositions no doubt sounded only natural to DuBois's 1890s readers, but they do show DuBois waffling on the implications of his empiricism. The modern reader can only surmise that these black Philadelphians might well have had more use for their "proverbial good nature" than any of the other mixed qualities for which DuBois gave them credit — since good jobs lay outside their reach.

Likewise, DuBois's references to Social Darwinism show him wrestling with fact that his understanding of the laws of Darwinism does not always converge with his research. Still speculating on black Philadelphia's failures in the labor market, he theorized that the best Negro laborers, "who are as bright, talented and reliable as any class of workmen . . . in untrammelled competition would soon rise high in the economic scale, and thus by the law of the survival of the fittest we should soon have left at the bottom those inefficient and lazy drones who did not deserve a better fate." Recognizing that this happy outcome could not be seen in Philadelphia's black labor market, DuBois was forced to modify his conception of Darwinian law, adding that "in the realm of social phenomena the law of survival is greatly modified by human choice, wish, whim and prejudice" (p. 98).

Insights from his research did not change DuBois's mind overnight. Optimistic readings of social Darwinism held powerful appeal for black leaders of his generation, since such readings could be easily fused with much older ideas about black uplift to create a social theory that predicted a glorious racial destiny for the black race. It was a destiny that DuBois encouraged his race to find in "The Conservation of the Races," and would continue to half-believe in for most of his life. But *The Philadelphia Negro* both illustrates and embodies the early erosion of his scientific belief in Darwinian laws. DuBois would continue to talk about race development in evolutionary terms for several years, writing as late as 1904 that study of American Negroes in the United States could hope to record "the evolution of a vast group of men from simpler primitive conditions to higher and more complex civilizations."[44]

But by the end of that decade he had decisively rejected Spencer's vast "biological analogy." "The elaborate attempt to compare the social and animal organism failed because analogy implies knowledge but does not supply it," he then wrote in an unpublished essay " — suggests but does not furnish lines of investigation."[45] DuBois's repudiation of Spencer suggests how much he ultimately learned from his research for *The Philadelphia Negro*. The investigative and inductive methodology he developed for his study informed his ultimate break with Darwinian laws.

More generally as well, the data he gathered for the study led him away from racial explanations for Negro problems — even if he did not escape them entirely in *The Philadelphia Negro*. Nowhere is this more evident than in a talk he gave at Atlanta University after his study of Philadelphia was complete. Speaking at a meeting of the black university's Sociological Society, he summed up his findings with a thumbnail sketch presenting a thesis that analyzed the social problems of black Philadelphia as a labor question rather than as a race question. "Where sociological inquiry reveals great differences in the conditions of people this is usually evidence of an unseen cause which makes the variation," he observed. He then drew two contrasting graphs charting with the occupations of Philadelphians by race, which showed that the vast majority of the black populations to be clustered in menial occupations (see Figure 4). "What is the meaning of this striking difference?" he asked. "It is explained fully by one comprehensive word SLAVERY. Thus history writes itself in figures and diagrams."[46]

DuBois did not present this simple and radical thesis in *The Philadelphia Negro*. Indeed, as his biographer notes, the study is full of "moralizing, and stern admonitions to black people to behave like lending library patrons."

All the same, however, the book captured the subversive economic determinism that lay behind DuBois's analysis of the social problems of black Philadelphians when it spoke "calmly yet devastatingly to the history and logic of poverty and racism."[47]

In addition to subverting the essentialist explanations for Negro problems posed by white scientists, *The Philadelphia Negro* sought to move the black antiracist argument to new secular ground, again combining innovation with ambivalence. DuBois's study eschewed the traditional appeals that black authors made to monogenism as the basis for racial unity, forging a secular argument against racial discrimination. Unlike many other contemporaneous discussions of black people by black authors, *The Philadelphia Negro* neither begins with nor ultimately contains any ringing argument for the unity of the races or an affirmation of the potential of the black race. Indeed, DuBois postpones any sustained discussion of the question of human differences, and black capacities, until the end of the book, and takes the subject up only briefly in his closing, "A Final Word."

Yet when he finally addressed the subject his African American contemporaries usually put first, DuBois did consider the question of human differences. In his formulation, however, human differences were so broadly conceived that the question of Negro capacities became question of the capacities and relations of all people. Are Negro problems "more hopelessly complex" than other people's problems, he asks in *The Philadelphia Negro*. "They are after all the same difficulties over which the world has grown gray" (p. 385). Having successfully sidestepped the whole question of the origins of the races by considering the question of differences among all peoples, DuBois then betrayed the authority the scriptures still held in the language of his answer:

the question as to how far human intelligence can be trusted and trained; as to whether we must always have the poor with us; as to whether it is possible for the mass of men to attain righteousness on earth; and then to this is added that question of questions: after all who are Men? Is every featherless biped to be counted a man and a brother? (385–86)

Never really answering his own question, DuBois went to make a few pointed, purely secular arguments against racial discrimination. African Americans, he pointed out to those whites who hoped that Darwin's natural laws would solve the race problem by attrition, were not likely to die out any time soon: "a nation that has endured the slave-trade, slavery, reconstruction, and present prejudice three hundred years, and under it increased in numbers and efficiency, is not in any immediate danger of extinction" (p. 388). Too numerous to get rid through any colonization scheme, DuBois argued, black people were in America to stay, and advances in their prosperity could only benefit both races. Discrimination was "morally wrong, politically dangerous, industrially wasteful, and socially silly" (p. 394).

Conclusion

As the twentieth century opened, DuBois and other black intellectuals would be the first Americans to enlist in what one scholar has called Franz Boas's "war on the idea differences in culture [that] were derived from differences in capacity."[48] Widely cited and published in black journals and magazines, Boas's ideas supported the arguments for black equality that African Americans had made for centuries.[49] Boas's culture concept, nonetheless, heralded a paradigm shift in black as well as white thought. For African American thinkers the shift from race to culture would be a shift from biblical arguments defending the equal, if not identical, character of the races to scientific arguments that dismissed race as a fallacy. It would also entail giving up Social Darwinist ideas of race development that promised an ultimate triumph for the African race in the Darwinian struggle. In short, black thinkers would have to reconfigure their own ideas before they could emphasize culture rather than race as the arbitrator of human differences. *The Philadelphia Negro* illustrates that such a reconceptualization of race was already underway among African American intellectuals during the years Boas was developing his ideas.

Boas's ideas — his conception of culture — would be still revelatory to DuBois, who met him in 1906. Recording the impact of Boas, DuBois later wrote, "When the matter of race became a matter of comparative culture I was in revolt. I began to see that the cultural equipment attributed to any people depended largely on who estimated it." In particular, DuBois learned much from the German anthropologist's research on non-Western cultures, realizing that his education had been "suppressed concerning Asiatic and African culture."[50] Yet, in other ways, as we have just seen, DuBois was already primed for revolt when he encountered Boas. By the late 1900s, DuBois and a few other black academics such as Kelly Miller, who published a purely secular attack on Frederick L. Hoffman's racist reading of the census, had begun to consider the problems and peculiarities of African Americans in cultural rather than theological or biological terms. African Americans, Miller had told Hoffman in 1897, faced a "condition" rather than a predetermined racial destiny — a point that DuBois's *Philadelphia Negro* richly documented.[51]

The conceptual advances in *The Philadelphia Negro* have been obscured by later developments in American social sciences, which made the study's secular and empirical approach to the study of Negro problems seem commonplace. Moreover, they have also been overshadowed by the twentieth-century evolution of DuBois's thought, which took him from science to activism. Reviewing his scientific career late in his life, DuBois looked back ruefully on his old faith in the liberatory power of empiricism. He had gone to Philadelphia thinking that "the world was thinking wrong about race, because it did not know. The ultimate evil was stupidity. The cure for it was knowledge based on scientific investigation." He later realized that he had put too much faith in truth. "I was not at the time sufficiently Freudian to understand how little human action is based on reason; nor did I know Marx well enough to appreciate the economic foundations of human history."[52] Yet DuBois's attempts to develop a scientific approach to African American problems were no less necessary for being transitional. In all his accounts of the book, DuBois always emphasized how much he had learned from *The Philadelphia Negro*, noting more than once that he "had learned far more from the Philadelphia Negroes than I had taught them concerning the Negro Problem."[53]

Notes

1. W.E.B. DuBois, *Darkwater: Voice from Within the Veil* (1920; reprint, New York: Schocken Books, 1969), p. 20.

2. The literature on DuBois's achievements as a sociologist is extensive. See, for example, Dan S. Green and Edwin D. Driver, "W.E.B. DuBois: A Case Study in the Sociology of Sociological Negation," *Phylon* 37, no. 4 (1976): 308–33; David Turley, "Black Social Science and Black Politics in the Understanding of the South: Du Bois, the Atlanta University Studies, and the Crisis, 1897–1920," in *Race and Class in the American South Since 1890*, ed. Melvyn Stokes and Rick Halpern (Providence, R.I.: Berg, 1994). For a more complete list of assessments of DuBois's sociological achievements in *The Philadelphia Negro*, see David Levering Lewis, *W.E.B. DuBois: The Biography of a Race* (New York: Henry Holt, 1993), p. 642 n. 31.

3. Council Taylor, "Clues for the Future: Black Urban Anthropology Reconsidered," *Race Change and Urban Society*, ed. Peter Orleans and William Russell Ellis (Beverly Hills, Calif.: Sage, 1971), p. 608. See also Werner J. Lange, "W.E.B. DuBois and the First Scientific Study of Afro-America," *Phylon* 44 (1983): 135–46; and Faye V. Harrison, "The DuBoisian Legacy in Anthropology," *Critique of Anthropology* 12, no. 3 (1992): 239–60.

4. On *The Philadelphia Negro* as urban history, see Kenneth Kusmer's assessment in "The Black Urban Experience in American History," in *The State of Afro-American History*, ed. Darlene Clark Hine (Baton Rouge: Louisiana State University Press, 1986), pp. 91–92; on the economic significance of DuBois's early work see Thomas D. Boston, "W.E.B. DuBois and the Historical School of Economics," *American Economic Review* 81, 2 (May 1991): 303–6.

5. Nancy Leys Stepan and Sander L. Gilman, "Appropriating the Idioms of Science: The Rejection of Scientific Racism," in *The Bounds of Race: Perspectives of Hegemony and Resistence*, ed. Dominic LaCapra (Ithaca, N.Y.: Cornell University Press, 1991), p. 74.

6. The sentence I quote is in DuBois's preface, although it is out of order there; one clause has been misplaced and appears out of context at the bottom of p. iii, instead of p. iv, where it belongs. My quote corrects the error.

7. Franz Boas, "Human Faculty as Determined by Race," *Proceedings of the American Association for the Advancement of Science* 43 (1894): 301.

8. W.E.B. DuBois, "My Evolving Program for Negro Freedom," in *What the Negro Wants*, ed. Rayford V. Logan (Chapel Hill: University of North Carolina Press, 1944), p. 44.

9. DuBois, "Evolving Program," pp. 43–44.

10. Lewis, *DuBois*, p. 180.

11. Aptheker, "Introduction" to the 1973 edition, p. 7.

12. Vernon Williams, *From a Caste to a Minority: Changing Attitudes of American Sociologists Toward Afro-Americans* (New York: Greenwood Press, 1989), p. 21.

13. Robert C. Bannister, *Social Darwinism: Science and Myth in Anglo-American Social Thought* (Philadelphia: Temple University Press, 1979), p. 188.

14. Bannister, *Social Darwinism*, p. 192.

15. W.E.B. DuBois to Walter Francis Willcox in *The Correspondence of W.E.B. DuBois*, ed. Herbert Aptheker (Amherst: University of Massachusetts Press, 1973), 1: 75.

16. DuBois, "Evolving Program," p. 44.

17. Stepan and Gilman, "Appropriating the Idioms," p. 85.

18. On nineteenth-century black ethnology see Stepan and Gilman, "Appropriating the Idioms"; Mia Elisabeth Bay, "The White Image in the Black Mind: African-American Ideas About White People, 1830–1925" (Ph.D. dissertation, Yale University, 1993), chapters 1–3.

19. Frederick Douglass, "The Claims of the Negro Ethnologically Considered: Speech delivered to the prestigious Philozetian and Phi Delta Societies of Western Reserve College in Hudson Ohio, 12, July, 1854," in *The Frederick Douglass Papers, Series One: Speeches, Debates, and Interviews*, vol. 2, *1847–1854*, ed. John W. Blassingame (New Haven, Conn.: Yale University Press, 1982), p. 500.

20. The monographs written by these men on this subject include: Benjamin Tucker Tanner, *The Descent of the Negro* (n.p.: [1898]), and *The Negro's Origins* (n.p.: [1869]); Joseph Hayne, *The Black Man; or, Ham and His Immediate Descendants* (Spartanburg, S.C.: W. DuPres, 1893), and *The Negro in Sacred History* (Charleston, S.C.: Walker, Evans and Cogswell, 1887); Harvey Johnson, *A Gross Theological Error Corrected: White Men Were the First Slaves. Ham, the Son of Noah not Cursed, but Canaan, Ham's Youngest Son* (Baltimore: J. B. Clarke, Printer, n.d.); and *The Nations from a New Point of View* (Nashville, Tenn.: National Baptist Publishing Co., 1903).

21. George Washington Williams, *History of the Negro Race in America from 1619 to 1880* (New York: G. P. Putnam's Sons, 1885); John Wesley Crogman and H. F. Kletzing, *The Progress of a Race* (Atlanta: J. L. Nichols and Co., 1897).

22. E. R. Carter, *The Black Side: A Partial History of the Business, Religious, and Educational Side of the Negro in Atlanta, Ga.* (Atlanta: n.p., 1894), p. v. Its author, Edward Randolph Carter, was a Baptist minister as well as an author, journalist, educator, service industry employee, and civic leader. But his voluminous compilation of biographies, facts, and figures documenting the achievements of Atlanta's blacks is not otherwise focused on religion or theology. Henry MacNeal Turner's pamphlet on ethnology is called *The Negro in All Ages: A Lecture Delivered in the Second Baptist Church of Savannah* (Savannah, Ga.: D. G. Patton, Steam Printer, 1983).

23. W.E.B. DuBois, "The Conservation of the Races (1897)," in *Writings* (New York: Library of America, 1986), p. 815.

24. Anthony Appiah, "The Uncompleted Argument: DuBois and the Illusion of Race," in *"Race," Writing, and Difference*, ed. Henry Louis Gates, Jr. (Chicago: University of Chicago Press, 1986), pp. 21–37.

25. DuBois, "Conservation of the Races," pp. 816, 817.

26. DuBois, "Conservation of the Races," p. 816.

27. DuBois, "The Study of Negro Problems," *Annals of the American Academy* 11 (January 1898): 19.

28. W.E.B. DuBois, "The Laboratory in Sociology at Atlanta University," *Annals of the American Academy of Political and Social Science* 21 (May 1903): 503.

29. Gertrude Himmelfarb, *Poverty and Compassion: The Moral Imagination of the Victorians* (New York: Alfred A. Knopf, 1991), p. 95.

30. Lewis, *DuBois*, p. 190.

31. Himmelfarb, *Poverty and Compassion*, pp. 122, 124.

32. Lewis, *DuBois*, p. 209.

33. Francis L. Broderick, "German Influence of the Scholarship of W.E.B. Du-Bois," *Phylon* 18 (1958): 369.

34. Broderick, "German Influence," p. 370.

35. DuBois, "Study of Negro Problems," p. 12.

36. DuBois, "A Program for a Sociological Society," typescript draft, W.E.B. Du-Bois Papers, reel 80, p. 15 (Manuscript Division, University of Massachusetts at Amherst).

37. DuBois, "Study of Negro Problems," 18.

38. *Colored American*, January 26, 1839.

39. DuBois, "Study of Negro Problems," pp. 14–15.

40. Lewis, *DuBois*, p. 210.

41. Lewis, *DuBois*, p. 189.

42. On racial stereotypes in nineteenth-century black thought, see Wilson Jeremiah Moses, *The Golden Age of Black Nationalism, 1850–1925* (New York: Oxford University Press, 1978).

43. Lange, "Scientific Study," p. 138.

44. W.E.B. DuBois, "The Atlanta Conferences," *Voice of the Negro* 1, 3 (March 1904): 85–86.

45. W.E.B. DuBois, "Sociology Hesitant," manuscript, W.E.B. DuBois Papers, reel 82, pp. 4–5.

46. The diagram is in both drafts of DuBois's unpublished paper "A Program for a Sociological Society." The diagram I have photocopied is from the handwritten version. See W.E.B. DuBois Papers, reel 80, p. 11.

47. Lewis, *DuBois*, p. 190.

48. Carl N. Degler, *In Search of Human Nature: The Decline and Revival of Darwinism in American Social Thought* (New York: Oxford University Press, 1991), p. 62.

49. On Boas and black thinkers see Bay, "White Image," chap. 6; John David Smith, *A New Creed for the Old South: Proslavery Ideology and History, 1865–1918* (Westport, Conn.: Greenwood Press, 1985), pp. 202–3, 214; Vernon J. Williams, "The Boasian Paradox, 1894–1915," *Afro-Americans in New York History and Life* 16 (July 1992): 69–85.

50. W.E.B. DuBois, *Dusk of Dawn* (New York: Schocken, 1974), p. 99.

51. Kelly Miller, *A Review of Hoffman's Race Traits and Tendencies of the American Negro* (Washington, D.C.: American Negro Academy, 1897), p. 36.

52. *The Autobiography of W.E.B. DuBois: A Soliloquy on Viewing My Life from the Last Decade of its First Century* (New York: International Publishers, 1968), pp. 197, 228.

53. "Evolving Program," p. 45. One lesson DuBois seems to have been just beginning to learn during his research on Philadelphia's Negroes was on the need for activism, as can be seen in an anecdote he told about his research in 1897: "I was once pursuing an elaborate piece of investigation in regard to Negroes in a certain city," DuBois told the Sociology Club at Atlanta University, "when I came across a woman who could if she would give me much valuable matter. She looked at me suspiciously and said 'What's the object of this investigation?' 'Simply to get at the truth,' I answered. . . . 'Then you are only trying to get facts and not to better things,' she said. 'Yes,' I answered. 'Humph,' she replied and I'm still waiting for that information. Now this illustrates well the attitude of many toward the careful and systematic collection of minute facts," DuBois commented disapprovingly. "Program for a Sociological Society," pp. 14–15.

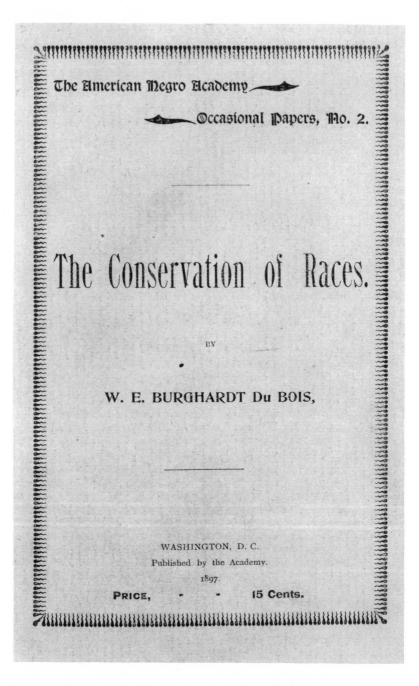

The American Negro Academy

Occasional Papers, No. 2.

The Conservation of Races.

BY

W. E. BURGHARDT Du BOIS,

WASHINGTON, D. C.
Published by the Academy.
1897.
PRICE, - - 15 Cents.

Figure 5. Title page for *The Conservation of Races.* Courtesy of The Library Company of Philadelphia.

Chapter 2

W.E.B. DuBois's Archaeology of Race

Re-Reading "The Conservation of Races"

Thomas C. Holt

Perhaps few words have proved as prophetic as that ringing phrase with which W.E.B. DuBois opened the second essay of *The Souls of Black Folk*: "The problem of the twentieth century is the problem of the color-line, — the relation of the darker to the lighter races of men in Asia and Africa, in America and the islands of the sea."[1] Significantly, this essay—following immediately upon his discussion of the problem of black identity in the first essay—addressed the issues of slavery emancipation and Reconstruction. This is significant, I believe, because these essays in tandem frame just what "the problem of the color-line" was all about. It was first of all a problem of identity and difference in the modern world; second, it was a problem *because* that world had been profoundly shaped by slavery, by emancipation, and by imperialism. And, finally, at the root of the problem were the social relations of labor exploitation: a people denied the fruits of their labor could not claim their cultural birthright either. These three sets of *interrelated* problems defined nothing less than the *problematic*[2] of race relations in the modern world.

Much of the remaining text of *Souls*, indeed much of DuBois's future work, can be understood, in part, as largely a reworking and elaboration of aspects of this problematic. This, of course, is not to say that those works were always coherent or even always internally consistent. As he himself would later concede, his thinking would undergo many more changes of direction, of emphasis, of influence over the course of his remaining sixty years.[3] Nonetheless, I will argue that at the dawn of the twentieth century and relatively early in his career, DuBois had succeeded in sketching the protocols of a racial problematic that have continuing — perhaps even intensifying — resonance, even as that century draws to a close.

Admittedly, such a claim must contend with a formidable cohort of interpretations of DuBois's work—especially of that completed during the period examined here—that emphasize his inconsistencies, his incoherences, his virtual entrapment by Victorian ideas of race and historical process. David Levering Lewis, for instance, has sketched a compelling portrait of a man struggling with personal angst about his own racial identity, which decisively colored his articulation of both the problem of race and its solution.[4] Others, as well, have made strong cases for the intellectual derivativeness of many of DuBois's key ideas about race and history: derivative from his mentor Alexander Crummell, from Hegel, from his high German education.[5] Despite their significant contributions and insights, however, such analyses always risk—and often succumb to—a reductionist logic, wherein DuBois can never rise above his sources. As a consequence, the various searches for the intellectual and personal derivation of DuBois's thinking often seem merely to trap and desiccate that thought, leaving an enervated portrait of the thinker strangely incongruent with the manifestly enduring power of the thought.

We might capture something of that power—and staying power—by recognizing the evolutionary, experimental nature of this period in DuBois's thought. He cobbled most of *Souls of Black Folk* together from disparate pieces composed and published over the six-year period 1897 to 1902, a fertile period of self-conscious reflection about the problem of race and how it might be studied. The very multivocality of *Souls*—by turns lyrical, sociohistorical, hortatory, self-revelatory—reflects the diverse goals, approaches, and strategies that his work essayed. His major scholarly effort during this period, of course, was the sociological study of Philadelphia's Seventh Ward, which he began in the summer of 1896 and published in 1899 as *The Philadelphia Negro*. During that interval, however—in fact, over a mere ten months—he delivered an address, in November 1896 to the Academy of Political Science on "The Study of the Negro Problem"; delivered a paper at the inaugural meeting of the American Negro Academy in March 1897 on "The Conservation of the Races"; undertook in the summer of 1897 a survey of black life in Farmville, Virginia for the Bureau of Labor Statistics; and published the preliminary version of the essay that opens *Souls of Black Folk*, "Strivings of the Negro People," in the August 1897 issue of *Atlantic Monthly*. In each of these works DuBois attacked some aspect of that larger problematic to which he had determined to devote his life. Taken together these essays framed that problematic: What (and how) does race mean? How is it related to the larger history of humankind? How does one study it? How can one understand and overcome its pernicious effects on human life and aspirations?

Of these pieces, the essay "The Conservation of Races" is DuBois's earliest effort to elaborate a comprehensively theoretical *and political* analysis of the race concept. In that sense it might be regarded as a foundational piece, a seminal article that both informs and is informed by the other works he undertook during this period, including his major academic work, *The Philadelphia Negro*. The fall 1896 address, "The Study of Negro Problems," provided the methodological template—at once empirical, comparative, and historical—for both the Philadelphia and Farmville studies that followed. The "Conservation" essay, on the other hand—composed during the months of intensive fieldwork in the Seventh Ward but well before *The Philadelphia Negro* could have been written—can be read as its conceptual and political complement.

"The Conservation of Races" is also one of DuBois's most controversial and difficult pieces. Indeed, rather than anchoring our understanding of his evolving thinking about race during this period, it is more often invoked to undermine the credibility of that thought. For example, an influential dissection of this piece by the philosopher Anthony Appiah all but dismisses it as DuBois's "illusion of race."[6] Modern genetics has thoroughly undermined any significant biological criteria for race as a basis for differentiating among human beings, but Appiah goes further. He insists—by an exercise of philosophical logic, a kind of reductio ad absurdum—that we should eliminate any nonbiological basis as well, because it, too, must be inevitably tainted by biological presumptions. In this article, therefore, Appiah uses DuBois's life's work to illustrate the formidable problem of freeing ourselves from "the race idea," because in DuBois, he argues, we witness the difficulty of a highly intelligent man's struggle with the same problem, despite his own embrace of the new genetic evidence refuting race. In sum, Appiah argues that DuBois *began* the task of dismantling the illusion of biological race, but did not or could not finish it; thus his was an "uncompleted argument."

But it is demonstrably incorrect—even by the evidence Appiah himself cites—to say that DuBois remained captive to a biological idea of race in any substantial way; indeed, his was an uneasy relationship with that notion from the start. Ultimately, then, Appiah's argument appears to be that *any* invocation of race—of which DuBois was certainly guilty—necessarily entails invoking its biological traces as well, simply because there is no legitimate, parsimonious, nonbiological criterion for expressing racial bonding or difference.

The idea that race provides little basis as a scientific criterion for distinguishing among humans is relatively unexceptional in most academic discussion today. But to show that race is more a product of imagination than biology is not sufficient to the claim that it is an "illusion" that should be banished from our discourse. Race is not the only socially constructed category that remains nonetheless essential to both academic and lay analyses of social processes. For example, "nation"[7] and "gender"[8] are similarly "imagined" entities. What is important is to recognize that all such entities are not only socially constructed but also politically and historically constructed; that is, their very forms and utilities involve relationships of power and the deployment of power that have evolved over time. A *re*-reading of "The Conservation of Races" against these insights suggests a perspective on Du-Bois's thinking about the politics of race that may in turn sharpen contemporary observations more generally about the political utilities and implications of all such ostensibly "illusory" concepts.

How we think about these matters can have far-reaching consequences for us, as they did for DuBois when he authored the prophesy quoted above. Our daily newspapers alert us to the terrible dangers of "the race idea," and the horrible crimes committed in its name should be well known to us. It is not only peoples of African descent who have been victimized by racialized stigmas, but Muslims in a dismantled Yugoslavia and Turks in a unified Germany. Thus, even as we find that we cannot yet dispense with "the race idea" in our analyses or in our politics, there remains the legitimate problem of how to mobilize on the basis of identity without reifying difference. At stake in our response to this problem are a wide range of issues: for example, the legitimacy and mode of implementation of affirmative action; the justification of group-identified institutions, like universities (African American and women's colleges, for example) or programs of study within universities (African American studies or women's studies); and the accessible as well as acceptable forms for progressive political mobilizations.

The problem of how to politically mobilize an excluded group seeking inclusion acutely informed the intellectual task of "The Conservation of Races."[9] Written for the inaugural meeting of the American Negro Academy, the essay addressed a primarily black audience, one DuBois apparently thought inclined to deny its race in its pursuit of universal human brotherhood. Thus he sought to establish not only the intellectual and moral validity of the race concept but that race consciousness was an essential tool for black progress. As the paper's very title suggests, he wanted to *conserve* the "race idea" and racial integrity.

The fact of racial differences is a reality that we must acknowledge "in our calmer moments," he began, and black intellectuals needed to "rise above the pressing, but smaller questions of separate schools and cars, wage-discrimination and lynch law" in order "to survey the whole question of race in human philosophy" so as to lay a foundation for "those large lines of policy and higher ideals which may form our guiding lines and boundaries in the practical difficulties of every day." And this required recognizing "the hard limits of natural law, and that any striving, no matter how intense and earnest, which is against the constitution of the world, is vain." Thus the questions he posed to guide this inquiry were: "What is the real meaning of Race; what has, in [the] past, been the law of race development, and what lessons has the past history of race development to teach the rising Negro people?"

One finds at the outset, then, a seeming commitment a priori to the reality of race, as a fact of life and as a category of intellectual analysis. Indeed, the task of elaborating the race idea seems to take priority over "smaller," presumably subordinate, matters like *actual* racial discrimination. And yet, DuBois recognized full well that the common physical criteria by which we recognize race — "color, hair, cranial measures, and language" — were all unreliable indicators because they do not correlate very well and thus do not constitute consistently distinguishable categories for distinctions among humans. And although science had defined, in his time, three "great families of human beings" — white, Negro, and yellow — the crudeness of such broad categories was itself an indicator of the unreliability of physical criteria in determining race. "This broad division of the world's races," he writes, "is nothing more than an acknowledgement that, so far as purely physical characteristics are concerned, the differences between men do not explain all the differences of their history." It is worth noting here that the raison d'être for making racial distinctions at all is to somehow account for differences in the histories of groups. Indeed, from the statement that follows, it appears that it is history as such that undermines the validity of physical criteria for race: "the wonderful developments of human history teach that the grosser physical differences of color, hair and bone go but a short way toward explaining the different roles which groups of men have played in Human Progress." But this phrase is a caveat qualifying another in which he reasserts his belief that "yet there are differences — subtle, delicate and elusive, though they may be — which have silently but definitely separated men into groups." These subtler phenomena cannot be accounted for by physical differences; indeed, "they transcend scientific definition" but "are clearly defined to the eye of the Historian and Sociologist."

From these premises, DuBois goes on to propose a working definition of "a race." "It is a vast family of human beings, *generally* of common blood and language, [but] *always* of common history, traditions and impulses, who are both voluntarily and involuntarily striving together for the accomplishment of certain more or less vividly conceived ideals of life." One should take note of the key words in this passage: "family," "history," "tradition," "striving," "ideals of life," for they suggest that race is formed by social and cultural processes rather than established as a fixed category.

Based on these criteria, however, DuBois goes on to identify "eight distinctly differentiated races, *in the sense in which History tells us the word must be used*" (emphasis added). But, again, the latter phrase signals something more contingent than the fixed categories suggested by the first half of the sentence, which goes on to elaborate a somewhat quaint list of Negroes in Africa and America, Slavs, Teutons, English, Mongolians, Hindoos, Semites, and people speaking Romance languages. Whatever one might think of these categories, it would appear that what "History" had wrought was something he could describe only in national or cultural rather than biological terms.

As if to underscore this point, DuBois followed this list with a declaration that none of these races was "pure" in a biological sense, with "negroes . . . perhaps, the most indefinite of all." DuBois did not seek to totally exclude physical difference as a criteria, however; indeed, "with wide exceptions and qualifications," he writes, "these eight great races of today follow the cleavage of physical race distinctions, . . . But no mere physical distinctions would really define or explain the deeper differences — the cohesiveness and continuity of these groups. *The deeper differences are spiritual, psychical, differences —* undoubtedly based on the physical, *but infinitely transcending them.*" As a consequence, the "more important" bases for these racial categories were "a common history, common laws and religion, similar habits of thought and a conscious striving together for certain ideals of life." In fact, he argues that the "whole process" by which these races have formed involved increasing differentiation of their "spiritual and mental" character and greater "*integration* of physical differences" (emphasis added).

Here DuBois sketches simultaneous *historical* processes by which "tribal" differences coalesced into larger "racial" groupings at the same time as the broad racial groupings were themselves differentiated and were then able to develop what he called their unique "gifts" and "strivings." The passage captures DuBois's vision of historical process so well that it deserves quotation in full.

The age of nomadic tribes of closely related individuals represents the maximum of physical differences. *They were practically vast families, and there were as many groups as families.* As the families came together to form cities the physical differences lessened, purity of blood was replaced by the requirements of domicile, and all who lived within the city bounds became gradually to be regarded as members of the group; ie., there was *a slight and slow breaking down of physical barriers.* This, however, was accompanied by *an increase of the spiritual and social differences* between cities. This city became husbandmen; this, merchants; another warriors; and so on. The *ideals of life* for which the different cities struggled were different.

When at last cities began to coalesce into nations there was another breaking down of barriers which separated groups of men. The larger and broader differences of color, hair and physical proportions were not by any means ignored, but myriads of minor differences disappeared, and *the sociological and historical races of men began to approximate the present division of races as indicated by physical researches.* At the same time the spiritual and physical differences of race groups which constituted the nations became deep and decisive. The English nation stood for constitutional liberty and commercial freedom; the German nation for science and philosophy; the Romance nations stood for literature and art, and the other race groups are striving, each in its own way, to develop for civilization its particular message, its particular ideal, which shall help to guide the world nearer and nearer that perfection of human life for which we all long, that "one far-off Divine event." (3–4, emphasis added except for "ideals of life")

The process of "race-making," therefore, is preeminently historical and, one might add, at root, materialistic. Given the endogamy of a nomadic, primitive existence, biology was a reliable, consistent basis for marking social boundaries and identities — groups approximated families and there were "almost as many groups as families." But with the development of settled communities — that is, cities — economic and social needs broke down the barriers of blood *within* each community, while at the same time new differences — but apparently ones based originally on a diversity of material interests — developed *between* communities. It should be noted that the examples that DuBois gives of what he calls the "spiritual and social differences between cities" are socio-economic: "This city became husbandmen, this, merchants; another warriors; and so on." It is out of these social differences, apparently, that there developed different "*ideals of life* for which the different cities struggled." The historical process by which cities developed is repeated in the formation of nations and, presumably, supranational entities like civilizations and language groups. Notably, this was a process that entailed the "breaking down of barriers which separated groups of men" as an essential part of raising new "racial" entities. And although DuBois is not yet ready to jettison the notion that these entities somehow still "approximate the present division of races as indicated by physical researches," he makes clear that it is their "sociological and historical" character that is "deep and decisive."

Rather than emphasize how much DuBois was still entangled in nineteenth-century ideas about race and nation, therefore, I find far more interesting the strides he had already made toward a late twentieth-century conception of race as a social/historical construction. There is no denying that he was certainly mesmerized by an almost teleological notion of what he called "the race idea, the race spirit, the race ideal," which was "the vastest and most ingenious invention for human progress." Through race consciousness each group develops its unique, divinely ordained mission, which is "to develop for civilization its particular message." But as we have seen in his account of the development of city-states, the ultimate roots of this consciousness are socioeconomic. Each group — whether city, nation, or race — develops perspectives and talents in the course of its particular struggles ("strivings") in life. It is in the interest of human-kind as a whole, a God-given right of all, that each group be allowed to develop *its* message and deliver it to the world.[10]

DuBois accepts that the Negro's "full, complete" message for or contribution to civilization has not been fully articulated as yet, despite the still open question in his mind as to how much of the ancient Egyptian civilization was in fact a Negro contribution. The current generation's task, therefore, is to determine what shall be the Negro race's future function, its message for the world. "The answer is plain: By the development of these race groups, not as individuals but as races." And with this, we get some inkling about exactly what was at stake in all this for DuBois — epistemologically and politically. "We, who have been reared and trained under the individualistic philosophy of the Declaration of Independence and the laissez-faire philosophy of Adam Smith," he wrote, "are loath to acknowledge this patent fact of human history. We see the Pharaohs, Caesars, Toussaints and Napoleons of history and forget the vast races of which they were but epitomized expressions." Contrary to this methodological individualism, he argued, "the history of the world is the history, not of individuals, but of groups, not of nations, but of races, and he who ignores or seeks to override the race idea in human history ignores and overrides the central thought of all history."

Thus DuBois failed to interrogate more thoroughly the Victorian "race-idea," perhaps because his sights were set on mobilizing it against that era's more powerful fixation on the nostrums of classical liberalism. What was at stake, moreover, was history itself, in at least two fundamental senses: first, there was the historical record and its fulfillment in the immanent unfolding of the historical destiny of black people, their contribution to world civilization; and second, there was the *study* of history itself, the necessity for a different understanding of historical process, one that repudiated the bourgeois, individualist ethos of his day; that, rejecting any Carlylean notion of history as hero worship, saw it as the creation of ordinary folk. Within this latter point, perhaps, lay the seeds of a larger critique of modernity itself— one not dissimilar to that of the other great sociologists of that time, and one that would flower after the Great War.

DuBois goes on in the balance of the essay to argue a political position and offer an intellectual program based on racial solidarity and study. He would elaborate both in future writings and in his active opposition to Booker T. Washington in the early twentieth century. Both the study and the theory were based on an evolving theory of race that would continue to be elaborated during the first half of the next century.

But even as that theory stood in 1897, one can discern the process by which DuBois sought to reconcile his career as both empirical scholar and "race-man." *The Philadelphia Negro,* for example, was the epitome of an empirical, scientific work—a door-to-door survey and statistical portrait of a black community (one repeated in miniature in Farmville later that year). And yet, the Philadelphia study begins with a comprehensive history of black life in that city, and each major element of the study (demography, education, religion, employment, crime, class formation) is elaborated in historical detail. His method suggests that the relations between the races and the interrelations of various class segments within the black race could be understood only as the outcome of historical processes. In short, the meaning of racial identity and the nature of race relations are historical and socially made.

Those who contend, therefore, that DuBois embraced certain elements of the nineteenth-century conceptions of race, even as he struggled to free himself from their biological genesis, are only partially correct. They are wrong in not crediting DuBois with going a much greater distance in refiguring the nineteenth-century "race idea" that he had inherited. But even more important is our own intellectual loss in not recognizing and building upon DuBois's insights into the relation between "the race idea" and history.

Of course, Anthony Appiah would deny any such insights, insisting that DuBois's "history" merely camouflages biology. Conceding that DuBois leaned more on a sociohistorical than a biological basis for understanding race, Appiah argues, nonetheless, that (1) the sociohistorical argument provides no better criterion for racial definition than the biological one; and (2) that DuBois's usage of the sociohistorical reduces to merely *disguised* biology, bringing it in through a back door, so to speak.

If common history is the basis for black racial identity, then why is DuBois, whose grandfather was Dutch, not a Teuton rather than a Negro, Appiah asks. The explanation, he asserts, is obviously that "the Dutch were not Negroes; DuBois is." That is to say, DuBois is thought to have a common history with Africans rather than with the Dutch only because he has been classified a priori as a Negro rather than a Dutchman. This is a circular argument, Appiah insists, because the identity to be attributed via a common history must precede the historical event by which the identity becomes known; therefore, "it is only because they are [already] bound together that members of a race at different times can share a history at all." Put yet another way, it is simply a matter of a rather arbitrary choice of *which* "common history" black peoples identify with, since that history can be common only to the extent they have preselected the group with whom they wish to identify.[11]

In Appiah's usage history appears to be a fairly passive category—a mere temporal space in which "events" happen to "someone." "My general point is this," he writes, "in order to recognize two events at different times as part of the history of a single individual, we have to have a criterion for identity of the individual at each of those times, independent of his or her participation in the two events." The individual is the only actor here, and time is empty space—"a string or series of isolated moments or 'nows' "[12]—in which action transpires. In this conception, history is not part of the action, not *the process by which* an "individual" is brought *into being* in the first instance. If one does imagine history as an active process rather than simply as empty temporal space, however, it becomes clearer how identity in time-past can be linked to identity in time-present.

Martin Heidegger's work is suggestive in this regard since he wrestles with issues quite similar to those Appiah poses, but with quite different results. At the core of Heidegger's rethinking of the problem of independent verification of existence was the problem of the knowing subject: How does one know that one exists, that one *is* who one *was*? The proof for Heidegger lies in the myriad encounters in the everyday, encounters that make the self knowable, and thus constitute the subject. Individual identities are constituted through such encounters through time. Heidegger's short answer to Appiah's problem, therefore, is that there is no means of validating an individual identity independent of the living history of that individual. Indeed, it is only in historical time that identity *can* exist at all.[13]

It seems to me that this latter usage of history — as a process — is precisely the one that DuBois was trying to articulate. Thus when DuBois writes in *Dusk of Dawn* that his links with Africa are not in any important way biological, but a product of European expansion in the fifteenth century (a passage Appiah cites at length but with a different interpretation), he is offering us a protean appreciation of precisely how race was and is socially and historically constructed *and* of the legitimate *political* claims of a pan-Africanist consciousness. Indeed, this passage reads virtually like a response to Appiah's earlier question of why DuBois is Negro rather than Dutch: it is simply because the *relevant* historical coincidence, the commonality, is not the "blood" of an ancestral Dutch slavemaster, but the *experience* of enslavement with other Africans. This is not a "disguised" reversion to a biological link.[14]

Despite the encumbrance of nineteenth-century ideas about race, therefore, DuBois succeeds in shifting the emphasis of the ongoing discussion of "the Negro Problem" fairly emphatically to the common historical experience and the common relations to power that their New World experience had entailed for African Americans. This becomes more and more evident in his writings over the course of the first half of the twentieth century and is certainly fully evident by the publication of *Dusk of Dawn* in 1940. It is very clear from numerous texts that racial reality is not some a priori category for DuBois, but rather something one *discovers*. This is the essential import of his description in *Souls of Black Folk* of his rejection by a white schoolmate, a newcomer, in a child's game. Similar descriptions of how race is *learned* appear in other texts, like his "The Shadow of Years" essay of 1918, where he writes, "Very gradually, — I cannot now distinguish the steps, though here and there I remember a jump or a jolt — but very gradually I found myself assuming quite placidly that I was different from other children." If the difference had been merely physical or a priori, it would not have to be learned or discovered. His coming of age at Fisk and Harvard added other experiences that furthered his education about the material and ideological basis of group identities and differences.

But it was during his sojourn as a student in Germany that he experienced what might be called a *second* discovery of race: "On mountain and valley, in home and school, I met men and women as I had never met them before. Slowly they became, not white folks, but folks."[15] But race is not only learned from one's environment; it is externally imposed. Thus the racial consciousness he had formed after two years in Europe — which was marked by a "broader sense of humanity and world-fellowship — changed upon his return to " 'nigger'-hating America!" The racial violence in Georgia and elsewhere during these years definitively reshaped his consciousness of self (his identity) and ultimately his career commitment, which entailed leaving the university for the NAACP and engaging in a "hot and indignant defense" of the race.

But the learning process by which one takes on an identity — willingly or unwillingly — is not confined simply to the excluded and oppressed. If "black" is socially constructed, so too is "white." In 1918, he wrote:

The discovery of personal whiteness among the world's peoples is a very modern thing, — a nineteenth and twentieth century matter, indeed. The ancient world would have laughed at such a distinction. The Middle Age regarded skin color with mild curiosity; and even up into the eighteenth century we were hammering our national manikins into one, great, and Universal Man, with fine frenzy which ignored color and race even more than birth. Today we have changed all that, and the world in a sudden, emotional conversion has discovered that it is white and by that token, wonderful![16]

DuBois's analysis of the causes of the race riot in East Saint Louis brings his intuitions about how race is socially and historically constructed sharply into focus. A war-induced boom had produced a historic conjunction in that city of northern capitalists, eastern poor white labor, and southern impoverished blacks. The latter two groups might have logically found common cause and community in their basically similar relation to northern capital, but instead white labor came to see its interests and itself as somehow fundamentally different from black labor. "They saw something at which they had been taught to laugh and make sport; they saw that which the heading of every newspaper column, the lie of every cub reporter, the exaggeration of every press dispatch, and the distortion of every speech and book had taught them was a mass of despicable men, inhuman; at best, laughable; at worst, the meat of mobs and fury."[17] Notably, the instruments for their self-recognition were all media of communication. White laborers were *learning* from it the discourse of race, and through it conceived of themselves as "white." "Whiteness" justified barbarous deeds in East Saint Louis.

But by this time DuBois himself was developing a slightly different discourse from what he had written two decades earlier:

There are no races, in the sense of great, separate, pure breeds of men, differing in attainment, development, and capacity. There are great groups, — now with common history, now with common interests, now with common ancestry; more and more common experience and present interest drive back the common blood and the world today consists, not of races, but of the imperial commercial group of master capitalists, international and predominantly white; the national middle classes of the several nations, white, yellow, and brown, with strong blood bonds, common languages, and common history; the international laboring class of all colors; the backward, oppressed groups of nature-folk, predominantly yellow, brown, and black.[18]

This passage echoes many, even as it repudiates some others, of the central themes of "Conservation of Races." The idea that "common experience and present interest" undermine bonds based on blood alone echoes the historical sociology found in "Conservation of Races": as diverse racial families develop common interests vis-à-vis the outside world, they form new combinations of socioeconomically based kinship. In the global economy of the twentieth century these "sociological and historical" races had become broad hierarchical groupings in which class and color were highly correlated, but whose raison d'être was class interests rather than biology. Thus capital and labor were now international-scale groupings with their respective linkages based on the commonality of their experiences as exploiter and exploited; racially, the former was white and the latter mixed. By contrast, the self-consciousness of both the middle and unproletarianized classes tends to be geographically delimited — confined within national or regional boundaries; but they, too, were racially heterogenous (although blacks were largely excluded from the middle group). Biology appears to have little, if any, bearing on this classification scheme; rather, it is history — and recent history at that — that determined these "racialized," rather than racial, categories. Consequently, one could not possibly analyze or attack this system solely in racial terms; it was equally clear — contrary to many socialist contemporaries who emphasized only class — that race was a central feature of the system. Class was "racialized" in this hierarchical scheme: capital ruled, but the capitalists were white.

In order to appreciate this shift in his thinking, one must realize that the sociohistorical process and the relevant historical era had shifted for Du-Bois. It was no longer a question of locating race in antiquity, in some primordial processes by which peoples abandoned their nomadic clans to live in multiethnic cities. It was no longer a burning question, as in "Conservation of Races," of whether Africans could claim partial credit for Egyptian civilization. Race is a phenomenon of the modern era and that vast transformation of human life which that era brought forth. The origins of that era he dates from the expansion of Europe and its subsequent accumulation of capital on a world scale. Central to that process, DuBois would argue — a quarter century before Eric Williams's *Capitalism and Slavery*—was the development of the Atlantic slave trade, because it was in the slave trade that we discover the origin of commerce on a truly world-scale. Africa's was not a separate history from Europe's; rather, they were inextricably bound together in one compelling narrative. DuBois's vision was a global one in which issues of world economy were imbricated within the everyday, linked to issues of representation, and thereby to issues of self-consciousness and identity. Indeed, it is with an amazingly "postmodern" vision of modernity that he writes:

One cannot ignore the extraordinary fact that a world campaign beginning with the slave-trade and ending with the refusal to capitalize the word "Negro," leading through a passionate defense of slavery by attributing every bestiality to blacks and finally culminating in the evident modern profit which lies in degrading blacks, — all this has unconsciously trained millions of honest, modern men into the belief that black folk are sub-human.[19]

This belief is based on neither science, history, nor modern sociology — all of which refute it — but on a "simply passionate, deep-seated heritage, and as such can be moved by neither argument nor fact. Only faith in humanity will lead the world to rise above its present color prejudice."[20] He then goes on to equate the overthrow of racism to the overthrow of "our belief in war," "our international hatreds," "our old conception of the status of women," "our fear of educating the masses," and "our belief in the necessity of poverty."

Interestingly, this list of reform objectives also exposes the tenacity of DuBois's idealist conception of history and politics. If only one could change the way people think — their "belief[s]," "hatreds," "conception[s]," and "fear[s]" — or inculcate a "faith in humanity," we could stop oppression; we could truly make the world safe for democracy. A decade later, of course, he had become much less optimistic.[21]

Two additional points are worth noting here as well: (1) that the maturing of this particular historical vision of race came in the context of DuBois's critique of World War I, which he blamed on European imperialism and (2) that the terrible carnage of that war discredited in his mind any claim Europeans might have had to possessing a superior culture and civilization. If further impetus were needed for a break with Victorian era notions about race, history, and progress, the war almost certainly provided it.

DuBois was in his fifties when that war ended, but his ideas would continue to evolve and deepen over the forty-odd remaining years of his life. Far from an "uncompleted argument" about race, his was a persistent interrogation of the concept and a determined struggle against its pernicious effects. That interrogation and struggle have left us one clear message — which we can critique but should not ignore: race, as we know it, is a social, political, and historical construction of the modern era, linked to the expansion of European capital; as such, it is an illusion, but one so thoroughly implicated in the genesis and continued hegemony of the modern world order that no social revolution can succeed that does not try to extirpate it. There must be a socialist revolution, DuBois argued, but it must proceed in tandem with the destruction of race prejudice. "What we must decide sometime," he wrote, "is [just] who are to be considered 'men.'" After the structure of socialism must come its spirit, he wrote, "the Will to Human Brotherhood of all Colors, Races, and Creeds; the Wanting of the Wants of All. Perhaps the finest contribution of current Socialism to the world is neither its light nor its dogma, but the idea back of its one mighty word — Comrade!"

Having tried in this essay to put DuBois's ideas in their temporal context, which tends to emphasize the changes and evolution of his thinking, I would like as a measure of balance to end by reasserting what was fundamental, what was consistent in his ideas. And this was his basic commitment to comradeship, to human brotherhood and sisterhood. As he had written at the dawn of this century, his struggle, his striving was "in the name of an historic race, in the name of this the land of their fathers' fathers," but it was also — and ultimately — "in the name of human opportunity."

This paper was completed while I was a fellow at the Center for Advanced Study in the Behavioral Sciences. I am grateful for the partial financial support provided for that fellowship by the John D. and Catherine T. MacArthur Foundation and the Andrew W. Mellon Foundation. I am also grateful to Robin Kelley and Michael Katz for their insightful critiques of earlier drafts. A preliminary version of this paper was delivered as the annual Rayford A. Logan Lecture at Howard University in April 1993.

Notes

1. W.E.B. DuBois, "Of the Dawn of Freedom," in *The Souls of Black Folk* (Chicago: McClurg, 1903), 13. This essay had been published earlier as "The Freedmen's Bureau," *Atlantic Monthly* 87 (March 1901): 354–65. The basic idea had been expressed even earlier, however, in an address — "The Present Outlook for the Dark Races of Mankind," *AME Church Review* 17 (October 1900): 95–110. There DuBois, declaring that the American Negro Problem must be considered in "its larger world aspect in time and place," described how "the color line belts the world and that the social problem of twentieth century is to be the relation of the civilized world to the dark races of mankind."

2. I use the word "problematic" not simply to denote problems, but the interrelated set of assumptions, questions, and answers as situated within an "ideological field." This definition is indebted, but not rigidly tied, to the discussion in Louis Althusser's *For Marx*, trans. Ben Brewster (London: Verso, 1990), pp. 66–70.

3. See, for example, his introduction to the fiftieth anniversary edition of *The Souls of Black Folk* (New York: Blue Heron Press, 1953); and *The Autobiography of W.E.B. DuBois* (New York: International Publishers, 1968).

4. David Levering Lewis, *W.E.B. DuBois: Biography of a Race, 1868–1919* (New York: Henry Holt, 1993), pp. 148–49, 161–68, 170–73, 199.

5. Among others, see Wilson Jeremiah Moses, *Alexander Crummell: A Study of Civilization and Discontent* (New York: Oxford University Press, 1989), pp. 264–65, 293–95; and Joel Williamson, *The Crucible of Race: Black-White Relations in the American South Since Emancipation* (New York: Oxford University Press, 1984), pp. 399–413.

6. Anthony Appiah, "The Uncompleted Argument: DuBois and the Illusion of Race," in *"Race," Writing, and Difference*, ed. Henry Louis Gates (Chicago: University of Chicago Press, 1986), pp. 21–37. See also "Illusions of Race," in *In My Father's House: Africa in the Philosophy of Culture* (New York: Oxford University Press, 1992), pp. 28–46.

7. See Benedict Anderson, *Imagined Communities: Reflections on the Origin and Spread of Nationalism* (London: Verso, 1983).

8. See Denise Riley, *"Am I That Name?" Feminism and the Category of "Women" in*

History (Minneapolis: University of Minnesota Press, 1988); and Judith Butler, *Gender Trouble: Feminism and the Subversion of Identity* (New York: Routledge, 1990).

9. Reprinted in *Pamphlets and Leaflets by W.E.B. DuBois,* comp. and ed. Herbert Aptheker (White Plains, N.Y.: Kraus-Thomson, 1986); original found in American Negro Academy, *Occasional Papers* 2 (Washington, D.C., 1897), pp. 5–15.

10. It should be noted that DuBois seems to envision some fundamental cultural differentiation among peoples without any serious differences in their basic goals and ends. Unstated but *logically* apparent is some end point when there will be a grand synthesis of all these messages, the product of these diverse "strivings," for the common benefit of humankind. Yet, for DuBois, that synthesis apparently does not include any biological amalgamation, even though such amalgamation brought the existing "great" races into being in the first place.

11. Appiah, "The Uncompleted Argument," p. 27. "To put it more simply: sharing a common group history cannot be a criterion for being members of the same group, for we would have to be able to identify the group in order to identify *its* history. Someone in the fourteenth century could share a common history with me through our membership in a historically extended race only if something accounts both for his or her membership in the race in the fourteenth century and for mine in the twentieth. That something cannot, on pain of circularity, be the history of race." By these terms race can never be itself a creation of historical conjunctures. The slave trade, for example, goes a long way toward providing the link between "race then" and "race now" that Appiah seeks.

12. The phrase is Michael Gelven's from *A Commentary on Heidegger's Being and Time,* rev. ed. (DeKalb: Northern Illinois University Press, 1989), p. 182.

13. See Martin Heidegger, *Being and Time,* trans. John C. Macquarrie and Edward Robinson (San Francisco: HarperSanFrancisco, 1962), esp. 208–41. Also see Thomas C. Holt, "Marking: Race, Race-Making, and the Writing of History," *American Historical Review* 100 (February 1995): 1–20.

14. Despite my strong disagreement with many aspects of Appiah's reading of DuBois, however, I would still want to draw attention to important implications of and insights in his critique. Still unresolved is the problem of the independent status of "experience" itself as a legitimate basis for identity and politics. Indeed, it is a problem that remains implicit even in Appiah's query as to why a Negro rather than a Dutch identity for DuBois. It is a question to which feminist historian Joan Scott has recently drawn our attention in an article entitled "The Evidence of Experience." *Critical Inquiry* 17 (Summer 1991): 773–97. Examining the general problematic of how historians are to study and activists to act on our understandings of the countervailing identities and experiences of oppressed groups, Scott argues that experience as a category of analysis must be understood as discursively constituted. That is, its meaning cannot be apprehended outside a given discursive system. Also see my exchange with Scott on this point in *The Question of Evidence: Proof, Practice, and Persuasion Across the Disciplines,* ed. James Chandler, Arnold I. Davidson, and Harry Harootunian (Chicago: University of Chicago Press, 1994), 388–400.

15. This is not to say that the racial awareness learned in Germany was not also marked by ambiguities, rejections, and illusions. See the interesting and provocative discussion of DuBois's psychological state during these years in Lewis, *DuBois,* pp. 130–39.

16. W.E.B. DuBois, "The Souls of White Folk," *Darkwater* (1918): 30.

17. W.E.B. DuBois with Martha Gruening, "The Massacre of East St. Louis," *Crisis* 14 (September 1917): 219–38; reprint as "Of Work and Wealth," in *Darkwater,* pp. 81–104.

18. "Massacre of East St. Louis," p. 98.

19. W.E.B. DuBois, "The African Roots of War," *Atlantic Monthly* 115 (May 1915): 707–104; reprint as "The Hands of Ethiopia," in *Darkwater*, pp. 72–73.

20. DuBois, "Hands of Ethiopia," p. 73.

21. See Thomas C. Holt, "The Political Uses of Alienation: W.E.B. DuBois on Politics, Race and Culture, 1903–1940," *American Quarterly* 42 (June 1990): 100–115 and a series of articles in the *Crisis* between 1931 and 1934.

Chapter 3

Giant Steps

W.E.B. DuBois and the Historical Enterprise

Robert Gregg

W.E.B. DuBois's historical scholarship has received insufficient attention from American historians, especially considering its importance to developments within the profession. In *Nothing but Freedom*, Eric Foner reveals his own debt to DuBois and notes sardonically that *Black Reconstruction in America* has never been reviewed in the *American Historical Review*.[1] Perhaps the most celebrated text on the formation of the historical profession, Peter Novick's *That Noble Dream*, barely mentions DuBois's name, and certainly gives little weight to his work and contributions to the profession.[2] Even August Meier and Elliott Rudwick, in *Black History and the Historical Profession*, pay relatively little attention to DuBois. Their main focus for the early part of their study is Carter G. Woodson, and DuBois is featured mainly insofar as he responded to this other historian's work. While they note that DuBois was a "pioneer in black history" and "the most widely learned Negro scholar of the era," they focus only on his earlier histories (*The Suppression of the African Slave-Trade* and *The Negro*). With a rather dismissive wave they mention *Black Reconstruction in America*'s "controversial interpretive framework." They refer to it as an inspiration for "recent generations of scholars, black and white," but do not elaborate on who these people may be and how it gained this status given its framework. Moreover, such references occur as part of the chapter on Woodson, rather than as part of the chapter on generational change, further obscuring DuBois's impact on African American history.[3] This paper, then, endeavors to compensate for this neglect among Americanists by highlighting the richness and importance of DuBois's historical writings. In the process it focuses on the various stages of DuBois's development as a historian from his earliest work, *The Suppression of the African Slave-Trade*, to *Black Folk: Then and Now* published in 1939.

Figure 6. DuBois in the offices of *The Crisis*. Courtesy of the Schomburg Center, New York Public Library.

DuBois's historical writings can be broken up into three groups—the social scientific, the cultural materialist, and the Marxist—each marking a phase in DuBois's development. These parallel the stages of the historical profession's early development outlined by Novick in *That Noble Dream:* first, the emergence of the notion of objectivity, with its belief in "facts" and the inductive method; second, the gradual emergence of a "genteel insurgency" among Progressive historians promoting deductive reasoning; and last, "the stalling of the professional project" in "divergence and dissent" in the period following World War One.[4] While DuBois paralleled these changes, he either remained apart from the profession's development or, when involved, was virtually unrecognized for his contributions. In part, this was because at each stage of his development DuBois consciously deviated from the work of his white counterparts.

DuBois's early writings, reflected in *The Suppression of the African Slave-Trade* and *The Philadelphia Negro*, resembled the output of many scientific historians working at this time, except that in both books he only half-suppressed his idealism and allowed tensions and subtleties to surface that would seldom be evident in other historians' works. The presence of these tensions, I argue, gave texts like *The Philadelphia Negro* a dialectical or dynamic quality wherein the main body of the work articulated a thesis while some of the conclusions seemed to reach for its antithesis. In addition, the fact that DuBois was continually migrating intellectually (in the way Malcolm X would later describe his own intellectual development),[5] meant that when a text was viewed in conjunction with others, this dialectic appeared as an effort to step from one level of analysis or political theory to another.

DuBois's writings during the second phase, particularly *The Souls of Black Folk, John Brown*, and *The Negro*, were "insurgency" plain and simple and not the least "genteel," even though they incorporated ideas that resembled the cultural materialism to be found among some other Progressives.[6] Here, too, DuBois's work was in motion and could be readily misunderstood if stopped or taken in isolation. Notions like "The Talented Tenth" or his conception of "the Race" might be seen as elitist and, some have argued, even racist, when analyzed separately. When placed alongside one another, they appeared as the internal contradictions that propelled DuBois to newer and more radical interpretations of class and race than those emanating from the intellectuals, like Thomas Carlyle or Alexander Crummell, who had inspired him.

The third period, reaching its fruition with the publication of *Black Reconstruction in America* and *Black Folk*, witnessed DuBois's rejection of many Progressive notions and the adoption of Marxist terminology, taking him down paths that few, if any, white American historians were willing to follow. And here Novick's virtual omission of DuBois is crucial, for the latter provided one of the most significant voices of "divergence and dissent" following the Great War. If one were to observe American historians from outside the borders of the United States and to recognize their contributions to a transatlantic dialogue with German, French, and British as well as Caribbean, African, and Indian scholars, then DuBois would appear less marginal to the development of the profession as a whole. His work represented one part of an "assault on the civilizing mission," to use Michael Adas's term, that was occurring in response to colonialism on the American mainland, in the Pacific rim, and in Africa and South Asia.[7]

By embracing Marxian categories, DuBois made a self-conscious effort to test the foundation stones of the historical profession—objectivity and progress, as defined by the White Man's Burden. In *Black Reconstruction in America*, he endeavored to highlight the limitations of American history and to question its propagandist or mythological aspects.[8] In the process, his work has become a valuable guide (along with the work of other anticolonial and antiracist writers of the period, from C.L.R. James, Eric Williams, George Padmore, and Kwame Nkrumah within the African diaspora, to Jawarhalal Nehru in India) for historians who wish to move beyond strict class and race analyses toward a history that weaves together class, race, gender, and imperialism.[9]

"The One Thing Needful"

The 1880s and 1890s have been described by Peter Novick and others as the time when notions of objectivity and fact gained ascendancy, when practitioners of "scientific history" came to the fore.[10] A majority of historians embraced an inductive method and rejected the deductive moralism of their predecessors (moralism that had contributed to antislavery movements and the northern position during the Civil War and Reconstruction). A few historians remained committed to the deductive method, like Henry Adams, who challenged others to find the laws on which historical study could be founded, John William Burgess, who applied the Hegelian dialectic to American history, and Frederick Jackson Turner, creator of the frontier thesis.[11] But they were few in number. The more popular approach to scientific history derived from the German Leopold von Ranke. Ranke had managed to overturn the Hegelian tradition in Germany, replacing it with a belief that "facts" should be treated objectively and not reshaped to meet the demands of philosophy.[12] This approach was adopted in America by historians like James Ford Rhodes, who wished to rid history of its preconceived notions and theories (or at least those that attacked businessmen like himself); like William A. Dunning, who saw history as "[t]he absorbing and relentless pursuit of the objective fact—of the thing that actually happened in exactly the form and manner of its happening"; like Albert J. Beveridge, biographer of Abraham Lincoln and self-proclaimed imperialist, who maintained that "facts when justly arranged interpret themselves"; and by Edward Channing, who would be Carter G. Woodson's teacher at Harvard University.[13]

The gap between the two approaches was not unbridgeable.[14] Adams attacked the lack of philosophic integration among the members of the other school, but even so, he himself owed much to Ranke.[15] He would have accepted the compromise between the two schools of thought theorized by Albert Bushnell Hart, DuBois's teacher at Harvard University. In his 1910 article, "Imagination in History," Hart wrote:

Did not Darwin spend twenty years in accumulating data, and in selecting typical phenomena, before he so much as ventured a generalization? In history, too, scattered and apparently unrelated data fall together in harmonious wholes; the mind is led to the discovery of laws; and the explorer into scientific truth is at last able to formulate some of those unsuspected generalizations which explain the whole framework of the universe.[16]

And if Darwin's empirical method was insufficient to convince many historians, it was clear enough to an American historian in the nation's imperial heyday that deduction and induction would probably arrive at similar conclusions. After all, "What do speculations of any kind matter?" Hart wrote. "The Harvard baseball team will play Yale just the same, the President will build his freshman dormitories, the Panama Canal will be completed, Theodore Roosevelt will come out on top: why should anybody philosophize?"[17]

DuBois conformed to this compromise method. If Arnold Rampersad is correct that DuBois's career was divided between his sociological emphasis and his cultural criticism, then in this first period sociology dominated;[18] and DuBois's sociological method corresponded closely with the inductive method popular among historians. DuBois would write later that

it was James with his pragmatism and Albert Bushnell Hart with his research method, that turned me back from the lovely but sterile land of philosophic speculation, to the social sciences as the field for gathering and interpreting that body of fact which would apply to my program for the Negro.[19]

Hart was not noted for racial egalitarianism and believed both that democracy was a Teutonic invention and that "the average of the Negro is very much below that of the white race." And yet Hart had taken a special interest in DuBois, suggesting that the latter write his dissertation on the suppression of the slave trade, promoting its publication, and arranging for DuBois to appear at the American Historical Association's conventions of 1891 and 1909 (the two occasions when he was that organization's president).[20] But, while Hart's dismissal of philosophic speculation held sway over any residual Hegelianism DuBois might have brought back from Germany, the inductive research method was unable to eradicate many of the idealistic assumptions that the former student held about race, culture, the state, and civilization. Of course, for Hart that would hardly matter. DuBois's speculations, whether or not they were given center stage, would not stop the Panama Canal from being built or Roosevelt coming out on top.[21]

DuBois's *The Suppression of the African Slave-Trade to the United States of America, 1638–1870* deserved the praise Hart afforded it at the time by making it the first monograph in the series of Harvard Historical Studies, and that other scholars, including Eugene Genovese, A. Norman Klein, David Levering Lewis, and DuBois himself, also gave it.[22] In addition to showing the extent of American involvement in the slave trade from 1830 to the Civil War,[23] DuBois paid particular attention to the significance of Toussaint Louverture and the revolution in Saint Domingue for developments in American history—a theme he would return to on many occasions.[24] While this was not the first notice given to the significance of this man and the revolution he led (Henry Adams in his indictment of Thomas Jefferson had noted some of the same facts),[25] DuBois devoted a pivotal chapter to this subject. According to DuBois:

The role which the great Toussaint, called L'Ouverture, played in the history of the United States has seldom been fully appreciated. Representing the age of revolution in America, he rose to leadership through a bloody terror, which contrived a Negro "problem" for the Western Hemisphere, intensified and defined the anti-slavery movement, became one of the causes, and probably the prime one, which led Napoleon to sell Louisiana for a song, and finally, through the interworking of all these effects, rendered certain the final prohibition of the slave-trade by the United States in 1807. (p. 70)[26]

Two Afro-Trinidadians, Eric Williams and C.L.R. James, would expand on this interpretation, so that many Americanists are now aware that American expansion owed as much to the actions of Haitian revolutionaries as to Jefferson's republican ideology, and, further, that Jefferson was so obsessed by the need to undermine the "slave republic" that he was prepared to try anything to achieve this, even risking an expanded French imperial presence on the American mainland.[27] Safeguarding slavery, as DuBois knew, was as important to men like Jefferson as expansion west. Such conclusions would give *Suppression* a freshness that remains today in spite of Hart's cumbersome methods.

DuBois's *The Philadelphia Negro: A Social Study* now has a secure place in the foundational narrative for sociology; this is not so for history. This is unfortunate for a number of reasons. First, the lines between sociology and history were often blurred in spite of attempts by some of the professionals concerned to clearly demarcate them. Second, the black community of Philadelphia was a product of many forces—slavery, emancipation, the underground railroad, migration, and so on—that had occurred long before 1896, when DuBois arrived in the city. Being aware of this, DuBois could not help make the study a work of history as well as sociology.

DuBois was brought to Philadelphia largely on the initiative of Susan P. Wharton, a member of one of the city's oldest and most prominent Quaker families, a family that had endowed the Wharton School at the University of Pennsylvania. Wharton was also a member of the executive committee of the Philadelphia College Settlement, which had been founded in 1892. Her concern for African Americans in South Philadelphia, matched by that of other members of the University community, followed in the wake of the University's relocation from South Philadelphia to West Philadelphia, partly to take advantage of the more open space and cheaper land in that area, but also to escape what was perceived to be a harsh and unsavory environment in South Philadelphia (Provost Charles J. Stillé had referred to this area as "A vile neighborhood, growing viler every day").[28] It also coincided with the University's attempts to acquire more land from the city of Philadelphia, and showing a commitment to the city by attempting to combat some of its "social problems" was politic at such a time.[29] According to E. Digby Baltzell, Wharton prevailed on the new provost, Charles C. Harrison, to undertake a study of "the Negro Problem" in the city's Seventh Ward, and Samuel Mc-Cune Lindsay, a member of the sociology department, secured DuBois's services. The latter arrived in the city in August 1896 and stayed in Philadelphia, living in the heart of the Seventh Ward until January 1898.[30]

DuBois had learned his sociological method during his sojourn in Germany as a result of his contact with Gustav von Schmoller, Adolf Wagner and Max Weber. Feeling that the "Negro Problem" was essentially a result of ignorance, the accumulation of facts required by this method seemed most appropriate to him, "The Negro problem was in my mind a matter of systematic investigation and intelligent understanding. The world was thinking wrong about race, because it did not know. The ultimate evil was stupidity. The cure for it was knowledge based on scientific investigation."[31] So, while living in South Philadelphia, DuBois plunged into the work of gathering data. In so doing, he was conforming to the practice of sociologists and historians of his day, and facing many of the same pitfalls as well.

These pitfalls were most obvious in the moralistic characterizations of the community that appeared throughout *The Philadelphia Negro*. Borrowing from the earlier sociological studies of Henry Mayhew and Charles Booth, DuBois defined African Americans according to whether they were "good, bad, [or] indifferent," and many even were included in a category for "dregs" (p. 305).[32] The pitfalls were also evident in DuBois's assumptions about the future of certain forms of religious worship among African Americans. While DuBois questioned the widely accepted notion that Christians of African descent necessarily worshiped with more mysticism and fervor than did their white counterparts because of their race, he also felt (and here he was a precursor of E. Franklin Frazier) that where "little noisy missions" led by "wandering preachers" survived in the city, these represented "the older and more demonstrative worship," and "customs [that] are dying away" (pp. 220–21).[33] Such analysis was based upon his assumption that because secularism and more "rational" approaches to religion were on the rise, these more emotive practices had to be dying out. A closer study of the many the storefront churches appearing in the Seventh Ward at this time would have forced DuBois to draw a different conclusion.[34]

While such pitfalls were present, DuBois clearly transcended the work of other sociologists and historians and took his study well beyond the design and intention of his university sponsors. In particular, he showed clearly what no one had done before — that the black community was both sophisticated and multilayered.[35] With regard to the church, once more, he revealed the "differentiating" aspect of black religious life, showing that while the church was "the world in which the Negro moves and acts" (p. 201), this could mean very different things for African Methodists as compared to the more elite Episcopalians and Presbyterians, and the usually less well situated Baptists (pp. 203–4).[36] Moreover, while he employed moralistic categories to describe class differences, he nevertheless showed that these differences existed. There was clearly a black elite which, although embattled (it seemed to be losing some of its privileges to the new immigrant groups), nevertheless had a long history of achievements (pp. 111–31). There was also a large middling group of the "respectable working class," servants and regularly employed laborers ("responsible workers") who provided the backbone for the community's many social organizations (pp. 131–46). In addition, DuBois highlighted the tensions that seemed to be emerging around issues of migration and regionalism, suggesting that the migration of single, unattached women into Philadelphia was creating a social problem of some magnitude for the black community (pp. 65–78).[37] But here too, DuBois did not rely solely on negative perceptions of the migrants. While working on *The Philadelphia Negro*, he also undertook a study of African Americans in rural Virginia, later published as "The Negroes of Farmville," in which he showed clearly the variegated nature of a black community that was a typical source of Philadelphia's southern migrants at this time.[38]

"The Final Word" revealed both the strengths and weaknesses of DuBois's analysis. In it, he laid down several "axiomatic propositions" arising from his work. Among these were the fact that "the Negro is here to stay," and the suggestion that "It is to the advantage of all . . . that every Negro should make the best of himself" (p. 388). Here idealistic language entered the text, for instead of the abstractions "to the advantage of all" and "making the best of himself," he might merely have couched his analysis in the less "static or consensual" language of natural rights (whether or not they are making the best of themselves, whatever that may mean, people cannot be denied equal opportunity and treatment). Eliding at this stage the question of rights, partly in an attempt to appeal to white Philadelphians (since to focus on rights might have seemed "sharp with subversive possibilities"[39]), DuBois moved down the road toward a justification of the status quo. Thus, his third axiom was: "It is the duty of the Negro to raise himself by every effort to the standards of modern civilization and not to lower those standards by any degree." Implicitly, therefore, DuBois was suggesting that many African Americans were not raising themselves to that "standard of modern civilization." And the fourth axiom read: "It is the duty of white people to guard their civilization against debauchment by themselves or others; but in order to do this it is not necessary to hinder and retard the efforts of an earnest people to rise, simply because they lack faith in the ability of that people" (pp. 388–89). Even though DuBois had faith in the earnestness of "his people," he here found them trailing behind a civilization that, however racist and class infected, could be looked up to. And so, by the time DuBois returned to the language of rights and equal opportunity in the final axiom, the damage had been done: "With these duties in mind and with a spirit of self-help, mutual aid and co-operation, the two races should strive side by side to realize the ideals of the republic and make this truly a land of equal opportunity for all men" (p. 389). It is hard not to conclude with DuBois's own words regarding Booker T. Washington, that here he "practically accept[ed] the alleged inferiority of the Negro races."[40]

But even with these pitfalls, DuBois was able to point the way ahead to a new position regarding "the race." For in *The Philadelphia Negro*, DuBois believed he had shown that "the Negro problems are not more hopelessly complex than many others have been." He continued:

Their elements despite their bewildering complication can be kept clearly in view: they are after all the same difficulties over which the world has grown gray: the question as to how far human intelligence can be trusted and trained; as to whether we must always have the poor with us; as to whether it is possible for the mass of men to attain righteousness on earth; and then to this is added the question of questions: after all who are Men? Is every featherless biped to be counted a man and brother? Are all races and types to be joint heirs of the new earth that men have striven to raise in thirty centuries and more? (pp. 385–86)

Clearly, assumptions about progress framed such analysis and legitimated fears that "we not swamp civilization in barbarism and drown genius in indulgence" by seeking "a mythical Humanity" (p. 386). DuBois wished to reassure readers by suggesting that just as the privileged classes of old feared the expansion of democracy and were unwarranted in doing so, those who now feared such extension in America were also misguided:

We who were born to another philosophy hardly realize how deep-seated and plausible this view of human capabilities and powers once was; how utterly incomprehensible this republic would have been to Charlemagne or Charles V or Charles I. We rather hasten to forget that once the courtiers of English kings looked upon the ancestors of most Americans with far greater contempt than these Americans look upon Negroes — and perhaps, indeed, had more cause. We forget that once French peasants were the "Niggers" of France, and that German princelings once discussed with doubt the brains and humanity of the *bauer.* (p. 386)[41]

For DuBois, the world had "glided by blood and iron into a wider humanity, a wider respect for simple manhood unadorned by ancestors or privilege" (p. 386), so it was now possible to see that what separated oppressor from oppressed was not the fact that one was civilized and the other was not, but that one group had the privilege to *claim* itself civilized and the other did not.

"This widening of the idea of common Humanity is of slow growth and today but dimly realized," DuBois wrote, and so it was in his work at this stage. But the direction of his thought leading toward *The Souls of Black Folk* was clear:

We grant full citizenship in the World Commonwealth to the "Anglo-Saxon" (whatever that may mean), the Teuton and the Latin; then with just a shade of reluctance we extend it to the Celt and the Slav. We half deny it to the yellow races of Asia, admit the brown Indians to an ante-room only on the strength of an undeniable past; but with the Negroes of Africa we come to a full stop, and in its heart the civilized world with one accord denies that these come within the pale of nineteenth-century Humanity. (pp. 386–87)

DuBois had started out his work believing that ignorance was the problem, but by its end he had come to realize that the problem was really just the denigration of and denial of status to African Americans. Others who had similar backgrounds to African Americans were entitled to "whiten" themselves, and were given a status never afforded to blacks. Writing in a vein similar to those who are now interrogating the concept of "whiteness,"[42] DuBois wrote:

we have, to be sure, a threatening problem of ignorance but the ancestors of most Americans were far more ignorant than the freedmen's sons; these ex-slaves are poor but not as poor as peasants used to be; crime is rampant but not more so, if as much, as in Italy; but the difference is that the ancestors of the English and the Irish and the Italians were felt to be worth educating, helping and guiding because they were men and brothers, while in America a census which gives a slight indication of the utter disappearance of the American Negro from the earth is greeted with ill-concealed delight. (p. 387)

Certainly, elitist and modernist presumptions about "the ignorance" of all ancestors and the need for "uplift" remained embedded in these pronouncements. Yet such pronouncements were sufficiently democratic in emphasis and in conflict with much of his own elitism to propel DuBois into the cultural relativism found in the next stage of his historical writing. Now "the battle involve[d] more than a mere altruistic interest in an alien people." It would be "a battle for humanity and human culture" (p. 388).

"Another Thing Needful"

During the period in which he wrote *The Souls of Black Folk* (published in 1903), *John Brown* (1909), and *The Negro* (1915), and for much of the time that he served as editor of the National Association for the Advancement of Colored People's *Crisis,* DuBois contributed to a Progressive insurgency, sharing the stage with such historians as Carl L. Becker and Charles and Mary Beard. But while other Progressives focused their histories on particular kinds of nonracial social divisions (frequently a non-Marxian, populist version of class struggle), DuBois centered his work on the category of race. This emphasis on race gave DuBois's writings a less than "genteel" air, particularly in the face of this "nadir" in post-Civil War race relations — the rising tide of lynching, race riots, segregation, disfranchisement, and imperialism.[43] And while other Progressives usually endorsed notions of progress associated with "the White Man's Burden," DuBois took an early stand against American expansionism. Thus, although his own category of race harbored romantic assumptions, it nevertheless pushed him toward the anti-imperialist Marxism of his later years.

Having allowed the pragmatism of James and the historical method of Hart to shape his work of the 1890s, DuBois now returned to Hegel and other Idealists, especially Thomas Carlyle. According to David Levering Lewis, DuBois felt an "affinity" for Hegel, "from whose *Phenomenology of Mind* he borrowed more or less intact notions of distinct, hierarchical racial attributes." Further, "[he] found in the Hegelian World-Spirit, dialectically actualizing itself through history, a profoundly appealing concept." Lewis continues:

"Lordship and Bondage," Hegel's lodestar essay, explicated a complex reciprocity of master and slave in which the identities of both could be fully realized only to the extent that the consciousness of one was mediated through that of the other. If the master understood dominance, it was the slave who truly understood the sovereign value of freedom.[44]

Understanding the history of freedom in American society, DuBois believed, necessitated studying slavery, emancipation, and continuing racial discrimination, so that African Americans had to be central to the story.[45] But since Hegel himself had deliberately excluded Africans from his analysis, it seemed obvious to DuBois that history had been abused: a "Veil" had been placed in front of it and, in the process, people of African descent had been stripped of their "manhood."

It was this veil that had confounded his earlier social scientific work, DuBois now felt. Clearly, ignorance alone had not been the problem. Racism interfered in important ways with science, preventing the collection of certain facts and distorting those already accumulated. Science and scientific history, for DuBois, were too myopic in their present form to deal with racism, and historians gathered only those facts that were agreeable to themselves and their society. "Before that nameless prejudice," DuBois would write,

[the Negro] stands helpless, dismayed, and well-nigh speechless; before that personal disrespect and mockery, the ridicule and systematic humiliation, the distortion of fact and wanton license of fancy, the cynical ignoring of the better and the boisterous welcoming of the worse, the all-pervading desire to inculcate disdain for everything black, from Toussaint to the devil.[46]

This veil, then, was a close relative of "Orientalism."[47] Once DuBois acknowledged its existence, he could begin to contemplate alternative cultures, and argue that they were creative and valid on their own terms, turning his reading of Thomas Carlyle into a rigorous critique of American society.[48] Hence DuBois's emphasis on the Sorrow Songs. These songs symbolized the highest ideals of "the race" and yet they had never been given serious treatment by scholars. DuBois made them central to *The Souls*, embracing their message of hope for a changed world and their implicit critique of exploitation.[49] Attributing value to black music broadened the confines of Carlyle's criticism of the "cash nexus" and capitalist society from a romanticization of the past and its elites to a belief in the potential of a future based on human creativity.[50]

Employing this cultural critique as his tool, DuBois attempted to "lift the Veil" that had been placed in front of the historical record. In "Of the Dawn of Freedom," DuBois contested many of the conclusions about Reconstruction that were then gaining hold in history departments around the country. Slavery was being downplayed as a cause for the Civil War, but DuBois was categorical in his assessment that the war revolved around the status of Africans in America (*Souls of Black Folk*, p. 10). Most historians were deriding the Freedman's Bureau as a site of corruption and a cause of Reconstruction's failure (for attempting to give too much power and autonomy to the former slaves), but DuBois insisted that the Bureau was "one of the great landmarks of political and social progress" (p. 17). Its failure, DuBois felt, was not in going too far but in being unable or unwilling to go far enough (p. 29). And yet, though he was able to dismiss the conclusions of the new Southern School historians, he remained tied to the old northern interpretations. Thus, he found that the Freedman's Bureau had been held back by "the tyrant and the idler, — the slaveholder who was determined to perpetuate slavery under another name; and the freedman who regarded freedom as perpetual rest, — the Devil and the Deep Sea" (pp. 22–23). While the older vision was preferable to the new, it still harbored prejudices of its own.

DuBois's *John Brown*, published in 1909, was also shaped by his attempt to dismantle the Veil. This was shown explicitly in the book's preface:

After the work of Sanborn, Hinton, Connelley and Redpath, the only excuse for another life of John Brown is an opportunity to lay new emphasis upon the material which they have so carefully collected, and to treat these facts from a different point of view. The viewpoint in this book is that of the little known but vastly important inner development of the Negro American.[51]

DuBois's commitment to a deductive method could not be more clearly stated. He saw John Brown as a Carlylean hero who understood the nature of the "Negro Problem" and acted upon it. DuBois wrote, "this book is at once a record of and a tribute to the man who of all Americans has perhaps come nearest to touching the real souls of black folk."[52] That "the Negro Problem" was central to *John Brown* can be illustrated by comparing it briefly with another work on Brown, written by Oswald Garrison Villard a year after DuBois's work. For DuBois, Brown's awareness of the significance of slavery led him to take the desperate action at Harper's Ferry. He had realized the manner in which slavery had held back American society, for he had assimilated one truth: "The cost of liberty is less than the price of repression" (p. 435). Above all, Brown was not a "crackpot." For Villard, Brown's actions had little effect on the events leading up to the Civil War, and he was no more than an insane man who, after a "deliverance" behind bars, recognized that his actions had been wrong.[53] For DuBois, repression was "fraught with the gravest social consequences" (p. 435) undermining social progress and the spiritual strength of a society, and tending "ever to explosion, murder and war" (p. 442), of which Brown's actions were but the logical extension.

DuBois turned both Carlyle and Hegel on their heads by inverting their views of race. In the process, however, he romanticized the category of race and created a mirror image of their historicism. In his study of Africa in the philosophy of culture, Kwame Anthony Appiah argues that DuBois attempted to overcome racism by developing an alternative category of race. According to DuBois, racial characteristics were not related to biological or intrinsic moral differences, but were sociohistorical in nature — in other words, they were socially constructed. And yet, having taken form, they developed histories and cultures, and these gave races meaning. Thus DuBois could write, "the history of the world is the history, not of individuals, but of groups, not of nations, but of races."[54] In this history, "races have a 'message' for humanity," and each one differed. One was not better than another; it was merely different. Thus DuBois wished to take a concept of race that was constructed along a vertical, hierarchical axis (one race is better than another) and give it a horizontal reading. But while the attempt to highlight certain "race abilities" might lead to a more equitable estimation of the different contributions of the races, "it might just as easily," according to Appiah, "lead to chauvinism or total incomprehension."[55] Racial stereotyping might be a by-product of such a method.

Perhaps, then, *The Negro*, published in 1915, represented the culmination of this approach to the analysis of African Americans and race. In this work DuBois brought to bear the latest historical and anthropological knowledge about the African diaspora. With the aid of the then recently published work of Franz Boas (with whom he came in contact while at Atlanta University), DuBois undertook a sophisticated discussion of the history of the cultures of Africa south of the Sahara.[56] The romantic racialism evident in *The Souls of Black Folk* was very much present in this path-breaking study, but the concern for what lay beyond African American experiences was crucial. Focusing on Africa gave DuBois an acute appreciation of the European colonialism following "the Scramble for Africa" as well as of the efforts of African peoples to resist European power. At a time when European notions of progress still prevailed, DuBois's romanticism would place him nearer to Alexander Crummell (who suggested that African Americans could help lead and "uplift" the people on this "dark" continent)[57] than it would to the anticolonial writers of twenty years later. But as DuBois commenced writing *The Negro*, the First World War had already begun in Europe; and though its consequences remained unclear to him at this time, the imperial world would be "changed utterly" and "a terrible beauty . . . born."

"Philosophical"

This "terrible beauty" was anticolonial Marxism, or "Black Marxism," as Cedric Robinson has described it (though its adherents reached beyond the African diaspora).[58] It was certainly not conceived in the war, since anticolonialism of different forms had already been witnessed in many parts of the world (Haiti, Virginia and Demerara, and the western and southern frontiers of the United States in the New World, along with India, Nyasaland, and the Philippines elsewhere, to name but a few).[59] So too, Marxism was hardly new when the war began. What the war did, in essence, was bring all opponents of imperial capitalism into dialogue. On the one hand, a man like DuBois could now look to the Russian Revolution for an alternative to that "cash nexus," which he had found so disquieting in "Of the Wings of Atalanta" and "Of Mr. Booker T. Washington and Others." On the other hand, in seeking their internationalism, European Marxists now had to consider, though not necessarily welcome, the anticolonial movements developing from India to Africa, Ireland, and (with Garvey) the Americas. Radicals who spoke in terms of class conflict would need to address those who talked in terms of race — Lenin and Stalin would have to speak to the descendants of Louverture and Chilembwe — when before there had seemed no need.[60]

Having earlier criticized Marxian socialists (like Debs) for their failure to consider issues of race, W.E.B. DuBois had, by the 1930s, moved toward his own brand of Black Marxism. This represented a substantial shift in his writing brought on by a number of events that pushed him into conflict with his Progressive colleagues at the NAACP. First, there was the campaign in 1916 against *The Birth of a Nation*, the movie that had been so carefully crafted around the leading historical interpretations of the Civil War and Reconstruction. This was followed by the U.S. intervention in the First World War, which DuBois had so clearly described as an imperial war, but which he supported in the hope that it would improve the position of "dark" peoples around the world. Following the war, however, the race riots of Chicago and East St. Louis, and the manner in which the world leaders both refused to hear Pan-African demands at the Paris Peace Conference and, endorsed by Woodrow Wilson, reestablished colonialism, brought home to DuBois his mistake. Finally, his increasing consternation was accompanied by a growing awareness (made possible through his Pan-African commitments) that racism in the United States was not exceptional and that colonialism in Africa was matched by colonialism in China, India, and the Philippines.[61] These multiple experiences of racism, he now felt, could be observed collectively using class analysis.

DuBois's own criticism of his early work *The Suppression of the African Slave-Trade* reveals the degree to which he felt he had adopted Marxist analysis in his work. In 1954, he claimed that he had earlier been ignorant "of the significance of the work of Freud and Marx." After outlining how his education at Harvard and in Germany had made him feel that Marx had already been "superseded" and so he had given "little time to firsthand study of his work," he wrote:

This was important in my interpretation of the history of slavery and the slave-trade. For if the influence of economic motives on the action of mankind ever had clearer illustration it was in the modern history of the African race, and particularly in America. No real conception of this appears in my book. There are some approaches, some allusions, but no complete realization of the application of the philosophy of Karl Marx to my subject. That concept came much later, when I began intensive study of the facts of society, culminating in my *Black Reconstruction* in 1935.

Finally, he concluded his assessment of both the earlier work, and implicitly the method of history from which it sprang: "What I needed was to add to my terribly conscientious search into the facts of the slave-trade the clear concept of Marx on the class struggle for income and power, beneath which all considerations of right or morals were twisted or utterly crushed."[62]

This twisting of right and morals was most clearly evidenced in the development of the historical profession and in its commitment to "scientific history." DuBois's radical interpretation of Reconstruction would appear so "controversial" because the acceptance of white supremacy and the Southern solutions to the "Negro Question" had become widespread, either implicitly or explicitly, among American historians. In the final chapter of *Black Reconstruction in America*, entitled "The Propaganda of History," Du-

Bois demonstrated the extent of this acceptance of white mythology. "We have too often a deliberate attempt so to change the facts of history," he wrote, "that the story will make pleasant reading for Americans."[63] In short, propaganda enabled racist histories to remain unquestioned.

DuBois was keenly aware that the archive that historians had developed was hopelessly biased in favor of elites. "The chief witness in Reconstruction, the emancipated slave himself, has been almost barred from court," he wrote.

His written Reconstruction record has been largely destroyed and nearly always neglected. Only three or four states have preserved the debates in the Reconstruction conventions; there are few biographies of black leaders. The Negro is refused a hearing because he was poor and ignorant. It is therefore assumed that all Negroes in Reconstruction were ignorant and silly and that therefore the history of Reconstruction in any state can quite ignore him. The result is that most unfair caricatures of Negroes have been carefully preserved; but serious speeches, successful administration and upright character are almost universally ignored and forgotten.

Treating African Americans "with silence and contempt" in this way enabled American writers, "with a determination unparalleled in science," to distort "the facts of the greatest critical period of American history as to prove right wrong and wrong right" (p. 721).

"I stand at the end of this writing, literally aghast at what American historians have done to this field" (p. 725), DuBois pronounced. What had the leading American historians, like John William Burgess and William A. Dunning, done? According to DuBois, Burgess was both "frank and determined in his anti-Negro thought" and "a Tory and open apostle of reaction" (pp. 718–19). Yet, DuBois could write, "Subtract from Burgess his belief that only white people can rule, and he is in essential agreement with me" (p. 726). Throughout his major work, *Reconstruction and the Constitution* (1905), Burgess illustrated his racism:

The claim that there is nothing in the colour of the skin from the point of view of political ethics is a great sophism. A black skin means membership in a race of men which has never of itself succeeded in subjecting passion to reason, has never therefore, created any civilization of any kind.[64]

Founding his work on this premise, Burgess suggested that "it is the white man's mission, his duty and his right, to hold the reins of political power in his hands for the civilization of the world and the welfare of mankind" (p. 719).[65] Burgess's quirky Hegelian approach to history obviously did not allow for the incorporation of black people in his unfolding dialectic. The evolution toward "more and more individual liberty" granted by the American state would exclude African Americans.[66] And while Burgess would argue that the South had failed to understand "the plans of Providence," southerners were at least correct in believing that these plans were completely lost on people of African descent.

William A. Dunning was less dogmatic than Burgess, and DuBois believed that his statements were often judicious.[67] But even Dunning could declare, in *Reconstruction, Political and Economic,* that during Reconstruction "all forces (in the South) that made for civilization were dominated by a mass of barbarous freedmen." Consequently, he maintained that slavery, or some other system like segregation, was necessary as a method of race control.[68] Under his aegis "Bourbon historiography," or the school of "political fable," as DuBois described it,[69] became established at Columbia University. This school produced monograph after monograph detailing the "horrors" of Reconstruction and the grandeur with which rulers of the South had managed to restore "civilization."[70] At Columbia, Dunning trained historians like Walter L. Fleming, Ulrich Bonnell Phillips, J. G. de Roulhac Hamilton, and Charles W. Ramsdell to use scientific methods in conjunction with the propagation of racist belief. According to DuBois, the results of this method were "first, endless sympathy with the white South; second, ridicule, contempt or silence for the Negro; third, a judicial attitude towards the North, which concluded that the North under great misapprehension did a grievous wrong, but eventually saw its mistake and retreated."[71] This amounts to a precis of the screenplay for *The Birth of a Nation*, which DuBois had played such a large part in protesting after its release to general fanfare and presidential acclaim.

Historians and historical novelists[72] had turned history into an exercise in propaganda—the establishment of white myths. It was now "useless as science and misleading as ethics," DuBois wrote. "It simply shows that with sufficient general agreement and determination among the dominant classes, the truth of history may be utterly distorted and contradicted and changed to any convenient fairy tale that the masters of men wish" (*Black Reconstruction*, pp. 725–26). And if this was true for the history of Reconstruction, it was likely to be the case for American history, and beyond that for people outside the United States. DuBois turned his attention to finding out whether this was true, and if so, replacing propagandist narratives with an alternative, if incomplete, counternarrative.

The result of this endeavor was *Black Folk: Then and Now,* in which DuBois challenged Eugene Guernier's 1933 repetition of "the ancient lie of 1833" (Hegel): "Seule de tous les continents, l'Afrique n'a pas d'histoire."[73] He understood the incompleteness of his project, that it would rely in some places on "conjecture and even guesswork," but felt this was preferable to the "widespread lack of knowledge" and the "irritating silence" with regard to Africa and people of African descent (p. vii). Moreover, learning from his survey of American historians and their pretensions to objectivity, DuBois announced his own presuppositions in his preface:

I do not for a moment doubt that my Negro descent and narrow group culture have in many cases predisposed me to interpret my facts too favorably for my race; but there is little danger of long misleading here, for the champions of white folk are legion. The Negro has long been the clown of history; the football of anthropology; and the slave of industry. I am trying to show here why these attitudes can no longer be maintained. I realize that the truth of history lies not in the mouths of partisans but rather in the calm Science that sits between. Her cause I seek to serve, and wherever I fail, I am at least paying Truth the respect of earnest effort. (p. ix)

Truth was for someone in the future to determine; DuBois saw his task less in the effort to establish encyclopedic facts than in debunking false assumptions and lies.[74]

This task was particularly important as the world that American Reconstruction had helped to make, the imperial world of the Scramble for Africa, appeared to be on the verge of implosion in the wake of World War I and the rise of German and Italian fascism. What DuBois wished to do in this study was highlight not only the ways Africans had been sucked into other people's history through slavery and the slave trade, but how through resistance — from Toussaint Louverture to anti-colonial rebels in the Congo, Nyasaland, Kenya, Ghana, and South Africa — they had made that world their own; or to borrow from Paul Gilroy, how they had established a "Black Atlantic."[75]

DuBois's Marxism, then, was anticolonial in essence. This he made abundantly clear in the volume's closing passage:

The Proletariat of the world consists not simply of white European and American workers but overwhelmingly of the dark workers of Asia, Africa, the islands of the sea, and South and Central America. These are the ones who are supporting a superstructure of wealth, luxury, and extravagance. It is the rise of these people that is the rise of the world. (*Black Folk*, p. 383)

Precisely "the modern history of the African race" and the manner in which it linked up to other "subaltern" histories exemplified the Marxian philosophy. Nevertheless, when DuBois finally announced his membership in the U.S. Communist Party in October of 1961, from his new home in Accra, he was not only confirming this link between Marxism and anti-colonialism; he was also transcending Marx, since the latter had stuck to the Eurocentric Hegelian vision of African history.[76]

Conclusion

In this intellectual journey from positivism to anticolonial Marxism, the significance of *The Philadelphia Negro* was profound. Within this work could be found both the highest expression of empirical social science much touted during the 1890s and a glimmering of the idealism of *The Souls of Black Folk*, which ultimately would lead to an assault on positivism similar in content and scope to Marx's assault on classical political economy. The very dynamic quality of the Philadelphia study highlighted the fact that DuBois's gradual self-transformation from *The Suppression of the African Slave-Trade* through *The Souls of Black Folk* to *Black Reconstruction in America* was no leap from the mainstream of the historical profession into polemical essays and "controversial interpretive frameworks," but was rather a series of well-considered steps prompted by the limitations found in each methodology encountered and employed along the way. As such, DuBois's giant steps provide comments on the nature of that profession, its polemical bases, and its propagandist intentions that historians at the end of DuBois's century would do well to heed.

The author would like to thank the participants in the W.E.B. DuBois symposium, especially Robin Kelley, Carl Nightingale, Tom Sugrue, Mia Bay, and Michael Katz, for their comments on an earlier version of this paper.

Notes

1. Eric Foner, *Nothing but Freedom: Emancipation and Its Legacy* (Baton Rouge: Louisiana State University Press, 1983), pp. 5–6; Foner relies on Herbert Aptheker, *Afro-American History: The Modern Era* (New York: Citadel Press, 1971), p. 67.

2. Peter Novick, *That Noble Dream: The "Objectivity Question" and the American Historical Profession* (New York: Cambridge University Press, 1988).

3. August Meier and Elliott Rudwick, *Black History and the Historical Profession, 1915–1980* (Urbana: University of Illinois Press, 1986). Meier and Rudwick, *Black History*, pp. 5–6; p. 71. Since the book intends to "illuminate the rise and the transformation of black history as a research field" (p. xi) this treatment of DuBois is problematic.

4. Novick, *That Noble Dream*, chaps. 1, 4, 7, and 8.

5. "My whole life had been a chronology of *changes*," *The Autobiography of Malcolm X* (New York: Ballantine Books, 1973), p. 346.

6. Particularly Randolph Bourne, *War and the Intellectuals* (New York: Harper and Row, 1964).

7. Michael Adas, "Contested Hegemony: The Great War and the Afro-Asian Assault on the Civilizing Mission Ideology" (paper presented to the Annenberg Seminar in History, Department of History, University of Pennsylvania, April 20, 1995); see also Adas, *Machines as the Measure of Men: Science, Technology, and Ideologies of Western Dominance* (Ithaca, N.Y.: Cornell University Press, 1989), chap. 6.

8. Robert Young, *White Mythologies: Writing History and the West* (London: Routledge, 1990).

9. Paul Gilroy, *The Black Atlantic: Modernity and Double Consciousness* (London: Verso, 1993).

10. Novick, *That Noble Dream*, pp. 21–46.

11. W. Stull Holt, *Historical Scholarship in the United States* (London: University of Washington Press, 1967), p. 21.

12. This was an inductive approach very similar to that promoted at the same time by Thomas Babington Macaulay in England. See Macaulay's essay on Ranke in *Critical and Historical Essays* (London: J. M. Dent, 1907), pp. 38–72.

13. Holt, *Historical Scholarship*, pp. 22–23.

14. As Carl L. Becker and Charles A. Beard would point out later, the notion of objectivity employed by the inductive school was itself a theory, and adherence to it entailed implicit assumptions. Becker, "Everyman His Own Historian," *American Historical Review* 37, 2 (January 1932): 221–36; Beard, "Written History as an Act of Faith," *American Historical Review* 39, 2 (January 1934): 219–29. E. P. Thompson overlooked this point in his critique of Louis Althusser in *The Poverty of Theory and Other Essays* (New York: Monthly Review Press, 1978), pp. 1–210.

15. According to Harvey Wish, "Adams's actual histories were well within Ranke's canons of scientific history; and his own formulas derived from natural science produced no history whatsoever." *The American Historian* (New York: Oxford University Press, 1960), p. 162. See also Henry Steele Commager in *Essays in Historiography*, ed. Marcus Jernegen (Chicago: University of Chicago Press, 1937), p. 191.

16. Holt, *Historical Scholarship*, p. 21.

17. Novick, *That Noble Dream*, p. 30. The conflict between inductive and deductive historians was not as significant as many felt at the time. Even though heated debates were common, like the one between James Mill and Macaulay in England at the beginning of the nineteenth century, those debates would dissipate when conclusions were drawn about the direction of history. Whether or not the inductive or the deductive methods were adopted, both Mill and Macaulay concluded that the history of civilization justified British imperialism in India. For American historians at the end of that century, as Novick writes, "optimism was the great solvent of doubt in the epistemological as in the ideological realm." *That Noble Dream*, p. 105.

18. Arnold Rampersad, in "A Divided Career," *The Art and Imagination of W.E.B. DuBois* (New York: Schocken Books, 1990), pp. 48–67.

19. DuBois, "My Evolving Program for Negro Freedom," in Rayford Logan, ed., *What the Negro Wants* (Chapel Hill: University of North Carolina Press, 1944), p. 39; quoted in Baltzell, introduction to the 1967 edition of *The Philadelphia Negro*, p. xvi.

20. Quoted in Meier and Rudwick, *Black History*, p. 5.

21. Most of the abstract formulations in *The Suppression of the African Slave-Trade* (New York: Schocken Books, 1969) were to be found in the conclusion, where DuBois discussed the dangers of nations engaging in "moral wrong" and the need for "nations as well as men to do things at the very moment when they ought to be done" (p. 199).

22. Eugene Genovese republished the work in 1959; A. Norman Klein, introduction to the 1969 edition, in *Suppression*, pp. xi–xxvii; David Levering Lewis, *W.E.B. DuBois: Biography of a Race* (New York: Henry Holt, 1993), pp. 155–61; DuBois, "Apologia," in *Suppression*, pp. xxxi–iv.

23. DuBois, *Suppression*, p. 143; Lewis, *DuBois*, p. 153.

24. One of DuBois's last essays focused on Toussaint Louverture. Eric J. Sundquist, ed., *The Oxford W.E.B. DuBois Reader* (New York: Oxford University Press, 1996), pp. 296–302.

25. Henry Adams, *History of the United States of America During the First Administration of Thomas Jefferson* (New York: Charles Scribner's, 1921) 1:384–85.

26. See pp. 70–93.

27. Eric Williams, *Capitalism and Slavery* (London: Andre Deutsch, 1964); C.L.R. James, *The Black Jacobins* (New York: Vintage, 1963); Michael B. Zuckerman, "The Power of Blackness," in *Almost Chosen People: Oblique Biographies in the American Grain* (Berkeley and Los Angeles: University of California Press, 1993).

28. Edward Potts Cheyney, *History of the University of Pennsylvania, 1790–1940* (Philadelphia: University of Pennsylvania Press, 1940), p. 261.

29. The University's debt to the city is evident in "Proceedings at the Opening of

the Library of the University of Pennsylvania," pamphlet (Philadelphia: University of Pennsylvania Press, 1891).

30. Baltzell, "Introduction," to the 1967 edition of *The Philadelphia Negro*, p. xviii.

31. DuBois, *Dusk of Dawn*, pp. 3, 51; Baltzell, "Introduction," p. xviii.

32. Henry Mayhew, *London Labour and London Poor* (New York: Harper, 1851); Baltzell, "Introduction," pp. xvii–xviii.

33. E. Franklin Frazier, *The Negro Church in America* (New York: Schocken Books, 1963).

34. Robert Gregg, *Sparks from the Anvil of Oppression: Philadelphia's African Methodists and Southern Migrants* (Philadelphia: Temple University Press, 1993), chap. 3; Arthur Huff Fauset, *Black Gods of the Metropolis: Negro Cults in the Urban North* (Philadelphia: University of Pennsylvania Press, 1971).

35. He was far more sensitive to such divisions than was his contemporary William Dorsey. See Roger Lane, *William Dorsey's Philadelphia and Ours: On the Past and Future of the Black City in America* (New York: Oxford University Press, 1991).

36. Gregg, *Sparks*, chaps. 1–3.

37. For a discussion of this, see Joe William Trotter, Jr, "Introduction" to *The Great Migration in Historical Perspective* (Bloomington: Indiana University Press, 1991), pp. 2–3.

38. DuBois, "The Negroes of Farmville, Virginia: A Social Study," *Bulletin of the U.S. Department of Labor* 3 (January 1898).

39. Daniel T. Rodgers, *Contested Truths: Keywords in American Politics Since Independence* (New York: Basic Books, 1987), p. 47.

40. DuBois, *The Souls of Black Folk* (New York: Dutton, 1995), p. 36.

41. A recent version of this statement is to be found in the movie *The Commitments*, where the protagonist explains to the members of his band that they should play soul music because "the Irish are the blacks of Europe, and the Dubliners are the blacks of Ireland."

42. See David Roediger, *The Wages of Whiteness: Race and the Making of the American Working Class* (London: Verso, 1991); *Towards the Abolition of Whiteness* (London: Verso, 1994); and Theodore W. Allen, *The Invention of the White Race*, Vol. 1, *Racial Oppression and Social Control* (London: Verso, 1994).

43. Rayford W. Logan, *The Negro in American Life and Thought: The Nadir, 1877–1901* (New York: Dial, 1954).

44. Lewis, *DuBois*, pp. 139–40.

45. With this in mind, it is not surprising that DuBois should have both begun and ended his essay "Of the Dawn of Freedom," a study of the years 1861 to 1872, with the oft-quoted phrase: "The problem of the twentieth century is the problem of the color-line." *Souls of Black Folk*, pp. 10, 29.

46. DuBois, *Souls of Black Folk*, p. 7.

47. Edward Said, *Orientalism* (New York: Pantheon, 1978).

48. It must be remembered that Carlyle himself had denied the significance of Africans to history; Eugene R. August, ed., *Thomas Carlyle's "The Nigger Question" and John Stuart Mill's "The Negro Question"* (New York: Meredith Corporation, 1971). He provided inspiration for DuBois, however, in his characterization of any kind of work as important, for "all work, even cotton-spinning is alone noble." Thomas Carlyle, *Past and Present* (New York: New York University Press, 1965), p. 155. This approach to culture was later employed by scholars like Raymond Williams, *Culture and Society* (Middlesex: Penguin, 1975); and E. P. Thompson, *The Making of the English Working Class* (New York: Vintage, 1966), who endeavored to theorize and valorize working-class culture. See Gilroy, *Black Atlantic*, p. 11; Robert Young, *Colonial Desire: Hybridity*

in Theory, Culture and Race (London: Routledge, 1995), pp. 55–89 for related discussions of Matthew Arnold's *Culture and Anarchy*.

49. Just as William Morris was inspired by Icelandic people and their myths, and was able to move beyond feelings of stagnation and despair to realize that there were worlds beyond that of Gradgrind, so DuBois was inspired by the Sorrow Songs; E. P. Thompson, *William Morris: Romantic to Revolutionary* (London: Merlin Press, 1977), pp. 175–91.

50. See, for example, the final passage of *Souls of Black Folk*, p. 187. Gilroy, *Black Atlantic*, p. 125.

51. DuBois, *John Brown*, in Julius Lester, ed., *The Seventh Son: The Thought and Writings of W.E.B. DuBois* (New York: Random House, 1971), p. 432.

52. DuBois, *John Brown*. In *The Art and Imagination of W.E.B. DuBois*, Rampersad maintains that DuBois placed the Carlylean hero John Brown into the historical framework of Hippolyte Taine. According to Rampersad, Brown's martyrdom was shown to be the result of forces arising from his race, milieu, and moment, together with "those psychological qualities and accidents that set him apart from other men subjected to the same pressures" (p. 110). There is no evidence that DuBois used Taine directly, and his ideas were derived more from German than French thinkers. Nevertheless, slavery and "the Negro Problem" in DuBois's writings certainly corresponded to Taine's notion of the milieu.

53. Oswald Garrison Villard, *John Brown* (London: Constable, 1910), pp. 588–89.

54. Kwame Anthony Appiah, *In My Father's House: Africa in the Philosophy of Culture* (New York: Oxford University Press, 1992), p. 28. See Robert Gregg, "Beyond Boundaries, Beyond the Whale," *American Quarterly*, 45, 4 (December 1993): 631–38.

55. Appiah, *My Father's House*, p. 94.

56. DuBois, *The Negro* (Millwood, N.Y.: Kraus-Thomson, 1975); Meier and Rudwick, *Black History*, p. 6.

57. Appiah, *My Father's House*, p. 28.

58. Cedric Robinson, *Black Marxism* (London: Zed Press, 1983).

59. C.L.R. James's *A History of Pan-African Revolt* (New York: Charles H. Kerr, 1995) focuses on the African and African American revolts mentioned here. L. S. Stavrianos, in *Global Rift: The Third World Comes of Age* (New York: William Morrow, 1981), highlights this intersection of Marxism and anticolonialism following the First World War and the Russian Revolution, chaps. 19–22.

60. Robin D. G. Kelley, *Hammer and Hoe: Alabama Communists During the Great Depression* (Chapel Hill: University of North Carolina, 1990), pp. xi–xv, and 119–92 discusses this nexus between Marx and black protest.

61. Paul Gilroy has placed considerable emphasis on the novel *Dark Princess* (1928) in turning DuBois toward a more internationalist perspective. The importance of this text lies in DuBois's attempt to bring together an African American radical and a South Asian princess, who becomes a trade union radical and political activist in the United States. The work shows clearly DuBois's awareness that the experiences of exploitative labor were shared by a proletariat made up of "yellow, brown, and black peoples," and that, while unique in many respects, African experiences were not wholly exceptional. Many of the ideas put forward in *Dark Princess* were emerging in DuBois's thought as early as his comments on the war in the Philippines in *The Souls* and were influenced by his attendance at the London Races Conference of 1911, but the novel is very much a product of the 1920s. Gilroy, *Black Atlantic*, pp. 140–45. See also Lewis, *DuBois*, pp. 440–42.

62. DuBois, "Apologia," pp. xxxi–ii, xxxiv.

63. DuBois, *Black Reconstruction in America, 1860–1880* (New York: Atheneum, 1979), p. 713.

64. William Burgess, *Reconstruction and the Constitution* (New York: Scribners, 1903), pp. viii–ix, 133.

65. Wish, *American Historian*, p. 232; and DuBois, *Black Reconstruction in America*, p. 719.

66. For Burgess's brush with Hegelianism and his racism, see Rodgers, *Contested Truths*, pp. 164–66.

67. DuBois, *Black Reconstruction in America*, p. 719.

68. Wish, *American Historian*, p. 232.

69. DuBois in Herbert Aptheker, ed., *The Correspondence of W.E.B. DuBois* (Amherst: University of Massachusetts Press, 1973), p. 150.

70. DuBois in Herbert Aptheker, ed., *The Book Reviews of W.E.B. DuBois* (Amherst: University of Massachusetts Press), p. 14.

71. DuBois, *Black Reconstruction in America*, p. 719. See also his penetrating review of Ulrich Bonnell Phillips's *American Negro Slavery* (1918). DuBois wrote: "The Negro as a responsible human being has no place in the book. . . . Nowhere is there an adequate conception of 'darkies,' 'niggers' and 'negroes' (words liberally used throughout the book) as making a mass of humanity with all the usual human reactions." Phillips established arguments, according to DuBois, "by innuendo and assumption." Aptheker, *Book Reviews*, p. 58. See also I. A. Newby, *The Defense of Jim Crow* (Baton Rouge: Louisiana University Press, 1965), p. 3.

72. The line between historians and historical novelists was a fine one at this time. Woodrow Wilson's *History of the American People* (1895) inspired Reverend Thomas Dixon (a former Princeton student) to write *The Clansman* (1905), which in turn led to the creation of D. W. Griffith's *The Birth of a Nation* (1915). Thus looking only at the output of historians seriously underestimates their influence during the first three decades of the twentieth century.

73. DuBois, "Alone of all the continents, Africa has no history," *Black Folk: Then and Now* (New York: Kraus-Thomson, 1975), p. 219.

74. However, DuBois never gave up on the idea of producing an *Encyclopedia Africana*. Given the imperial genealogy of encyclopedias (the *Encyclopaedia Britannica* having one of its origins in the attempt of Scottish intellectuals at the end of the eighteenth century to improve their standing in the British empire), DuBois's commitment to this idea revealed the degree to which he remained unwilling to contest notions of "historical truth," even when it meant participating in the re-creation of a genre that had been instrumental in theorizing African inferiority.

75. DuBois, *Black Folk*. For DuBois's most extensive treatment of Toussaint and Saint Domingue, see pp. 145–76; for twentieth-century rebellions see pp. 380–81. Gilroy, *Black Atlantic*, pp. 1–40. See also James, *History of Pan-African Revolt*, which was similar to *Black Folk* in many respects.

76. Klein, Introduction to DuBois, *Suppression*, p. xi.

Part II

DuBois's Philadelphia

Figure 7. Black hod-carriers, circa 1924. A menial task on construction sites, hod-carrying was the type of heavy, unpleasant labor that typically employed African Americans. Courtesy of Temple University, Urban Archives.

Chapter 4

"Lifework" and Its Limits

The Problem of Labor in The Philadelphia Negro

Jacqueline Jones

Of the myriad issues W.E.B. DuBois explored in *The Philadelphia Negro*, "the question of employment" constituted "the most pressing of the day" (p. 141). DuBois understood that patterns of work lie at the heart of any society, that the kinds of jobs people do — where they work, for whom, and under what conditions — help to define the structure of every community. And in fact, *The Philadelphia Negro* contains a wealth of primary material that reveals the ways in which the deployment of labor, both black and white, male and female, profoundly affected the social and political economy of Philadelphia in the late nineteenth century. Out of a job structure specific to this time and city, a structure shaped by racial and gender discrimination, emerged identifiable patterns of black poverty, labor relations, health and family life, and crime. DuBois's great achievement was to highlight the significance of Philadelphia as a particular place — a place with a unique history, to be sure, but a place shaped also by larger historic forces that affected the economic well-being of African American communities throughout the country during this period. In essence, as a work that blends scholarship with implicit policy analysis, *The Philadelphia Negro* endures — it continues to instruct and to inspire — because DuBois built his study around the problem of jobs, and he placed that problem within a broad historical context. Late twentieth-century historians and social scientists alike would do well to look to his example.

Based on extensive, interdisciplinary research, DuBois's pioneering work suggests that racism functioned primarily as an amalgam of economic strategies that benefited the interests of certain groups of white people within certain social contexts. Indeed, racial prejudice stemmed from concrete social conflicts, and assumed a "tangible form" (p. 350). By the standards of late twentieth-century social-scientific research, *The Philadelphia Negro* devotes relatively little attention to African American "culture" — to gender relations, religious beliefs, and forms of oral expression, including music and rapping on the streets — or to politics and the role of black voters in the city's two-party system. At the same time, DuBois's book provides a compelling corrective to more recent studies of ghetto life, studies that almost as a matter of perverse principle downplay the long-term effects of structural unemployment and underemployment in shaping the African American past and present. DuBois reminds us that history matters, and that within history, the social division of labor matters most of all.

Despite his conviction that the problem of work was the "most pressing issue of the day" for blacks, DuBois was no crude material determinist. On the one hand, he stressed that in the job competition between working-class blacks and whites, whites invariably won. On the other hand, he pointed out that other groups of white Philadelphians who were not directly competing for wages with black men and women also indulged in discriminatory behavior, for a variety of reasons. Department store owners refused to hire black women as clerks, believing, rightly or wrongly, that their middle-class customers preferred to have whites wait upon them. Likewise, white professionals, from lawyers to physicians, feared that their own practices would be compromised by the presence of blacks, no matter how well qualified for their jobs. And the city's white elite ministered to the black poor in the belief that all black people were poor and "vicious," the whites complacent in their perception of the black "race" as degraded and inferior. These various forms of discrimination produced a job structure that relegated black men, women, and children to the lowest-paying employment, and condemned most Philadelphia blacks to lives of poverty and hardship.

DuBois's study is significant not only for the way it focuses on patterns of work to illuminate this particular community at this particular time, but also for the way it can help us to understand the class and racial dynamics of late twentieth-century, postindustrial America. Thus an examination of Philadelphia's labor force in the 1890s, and the attendant social dynamics flowing from it, has much to tell us about the struggles of various black communities over the last century, and about the discriminatory employment patterns that have remained at the core of those struggles. In other words, with some modification, *The Philadelphia Negro* can serve as a model of scholarly investigation that illuminates the complexities of local as well and national social hierarchies based on class, gender, age, and race. The book, I would argue, provides a text for our times, as well as a text of DuBois's times.

Woven into the narrative of *The Philadelphia Negro* are descriptions of the distinctive labor-market experiences that set African Americans of both sexes and all ages apart from their white coworkers. In terms of the work they did and the wages they earned, black people were part of Philadelphia's nineteenth-century working class, broadly defined. However, black workers occupied a unique place in the city's job structure, and they also possessed a unique, collective historical consciousness, one shaped by oppression, past and present.

As DuBois shows in a masterful way, to label black people's constricted job opportunities the end result of "racial discrimination" would be to oversimplify a number of complex historical processes. Recent research by historians has deepened our understanding of the major issues that DuBois pinpointed in his study. For example, it is certainly true that employers of manufacturing and clerical workers made clear their hiring preferences by reserving jobs in these two large sectors to whites exclusively. At the same time, the late nineteenth-century trend toward business consolidation and technological innovation worked against small craftsmen and entrepreneurs of both races, though blacks as a group were disproportionately harmed by this development. Moreover, inferior and inadequate educational institutions prevented black workers from gaining the various skills necessary to compete for jobs at all levels above manual labor in an emerging industrial society; for example, without the requisite training at a commercial high school, black job applicants had no hope of competing with their better educated white counterparts for secretarial and bookkeeping positions. Unlike immigrant groups from western and then later eastern Europe, black people were never able to establish their own secure "niches" that would insure them economic stability for the present, and opportunities for upward mobility (especially for their children) in the future.[1] Because of the stigma of slavery attached to domestic service and other kinds of menial labor, white workers eschewed these jobs, leaving black men and women clustered in the dirtiest, most disagreeable, ill-paid, and seasonal employment the city had to offer. And finally, throughout the century, black workers endured the wrath of certain groups of white workers who served as gatekeepers into their respective occupations (especially through hiring policies and union apprenticeship programs) and who put employers on notice that they would not tolerate blacks as either coworkers or prospective strikebreakers. In essence, the white working class organized to fight on two fronts—against employers, but also against blacks, their rivals for scarce jobs. It would be difficult to separate the racial prejudice of white workers from their determination to protect their economic prerogatives against groups weaker than themselves—in this case, African Americans.

In order to examine black Philadelphia in the 1890s, DuBois began at the beginning of the story—with a history of the city's racial division of labor. The institution of bondage was the seed that produced the city's subsequent labor relations. During the antebellum period, tensions developed between white immigrants and black urban in-migrants as these groups engaged in bitter competition for skilled and unskilled jobs. By the late-nineteenth century, the city's labor force had been transformed, as successive waves of black workers were displaced by a new economic order based on more complex forms of business organization and the need for workers with specialized education and training. DuBois showed clearly that when individual black workers lost their livelihoods and their places in the city's job structure, the black community registered these effects in dramatic and specific ways. With the erosion of a black economic base, families fragmented, crime increased, and class divisions within the community intensified. Meanwhile, groups of white skilled and menial workers and, by extension, their families and neighborhoods prospered by virtue of their privileged status relative to the black population.

Slaves occupied a wide variety of jobs in colonial Philadelphia; they served as skilled artisans and jacks-of-all-trades, as well as domestic servants.[2] Nevertheless, white elites became convinced early on that free blacks constituted an inherently anomalous and dangerous group, and these fears hardened into a formal ideology of black racial inferiority after formal emancipation. DuBois quoted the Pennsylvania legislature's declaration in 1726 that "free negroes are an idle and slothful people," and he suggested that whites by this time had begun to associate free blacks — that is, blacks living and working without the direction of an owner or the limitations placed on them by law — with poverty, crime, and social disorder in general (p. 15).[3]

In the eighteenth century, the badge of bondage remained fastened on the whole black population, slave and free, as well as on future generations. Philadelphia slaveowners were in a position to ignore the resentments of white craftsmen, men whose work possibilities were undercut by the availability of cheap slave labor. However, after the gradual abolition of slavery (1780–1808), black men, women, and children paid for their freedom with increased vulnerability to "a fierce economic struggle," as Irish and German immigrants launched concerted, violent attacks upon the black artisans of the city (p. 26). For over a decade, from 1829 to 1840, "a series of riots directed chiefly at the Negroes" gave expression to the fears of whites in a city undergoing rapid economic change and population growth. The result was a swift decline in the black artisanal class that had its roots in slavery. By the Civil War, the black labor force had assumed a form that would endure for many generations; black women workers were confined to domestic service, while their menfolk lacked a comparable source of steady, though ill-paid and menial, labor.[4] When DuBois began his study of Philadelphia in the 1890s, he found that the recent influx of European workers, combined with growing numbers of black migrants from the southern states, had depressed wage levels and made the rivalry for unskilled work among men of both races even more desperate than in earlier periods.[5]

DuBois documented the ways in which the traditionally black male occupations of barbering and catering declined under the pressures of job competition and technological change. During the early nineteenth century, some black men found a place in the catering business, and their relative success in serving the city's wealthiest white families provided the economic underpinnings for a small elite in Philadelphia's black community. By the postbellum period, however, the rise of large hotels had rendered black caterers increasingly superfluous, as a "large business built up by talent and tact" encountered "changed social conditions." DuBois noted, "if the Negro caterers of Philadelphia had been white, some of them would have been put in charge of a large hotel, or would have become co-partners in some large restaurant business" (p. 120). As it was, black caterers were forced to scale down their operations and attract middle-class white clients, and in the process compete with modest white caterers as well.

The fate of another entrepreneurial class, the barbers, was somewhat different. According to DuBois, by the 1890s, younger black men had begun to associate the job with domestic service, and they became increasingly sensitive to the "degree of contempt and ridicule" heaped upon the men who did it (p. 116). Too, the custom among black barbers of barring black customers from their shops out of deference to the prejudices of the whites they served was "particularly galling [to other blacks] and has led to much criticism and unpopularity for certain leading barbers among their own people" (p. 116). Finally, immigrant competitors administered the final blow to this particular group of black workers; German and Italian barbers "were skilled workmen, while skilled barbers were becoming scarce; they cut down the customary prices and some of them found business co-operation and encouragement which the Negroes could not hope for" (p. 116). DuBois concluded that a more general principle pertained here: "the application of large capital to the retail business, the gathering of workmen into factories, the wonderful success of trained talent in catering to the whims and taste of customers . . . the economic condition of the day militates largely against the Negro" (p. 123). The future belonged to men who could command capital and invest in new and sophisticated kinds of technology; throughout the city's commercial economy, then, small businesses (and hence virtually all black-owned businesses) remained at a distinct disadvantage in the race for customers and profits. Meanwhile, larger firms — whether factories or department stores — continued to favor white over black workers.

Here it would be appropriate to mention a relevant point that DuBois did not explore in any depth — the absence of black machine operatives in Philadelphia, which was one of the great urban industrial centers of late nineteenth-century America. Scholars who have studied the history of the city's diverse manufacturing economy, one based on the predominance of light industries, have been struck by the relative absence of blacks from the industrial sector. Though white women and even white children found places for themselves in the textile industry, for example, black people as a group were kept out of blue-collar semiskilled and skilled jobs. In contrast to successive waves of immigrants lacking formal skills and education — the Irish and Germans in the 1830s and 1840s, the Poles, Slavs, and Jews in the 1880s — black workers remained confined to the lowest echelons of the labor force well into the twentieth century. A 1936 survey of 2,500 of the city's workers in the textile and hosiery industries, the metal trades, and radio manufacturing found just seven black people employed in those jobs. Subsequent studies have shown that family connections often aided a young person in finding his or her first job; hence, the initial absence of blacks from manufacturing enterprises in the first half of the nineteenth century exerted a profound influence on the employment opportunities — or rather lack of them — for subsequent generations.[6]

The policies of the Midvale Steel Works, located near Germantown, outside of Philadelphia, provided an intriguing exception to the rule of blacks' exclusion from industrial pursuits. DuBois noted that black men were hired at Midvale because "a manager whom many dubbed a 'crank' . . . had a theory that Negroes and whites could work together as mechanics without friction or trouble" (p. 129). This bold manager was none other but the scientific-management efficiency expert Frederick Winslow Taylor, and though Midvale employed as many as 4,000 blacks by the start of World War I, neither Taylor's nor the company's integrationist impulses were entirely altruistic. Sociologist Isabel Eaton visited the Midvale work site, and she reported her findings in a footnote to *The Philadelphia Negro*. In 1895, the steelworks employed 1,200 men, one-sixth of whom were black and the rest about evenly divided between first- and second-generation immigrants from western Europe. In an interview with Eaton, Taylor suggested that black workers had been hired to counter "the clannish spirit of the workmen and [their] tendency to form cliques":

In steel manufacture much of the work is done with large tools run by gangs of men; the work was crippled by the different foremen trying always to have the men in their gang all of their own nationality. The English foreman of a hammer gang, for instance, would want only Englishmen, and the Irish Catholics only Irishmen. This was not good for the works, nor did it promote friendliness among the workmen. So we began bringing in Negroes and placing them on different gangs, and at the same time we distributed the other nationalities. Now our gangs have, say, one Negro, one or two Americans, an Englishman, etc. The result has been favorable both for the men and for the works. Things run smoothly, and the output is noticeably greater. (p. 130)

In fact, Taylor was less concerned about facilitating "friendliness" among his workers than he was determined to break down a system of ethnic loyalty among groups of workers who set their own piece-rate goals and refused to adhere to an employer-imposed pace of industrial discipline. Presumably, with blacks on the line, compatriots had less time to socialize with each other but workers had more incentive to compete with each other. However, according to historian Walter Licht, in the late 1890s, Midvale abandoned its experiment and instituted a strict system of racial segregation among its workers. In all probability, the offended sensibilities of white workers had inspired the switch in policy.[7]

As a preface to his discussion in the chapter "The Occupations of Negroes," DuBois observed that "it is sufficient to say in general that the sorts of work open to Negroes are not only restricted by their own lack of training but also by discrimination against them on account of their race; that their economic rise is not only hindered by present poverty, but also by a widespread inclination to shut against them many doors of advancement open to the talented and efficient of other races" (p. 98). The occupational data in *The Philadelphia Negro* tell a story that is as simple and straightforward as it is grim. During the last decade of the nineteenth century, in a city of more than one million people, blacks represented 4 percent of the population. Four out of every five black men under the age of twenty worked as porters or errand boys, domestic servants, or common laborers (p. 99). Similarly, 80 percent of all black adult males could be classified as either laborers or servants. DuBois further noted that the opportunities available to black female wage earners were "unusually narrow" (p. 333). Ninety percent of all wage-earning girls labored as servants or day workers, and three out of four black adult females served as domestics or day laborers (pp. 102–3). These figures did not necessarily reflect inferior levels of formal schooling achieved by black men, women, and children; in an era when relatively few working people of any ethnic background or either sex attended high school, blacks as a group boasted a literacy rate of 80 percent, slightly less than German immigrants in the city and higher than immigrants from Italy, Russia, Poland, and Hungary at the time (p. 92). Still, the job structure to some degree reflected the fact that within the public school system, "not only were the common schools separate [according to race], but there were no public high schools for Negroes, professional schools were closed to them, and within the memory of living men the University of Pennsylvania not only refused to admit Negroes as students, but even as listeners in the lecture halls" (p. 88).[8]

Domestic service formed the economic linchpin of the black community; therefore it is not surprising that DuBois appended Isabel Eaton's "Special Report on Negro Domestic Service in the Seventh Ward [of] Philadelphia" to his larger study. For many years, according to DuBois, black slaves and then freedpersons constituted the largest body of servants — "thus adding a despised race to a despised calling" (p. 136). Blacks saw service "as a relic of slavery, and they longed to get other work as their fathers had longed to be free" (p. 137). In the late nineteenth century, the ranks of Philadelphia black servants were filled with men and women who had aspired to, and in some cases trained for, other kinds of jobs, only to be denied those jobs "partly on account of lack of ability, partly on account of the strong race prejudice against them" (p. 137). Meanwhile, buoyed by their own corporate and industrial success, Philadelphia's white elite had begun to offer higher wages to specialized domestic workers — cooks, nursemaids, footmen, and coachmen — thus attracting greater numbers of native-born white men and women, and western European immigrants, into the occupation. Even in this type of employment, then, a process of displacement was affecting a large proportion of the black workforce, and DuBois suggested that the result was "an increase of crime, pauperism and idleness among Negroes: because while they are being to some extent displaced as servants, no corresponding opening for employment in other lines has been made" (p. 140).

DuBois revealed that black workers were thwarted in their aspirations every step up the ladder of social mobility; but he emphasized the role of white trade unions in preventing black men and boys from gaining entry-level positions in both skilled and unskilled jobs. For a people recently released from slavery, these barriers to entry into the stable working class proved devastating in limiting their options as individual workers, as family members, and as a group. Philadelphia's white working class reckoned according to a shortsighted equation: whatever enhanced the opportunities of black workers must limit the opportunities of white workers. White teamsters and carpenters had relatively little power over other workers in the city; they did not hire or fire anyone, and they could not set wage levels or establish working conditions. But they did serve as gatekeepers into the trades, and in that respect they wielded a great deal of power over black workers.[9]

DuBois offered a powerful indictment of the Philadelphia trade-union movement by suggesting that its object was "purely business-like; it aims to restrict the labor market, just as the manufacturer aims to raise the price of his goods" (p. 333). DuBois further observed that the discriminatory policies developed by unions were not the result of racial prejudice exclusively; rather, black workers represented a particularly vulnerable segment of the labor force. Without political power or white allies, blacks fell prey to the depredations of unionists eager to protect their relatively privileged place in Philadelphia's economy. "If they [native-born whites] could keep out the foreign-born workmen in the same way they would; but here public opinion within and without their ranks forbids hostile action," noted DuBois (p. 333).[10] Thus, white workers organized not out of a sense of class consciousness, but out of a sense of exclusivity; to "the natural spirit of monopoly and the desire to keep up wages" (p. 129) was added a socially sanctioned form of racial prejudice.

DuBois argued that, by virtue of their large numbers and their previous training that had prepared them for skilled industrial labor, white native-born and immigrant workers overwhelmed their black counterparts and effectively prevented them from entering the trades at any level. Given a great deal of latitude in admitting apprentices to their crafts and members to their unions, white tradesmen refused to work with "non-union men," and they also refused "to let colored men join the union." Some locals simply shut out blacks as a matter of formal, stated policy, while others used more circuitous means; they failed to act upon a black worker's bid for membership, or they set initiation and membership fees at prohibitively high levels. Obviously, the numerical superiority of whites over blacks in most fields facilitated this type of discrimination.[11]

On the other hand, DuBois cited the Philadelphia cigar makers as an exception to these rules; the "Cigar-makers' Union is a regular trades union with both white and Negro members. It is the only union in Philadelphia where Negroes are largely represented" (p. 227). He attributed their relatively favorable position to the fact that, in the cigar-making industry, "Negro labor [was] . . . competent and considerable" (p. 128). Moreover, the intense competition among Philadelphia's cigar manufacturers bolstered the position of the union even as it served as an incentive for the union to eliminate the threat of black strikebreakers.[12] Just as businesses had a vested interest in making peace with the Cigar Makers International Union (CMIU), so whites had a vested interest in bringing black workers into their fold.

The Philadelphia case of the integrated cigar makers union revealed the interplay between historical precedents and current political and economic realities. In other parts of the country, local conditions dictated different sets of policies of CMIU locals toward nonwhite workers. For example, in New Orleans in 1894, the CMIU showed little interest in organizing blacks, because, according to a white member, white cigar makers "are bitterly prejudiced against the colored ones."[13] In California, locals sponsored successful boycotts against non-union-made cigars, in order to drive Chinese workers from the occupation. DuBois acknowledged that trade unions differed in their approach to black members, according to time and region; in western Pennsylvania, black miners and ironworkers found a place in biracial unions, at least in part because they were a considerable portion of the workforce in both of those occupations (p. 128).[14]

In Philadelphia, white union members in a variety of other trades chose to sacrifice the potential gains of long-term class solidarity to the short-term satisfaction that derived from racial exclusivity; according to DuBois, "nineteen-twentieths of the population have in many cases refused to co-operate with the other twentieth, even when the co-operation means life to the latter and great advantage to the former" (p. 146). Many other unions throughout the country made the same calculation; only a few chose to organize black workers at all, and then usually only on the basis of racially segregated locals. In an era characterized by Jim Crow institutions of all kinds, in the North, as well as the South, the labor movement offered the only realistic hope of a meaningful alliance between blacks and whites in any sphere of public life.[15]

DuBois's discussion of unions, and his analysis of black labor force activity in general, provides insights into everyday contacts between members of the two races. Some of those contacts took place outside of the realm of employment—for example, when men and women of the two groups encountered each other in taverns and saloons (pp. 278–79). Yet by and large, job patterns shaped social patterns. Among unorganized workers, the scramble for jobs, no matter how lowly, heightened mutual suspicion and distrust; for example, noted DuBois, "the women day-laborers are, on the whole, poorly paid, and meet fierce competition in laundry work and cleaning" (p. 133). In the homes of whites, young black servant women remained vulnerable to sexual abuse from their white employers (p. 72). In all aspects of commercial life—in hotels, restaurants, and office buildings—well-to-do white people saw black people laboring as menials; on the streets, and on construction projects, passers-by might view segregated gangs at work, a daily reminder of the separate and unequal status of the black population in general. More significantly, however, was the fact that "the peculiar distribution of employments among whites and Negroes makes the great middle class of white people seldom, if ever, brought into contact with Negroes," and this fact, according to DuBois, was probably "a cause as well as an effect of prejudice" (p. 111).

DuBois offered a trenchant, if largely implicit, analysis of the impact of an emerging consumer culture on the constricted job opportunities for blacks; in a related vein, he stressed the fact that race was a social construction, an idea that existed apart from skin color per se. As department stores and service-oriented professions like the law began to assume a more prominent place in the city's economy, employers in these businesses went out of their way to avoid offending the racial prejudices of their customers. The new emphasis on personal "service" mandated the hiring of blacks out of the public eye, or in menial positions only.[16] Whether a very light-skinned black worker achieved a position "by sheer merit" or by "pluck," his or her "tenure of office" remained insecure (pp. 334–40). DuBois quoted from a study made by Isabel Eaton:

One very fair young girl, apparently a white girl, was employed as a clerk in one of the large department stores for over two years, so that there was no question of her competency as a clerk. At the end of this time it was discovered that she had colored blood and she was promptly discharged. One young woman who had been a teacher and is now a school janitress, teaching occasionally when extra help is needed, states that she had received an appointment as typewriter in a certain Philadelphia office, on the strength of her letter of application and when she appeared and was seen to be a colored girl, the position was refused her. She said that her brother—whom people usually take to be a white man—after serving in the barbershop of a certain hotel for ten years, was summarily discharged when it was learned that he was of Negro birth. (p. 337 n)

Eaton found that 15 percent of all Philadelphia black domestics possessed either a trade or some degree of higher education, but were unable to find positions in areas commensurate with their training; hence the powerful effect of prejudice based on a definition of race that ultimately did not depend on skin color. As the nation entered an era of mass merchandising, businesses of all kinds catered to, and reinforced, the discriminatory proclivities of white consumers.

A "businesslike" spirit of racial exclusion pervaded various organizations in the city; private and public, profit and not-for-profit enterprises sought to implement principles of efficiency and consolidation. For example, DuBois cited the case of a large church that claimed among its members a number of "the most respectable Negro families in the city," but refrained from hiring any black janitors. A member of the church's building committee justified this policy by explaining that the white janitors "would not wear uniforms with Negroes," and, he further noted, "[this church] is a business enterprise, to be run on business principles" (p. 340). For unstated reasons, the church wished to retain white employees, a factor that apparently precluded the hiring of any blacks. Thus, concluded DuBois, "the Christian church joins hands with trades unions and a large public opinion to force Negroes into idleness and crime" (p. 340). This example further suggests that white workers were wary of integrated workplaces altogether, for such places would seem to reveal the common condition shared by the descendants of "free men" (whites) and the descendants of slaves (blacks), a condition that the white working class refused to acknowledge.

Though attentive to local political and demographic factors, DuBois also pointed out that the structure of the Philadelphia labor force directly reflected patterns of prejudice elsewhere in the nation. The city was not a closed system insulated from the realities of African American life, whether on the Pennsylvania countryside or in the Deep South. Indeed, the urban in-migration among southern blacks — men and women fleeing terrorism and disfranchisement — was a significant factor in creating an oversupply of labor, which in turn heightened the racial animosities of white workers in the city. In addition, the seasonal influx of blacks from surrounding states reflected a lack of opportunities for blacks outside of Philadelphia.[17] DuBois observed that "the recent migration has both directly and indirectly increased crime and competition," and yet he also argued that behind the migration "is the world-view desire to rise in the world, to escape the choking narrowness of the plantation, and the lawless repression of the village, in the South" (p. 354). For these reasons he suggested that the migration "must be discouraged and repressed with great care and delicacy, if at all. The real movement of reform is the raising of economic standards and increase of economic opportunity throughout the South" (p. 354). In both its uniqueness and its representativeness, then, Philadelphia stood as one more emblem of white indifference — whether in the North or South, in the countryside or in the city—toward the plight of black people in general, regardless of where they lived and worked (p. 163).

The year after DuBois finished his research for *The Philadelphia Negro*, he initiated a corollary project, a study of the black community of Farmville, Virginia. His findings recorded in the published version of this study help to put into perspective his discussion of southern migrants who resided in Philadelphia. Located in Prince Edward County in the central part of the state, Farmville sent a goodly number of its residents, and members of farm families from the surrounding areas, into Norfolk and Richmond, and on up to mid-Atlantic cities like Baltimore and Philadelphia. DuBois's report, "The Negroes of Farmville, Virginia," published in an 1898 issue of the *Bulletin of the Department of Labor*, reveals the conditions of southern blacks in a small-town way station between rural life and city life. According to Du-Bois, Farmville acted "as a sort of clearing house, taking the raw country lad from the farm to train in industrial life, and sending north and east more or less well-equipped recruits for metropolitan life."[18] (He therefore antici-pated, and disputed, later scholars' contention that southern blacks were unable to find good jobs in the north because they failed to "adjust" prop-erly to a life more hectic and complex than that on the farm.) In this small-town "transition period," DuBois noted that family life suffered, for "The economic family in Farmville is the complement of the Negro family in a city like Philadelphia, and these two families are very often but parts of one family; for married couples often leave their children in Farmville, and single persons live alone in cities and are counted as families of one, etc. In this way the continual migration complicates the question of the size of Negro families" (p. 182).

DuBois discovered a thread of continuity linking the jobs of Farmville's black women to those of their Philadelphia counterparts; in both cases women's "range of employment [was] . . . peculiarly restricted" to domestic service (p. 173). However, while it was true that in Farmville the lowly posi-tion of black workers made "the term 'Negro' and 'servant' synonymous" (p. 179), black men enjoyed relatively more opportunities in the small-town South than in the big-city North. In the 1890s, large enterprises had not yet obliterated artisans and entrepreneurs among the self-employed of both races. Moreover, white unions were either nonexistent or too weak to exert much of an influence in barring blacks from the ranks of the skilled trades; hence, according to DuBois, "White and black mechanics are often seen working side by side on the same jobs, and get on without apparent friction, although there is some discrimination in wage" (p. 177).

Why the impulse to move north among so many of Farmville's black citizens? DuBois suggested that among the men, their "great demand is for steady employment which is not menial, at fair wages," and among the women, a desire for "industrial opportunities outside of domestic service, and of a kind compatible with decency and self-respect" (p. 180). He also noted but failed to explore the deeper significance of another group of ambitious persons migrating north in search of better opportunities to make money — the "street walkers and numerous gamblers and rowdies" (p. 193) who preyed upon their own people and, he implied, brought disgrace to the whole race.

DuBois located in Farmville the historical background for a whole host of other developments in Philadelphia's black community — the development of black religious and social organizations, and the emergence of a small middle class that attempted to differentiate itself from the laboring classes on the basis of wealth and color. It is significant that DuBois showed that all of these issues could be tied directly to the economic well-being of the community in general, and to the racial division of labor in particular. Indeed, his discussion of black labor patterns served as the groundwork for his analysis of several major themes, including the causes and effects of poverty. He argued that the economic distress suffered by blacks as a group resulted not from some supposed cultural or moral deficiencies on their part, not from laziness or an alleged desire to throw themselves on the mercy of the city's charities, but rather from the meagerness of their pay and the irregularity of their labor. With few exceptions, black boys and girls and men and women toiled at the lowest-paying jobs the city had to offer. No matter how well trained, few blacks could hope to become clerical workers, supervisors, skilled workers, or professionals of any kind. As teamsters, stevedores, and laborers in the building trades, the men especially found work only on a seasonal or irregular basis, and they were the first to lose their jobs in the event of recessions and economic downturns. Even in good times, as many as one-half of the people in the city's predominantly black neighborhood, the Seventh Ward, lived in poverty, "but in time of financial stress vast numbers of [the 'comfortable' upper half] fall below the line into the poor and go to swell the number of paupers, and in many cases of criminals" (p. 172). A study of impoverished families in the Seventh Ward revealed that more than three-quarters were suffering from a breadwinner's lack of work, or sickness or disability, or from the old age or the death of a breadwinner (p. 275). DuBois was careful not to confuse the symptoms of poverty — the broken families and attendant social ills — with the cause of poverty: that is, an unjust job structure.

Among the city's black population, poverty had circular and cumulative effects. For example, as domestic servants in private homes and large hotels and department stores, many black workers had to live near their places of employment; compared to their working-class white counterparts living in the proximity of factories, blacks paid higher rents for inferior housing. Noted DuBois, "much of the Negro problem in this city finds adequate explanation when we reflect that here is a people receiving a little lower wages than usual for less desirable work, and compelled, in order to do that work, to live in a little less pleasant quarters than most people, and to pay for them somewhat higher rents" (p. 296). Moreover, the poverty of the black population meant that its self-help and charitable organizations would remain overburdened, and always lacking sufficient financial resources. And finally, the fact that so many Philadelphia blacks were poor tended to confirm the deepest prejudices of whites, thus intensifying the discrimination aimed at black workers: "Many would explain the absence of Negroes from higher vocations by saying that while a few may now and then be found competent, the great mass are not fitted for that sort of work and are destined for some time to form a laboring class" (p. 329). Most white southerners would have agreed with this assessment of black life and labor.

The work available to Philadelphia's blacks directly affected family structure and the nature of family life. The relatively small size of black households (four persons) DuBois attributed to the type and extent of black people's employment. With its inferior, overpriced housing, the city's major black neighborhood was home to "lodgers and casual sojourners" (p. 165); couples with children could not afford to live there. As he stressed once again in his Farmville study, some southern migrants who were parents came to the city alone, leaving their children in the care of grandparents or other kin. In many cases the husband remained a lodger in the Seventh Ward while his wife "lived in" at the home of her employer; "such are the local conditions that affect greatly the size of families" (p. 165). Since DuBois was familiar with the plight of blacks in the rural South at the time, he knew that the exploitative system of sharecropping was conducive to large, two-parent families in a way that urban conditions were not. The circumstances of the city—housing and job patterns—produced a distinct family structure.[19]

Urban poverty helped to shape the demographic profile of the black family in other ways. Families were fragmented by death and disease. High mortality rates among blacks in the city stemmed from poor living conditions for people of all ages and both sexes; "excessive" death rates among children (no doubt related to poor prenatal care, inadequate nutrition, and the inability of working mothers to breastfeed their babies); and particularly unhealthful working conditions for men and boys. Tuberculosis accounted for almost one-half of the black mortality rate; noted DuBois, "Bad ventilation, lack of outdoor life for women and children, poor protection against dampness and cold are undoubtedly the chief causes of this excessive death rate. To this must be added some hereditary predisposition, the influence of climate, and the lack of nearly all measures to prevent the spread of disease" (p. 152).

DuBois also documented the origins of a peculiar set of gender relations characteristic of the Seventh Ward. In late-nineteenth-century Philadelphia, domestic service offered relatively steady employment to women, accounting for an unbalanced sex ratio among blacks in the city as a whole (4,501 men compared to 5,174 women [p. 64]). For black men and women, "late marriages among them undoubtedly act as a check to population; moreover, the economic stress is so great that only the small family can survive; the large families are either kept from coming to the city or move away, or, as is most common, send the breadwinners to the city while they stay in the country" (p. 165). Moreover, the lack of steady work and the low wages paid to those who did work served to discourage marriage altogether and disrupt the marital ties that existed among the black population as a whole. DuBois suggested that the result was "ill effects on the sexual morality of city Negroes" (p. 166).

The city's wage structure — the fact that unmarried white girls received higher wages and more frequent promotions, compared to those of adult black men (p. 346) — had disastrous consequences for the black family. Unlike contemporary white commentators and social scientists in our own day, DuBois avoided inflating the power and influence of black women who shouldered so much of their communities' economic burdens. Of the adult black female population, 43 percent served as breadwinners for their families (the comparable figure for white women was 16.3 percent [p. 111]). As the mainstays of their families, black wives and mothers received pitiful wages for long hours, and spent most, if not all, of their waking hours cooking and cleaning for white families to the detriment of their own. Discrimination among children in the workforce meant that boys and girls were called upon to keep house while their mother labored in the kitchen or parlor of a white household nearby (p. 111). As Tera Hunter points out in her essay for this volume, DuBois could at times express stern disapproval of black wives and daughters who refused to commit themselves body and soul to domestic service, women who sought out a rich associational life in the black community as a form of respite and relief from the demands of white housewives. At the same time, he rightly noted that the quality of black family life, the affective relations between men and women and parents and children, and the health and well-being of black individuals and households alike, derived from the ill-paid jobs to which black people of both sexes were confined.

DuBois took pains to outline the effects of discrimination and deprivation upon the collective psyche of black people in Philadelphia. Years of thwarted ambitions and dashed dreams took their toll upon individuals, and upon the group as a whole. DuBois alluded to the "many poverty-stricken people, decent but not energetic," who populated the Seventh Ward (p. 60). A variety of black workers, from porters and china packers to shipping clerks and cementers, received less pay compared to whites employed in the same jobs (p. 346). Black workers of both sexes daily lived with the indignity that came with the sight of comparably trained whites advanced to higher positions; for blacks, according to DuBois, the result was a "growing lack of incentive to good work, owing to the difficulty of escaping from manual toil into higher and better paid callings." In contrast, "the higher classes of white labor are continually being incorporated into the skilled trades, or clerical workers, or other grades of labor" (p. 134). Among the most poignant and powerful of the passages in *The Philadelphia Negro* are his descriptions of the determined men and women who managed to acquire specialized education as stenographers, pharmacists, mechanical engineers, and telegraph operators, or specialized skills as printers, sign painters, and typesetters, only to find themselves without any requisite job opportunities, and relegated to scrubbing floors, hauling boxes, or waiting on tables for the rest of their days.

> G—— is an iron puddler, who belonged to a Pittsburg union. Here he was not recognized as a union man and could not get work except as a stevedore.
> H—— was a cooper, but could get no work after repeated trials, and is now a common laborer. . . .
> J—— is a carpenter; he can only secure odd jobs or work where Negroes are employed.
> K—— was an upholsterer, but could get no work save in the few colored shops, which had workmen; he is now a waiter on a dining car. (p. 330)

No wonder, then, that "much discouragement results from the persistent refusal" to hire or promote black workers; but DuBois went further and suggested that critics who charged that blacks shunned menial labor were missing the point, for "If the better class of Negro boys could look on such labor as a stepping-stone to something higher it would be different; if they must view it as a lifework we cannot wonder at their hesitation" (p. 343). In DuBois's view, then, a particular kind of employment functioned as more than a way to make a living, day by day; a job represented the promise of an eventual reward for a task well done, a ticket to the future for a worker and his or her family. Whites might prattle on about the dignity of domestic, and all menial, labor, but the fact of the matter was that few of their own children would continue to labor at their first jobs for the rest of their lives. Wage labor ennobled only to the extent that it was fluid and full of possibility; a "lifework" of ill-paid toil symbolized the collective, and enduring, oppression of the race.

Employment discrimination had obvious ramifications for black children; taught by their parents that they could aspire only to positions as waiters and maids, they might "grow up satisfied with their condition," resentful of, yet acquiescent in, their lot in life. In contrast, other young people might simmer with ill-concealed rage; barred from advancement, they would "grow to despise their own people, hate the whites, and become embittered with the world" (p. 324). For many black youths, life offered a lesson only of "opportunities . . . limited, and . . . ambition circumscribed" (p. 350). A particular worker need not have much experience on the job market to take his or her clue from the experiences of parents, kin, and friends, and declare, "I never apply—I know it is useless" (p. 350). Thus, according to DuBois, racial prejudice daily touched all of Philadelphia's blacks "in matters of life and death"; discrimination served to "threaten their homes, their food, their children, their hopes" (p. 350). And the results were at once insidious and predictable — "increased crime, inefficiency and bitterness" (p. 350).

DuBois did not shrink from evidence of antisocial behavior among Philadelphia's blacks; rather, he confronted the issue head on, and drew a direct connection between illegal activity and the city's "legitimate" job structure. "Filled to an unusual extent with disappointed men," the ranks of black workers consisted of those who lacked a "natural outlet for [their] ability," and thus turned to illicit pursuits (p. 134). Recent southern immigrants and "young idlers" especially soon found it was "easier for them to live by crime or the results of crime than by work, and being without ambition — or perhaps having lost ambition and grown bitter with the world — they drift with the stream" (p. 313). He noted that of the 541 blacks charged with serious crimes in the previous ten years, three out of five were guilty of theft, robbery, or burglary. Apparently, the illegal appropriation of cash and goods offered to ambitious men a livelihood at once more lucrative, and even more secure, than menial wage work. (A double standard of criminal activity pervaded the public consciousness; thus, "embezzlement, forgery, and certain sorts of stealing" received lenient punishment, while the full force of the law came down hard on "petty thieving, breaches of the peace, and personal assault or burglary" [p. 249].) DuBois suggested that stealing in particular represented a carryover from plantation days among the large numbers of southern blacks who had migrated to Philadelphia; and he described theft as "the prevailing weakness of ex-slaves brought up in the communal life of the plantation, without acquaintanceship with the institution of private property" (p. 249). DuBois provided examples of black women servants who pilfered from their employers, and of persons of both sexes who specialized in robberies of physicians, jewelers, patrons of brothels, and well-dressed white pedestrians (pp. 260–62). Although not stated explicitly by DuBois, it is possible that, in Philadelphia, the rural southern moral economy (the redistribution of goods from well-to-do whites to poor slaves and, later, sharecroppers) underwent a transformation, as black men began to prey upon their own people, and an already impoverished community suffered accordingly.

Unlike white Philadelphians, who had historically linked the city's black population with undifferentiated criminal activity, DuBois took pains to distinguish among the various groups who made their living by engaging in illegal activities. In some cases the line separating legitimate wage earners from criminals was permeable — for example, when a porter laid off for a few weeks turned temporarily to illegal gaming operations for his livelihood, or when a domestic servant between jobs sought respite from the white woman's kitchen by working as a prostitute. In contrast, career criminals controlled the increasingly large and businesslike operations that were organized hierarchically and provided work for many employees — the large brothels that received formal police protection, the bookmaking outfits and policy shops that relied on sophisticated communication networks within the city. Nevertheless, although DuBois drew a distinction between what might be called casual versus career criminals, he hardly exonerated persons of either group who made their living from crime. His Victorian high-mindedness about the "evils" of illegal activities of all kinds made him indifferent to the social ramifications of criminals who assaulted or stole from their victims, in contrast to criminals like prostitutes and gamblers who provided services much in demand by willing customers of both races and all classes.

Once again, though, DuBois avoided viewing crime solely through a lens of moneymaking. He noted that "the connection of crime and prejudice is . . . neither simple nor direct. The boy who is refused promotion in his job as a porter does not go out and snatch somebody's pocketbook." Rather, it was a "social environment of excuse, listless despair, careless indulgence and lack of inspiration to work" (p. 351) that created a disposition toward crime. A relatively large concentration of men who suffered from chronic unemployment or underemployment was a breeding ground for disputes waged with fists or guns; the infusion of alcohol into the scene heightened the likelihood of bloodshed. Similarly, for men, women, and children alike, gambling seemed to offer the key to quick riches, in a way that ordinary jobs never could, and hopefulness quickly gave way to compulsion. DuBois quoted a journalistic investigation of the policy business (from an 1897 issue of the *Public Ledger*) to show that "Hundreds of poor people every day place upon the infatuating lottery money that had better be spent for food and clothing. They actually deny themselves the necessaries of life to gamble away their meagre income with small chance of getting any return." For those addicted to such games of chance, "the drain is constant" (p. 265). Substance abuse, gambling addiction, and violence were the inevitable outgrowth of discrimination in the workforce, making the links between crime and jobs "subtle and dangerous" (p. 351).

DuBois observed that a small class of criminals captured an inordinate amount of attention and resources from the city, to the detriment of workers who engaged in more mundane, less sensationalistic struggles for their daily bread. In the public, white mind, the solid, respectable "caterers of Addison street" were always associated with the "pickpockets and paupers of the race" (p. 310). Noted DuBois, "Nothing more exasperates the better class of Negroes than this tendency to ignore utterly their existence" (p. 310). The modest efforts of ordinary people to do their jobs and care for their families became lost amid melodramatic newspaper stories taken from the police blotter and the social worker's report. Law enforcement officials and the agents of the Department of Charities were vigorous in their attempts to highlight the depredations of criminals and to conflate the whole black population into a class of ne'er-do-wells; the existence of this class confirmed the prejudices of whites. Hence, for these blacks "the city teems with institutions and charities; for them there is succor and sympathy; for them Philadelphians are thinking and planning; but for the educated and industrious young colored man who wants work and not platitudes, wages and not alms, just rewards and not sermons—for such colored men Philadelphia apparently has no use" (p. 352).

In response to a form of prejudice based on social definitions of race as well as on class, Philadelphia's tiny elite—"the germ of a great middle class"—withdrew into itself and shunned association with less fortunate members of their own group. DuBois labeled this impulse as "sheer self-defence" (p. 177), suggesting that relatively prosperous blacks "do not relish being mistaken for servants; they shrink from the free and easy worship of most of the Negro churches, and they shrink from all such display and publicity as will expose them to the veiled insult and depreciation which the masses suffer" (p. 177). As a result, religious and benevolent associations in black Philadelphia were organized along class lines. Unwilling to associate with the poor or to serve in positions of power and influence that would force them to interact with "the masses," the black elite eschewed formal leadership roles, and the community as a whole lacked a unified political voice. In the end, according to DuBois, blacks constituted a readily identifiable group only to the extent that all members within it were bound together by ties of "blood and color prejudice" (p. 317). Abdicating their responsibility as "leaders or ideal-makers of their own group in thought, work, or morals" (p. 317), the black middle class remained the object of scorn and ridicule among their less well-to-do neighbors.

DuBois ended his book with a chapter titled "The Meaning of All This." In it he took the long view and reminded his readers that history afforded numerous examples of the proposition that mankind was moving inexorably "into a wider humanity, a wider respect for simple manhood unadorned by ancestors or privilege" (p. 386). Endowed with a characteristically Progressive-era optimism—a belief that the widespread dissemination of social-scientific data would educate people and inspire them to see their responsibility toward the less fortunate—DuBois outlined "The Duty of the Negroes" and "The Duty of Whites." He urged readers of both races to appreciate the personal and collective value to be gained from a non-discriminatory system of employment. To black criminals and idlers, DuBois exhorted, "Work, continuous and intensive; work, although it be menial and poorly rewarded; work, though done in travail of soul and sweat of brow, must be so impressed upon Negro children as the road to salvation, that a child would feel it a greater disgrace to be idle than to do the humblest labor" (p. 390). DuBois went on to urge whites to wake up and understand that they owed it to themselves to widen the "opportunities afforded Negroes for earning a decent living": the "cost of crime and pauperism, the growth of slums, and the pernicious influences of idleness and lewdness, cost the public far more than would the hurt to the feelings of a carpenter to work beside a black man, or a shop girl to stand beside a darker mate" (pp. 394–95).

DuBois concluded *The Philadelphia Negro* with an implicit expression of his faith that white people — with their capacity for politeness and sympathy, their delicacy and their generosity — could redeem the City of Brotherly Love (p. 397). However, developments during the time he conducted his study, and the time subsequent to its publication, reveal that his hope for a new and better day for the city's black community was misplaced. Based on DuBois's analysis, we can locate the Philadelphia of the 1890s within the historical "nadir" of black life, as described by Rayford Logan.[20] The small black population of the city played no formal role in partisan politics; it was divided among itself, on the basis of class; the white working class proved to be one of its most potent adversaries; and the federal government remained supremely indifferent to the problems of Jim Crow segregation, job discrimination, and issues related to health, welfare, and education.

Within the next fifty years or so, this situation would change, in some places more dramatically than in others. For example, the founding of the National Association for the Advancement of the Colored People in 1910 signaled the beginning of a movement headed by middle-class blacks (and some whites) to use the courts to dismantle American apartheid in all its manifestations; the victories of the NAACP would eventually benefit blacks of all classes all over the country, from peons in Alabama to college students in Mississippi. And the era of the First World War represented a departure in the history of American politics and race relations. The Great Migration inspired the founding of the National Urban League, again an organization headed by middle-class black men and women, and intended to serve as an advocate for poor blacks in the realm of jobs, housing, and social welfare. In some cities, black people began to emerge as a relatively powerful political presence for the first time.

The bloody labor struggles at home during World War I gave new life to a moribund biracial labor movement, especially in the southern extractive industries like lumbering, and coal and phosphate mining. It was during this period that the Industrial Workers of the World offered a vision of "One Big Union" that highlighted the discriminatory tactics of the American Federation of Labor and its affiliates. And too, during the Great Depression, the federal government, however tentatively, began to set explicit, nationwide standards related to wages and child labor, thereby welding localities, both north and south, urban and rural, into a larger national economy. By the late 1930s, the rise of the Congress of Industrial Organizations, combined with the New Deal coalition consisting of the overlapping groups of blacks, immigrants, and the working class, meant that the labor movement and party politics had emerged as the two major arenas for interracial cooperation and political activism on the local, as well as the national, scene. The fusion of party politics and labor politics in cities like Detroit, Chicago, and New York yielded militant black communities and influential black-white coalitions that contrasted greatly with the situation documented in DuBois's *Philadelphia Negro*.[21] The meaning of race continued to change according to time and place, throughout the country.

Therefore we cannot judge DuBois too harshly if he believed passionately, and ultimately naively, in the redemptive power of individual goodwill in transforming the racial division of labor in Philadelphia, and in all American cities. He could hardly foresee a future like the one outlined by Carl Husemoller Nightingale in his essay for this volume, and by others — a future of Third World global assembly lines and the increasing marginalization of "hypersegregated" black inner-city populations; a future of crack epidemics and murderous, high-tech images of the so-called good life; a future of postindustrial, best-selling renderings of Jim Crow theories of racial inferiority.[22] Yet just as significant as the major recent transformations in the city's relation to the larger international political economy was the persistence of traditional forms of racial discrimination in the urban job market. For example, in the mid-1990s, despite the emergence of a biracial labor movement in the building trades, and despite affirmative action hiring policies promoted by the federal government, black Philadelphia construction workers failed to receive their fair share of jobs compared to their white counterparts. One white foreman noted that when work became available, he tended to call other whites, because "they are the people I know best," regardless of individual blacks' qualifications to do the job. As a result of informal but entrenched practices like this, white unionists made on average 25 percent more than black union members — in 1995, $514 a week as opposed to $405.[23]

Nevertheless, I would like to end by stressing the relevance of *The Philadelphia Negro* for our study of poverty and prejudice today, a relevance borne of DuBois's vision of a just society based on a just system of employment and compensation. We have learned the hard way that political leaders might come and go, that mayors like Tom Bradley and Carl Stokes and Maynard Jackson, and yes, Wilson Goode, might give eloquent expression to the deepest fears and greatest hopes of their black constituents. Nevertheless, these leaders and other black politicians are helpless to effect meaningful changes in the social division of labor, and indeed they are helpless to prevent the massive loss of jobs that just a couple of decades ago sustained a vibrant black working class in some of the country's largest cities. Yet we live in a time when social commentators of all stripes, from journalists and policymakers to academics and politicians, persist in turning their back on the past, and debating a snapshot of black "culture" devoid of all its historical context. Lost in these debates is the hard truth that W.E.B. DuBois described with such understated passion and force in *The Philadelphia*

Negro—that good jobs, and the collective hope and personal dignity that go with them, are the foundation of a good society. As more and more groups of people, and not just African Americans, are condemned to a "lifework" of little pay and few possibilities for promotion, or to a "lifework" of no paid employment at all, DuBois's study will continue to illuminate the future, as well as the history, of American labor and social relations.

Notes

1. For a discussion of similar dynamics at work in New York City, see Suzanne Model, "The Ethnic Niche and the Structure of Opportunity: Immigrants and Minorities in New York City," in *The "Underclass" Debate: Views from History*, ed. Michael B. Katz (Princeton, N.J.: Princeton University Press, 1993), pp. 161–93.

2. See for example the works by Jean R. Soderlund, *Quakers and Slavery: A Divided Spirit* (Princeton, N.J.: Princeton University Press, 1985); and "Black Women in Colonial Pennsylvania," *Pennsylvania Magazine of History and Biography* 107 (January 1983): 49–68.

3. G. D. Rowe suggests that "the fact that blacks were historically associated with property offenses, and that property crimes came to loom larger in the concerns of white Philadelphians [after 1800], strained the courts' capacity for objectivity and presaged greater insensitivity among whites to black aspirations." "Black Offenders, Criminal Courts, and Philadelphia Society in the Late Eighteenth-Century," *Journal of Social History* 22 (Summer 1989): 706.

4. See, for example, Gary B. Nash, *Forging Freedom: The Formation of Philadelphia's Black Community, 1720–1840* (Cambridge, Mass.: Harvard University Press, 1988). For comparisons of Philadelphia's antebellum black community with those of other cities during the same period, see for example James Oliver Horton, *Free People of Color: Inside the African-American Community* (Washington, D.C.: Smithsonian Institution Press, 1993); Leon F. Litwack, *North of Slavery: The Negro in the Free States, 1790–1860* (Chicago: University of Chicago Press, 1961); Leonard P. Curry, *The Free Black in Urban America, 1800–1850: The Shadow of the Dream* (Chicago: University of Chicago Press, 1981).

5. A similar process was at work in Milwaukee during this period. See Joe Trotter, *Black Milwaukee: The Making of an Industrial Proletariat, 1915–1945* (Urbana: University of Illinois Press, 1985), pp. 13–15, 28.

6. Walter Licht, *Getting Work: Philadelphia, 1840–1950* (Cambridge, Mass.: Harvard University Press, 1992), p. 31; Bruce Laurie and Mark Schmitz, "Manufacture and Productivity: The Making of an Industrial Base, Philadelphia, 1850–1880"; and Theodore Hershberg, et al., "A Tale of Three Cities: Blacks, Immigrants, and Opportunity in Philadelphia, 1850–1880, 1930, 1970," in *Philadelphia: Work, Space, Family and Group Experience in the Nineteenth Century: Essays Toward an Interdisciplinary History of the City*, ed. Theodore Hershberg (New York: Oxford University Press, 1981), pp. 43–92, 461–91.

7. Licht, *Getting Work*, pp. 46, 109, 178. See also E. Digby Baltzell, "Introduction" to the 1967 edition of *The Philadelphia Negro*, pp. xxxvii–xxxviii.

8. See also Vincent P. Franklin, *The Education of Black Philadelphia: The Social and Educational History of a Minority Community, 1900–1950* (Philadelphia: University of Pennsylvania Press, 1979).

9. Both DuBois, in his study of white workers in the Reconstruction South, and David Roediger more recently, have suggested that whites benefited from a non-

monetary "psychological wage" — that is, feelings of superiority over black workers — as a result of discriminatory policies at all levels of the recruitment and hiring process. See W.E.B. DuBois, *Black Reconstruction in America, 1860–1880* (1935; reprint, New York: Atheneum, 1969); and David R. Roediger, *The Wages of Whiteness: Race and the Making of the American Working Class* (New York: Verso, 1991).

10. In Boston, Irish-controlled longshoremen locals did manage to discriminate against not only blacks, but more recent foreign immigrants as well. See Herbert Northrup, *Organized Labor and the Negro* (New York: Harper and Bros., 1944), p. 6.

11. On the relationship between the willingness of whites to welcome blacks into their unions on the one hand, and the numerical significance of the population of black workers on the other, see Eric Arnesen, "Following the Color Line of Labor: Black Workers and the Labor Movement Before 1930," *Radical History Review* 55 (1993): 58, 68.

12. Patricia A. Cooper, *Once a Cigar Maker: Men, Women, and Work Culture in American Cigar Factories, 1900–1919* (Urbana: University of Illinois Press, 1987), pp. 137–38.

13. Cooper, *Once a Cigar Maker*, p. 25.

14. On the coal miners and the United Mine Workers Union, see Ronald L. Lewis, *Black Coal Miners in America: Race, Class and Community Conflict, 1780–1980* (Lexington: University of Kentucky Press, 1987); Joe Trotter, *Coal, Class, and Color* (Urbana: University of Illinois Press, 1990); David Alan Corbin, *Life, Work, and Rebellion in the Coal Fields: The Southern West Virginia Miners, 1880–1922* (Urbana: University of Illinois Press, 1981).

15. See for example Eric Arnesen, *Waterfront Workers of New Orleans: Race, Class, and Politics, 1863–1923* (New York: Oxford University Press, 1991); Daniel Rosenberg, *New Orleans Dockworkers: Race, Labor, and Unionism, 1892–1923* (Albany: State University of New York Press, 1988).

16. On the "service" ethos within the retail-sales industry around 1900, see William Leach, *Land of Desire: Merchants, Power, and the Rise of a New American Culture* (New York: Vintage Books, 1993), pp. 112–50.

17. For a study of the way in which seasonal migration among southern black men gradually led to massive outmigration among large numbers of southern blacks in general, see Peter Gottlieb, *Making Their Own Way: Southern Black Migration to Pittsburgh, 1916–1930* (Urbana: University of Illinois Press, 1987).

18. "The Negroes of Farmville, Virginia," in *W.E.B. DuBois on Sociology and the Black Community*, ed. Dan S. Green and Edwin D. Driver (Chicago: University of Chicago Press, 1978), p. 168.

19. On the transition between large rural families and small urban families, see Herbert G. Gutman, *The Black Family in Slavery and Freedom, 1750–1925* (New York: Pantheon, 1976); Jacqueline Jones, *Labor of Love, Labor of Sorrow: Black Women, Work, and the Family from Slavery to the Present* (New York: Basic Books, 1985).

20. Rayford Logan, *The Betrayal of the Negro: From Rutherford B. Hayes to Woodrow Wilson* (1954; reprint, New York: Collier Books, 1970).

21. Lizabeth Cohen, *Making a New Deal: Industrial Workers in Chicago, 1919–1939* (Cambridge: Cambridge University Press, 1990); Robert Korstad and Nelson Lichtenstein, "Opportunities Found and Lost: Labor, Radicals, and the Early Civil Rights Movement," *Journal of American History* 75 (December 1988): 786–811.

22. Jacqueline Jones, "Back to the Future with *The Bell Curve*: Jim Crow, Slavery, and *G*," in *The Bell Curve Wars*, ed. Steve Fraser (New York: Basic Books, 1995).

23. Louis Uchitelle, "Union Goal of Equality Fails the Test of Time," *New York Times*, July 9, 1995, pp. 1, 18.

Figure 8. Black domestic workers in late nineteenth-century Georgia. Courtesy of Georgia Historical Collections, Atlanta.

Chapter 5

"The 'Brotherly Love' for Which This City Is Proverbial Should Extend to All"

The Everyday Lives of Working-Class Women in
Philadelphia and Atlanta in the 1890s

Tera W. Hunter

In 1871, an anonymous "colored woman" wrote a letter of rhetorical inquiry to the *Philadelphia Post*. "I take the liberty of asking you to explain to me why it is that when respectable women of color answer an advertisement for a dressmaker, either in families or with a dressmaker, [they] are invariably refused." In lieu of preferred jobs they are offered "a place to cook or scrub, or to do house work," she stated. She described the subterfuge used by shop owners and garment and textile manufacturers to rebuff the employment of African American women. Despite the advertisements in newspapers publicizing openings, black women were turned away repeatedly with advice to "call again" or to "return later" at some illusory time when they would be needed. "There are many respectable women of color competent to fill any of the above named positions," she reiterated. Yet these women "eke out a scanty livelihood sewing at home," wait for a more receptive job market in vain, or resort to domestic work. "The 'brotherly love' for which this city is proverbial should extend to all, irrespective color, race or creed," she insisted.[1]

This letter, though written during the era of Reconstruction, could have easily been written twenty-five years later as W.E.B. DuBois began his landmark social science study, *The Philadelphia Negro*. DuBois documented the thwarted ambitions of black women in a city that locked them out of the relatively diverse enterprises that employed native-born white and immigrant women. Even fifty years later the situation had improved little. The major difference was that by 1920 not only did most black women perform domestic work; nearly half of the women in domestic labor were black — a trend moving toward long-standing patterns in southern cities like Atlanta.[2]

This paper focuses on the everyday lives of working-class women, most of whom engaged in household work, in Philadelphia and Atlanta in the 1890s.[3] DuBois recognized the importance of these women's labor in the context of the transformation of capitalism, which changed from a preindustrial help system into a wage system in the industrial era. He discussed domestic work in the main body of his study and attached an appendix written by Isabel Eaton, a graduate student at Columbia University awarded a fellowship to collaborate with him. Eaton's "Special Report on Negro Domestic Service in the Seventh Ward" coincided with the publication of another pioneering book, *Domestic Service* (1897), written by her mentor and friend Lucy Maynard Salmon. Salmon's was the first social scientific study on the topic, though it treated black women only minimally. Salmon, Eaton, as well as DuBois conducted their research not simply as scholars, but also as Progressive reformers, settlement house leaders, and potential, if not actual, employers of domestic workers. Like other middle-class professionals in the Progressive era, they were preoccupied with the "servant problem" — how to make the occupation more efficient and how to improve the behaviors and attitudes of the workers.[4] The present chapter reexamines the mostly poor women who were the subjects of investigation and objects of social reform. It analyzes the everyday experiences and conditions of working-class women who frequented the pages of DuBois's study and reconsiders DuBois's own values that influenced his attitudes on working-class culture and women in particular.

The similarities and the differences in the lives of Philadelphia and Atlanta African Americans offer insight for broadening our understanding of urban women. Philadelphia, an inland port city sandwiched between the Schuylkill and Delaware Rivers, was a leading center of commerce dating back to the colonial era. Atlanta, an inland city, originated in the antebellum period as a tiny railroad depot but grew to maturity during the Civil War. The railroads were critical enterprises in both cities. Philadelphia was home to Jay Cooke, the railroad entrepreneur and owner of the Pennsylvania Railroad, the largest corporation in the United States, whose business tactics went awry and triggered the national depression of 1873. Atlanta was a child of the railroad and owed its sudden and spectacular growth during and after the Civil War to the steam locomotive. The Confederate Army favored the city's strategic location in shipping goods throughout the region and made the city a pivotal distribution and manufacturing center. Philadelphia was an industrial city heavily invested in iron, steel, and coal plants, as well as in sugar and oil refineries. Textile factories were the city's largest and biggest employers. At the turn of the century, Philadelphia was the largest producer of wool, silk, and cotton textiles in the world. Related enterprises like clothing and carpet production were spread out in small workshops and tenements occupied by European immigrants. Atlanta's textile industry was largely limited to cotton in an agricultural economy where cotton was king. The textile factory bore an ideological as well as economic burden of regenerating a new South and providing jobs to displaced white yeoman farmers. It was the central symbol in an aggressive public relations campaign spearheaded by local entrepreneurs, politicians, and journalists determined to make Atlanta the prototype for regional economic development. Heavy industry ruled the northern city's economy, but there were a variety of other economic enterprises—foundries and rolling mills, as well as cigar, wagon, box, broom, soap, and candy manufacturers. Atlanta, unlike most of the South, also developed a diversified economy—foundries, metalworks, and rolling mills, as well as wagon, book, paper goods, furniture, patent medicine, straw hat, and piano manufacturers.[5]

The character of the population of the two cities diverged in significant ways. Compared to other northern cities, Philadelphia was dominated by native-born whites. Foreign-born residents in 1880 made up only 24 percent of the population—half the proportion in the populations of New York and Chicago. But compared to Atlanta, with less than 4 percent foreign-born people, there were significantly more Irish, English, German, Italian, and Jewish immigrants in Philadelphia.[6] By 1890, the absolute number of African Americans in Philadelphia exceeded those in Atlanta, though they constituted only 4 percent of the population in the former and 40 percent in the latter.

The physical development of the two cities also differed but overlapped. Neither ghettos nor de jure segregation were apparent in the last two decades of either city. In Philadelphia, a city in which ethnic groups were clustered but dispersed, blacks were mainly concentrated in the inner city's Seventh Ward, though they also lived throughout the entire metropolitan area. Some wards of the city were heavily white or black, but none excluded either race entirely. In Atlanta, the city's wealthy residents and businesses dominated the urban core. Most African Americans lived in neighborhoods in outlying areas—close enough to walk to work within the urban core, but far enough to be out of sight of upper-class homes. They too were spread throughout the metropolitan areas.

Despite these characterizations, Jim Crow was clearly not just on the horizon but already operative in both places. Philadelphia had a reputation for being a city of homes. Rows of modest one-family houses lined the streets, unlike in other northern cities, which were dominated by overcrowded multifamily dwellings. Yet poor people of different ethnic groups lived in the worst areas of the inner city—in dark courtyards and narrow alleys, in substandard and overcrowded houses. Blacks as well as poor whites in Atlanta tended to live in the worst areas of the city as well, on low-lying areas subject to floods and sewage spills where waste products from the hilly middle- and upper-class residents literally poured down into the valleys below. Whites tended to live fronting streets, blacks in the rear or in alleys. In both cities the political and economic elites controlled the distribution of municipal services that were important to health and sanitation of the entire citizenry. Resources allocated for water supply, sewage disposal, and road and street construction and repair were mostly directed to the areas dominated by businesses and the residences of the elites. Atlanta did not implement its residential segregation laws until 1922, but the pattern had already been fixed in practice decades before.[7]

Philadelphia had the largest number of African Americans in the North at the time of DuBois's publication of *The Philadelphia Negro*. The majority of the black residents in this city, as in most other cities either in the North or South, were women. Nearly half of all black females were gainfully employed, and their families relied in part, and too often entirely, on their meager wages. Seventy percent of black families were headed by two parents in 1880, and 25 percent were headed by women. Similarly, 80 percent of white families were headed by two parents and 14 percent were headed by women. Blacks, however, were more likely to live in households with three generations or other extended kin, which was an important cultural adaptation for the survival of people of West African descent in the New World.[8]

The slightly higher percentage of female-headed households among African Americans, then as now, was judged derisively. According to the statistics DuBois collected, the rate of marriages of most black and white Philadelphians was virtually the same; the proportion of single (never married) women over age fifteen across the races was nearly identical. Despite this, DuBois insisted that the "greatest weakness of the Negro family is still lack of respect for the marriage bond," which he attributed to sexual immorality.[9] But the data available to DuBois indicated that the most significant difference in marital status across race was the relatively higher number of black widows. Extraordinarily high mortality rates of black men wreaked havoc on potential and actual marital relationships in diminishing the prospects of long-term survival.[10] Black women with living spouses were also more likely to be separated from their husbands than were white women, quite frequently because black men were forced to leave home in order to find work. Black family structure and conjugal relations were also more fluid and complex than DuBois understood, or was willing to accept, and could not be easily measured against standards of morality that failed to respect the distinctive history and culture of African Americans. DuBois criticized female-headed households because he believed they created other social problems, such as a disproportionate share of members of the "submerged tenth" — the most socially and economically debilitated among the lowest class (*Philadelphia Negro*, pp. 55, 66–68, 311–19).[11]

DuBois's conception of the "submerged tenth" bears a striking resemblance to recent constructions of the "underclass," which defines working-class people more by behavioral and moral infractions and deficiencies than by their economic conditions. Although *The Philadelphia Negro*'s detailed analysis of the structural roots of poverty and racism exceeded the narrow aims established by the white reformers in the College Settlement Association who sponsored it, DuBois shared their paternalism toward the poor. DuBois's pioneering work became one of the most influential sociological studies in the twentieth century, inspiring a body of insightful urban history, sociology, and ethnography. His condemnatory moralizing about black working-class deviations from presumed cultural norms, however, has also been recapitulated and ultimately rendered less multifarious by some social scientists who have followed him. His reproach of female-headed households sowed the seeds of the "black pathology" thesis that would be taken up by E. Franklin Frazier and Daniel Patrick Moynihan, and elaborated by a host of social scientists and policymakers in extended debates about the "underclass" problem in the late-twentieth century.[12]

DuBois's attitudes toward female-headed households also reflected his sympathy toward women who bore the burden of earning a disproportionate share of family income, compared to white women, regardless of marital status.[13] Black men were paid relatively higher wages than women, but even the combination of both spouses' wages was often insufficient for establishing a comfortable standard of living. Nor was marriage a guarantee of two steady incomes. Unemployment was a common experience for male common laborers; separation or death of a partner could reduce a family's resources unexpectedly to below the minimum standard of living. Ironically, though black women entered and remained in wage labor significantly longer than did their white counterparts in order to support their families, they had 20 percent fewer children. Black and white women gave birth to roughly the same proportion of children, but poor health, disease, and poverty create extraordinarily high rates of stillbirths and mortality of African American children under five. There is some evidence that black urban women also practiced contraceptive methods to limit the number of children they bore (pp. 150, 151, 158, 164–68).[14]

Nearly all the women wage earners who contributed to the coffers of black families were household workers. In the 1890s, at least 90 percent of all black female wage earners in both cities were domestics. The most obvious difference between women in the two cities was that black women monopolized domestic work in Atlanta, whereas they constituted only a minority and competed with whites for jobs in Philadelphia. By the end of the century, as European immigration climbed, black Philadelphians faced increasing competition from English and Swedish servants considered more fashionable by elite employers. Blacks were relegated to the bottom of the bottom of the labor market in the "plainer establishments" (p. 448).

Another significant difference that profoundly affected the experiences of domestic work was the preponderance of live-in workers in Philadelphia.

The majority of black women in Philadelphia lived in isolation from their families and communities in the homes of their employers, though they lived in less often than white women did. While 61 percent of single women lived in, only 28 percent of married women did so. More single women may have preferred to live in their own homes, but given the competition for jobs, they had to accommodate employers' demands. This pattern differed from domestic service in the antebellum period when the majority of free blacks working as domestics lived in their own homes (pp. 141, 448).[15] In Atlanta, the pattern of late-nineteenth-century Philadelphia was reversed. The overwhelming majority of black women desired to physically distance themselves from erstwhile masters and were able to exercise this preference because of their leverage in a labor market that employers incessantly claimed was in short supply. The workers perceived few advantages from live-in arrangements, material or otherwise. "Free" accommodations and food were usually meager, especially when added to isolation from family and friends and the lack of privacy. In Philadelphia, Eaton suggests that live-ins may have had a slight advantage in net income by saving money on room and board, since there was little variation between the wages of those who lived in compared to those who lived at home (pp. 453–54).[16]

Women in Atlanta entered the occupation between the ages of ten and sixteen and remained within it most of their lives. Women in Philadelphia, however, tended to enter service work as adults, because employers rarely hired black children. Very few black women wage earners found options outside domestic work, but some were able to make choices about particular jobs, which they often did according to changes in their life cycles. In Atlanta and the South, younger and single women tended to become general housemaids and child nurses, while older and married women, especially those with children, chose cooking and washing. Younger women concentrated in general service positions contributed to their parents' income. But once they married or began giving birth to children of their own, they made occupational choices, like laundry work, that gave them more time and flexibility for their new responsibilities. In Philadelphia, black women faced more constraints in meshing wage labor and child rearing. Employers often preferred to hire women unencumbered by children, especially those who lived in. This put mothers at a disadvantage in finding employment and safe, affordable child care. When no other options were available, some women sent their offspring to "baby farms" during the week—expensive institutions that absorbed their wages and put their young ones at risk. The most destitute mothers were forced out of jobs onto the streets, fired by employers who discovered their offspring, and were unable to find suitable work.[17]

Most women in both cities found jobs through casual networks or by knocking on doors of potential employers. But employment agencies were notorious for luring young and unsuspecting women in the South to move

North under false pretenses of lucrative job offers. Itinerant agents offered advances in the form of transportation, for those who could not afford the fee, and promised good wages, nice jobs, and desirable living conditions. Agencies propagated deceitful claims on billboards, like one DuBois noticed on the streets of Norfolk, Virginia, that enticed black women to believe there were plentiful jobs as stenographers and clerks in the North. Once they reached their destination, however, many migrants discovered they had been duped and were forced to take undesirable jobs at wages lower than promised. Some of the employment agencies were actually procurers for brothels furtively searching for prostitutes. Women migrants often arrived in the city indebted to these agencies for the cost of transportation and other fees and their personal effects were held hostage in order to coerce them into accepting substandard domestic work or prostitution. To counter these tactics, the Association for the Protection of Colored Women was formed in Philadelphia in 1905 to meet women migrants at the docks and train stations and escort them to decent boardinghouses and legitimate employment agencies (p. 118).[18]

Once hired, Philadelphia domestics made up for the loss of independence that accompanied live-in service by insisting on time off at least on Thursday afternoons and alternating Sundays. Black women demanded time off for themselves more often than white women did. They worked long hours, however, and were paid on average four to sixteen dollars per month. Cooks, laundresses, and janitors commanded the highest average wages in Philadelphia, while chambermaids, errand girls, and general domestics received the lowest. Their counterparts in Atlanta worked seven days a week, with the exception of laundresses, who usually worked six. Whatever time off they acquired was achieved by manipulating the perpetual "shortage" in the labor market by quitting and moving around. Their wages on average were half that of the workers in the North. The more remarkable characteristics of these rates was that they changed so little over time and across occupations. When variations existed, cooks tended to command the highest wages per hour and kitchen sculleries the lowest. Laundresses could increase their earnings by adding on clients and seeking help from family members (447–48). Domestic work in general, however, was poorly paid work, which made survival difficult for women; no wages made it even harder. Some employers were notorious for cheating their workers of rightful earnings on spurious grounds. Workers could be deprived of wages when employers decided that they had overspent their household budgets. Live-in workers were especially vulnerable to real or imagined financial shortfalls because they could be expected to weather such periods without compensation. Any worker could face deductions for behavioral infractions such as lost time or impudence or for the replacement of missing, broken, or consumed objects. Sometimes employers would substitute perishables or durable goods in lieu of cash for remuneration without the worker's consent.[19]

There were distinct, if overlapping, skills and talents involved in house-hold labor. But no matter what job they chose, African American women were assured arduous work. Even as the expectations of good housekeeping dovetailed with changes in the economy and family life, very little changed in the actual labor processes of housework in the nineteenth century. Tech-nological advances hardly ever reached individual homes, and the few that did made limited improvements.[20] Housework was a full-time job, which meant double duties for women working for wages and taking care of their own families' housekeeping chores.

The specific duties and work conditions of general domestics varied ac-cording to the economic means of employers and the number of other servants hired. Hauling water and tending fires consumed a large part of the daily routine. The work of servants in wealthy families was facilitated by their access to gas and indoor plumbing. This advantage, however, was offset by the ostentatious surroundings and lavish objects that required extra care. Servants working in more modest homes might have fewer articles to main-tain, but the work was harder if they lacked amenities such as piped-in water.

Any number of a dizzying array of chores were required of general domes-tics. Their work could require cooking, helping with preparing and preserv-ing foodstuffs, and maintaining the kitchen. Women hired to perform gen-eral duties would sometimes do the laundry, ironing, mending, and caring for children. Servants who lived with employers faced the added encum-brance of having to respond to unpredictable intrusions at any hour that diminished time off for themselves. Domestics not only performed physical labor, but also pomp and circumstance in signifying the hosts' social rank. In the South, hiring a black servant was itself a mark of racial privilege; in the North, employers were more likely to hire specialized workers, usually men and European immigrants to signify social caste.

Child nurses would arrive early in the day to keep children occupied and protected while their parents engaged in other remunerative and social activities. In the South, many girls were hired at a young age to perform tasks from rocking cradles to the full range of caretaking responsibilities for charges not much younger than themselves. An older nurse described the litany of her duties as follows: "I not only have to nurse a little white child, now eleven months old, but I have to act as playmate or 'handy-andy,' not to say governess, to three other children in the home, the oldest of whom is only nine years of age."[21] She washed, fed, and bedded the children, which required round-the-clock work according to the infant's and children's needs. But even when the children demanded little attention, the work did not end there. The women were also expected to perform other household tasks between their child-care duties.

Cooking required the most skill and creativity among household occupa-tions, though constantly working around a hot stove was fatiguing. Cooking was the only household chore to benefit from technological advances in this period. The cast-iron stove, common by the late-nineteenth century, was the most important improvement, replacing the open fireplaces that had reigned in earlier kitchens. Cast-iron stoves required less fuel, worked more efficiently and safely, and were built high enough off the ground to prevent constant bending by the cook. But the lack of built-in thermostats forced cooks to gauge the level of heat through trial and error—arranging dampers and drafts or placing foods in strategic spots according to estimates of the time and degree of heat required. In other respects, food preparation remained virtually the same in the 1890s as it had been in 1800.[22] Most cooks developed improvisational styles of food preparation that defied emergent notions of scientific housewifery. Black women were cognizant of the cerebral aptitude required for cooking. As one cook described her work: "Everything I does, I does by my head; it's all brain work."[23]

In addition to food preparation, cooks also washed dishes, mopped floors, and cleaned and maintained the stoves, pots, pans, and utensils. The degree of autonomy they enjoyed varied, but they generally planned the meals and marketed for groceries. In the South cooks took on additional emotional roles. The comfort and intimacy evoked by the warmth and pleasant smells of the kitchens made them a prime social space, especially for children of the employing household in search of comfort and treats.[24] Black cooks conjured the stereotype of "Mammy" perhaps as much as child nurses did in the minds of white southerners.

If cooking required the most inventiveness, laundry work was the most difficult job of all. Unlike cooking, laundry work became more demanding as a result of industrialization. Manufactured cloth not only expanded individual wardrobes; wider availability of washable fabrics such as cotton increased the need for washing. Laundry work was the single most onerous chore in the life of a nineteenth-century woman and the first chore she would hire out whenever the slightest bit of discretionary income was available. Even some poor urban women sent out at least some of their wash. In the North, white women who lived in tenements and lacked the proper equipment might send their dirty clothes to commercial laundries.[25] In the South, however, where the adoption of technology lagged and manual labor predominated, many poor whites sent out part or all of their wash to black women.[26]

Atlanta, and the urban South more generally, had the highest concentration of domestic workers per capita in the nation. This regional disparity is accounted for not only by the cultural significance of domestic service as a racial signifier, but also by the large number of laundresses.[27] In marked contrast to the stereotype of the obsequious "Mammy" faithfully wedded to white families, the independent washerwoman was the archetype laborer in Atlanta. In Philadelphia, the general domestic working in isolation in a one-servant home was the typical black female laborer. Most of the laundresses hired in Philadelphia worked in the homes of employers, as did other domestics, though they were usually hired by the day. Eaton counted only thirty-one independent laundresses in the Seventh Ward, and they faced competition from businesses run by whites, and Chinese, as well as by a few African Americans (pp. 102–3, 143, 504).[28]

In Atlanta, the work of the washerwoman began on Monday morning and continued throughout the week until she delivered clean clothes on Saturday. Hundreds of pounds of water had to be toted from wells, pumps, or hydrants for washing, boiling, and rinsing clothes. Many women made their own soap from lye, starch from wheat bran, and washtubs from beer barrels cut in half. They supplied washboards, batting blocks or sticks, workbenches, fuel, and cast-iron pots for boiling. Different fabrics required varying degrees of scrubbing and then soaking in separate tubs with appropriate water temperatures. When the weather permitted, the preference was to perform the work outdoors under the shade of trees and to hang saturated garments on clotheslines, plum bushes, or barbed wire fences — to be marked by the telling signs of three-pronged snags on freshly cleaned fabric. When inclement conditions moved the work inside, clotheslines were hung across the main room. Once the clothes were dry, several heavy irons were heated on the stove and used alternately. After each use, the irons were rubbed with beeswax and wiped clean to minimize the buildup of residue, and, one by one, items were sprayed or dampened with water or starch and pressed into crisp form.[29]

Flexibility marked the main advantage of laundry work, especially for women with children. They could intermingle washing with other obligations and incorporate help from family members. Male relatives or hired draymen sometimes picked up dirty clothes in wheelbarrows or wagons. Children could also help with pickup and deliveries, assist with maintaining the fire, or beat the clothes with sticks. Laundry work was the best alternative among job options available to most black women in the urban South.

No matter what particular domestic job black women occupied, they fought to use whatever leverage and resources available to make wage labor fit their needs as mothers, wives, sisters, and daughters. The predominance of domestics who lived and worked in their own homes in Atlanta was the result of concessions they won. While some employers undoubtedly welcomed the absence of live-ins, many resented the loss of control that resulted from domestics returning to their own communities at night.[30]

DuBois criticized domestics who lived in their own homes because of the temptations it offered them after work. In his view, it was better for them to be cloistered in middle-class homes to avoid the temptations of "vice" that awaited them in their own neighborhoods. Living outside of the watchful eye of employers left black women "free at night to wander at will, to hire lodgings in suspicious houses, to consort with paramours, and thus to bring moral and physical disease to their place at work" (p. 141). DuBois's protestations ignored his own acknowledgment that white households were not necessarily safe havens for black women vulnerable to sexual exploitation by white men; he reinforced the fears of white employers already predisposed to seeing black domestics as profligate and contagious. The fear that black domestics were fecund with disease led the medical establishment to take note of black health issues, especially as migration increased after the turn of the century. Similar sentiments in Atlanta, however, aroused a more pejorative public health campaign that scapegoated black domestics as the primary carriers of tuberculosis infecting the white populace.[31]

African American women devised a number of other strategies to maximize autonomy and relief from poorly rewarded work. In Atlanta, where most workers were not given time off, quitting work was a routine method of usurping time and expressing discontent. Though quitting did not usually assure better wages and conditions, it expressed a refusal to submit to unfair treatment. Women also quit work for temporary periods, to take care of sick family or to participate in social activities. When church groups or secret societies sponsored train "excursions" as fund-raising and social events, employers were guaranteed sudden departures of their household help. In Philadelphia, seasonal departures occurred during the spring and summer as wealthy northerners headed for coastal resorts. Black Philadelphians, and some competitors from the upper South, took advantage of this opportunity to find temporary work outside of the city. Employers often complained of the "migratory turn of mind" of black servants predisposed to quit work at will (pp. 135, 488).[32]

Quitting was a thriving strategy for resisting onerous aspects of domestic work precisely because it was not easily defeated in a free labor system. Though some workers may have openly confronted their employers before departing, quitting did not require open or direct antagonism. Workers who had the advantage of living in their own homes could easily make up excuses for leaving, or leave without notice at all. These small and fleeting victories of individuals accumulated into bigger results as workers throughout Atlanta repeatedly executed this tactic, frustrating the nerves of employers.[33]

Household workers also reappropriated the material assets of their employers for their own use. The "pan-toting" custom of taking away table scraps or dry goods presents a microcosm of the competing expectations of workers and employers and the encroachment of the wage system. Household laborers expected employers to acknowledge openly their obligation to insure their workers basic subsistence by supplementing wages with leftover foodstuffs, or else they literally reclaimed the fruits of their labor without the employers' consent. DuBois and Eaton did not perceive "pan-toting" as customary vails or perquisites dating back centuries, nor did they recognize the retribution sought by workers who often had few, if any, legal remedies to redress grievances. Instead, they emphasized pilfering as theft — pure and simple matters of dishonesty among workers (pp. 260–61, 485–86).[34]

For black women in the South, pan-toting helped to alleviate some of the onerous consequences of low-wage labor. Some employers conceded to the practice, openly admitting that they paid low wages with table scraps in mind. Even though domestics sometimes used pan-toting to counter employers' dishonest tactics, critics attacked the custom as theft. Conflict over this matter was often resolved to the benefit of employers, who called for the police to arrest black women. Domestic workers, however, had no such recourse when duped by employers, who too frequently defined "free" labor as their right to expropriate labor without compensation. Outright refusals to pay wages, the use of coercion to pawn off extraneous articles in lieu of cash, bilking workers of wages for trivial "offenses," and assessing "insurance fees" were common occurrences.[35]

"Stealing" breaks, feigning illness, and sloughing off at work were other strategies used by discontented workers. Child nurses scheduled walks or outings with their charges in order to conveniently pass through their own neighborhoods to conduct business they would otherwise neglect. Feigning illness was a popular tactic, especially for live-in workers, who had less control over their time during or after work. On the spur of the moment, a dispute resolved without satisfaction to a cook or general maid could lead her to take action immediately by performing her job poorly. Even servants who were considered "well-raised" and "properly" trained by their employers would show "indifference" to their work if they felt unduly provoked. As one employer explained: "Tell them to wipe up the floor, and they will splash away from one end of the room to the other; and if you tell them that is not the way to do it, they will either be insolent or perhaps give you a vacant stare as if they were very much astonished that you thought that was not the way to do it, and they will keep right on."[36] These everyday tactics of resistance brought moments of relief and satisfaction to domestic workers who had few other outlets for recourse.

Despite the limits of the urban occupational structure that limited black women's access to jobs outside private white homes, some managed to find other kinds of employment. The options in Philadelphia were more varied than in Atlanta. Some black women worked as janitors, office maids, waiters, and public cooks; while these were jobs very similar to domestic work in private homes, they offered better wages and more distance from vicissitudes of intense personal relations. The largest number of women outside domestic work were dressmakers and seamstresses, often independent artisans; a few owned their own shops and others worked at home. Despite the array of clothing manufacturers in the city, the jobs available for seamstresses in factories were limited, just as the anonymous "colored woman" cited earlier lamented. When Jewish women immigrants at a local factory struck in 1890, Gabriel Blum, spokesmen for manufacturers, promised to open the industry to black women. After announcements in churches and newspapers, five hundred black women eagerly lined up at the factory at the crack of dawn the next day, hoping for the break they had long awaited. Most were turned away empty-handed, except for a few who were given piecework to take home.[37] Though relatively few in number, seamstresses doing piecework were the largest group of home workers and were afforded the autonomy similar to that of Atlanta's washerwomen. A few dozen other women ran their own businesses in undertaking, hairdressing, and catering, and ran groceries, employment agencies, and hardware stores. Most cigar stores, which often included bicycle rentals, bootblack stands, and pool rooms, were operated for and by men, but a few women entered the businesses. There were several candy and notion stores that were primarily female-run enterprises. A few dozen women worked in the professions, as teachers and nurses; a smaller number earned a living as musicians, actors, and artists (pp. 97–123).

In Atlanta, black women were hired as domestics in boardinghouses, brothels, and hotels. Others established à la carte meal services or lunch carts — dozens of these six-by-nine-foot shacks were erected on busy streets. As in Philadelphia, the largest number of nondomestics were dressmakers, seamstresses, and milliners. And here too, some were skilled artisans and business owners, while most did piecework at home on sporadic contracts. Just as Atlanta was becoming a thriving manufacturing center for white women, black women were locked out of industries. Black women were more likely to work in sales and clerical work in the small but growing black-owned insurance companies and retail stores. A small number worked as schoolteachers and nurses.[38]

A nascent underground economy supplied black women with alternative sources of income and employment as gamblers, bootleggers, and prostitutes. In Philadelphia, "policy playing" was a popular betting sport among women as well as men (p. 265).[39] In Atlanta, some women found they could maximize their options and evade detection by the police if they maintained a semblance of legal employment in domestic labor. Games of chance offered fun and recreation as well as the potential to earn extra cash. Similarly, bootlegging granted women a way to evade laws prohibiting their entry into Atlanta saloons and gave them access to profits that accrued from peddling liquor in alleys and side streets. Prostitution could range from casual trading of sex for favors between people of acquaintance to street and brothel trafficking. Women who sold their bodies assumed risks of arrest and disease, but they earned more money than they could accumulate as domestic and other wage workers.[40]

Prostitution in Atlanta, at least for white women, was a thriving business at the end of the century as the city attracted large numbers of transient men doing business, visiting conventions, or passing through on the railroad. White women entrepreneurs controlled the brothels and tied their trade to the fortunes of real estate companies, landlords, police officers, and politicians who took a cut of the profits. There is no way to know how many

African American women worked as prostitutes, but most of the available evidence from the period enumerates a small number of black women compared to whites. The most visible women could be found streetwalking on Decatur Street, the city's red-light and amusement district, and in a few brothels.[41]

Though DuBois found only fifty-six black prostitutes in 1896, he estimated that there were probably twice as many practicing in the sex trade. He spotted them inhabiting the slums with the "criminal class" in alleys, back streets, and courtyards. He noticed their presence as next door neighbors to laundresses and as "well-dressed and partially undetected prostitutes" intermingling with some "estimable families." It was this kind of contamination by the "submerged tenth" with more respectable members of the working and middle-classes that disturbed DuBois most. DuBois was also bothered by what he saw as a misguided materialism in Gilded Age America that led some women into prostitution to support worldly desires and to buy fancy clothes for their idle men (pp. 61, 192–93, 313–14). DuBois expected to find more evidence of prostitution given his belief that common law marriages, cohabitation between unmarried couples, and moral laxity were widespread, yet he did not. Though later estimates would suggest that DuBois had undercounted prostitutes by a much wider margin than he anticipated, there are no reliable data on the number in the Seventh Ward or in greater Philadelphia.[42]

African American women pieced together livelihoods by wage work, casual jobs, and illegal endeavors, if necessary. They also engaged in non-remunerative labor in their own homes and neighborhoods that was life-sustaining. The significance of laundry work and the stark disparity between the number of independent washerwomen in Atlanta and Philadelphia is thrown into greatest relief in this context. Laundry work was critical to the process of community building because it encouraged women to work together in communal spaces within the neighborhoods, fostering informal kinlike networks of reciprocity that sustained them through health and sickness, love and heartaches, birth and death.[43] This support system also facilitated the management of child care; laundresses watched the children of neighbors left at home or in the streets to fend for themselves as their parents worked away. The intimacy of laundry work inspired unity, but it could also produce friction between women. Gossip cut both ways. Individuals used it to pass on vital — literally life-saving — information, but as rumor and innuendo it could evoke jealousy or rouse ill will. Sharing did not occur indiscriminately, for one's past actions determined one's reputation for adherence to social expectations. Nor did women redistribute scarce resources simply on the basis of abstract or sentimental principles; they anticipated reciprocity. Public brawls and street fights, not uncommon in working-class neighborhoods, were used as a method of airing grievances, seeking support, and obtaining resolution, with the sanction of the wider community when there were disagreements about conduct or the violation of social rules.

Communal labor also made it possible for women to use time during the day to salvage resources from nearby merchants. Early in the mornings, before the business day commenced in Atlanta, women and children rummaged through the garbage pails of groceries, restaurants, and fruit stands and in the public domain. Everything from discarded cinders to generate fuel for cooking or for doing laundry, to food, clothing, and furniture were refurbished for use, trade, or resale in neighborhood pawnshops in exchange for cash. Sometimes children were sent out on their own to collect items for their mothers.

Shopping for fresh foods and dry goods was a luxury that working-class women could not always afford. Backyard gardens and chickens spotted in Atlanta were evidence of rural migrants continuing to produce some of their own food once they arrived in the city. Chickens in bedrooms and goats in cellars were familiar to working-class immigrant communities in Philadelphia as well. Livestock and fertile plots supplied food to caretakers and also enabled them to share the fruits, vegetables, and meats that fostered sociability among family, friends, and neighbors.[44] When able to purchase foods, they bought what they needed in small quantities from street vendors, peddlers, and grocery stores near their homes. This meant, of course, they could not obtain volume discounts, which raised their food costs. Hardly a disregard for economy, as some of their contemporaries decried, minimal shopping prevented food spoilage and permitted budgeting of small, irregularly paid wages.[45]

Renting rooms to boarders also provided a source of income for working-class families to help defray living expenses. Commercial boardinghouses as well as bedding and meal services in private households were necessary in cities where hotels were still scarce and the performance of routine household chores was not a customary habit of single men. The sudden population explosion and influx of migrants in Philadelphia during the last few years of the century made such services imperative. Three to four times more black families in Philadelphia rented rooms to boarders than did in Atlanta. Many of these boarders were young, single women who not only provided extra income, but sometimes helped with baby-sitting and household production. DuBois pointed out the perils of renting rooms to strangers, especially for girls left unattended by their mothers and exposed to the predatory acts of designing men, such as waiters who often returned to their lodging places between meals. DuBois objected to boarding because it violated sacred family norms: "the privacy and intimacy of home life is destroyed, and elements of danger and demoralization admitted" (pp. 194, 164–67, 271).[46]

Subsistence strategies and wage labor consumed most of working-class women's lives, but women found ways of replenishing their spirits through activities that gave them joy and pleasure. Recreation and personal gratification, of course, could serve multiple purposes. Lunch carts generated income and meeting places on the streets. Bootlegging, gambling, and prostitution could satisfy emotional and social desires, as well as bring in cash.

Churches were central to the social lives of black urban working-class women in both cities. Aside from the regular church service on Sunday, rituals like funerals, weddings, and baptisms were important life-affirming events. Churches offered social and spiritual activities throughout the week. Though DuBois thought the "noisy missions" frequented by the working class were marred by illiterate preachers and ecstatic worship, he gave credit to churches for the social services they provided to the larger community. Thursday afternoon events such as concerts, solo musicals, receptions, reading circles, and literary recitations were designed especially for domestic workers in Philadelphia. Given these women's relatively high literacy rate, reading and literary events were popular activities. Church-sponsored night schools added to personal enrichment, and kindergartens provided safe havens for children while their mothers worked (pp. 197–221, 469–72).[47]

Mutual aid societies rivaled the influence of the church in the lives of the working class. These benevolent associations provided benefits for the sick, widows, orphans, and unemployed workers in exchange for regularly assessed fees. Some of the organizations owned halls that served as meeting places for education, political, and social events. In Atlanta, domestic laborers were active and visible members and leaders in such societies as the Daughters of Bethel, Daughters of Zion, Sisters of Friendship, and Sisters of Love. In Philadelphia, they joined the Sons and Daughters of Delaware, the Female Cox Association, and the Sons and Daughters of Moses. The groups proved indispensable to urban survival, race advancement, and personal enrichment and offered formal mechanisms for weaving together a tightly knit community. DuBois, however, questioned the benefits of working-class investments in dues and fees in some unscrupulous or "doubtful societies" that may have been better saved in banks or invested in property (pp. 185, 173, 221–30).[48]

Household workers in the South demonstrated their commitment to these organizations by taking leave from work to carry out their various membership duties and obligations. Despite the six- to seven-day a week schedule, many domestic workers were devoted to fulfilling their community obligations, even if it meant missing work. Moreover, organized mutuality offered group protection by bolstering their ability to quit work with confidence when their rights were violated. As one employer regretfully acknowledged, secret society membership "makes them perfectly independent and relieves them from all fear of being discharged, because when they are discharged they go right straight to some of these 'sisters.' "[49] Domestic workers often used secret societies to blacklist or boycott employers who violated their rights, transforming individual grievances into collective dissent.[50]

Other loci of urban leisure included alleys, side streets, front porches, dance halls, theaters, saloons, and gambling dens. Commercial entertainment centers in both cities were located downtown in and near black neighborhoods, where legal and illegal activities often overlapped. Atlanta had Decatur Street, known as the "melting pot of Dixie" because of the conspicuous interracial and ethnic commerce and social intercourse that stood in marked contrast to that of the rest of the city. African Americans gathered there to share news, purchase fish from the market, hang out at barbershops, exchange sundry items for cash at pawnshops, play cards, drink, gamble, and dance. Philadelphia had Seventh and Lombard Streets, as well as many other locations in the Seventh Ward, where similar activities were carried out in pool rooms, private houses, and on the streets. Theaters and travel excursions were also popular among working-class people. DuBois singled out balls and cakewalks as "the most innocent amusements," in contrast to many of the other activities listed above, which he discerned to be of questionable character and doubtful value to the advancement of the race (pp. 319, 61, 192, 265–67, 309–21).[51]

Working-class women pieced together their livelihoods through wage labor and a variety of nonremunerative consumption strategies described here that were critical both materially and socially. Scavenging, borrowing, and "pan-toting" increased provisions of poor people. Domestic workers transformed raw products into consumable goods in their own families, the same labor that they performed in the homes of their employers, albeit under austerity. They conducted much of this activity at the level of neighborhoods, creating informal social networks in communal laundry spots, on the streets, at lunch carts, and in dance halls and saloons. The casual mechanisms of mutual aid, in turn, facilitated the development of more formal institutions such as churches and mutual aid societies, which provided other outlets for social, spiritual, and political expression, as well as economic cooperation. Churches and secret societies, in turn, strengthened the ties that bound people together as family, friends, and neighbors.

DuBois recognized the structural problems of racial discrimination that perpetuated underemployment and unemployment of African Americans and constrained their human potential generation after generation. He acknowledged the burdens on black family life when women were forced into the labor market, locked into positions as servants, and kept in poverty. He substantiated the double obstacle of women confined to domestic labor as the occupation was declining due to industrialization, yet denied access to the best paid positions by competition from recent immigrants.[52] Yet DuBois coupled his dissection of the restrictions of the racist political economy with attributions of black volition for existing conditions. He blamed the intolerant practices, attitudes, and institutions of white employers and workers alike, and he criticized African Americans for making wrong choices within the structural limitations imposed on them. Women who took in boarders to defray living expenses or those who were forced to work without the benefit of safe child care were criticized for imperiling their unsupervised children. Yet domestics who chose to live with their own families, rather than with employers, were chastised for exposing themselves to temptations of the flesh. Even within the context of otherwise wholesome religious institutions, DuBois argued, there was "a tendency to let the communal church and society life trespass upon the home." He believed that African American churchgoers diminished the primacy of the nuclear family ideal by participating in too few "strictly family gatherings" (pp. 194–96).

An underlying assumption running throughout *The Philadelphia Negro* is a bifurcation between the private "home" and the public "street." DuBois privileged the sanctity of nuclear, private homes—black and white—over and above working-class neighborhoods and collective public culture. He attributed multiple signs of communal life outside the private family sphere to intractable "traces of plantation customs" brought by southern migrants and immoral proclivities of untrained newcomers and old-timers alike. DuBois constructed the "street" or "neighborhood life" as sites of danger and vice. Women and men seen "loafing and promenading" on the streets, in his view, demonstrated the absence of "home life." But DuBois singled out young domestic servant girls who skirted the margins of respectability by roaming the streets unsupervised or unescorted by proper men. He viewed the heterosexual sociability and casual mingling between strangers or acquaintances as open invitations to engendering a number of social ills: deemphasis on the nuclear family and emphasis on sex outside of marriage, illegitimacy, crime, and the pursuit of short-term pleasures that ultimately impaired the progress of the race (pp. 191–95, 249, 320–21, 391). In effect, DuBois condemned a broad range of everyday cultural practices that working-class women relied on to survive the racially circumscribed job market, daily insults at work, low wages, no wages, and unemployment. He derogated the ways they looked for moments of joy and pleasure in their workaday lives.[53] What he often defined as antisocial behavior or maladjustment of rural peasants to city life were, on the contrary, highly social and rational adaptations by migrants with prior urban experiences.[54]

DuBois's attitudes and assumptions were not unique, however; they reflected the Victorian sensibilities of middle-class America. DuBois subscribed to the idea of "uplifting" the race by reforming the masses. Racial uplift was partly a critique of notions of black inferiority, partly an expression of hope in the capacity of the poor to improve their circumstances through proper training, and partly a faith in a meritocracy where when blacks as a group could demonstrate and achieve standards of "civilization," they could overcome racism and be granted full citizenship rights. Middle-class spokespersons of racial uplift often assumed a position of moral superiority that inevitably denigrated the habits, traits, and behaviors they associated with the masses. Improving the home, protecting the nuclear family, and encouraging monogamous legal marriages were inextricably tied to the advancement of the race as much as was the advocacy of civil rights. Thus, DuBois's condemnation of cultural practices that appeared to him to devalue the family was consistent with the ideas of many middle-class people of the period.[55]

DuBois was also a product of the Progressive reform movement. Like other educated professionals inspired to use the tools of new academic disciplines such as sociology to improve society, DuBois set out to collect empirical data that would not only expose the inequities in Philadelphia, but would also prompt social change.[56] His formula for reform surpassed mainstream proposals of the era in advocating the transformation of institutions and practices that were impediments to democracy in the labor market, politics, and society. He sent a prescient and pointed warning to politicians and industrialists that "Negro prejudice costs the city something." He argued that dire consequences could result from "the atmosphere of rebellion and discontent that unrewarded merit and reasonable but unsatisfied ambition make" (p. 351).

DuBois, like other middle-class reformers, however, also wished to reshape the behavior and values of the masses to fit them to fulfill their lot, however unfairly it may have been assigned to them, in urban industrial America. In this regard, he failed to fully appreciate working-class people's own values and tactics, which emphasized autonomy and collective life and savored social spaces for respite and recovery from wage work. Wage labor in itself was not virtuous, not by the estimates of the people who labored by their hands and sought to minimize its degradations. Though African Americans worked hard by necessity, conforming to standards of chaste, disciplined, hard-driving workers granted them few rewards. African American working-class women devised strategies within the constraints of inequality in fin de siècle America that made the difference between starvation and subsistence, enduring indignities and preserving of self-respect. They creatively built sustaining neighborhoods in the urban North and South, drawing from a rich heritage and resilient culture that they continually reconstituted to meet the exigencies of urban life.

Notes

1. *Philadelphia Post*, November 1, 1871, in *We Are Your Sisters: Black Women in the Nineteenth Century*, ed. Dorothy Sterling (New York: W. W. Norton, 1984), pp. 423–24.
2. Joseph A. Hill, *Women in Gainful Occupations* (Washington, D.C.: U.S. Government Printing Office, 1929), p. 115.

3. For an in-depth analysis of women in Atlanta, see Tera W. Hunter, *To 'Joy My Freedom: Southern Black Women's Lives and Labors After the Civil War* (Cambridge, Mass.: Harvard University Press, 1997).

4. For an important critique of Salmon's flawed methodology and the influence of Progressive thinking on her book and the subsequent literature on domestic work, see Bettina Berch, " 'The Sphinx in the Household': A New Look at the History of Household Workers," *Review of Radical Political Economics* 16 (Spring 1984): 105–21.

5. Nathaniel Burt and Wallace E. Davies, "The Iron Age, 1876–1905," in *Philadelphia: A 300-Year History*, ed. Russell F. Weigley (New York: W. W. Norton, 1982), pp. 471–83; Roger Lane, *The Roots of Violence in Black Philadelphia, 1860–1900* (Cambridge, Mass.: Harvard University Press, 1986), pp. 7–13; James Michael Russell, *Atlanta, 1847–1890: City Building in the Old South and the New* (Baton Rouge: Louisiana State University Press); Don Doyle, *New Men, New Cities, New South: Atlanta, Nashville, Charleston, Mobile, 1860–1910* (Chapel Hill: University of North Carolina Press, 1990), pp. 1–21, 136–58; Jonathan McLeod, *Workers and Workplace Dynamics in Reconstruction Era Atlanta* (Berkeley and Los Angeles: University of California Press, 1989).

6. Burt and Davies, "Iron Age," pp. 488–94; Russell, *Atlanta*, pp. 152–53; Doyle, *New Men*, pp. 11–14.

7. Burt and Davies, "Iron Age," pp. 491–92; Lane, *Roots of Violence*, pp. 20–21; James Michael Russell, "Politics, Municipal Services, and the Working Class in Atlanta, 1865–1890," *Georgia Historical Quarterly* 66 (Winter 1982): 467–91; Doyle, *New Men*, 143–47; Jerry Thornbery, "The Development of Black Atlanta" (Ph.D. diss., University of Maryland, 1977), pp. 7–12; Dana F. White, "The Black Sides of Atlanta: A Geography of Expansion and Containment, 1870–1970," *Atlanta Historical Journal* 26 (Summer/Fall 1982–83): 199–225; John H. Ellis, "Businessmen and Public Health in the Urban South During the Nineteenth Century: New Orleans, Memphis, and Atlanta," *Bulletin of the History of Medicine* 44 (May–June 1970): 197–371; John H. Ellis and Stuart Gallishoff, "Atlanta's Water Supply, 1865–1918," *Maryland Historian* 8 (spring 1977): 5–22; Michael Leroy Porter, "Black Atlanta: An Interdisciplinary Study of Blacks on the East Side of Atlanta, 1890–1930" (Ph.D. diss., Emory University, 1974).

8. Frank F. Furstenberg, Jr., Theodore Hershberg, and John Modell, "Origins of the Female-Headed Black Family: The Impact of the Urban Experience," in *Philadelphia: Work, Space, Family, and Group Experience in the Nineteenth Century, Essays Toward an Interdisciplinary History of the City*, ed. Theodore Hershberg (New York: Oxford University Press, 1981), pp. 438–46; Herbert Gutman, *The Black Family in Slavery and Freedom, 1750–1925* (New York: Random House, 1976); Andrew Miller, "Social Science, Social Policy, and the Heritage of African-American Families," in *The "Underclass" Debate: Views from History*, ed. Michael B. Katz (Princeton, N.J.: Princeton University Press, 1993), pp. 254–92; Antonio McDaniel, "The Power of Culture: A Review of the Idea of Africa's Influence on Family Structure in Antebellum America," *Journal of Family History* 15, 2 (1990): 225–38.

9. The proportion of white single women was 38 percent and black women 37.8 percent. *Philadelphia Negro*, pp. 71–72.

10. It is important to stress here the assessment DuBois made of his own data. Recent scholars, however, have questioned the reliability of census statistics on black widows. The extremely high rate of black male mortality notwithstanding, it appears that the number of black widows was overreported by women or that errors were made by census enumerators. I thank Antonio McDaniel for calling this issue to my attention. See Samuel H. Preston, Suet Lim, and S. Philip Morgan, "African-

American Marriage in 1910: Beneath the Surface of Census Data," *Demography* 29 (February 1992): 1–15.

11. Furstenberg, Hershberg, and Modell, "Origins of the Female-Headed Black Family," 435–54; Miller, "Social Science," pp. 254–92; Stewart Tolnay, "Black Fertility in Decline: Urban Differentials in 1900," *Social Biology* 27 (Winter 1980): 256–57; Michael B. Katz, "The Urban 'Underclass' as a Metaphor of Social Transformation," in *"Underclass" Debate*, pp. 3–26.

12. On DuBois's influence on Frazier and Moynihan see the following: Elliot Rudwick, "W.E.B. DuBois as a Sociologist," in *Black Sociologists: Historical and Contemporary Perspectives*, ed. James E. Blackwell and Morris Janowitz (Chicago: University of Chicago Press, 1974), p. 25; David Levering Lewis, *W.E.B. DuBois: Biography of a Race* (New York: Henry Holt, 1993), pp. 209–10; Anthony M. Platt, *E. Franklin Frazier Reconsidered* (New Brunswick, N.J.: Rutgers University Press, 1991), pp. 111–20, 133–42.

13. Furstenberg, Hershberg and Modell, "The Origins of the Female-Headed Black Family," pp. 439–42; Kathryn M. Neckerman, "The Emergence of 'Underclass' Family Patterns, 1900–1940," in Katz, *"Underclass" Debate*, p. 200. Southern black women were three times more likely to participate in the labor force than southern white women, and married black women were nearly six times more likely than married white women. See Claudia Goldin, "Female Labor Force Participation: The Origin of Black and White Differences, 1870 and 1880," *Journal of Economic History* 37 (March 1977): 94; Janice L. Reiff, Michael R. Dahlin, and Daniel Scott Smith, "Rural Push and Urban Pull: Work and Family Experiences of Older Black Women in Southern Cities, 1880–1900," *Journal of Social History* 16 (Summer 1983): 39–48; Thornbery, "Black Atlanta," p. 34; Jacqueline Jones, *Labor of Love, Labor of Sorrow: Black Women, Work, and the Family from Slavery to Freedom* (New York: Basic Books, 1985), p. 113; Gutman, *Black Family*, pp. 442–50, 624–42.

14. Tolnay, "Black Fertility Decline," pp. 249–60. For a misinterpretation of low fertility to bolster a black family "pathology" thesis, see Roger Lane, *Roots of Violence*, p. 158. Lane concluded that the small family size can be attributed to a large percentage of black women prostitutes and infertility caused by gonorrhea. This claim is made without providing any evidence of the incidence of gonorrhea, by exaggerating the number of prostitutes and by ignoring live birth, stillbirth, and infant mortality rates. Lane dismissed other factors for low fertility, such as the possibility that black women had fewer children voluntarily, either through birth control or abstinence. For an explicit rejection of the correlation between low fertility and venereal disease, see Tolnay, "Black Fertility in Decline." Lane continued this line of thought, slightly modified, in a subsequent study. He argued that low rates of marriage, high rates of infant mortality, and diseases from prostitution accounted for small black family sizes — except for "the most distinguished" black Philadelphians. The small family sizes of the elite can be attributed "not as the result of disease or desperation but of decision." See Lane, *William Dorsey's Philadelphia and Ours: On the Past and Future of the Black City in America* (New York: Oxford University Press, 1991), p. 305. According to Tolnay's data from the 1900 census, better-off families had fewer children than did the poor among black urbanites. If Lane accepts this data, his conclusions are inconsistent, since poor women had *more* children and he associates infertility, prostitution, and venereal disease with poor women. DuBois's conclusions concur with Tolnay. See *Philadelphia Negro*, p. 319.

15. Faye Dudden, *Serving Women: Household Service in Nineteenth-Century America* (Middletown, Conn.: Wesleyan University Press, 1983), p. 64; Nash, *Forging Freedom*, pp. 146, 150; Lane, *William Dorsey's Philadelphia*, pp. 77–80.

16. Hill, *Women in Gainful Occupations*, pp. 334–36; David Katzman, *Seven Days a Week: Women and Domestic Service in Industrializing America* (New York: Oxford University Press, 1978), pp. 87–91.

17. Lane, *William Dorsey's Philadelphia*, 88.

18. Frances A. Kellor, *Out of Work: A Study of Employment Agencies, Their Treatment of the Unemployed, and Their Influence upon Homes and Business* (New York: G. P. Putnam's Sons, 1905); Dorothy Salem, *To Better Our World: Black Women in Organized Reform, 1890–1920* (New York: Carlson Publishing, 1990), pp. 45–46; Charles Ashely Hardy III, "Race and Opportunity: Black Philadelphia During the Era of the Great Migration, 1916–1930" (Ph.D. diss., Temple University, 1989), p. 450; Ruth Rosen, *The Lost Sisterhood: Prostitution in America, 1900–1918* (Baltimore: Johns Hopkins University Press, 1982), p. 81.

19. See for example entries for 1880–99, Edwin Edmunds Account Book, 1838–92, Southern Historical Collection, University of North Carolina, Chapel Hill; Berch, "Sphinx in the Household," pp. 114–15; Dudden, *Serving Women*, pp. 87–93.

20. Susan Strasser, *Never Done: The History of American Housework* (New York: Pantheon, 1982).

21. A Negro Nurse, "More Slavery at the South," *New York Independent* 72 (January 25, 1912): 196.

22. Strasser, *Never Done*, pp. 36–46; Kathleen Ann Smallzried, *The Everlasting Pleasure: Influences on America's Kitchens, Cooks, and Cookery, from 1565 to the Year 2000* (New York: Appleton-Century-Crofts, 1956), pp. 93–102.

23. Quoted in Elizabeth Ross Haynes, "Negroes in Domestic Service in the United States," *Journal of Negro History* 8 (October 1923): 411.

24. See for example, Polly Stone Buck, *The Blessed Town: Oxford, Georgia, at the Turn of the Century* (Chapel Hill: University of North Carolina Press, 1986), p. 16.

25. Strasser, *Never Done*, pp. 105–21; Ruth Schwartz Cowan, *More Work for Mother: The Ironies of Household Technology from the Open Hearth to the Microwave* (New York: Basic Books, 1983), pp. 65, 98.

26. Katzman, *Seven Days a Week*, pp. 185–87; Ray Stannard Baker, *Following the Color Line: American Negro Citizenship in the Progressive Era* (1908; reprint, New York: Harper and Row, 1964), p. 53; Walter L. Fleming, "The Servant Problem in a Black Belt Village," *Sewanee Review* 8 (January 1905): 14, W.E.B. DuBois, "Negroes of Farmville, Virginia," *Bulletin of the Department of Labor* 14 (January 1898): 21; Dolores Janiewski, *Sisterhood Denied: Race, Gender, and Class in a New South Community* (Philadelphia: Temple University Press, 1985), pp. 43–44, 127–29.

27. Katzman, *Seven Days a Week*, pp. 60–62; U.S. Department of Commerce and Labor, Bureau of the Census, *Special Reports: Occupations at the Twelfth Census* (Washington, D.C.: U.S. Government Printing Office, 1904), pp. 486–89.

28. It is difficult to calculate the number of laundresses in Philadelphia. DuBois and Eaton referred to laundresses working in employers' homes as "day workers" and included housewives and seamstresses in this category.

29. For descriptions of laundry work, see Sarah Hill, "Bea the Washerwoman," Federal Writers Project, Southern Historical Collection, University of North Carolina, Chapel Hill (hereinafter FWP, SHC); Jasper Battle, "Wash Day in Slavery," in *The American Slave: A Composite Autobiography* (Westport, Conn.: Greenwood Press, 1972–79), vol. 2, pt. 1, p. 70; Buck, *Blessed Town*, pp. 116–20; Katzman, *Seven Days a Week*, pp. 72, 82, 124; Daniel Sutherland, *Americans and Their Servants: Domestic Service in the United States from 1800 to 1920* (Baton Rouge: Louisiana State University Press, 1981), p. 92; Dudden, *Serving Women*, pp. 224–25; Patricia E. Malcolmson, *English Laundresses: A Social History, 1850–1930* (Urbana: University of Illinois Press, 1986), pp. 11–43; Strasser, *Never Done*, 105–21.

30. See Don L. Klima, "Breaking Out: Streetcars and Suburban Development, 1872–1900," *Atlanta Historical Journal* 30 (Summer–Fall 1982): 67–82; Testimony of Albert C. Danner, in U.S. Senate Committee on Education and Labor, *Report upon the Relations Between Labor and Capital* (Washington, D.C.: U.S. Government Printing Office, 1885), 105 (hereinafter *Labor and Capital*).

31. David McBride, *Integrating the City of Medicine: Blacks in Philadelphia Health Care, 1910–1965* (Philadelphia: Temple University Press, 1989), pp. 34–35; Hunter, *To 'Joy My Freedom*.

32. Lane, *William Dorsey's Philadelphia*, p. 81.

33. *Atlanta Journal*, March 3, 1883; Testimony of Mrs. Ward, *Labor and Capital*, pp. 328, 343; Katzman, *Seven Days a Week*, 195–97; Tera W. Hunter, "Domination and Resistance: The Politics of Wage Household Labor in Atlanta," *Labor History* 34 (Spring–Summer 1993): 208–11.

34. For comparison of vails and customary rights in seventeenth- and eighteenth-century London, see Peter Linebaugh, *The London Hanged: Crime and Civil Society in the Eighteenth Century* (Cambridge: Cambridge University Press, 1992), pp. 250–55; Roger Lane argues that black domestics had some legal recourse when falsely accused of stealing in Philadelphia or when employers invaded their privacy by opening their mail, though he also acknowledges that only a few who were mistreated made formal complaints. *William Dorsey's Philadelphia*, p. 79.

35. For the controversy on pan-toting see Negro Nurse, "More Slavery at the South," p. 199; "The Negro Problem: How It Appeals to a Southern White Woman," *Independent* 54 (September 18, 1912): 22–27; Fleming, "Servant Problem," p. 8; Haynes, "Negroes in Domestic Service," pp. 412–13; Testimony of Mrs. Ward, *Labor and Capital*, p. 343; Elizabeth Kytle, *Willie Mae* (New York: Knopf, 1958), pp. 116–17; E. P. Thompson, "The Moral Economy of the English Crowd in the Eighteenth Century," *Past and Present* 50 (February 1971): 76–135. For an insightful discussion of "social wages" see Marcus Rediker, *Between the Devil and the Deep Blue Sea: Merchant Seamen, Pirates, and the Anglo-American Maritime World, 1700–1750* (Cambridge: Cambridge University Press, 1987), pp. 116–52.

36. Testimony of Mrs. Ward, *Labor and Capital*, p. 343. On resistance see Hunter, "Domination and Resistance," pp. 205–20; James C. Scott, *Domination and the Arts of Resistance: Hidden Transcripts* (New Haven, Conn.: Yale University Press, 1990).

37. Lane, *William Dorsey's Philadelphia*, 78.

38. U.S. Department of the Interior, Bureau of the Census, *Report of the Population of the United States at the Eleventh Census: 1890* (Washington, D.C.: U.S. Government Printing Office, 1897), pt. 2, p. 634; McLeod, *Workers and Workplace*, pp. 41, 100; Gretchen Maclachlan, "Women's Work: Atlanta's Industrialization and Urbanization, 1879–1929" (Ph.D. diss., Emory University, 1992), pp. 13–20.

39. Lane, *Roots of Violence*, pp. 116–22.

40. See *Atlanta Constitution*, May 15 and June 18, 1900, November 30, 1902; *Atlanta Journal*, April 12 and August 12, 1901; *Atlanta Independent*, September 22, 1906; "Condition of the Negro in Various Cities," *Bulletin of the Department of Labor* 2 (May 1897): 257–359.

41. Maclachlan, "Women's Work," 203–25; "Reports of the Martha Home," 1913–15, in Christian Council Papers, Men and Religion Forward Movement, Atlanta History Center; Minute Book, 1908–18, Neighborhood Union Papers, Robert W. Woodruff Library, Clarke Atlanta University; Ruby Owens, tape-recorded interview by Bernard West, January 23, 1976, Living Atlanta Collection, Atlanta History Center.

42. Though Roger Lane acknowledged that there are no direct figures on black women prostitutes, he made questionable calculations nonetheless. He derived the estimate of 2,000 to 2,500 black prostitutes (20 to 25 percent of the total presumed

number) by arguing that black women accounted for 29 percent of prosecutions for infanticide, 40 percent of known deaths from abortion, and 20 percent of official deaths caused by syphilis. How all of these morbidity and mortality measures, problematic in themselves, are linked to prostitution and prostitution alone is never substantiated or explained. Lane overreached his evidence even further to claim that "perhaps" as many as 25 percent of *all black women* in Philadelphia (e.g., over 5,000 women in 1890), by the end of their childbearing years "had at some time had exposure to the disease and habits associated with prostitution." There is no evidence presented here or elsewhere to sustain this conjecture—he cites two newspaper articles from 1863 and 1880. See *Roots of Violence*, pp. 107–9, 122–33, 159.

43. See "Bea the Washerwoman," p. 4; Julia Campbell Buggs, Mary Campbell, and Dinah Campbell, "Three Sisters," pp. 5, 9, FWP, SHC.

44. See Thornbery, "Black Atlanta," 210; Strasser, *Never Done*, 16–31.

45. On women's neighborhood networks and subsistence strategies see Neckerman, "Emergence of 'Underclass' Family Patterns," pp. 197–205; Christine Stansell, *City of Women: Sex and Class in New York, 1789–1860* (New York: Alfred A. Knopf, Inc., 1986), pp. 41–62; Ellen Ross, "Survival Networks: Women's Neighborhood Sharing in London Before World War I," *History Workshop* 15 (spring 1983): 4–27; Jeanne Boydston, "To Earn Her Daily Bread: Housework and Antebellum Working-Class Subsistence," *Radical History Review* 35 (1986): 7–25.

46. Maclachlan, "Women's Work," 163–85; Neckerman, "Emergence of 'Underclass' Family Patterns," 197–205.

47. DuBois, ed., *Efforts for Social Betterment Among Negro Americans* (Atlanta: Atlanta University Press, 1898), pp. 11–16; Porter, "Black Atlanta," pp. 68–75; Thornbery, "Black Atlanta," pp. 147–69.

48. U.S. Department of Treasury, Register of Signatures of Depositors in the Branches of the Freedmen's Savings and Trust Company, Atlanta Branch, 1870–74 (microfilm) National Archives, College Park, Maryland; DuBois, *Efforts for Social Betterment*; *American Missionary* (October 1889): 292; Porter, "Black Atlanta," 75–76.

49. Testimony of Mrs. Ward, *Labor and Capital*, p. 344; Ma [Margaret Cronly] to darling Rob [Cronly], June 29, 1881, Cronly Family Papers, William R. Perkins Library, Duke University.

50. This tactic of resistance evoked much controversy among employers in Atlanta as demonstrated by the attention it received in Joseph E. Brown's antiblack and antilabor U.S. Senate campaign in 1914. See 1914 campaign literature, Joseph M. Brown Papers, Atlanta History Center; *Atlanta Constitution*, March 31, 1910. Brown vowed to ease the burdens of "helpless" white housewives by eradicating domestic workers' organizations.

51. *Atlanta Constitution*, July 20, 1881; Porter, "Black Atlanta," pp. 254–61; Lane, *Roots of Violence*, 109–25.

52. Jacqueline Jones does an excellent job in the essay in this volume in explicating these strengths in DuBois's work and demonstrating how he understood the racially circumscribed labor market as the central problem affecting other aspects of black life.

53. I disagree with points raised in Jacqueline Jones's essay in this volume, which state that DuBois "devotes relatively little attention 'to African American culture.'" Jones implicitly defines culture as mainly aesthetics and artistic expression. She also defines culture as gender relations and argues that DuBois is inattentive to this issue as well. I treat culture as the collective life and everyday, routine practices of people. DuBois does not ignore culture; he treats it throughout the text in great detail and often with great insight, though with bias as well. I am concerned here with the way in which he derogates working-class culture and women's participation and contri-

bution to it. My views are more consistent with Mia Bay's and Antonio McDaniel's essays in this volume.

54. Recent literature on black migration indicates that more African Americans had prior urban experiences than previously assumed. Blacks usually migrated incrementally from rural areas to southern cities, rather than moving directly from the rural South to the urban North. DuBois discussed the urban origins of many migrants from the upper South in *The Philadelphia Negro*, but his descriptions of southern migrants as a group usually depicted them as rural peasants inexperienced in urban life. See Peter Gottlieb, *Making Their Own Way: Southern Blacks' Migration to Pittsburgh, 1916–1930* (Urbana: University of Illinois Press, 1987), pp. 23–30; Joe William Trotter, ed., *The Great Migration in Historical Perspective: New Dimensions of Race, Class, and Gender* (Bloomington: Indiana University Press, 1991); James R. Grossman, *Land of Hope: Chicago, Black Southerners, and the Great Migration* (Chicago: University of Chicago Press, 1989); Carole Marks, *Farewell — We're Good and Gone: The Great Black Migration* (Bloomington: Indiana University Press, 1989).

55. See for example, Robert Gregg, *Sparks from the Anvil of Oppression: Philadelphia's African Methodist and Southern Migrants, 1890–1940* (Philadelphia: Temple University Press, 1993), pp. 3–5, 109–11; Willard B. Gatewood, *Aristocrats of Color: The Black Elite, 1880–1920* (Bloomington: Indiana University Press, 1990); Evelyn Brooks Higginbotham, *Righteous Discontent: The Women's Movement in the Black Baptist Church, 1880–1920* (Cambridge, Mass.: Harvard University Press, 1993); Claudia Tate, *Domestic Allegories of Political Desire: The Black Heroine's Text at the Turn of the Century* (New York: Oxford University Press, 1992); Lewis, *DuBois*, pp. 189, 205. Too little research has been done on how the working class defined, challenged, or embraced "racial uplift" ideology. "Uplift" ideals were not necessarily limited to the black middle or upper classes, as many working-class people participated in the popular discourse about race advancement by attending public lectures, debates, and sermons, and by reading and discussing novels and serialized fiction and nonfiction in newspapers, such as the *AME Church Review*, published in Philadelphia.

56. *The Philadelphia Negro* makes explicit DuBois's many recommendations for changing policies, institutions, and individual behaviors. As Rudwick argued, DuBois enthusiastically embraced the double role of social scientist and social reformer. See Rudwick, "W.E.B. DuBois as a Sociologist," pp. 28, 38; Lewis, *DuBois*, pp. 183–210; Mary Jo Deegan, "W.E.B. DuBois and the Women of Hull-House, 1895–1899," *American Sociologist* 19 (Winter 1988): 301–11.

Part III

The Problem of the Twentieth Century

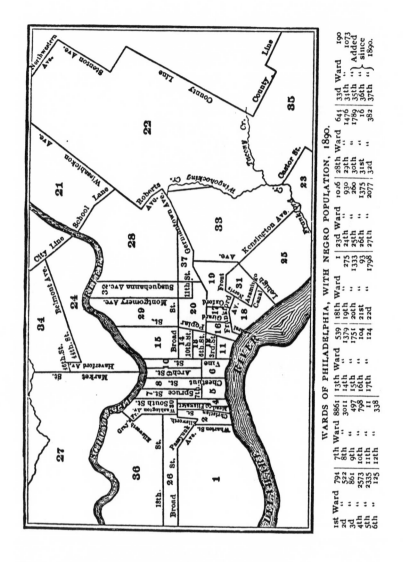

Figure 9. DuBois's map of the "distribution of Negroes" by ward in the City of Philadelphia, 1890. *Philadelphia Negro*, p. 59.

Chapter 6

The "Philadelphia Negro" Then and Now

Implications for Empirical Research

Antonio McDaniel

The Philadelphia Negro is William Edward Burghardt DuBois's quintessential empirical sociological production. He was a pioneer in the pursuit of empirical social science research at the dawn of the discipline in the United States, especially during the formative years between 1894 and 1910.[1] Published in 1899, *The Philadelphia Negro: A Social Study* was the first social science study of race in urban America.[2] DuBois rejected the racist grand theorizing that dominated sociological research during this period and charged the major sociological theorists, such as Herbert Spenser, Charles Ellwood, and Lester Ward, with substituting metaphysical figures from their own imaginations for actual observation of human action. In place of this creative imagining, DuBois advanced the need for empirical research. Additionally, *The Philadelphia Negro* presents the first population study of African Americans.

For DuBois, empirical observation of human action was essential for understanding and changing society.[3] *The Philadelphia Negro* shows clear signs of being influenced by the positivist revolts in economic history lead by Gustav von Schmoller and Adolph Wagner, DuBois's German professors.[4] The book's research design was greatly influenced by the empirical work of Charles Booth. DuBois's empirical method consequently was based heavily on descriptive statistics that he used to advocate social change. He added to these methods his desire to advance the status of the African American community.

Usually, empirical sociologists do not reflect on how their values and morals affect the interpretation of their empirical results, but DuBois did consider these matters as he contemplated the significance of *The Philadelphia Negro.* "We must study, we must investigate, we must attempt to solve; and the utmost that the world can demand is, not lack of human interest and moral conviction, but rather the heart-quality of fairness, and an earnest desire for the truth despite its possible unpleasantness" (p. 3). As we shall see, DuBois's moral conviction influenced his views of the African American community, and his views of the African American community influenced his interpretation of the empirical findings in *The Philadelphia Negro*.

Writers use language and symbolism with a particular audience in mind. For whom was DuBois writing *The Philadelphia Negro*? The Philadelphia branch of the College Settlement Association, the driving force behind the effort to have DuBois write the book, was a welfare organization with affiliations at the Wharton School of the University of Pennsylvania. The Association wanted DuBois's research to supply an empirical basis for its political reform agenda, which included its sought-for moral reforms; his services were solicited through the Association's efforts.[5] This arrangement put DuBois in the position of reporting on Philadelphia's African community as an outside observer, to an outside agency. He was very much aware of his outside audience, of the distance this intellectual orientation placed between him and the community and of the tensions that accompanied that distance. As he noted in *The Autobiography of W.E.B. DuBois*, "The colored people of Philadelphia received me with no open arms. They had a natural dislike to being studied like a strange species."[6] The very nature of his investigation presented the objects of his study—the African American community of Philadelphia—as a "strange species" from which he would gain information for the College Settlement Association. Yet the community did not fancy itself as an Other in need of a great intellectual savior; indeed, there was an obvious tension between DuBois and the city's African American elite. In the end, DuBois interpreted the community's aloof reception of him as an indication that he "did not know so much" about his "own people." "First of all I became painfully aware that merely being born in a group, does not necessarily make one possessed of complete knowledge concerning it. I had learned far more from Philadelphia Negroes than I had taught them concerning the Negro Problem." Yet, he maintained that his book did serve a positive purpose. "It revealed the Negro group as a symptom, not a cause, as a striving, palpitating group, and not an inert, sick body of crime; as a long historic development and not a transient occurrence."[7]

DuBois's analysis presented two pictures of Philadelphia's African community. In one view, the problems of African Americans resulted from enslavement and capitalism within the United States; in the other, they stemmed from African Americans' moral failings and included their lack of integration into the "greatest of the world's civilizations" (p. 388). DuBois sought to explain the African Americans' plight from a moral perspective that was both Eurocentric and socially conservative. He attributed moral failure to a lack of culture among African Americans. This lack of culture, he argued, resulted from racial exclusion. He suggested the need for more acculturation with European Americans. This culturally conservative perspective influenced DuBois's interpretation of his empirical results.

In this essay, I examine two aspects of DuBois's efforts in *The Philadelphia Negro*. First, I review its demographic analysis in the context of current knowledge about the city's population history and consider what demographic changes since the 1890s tell us about the subsequent development of African American Philadelphia. Second, I reflect on the implications of DuBois's moral convictions for his empirical research and the legacy of his stance for subsequent African American scholars. An understanding of those convictions reveals why DuBois reached certain conclusions and advanced particular social policies.

A Demographic History Since *The Philadelphia Negro*

Size and Racial Composition

European settlement along the Delaware River began in the seventeenth century with the arrival of Swedish colonists. By 1790, Philadelphia was considered the first city in a new nation. Even at this early date, Philadelphia embodied the multiracial reality of American society; about 5 percent of its population was of African origin, denoting a significant African American presence. Figure 10 graphically presents the city's changing racial composition. The African American percentage of the population has varied during the last two centuries; however, since the days of *The Philadelphia Negro*, that percentage has been on the rise. This increase in size has had many implications for African Americans.

Figure 10 does not show the impact of the formation of Philadelphia on the American Indian population. The first Europeans to travel to the Americas were, in effect, disease carriers; when they made contact with indigenous inhabitants who lacked immunity to these diseases, massive epidemics resulted that killed millions of people. Locally, diseases such as smallpox demolished the large American Indian tribes of Pennsylvania and New Jersey. The Delaware, the Munsee, and the Conestoga are believed to have lost 90 percent of their population to immigrant-related epidemics, particularly smallpox, by the middle of the seventeenth century.[8] It is surprising that DuBois did not discuss this issue, given his attention to historical detail. With the demise of the indigenous population, immigrants poured in from Europe and, later, Africa (via the southern United States).

With the exception of the post-Reconstruction period, the African American population has experienced a pattern of consistent growth in Philadelphia. Between 1790 and 1890 — the period covered in *The Philadelphia Negro* — the number of African Americans rose, climbing from 2,489 to 39,371. The rate of increase fluctuated in response to various social and economic factors, going down or stagnating, for example, during the pe-

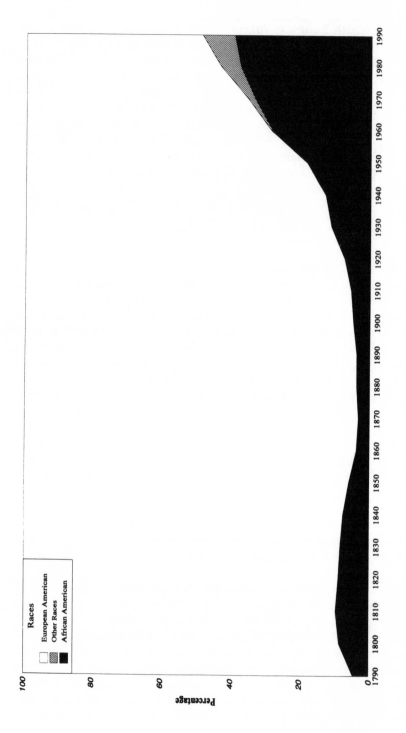

Figure 10. Racial distribution of the City of Philadelphia, 1790–1990 (percentages). Sources: DuBois, *The Philadelphia Negro*; U.S. Bureau of the Census, *Census of Population and Housing: Philadelphia (1960–1990)*.

riod's two major wars (1810–20 and 1850–70). The period following 1840 witnessed the continued arrival of immigrants from Europe, a surge that increased the European American share of the population for the next thirty years. Many of the earliest African American migrants to Philadelphia were refugees from enslavement in America's southern cotton kingdom. They flowed into the city by the hundreds. While many remained, a significant number passed through to Canada and to other areas in the eastern United States, making Philadelphia an essential terminal on the Underground Railroad.

With the onset of the industrial era, between 1880 and 1930, Philadelphia's population increased substantially, exceeding the one million mark by 1890. This growth was primarily the result of immigration from Europe, but was supplemented by the Great Migration north of southern-born African Americans during and after World War I. From 1854, when the city and county of Philadelphia were consolidated, until 1910, African Americans remained around 4 to 5 percent of the population. By 1990, their numbers had so grown that some 40 percent of Philadelphia residents were African American.

In 1890, 22 percent of the African American population resided in the Seventh Ward, making it the largest African American ward in Philadelphia. A large proportion of the African American population of DuBois's day lived in what he termed the "worst slum districts and most unsanitary dwellings of the city." The Seventh Ward, along with other central city wards (such as the Fifth and Sixth Wards), was, in fact, an area of the city with the lowest quality of life. Despite the size of its African American population, however, the Seventh Ward was not a "typical" African American community. DuBois noted that the Seventh and Eighth Wards were exceptional in that they simultaneously counted as among "the worst wards" in terms of living conditions and as wards with "large sections inhabited by the best people of the city," with below-average mortality (pp. 154–55). In 1990, the African American population continued to reside in various areas around the city, such as the West, South, North, and Southwest sections of modern Philadelphia. The distribution of the city's African American population one hundred years after *The Philadelphia Negro* may been seen in the accompanying map (see Figure 11). DuBois presented a similar map (see Figure 9). In addition to replicating DuBois's map, I have provided a percentage distribution of the African American population by block group in Figure 12. This figure graphically presents the African American residential concentration suggested by Figure 11 and Table 1 below. As in the time of *The Philadelphia Negro*, the African American community's place of residence continues to be influenced by race and space.

The Philadelphia Negro was in large part an intensive study of the Seventh Ward. That ward took the form of a long narrow strip, beginning at South Seventh Street and extending west, with South and Spruce Streets as bound-

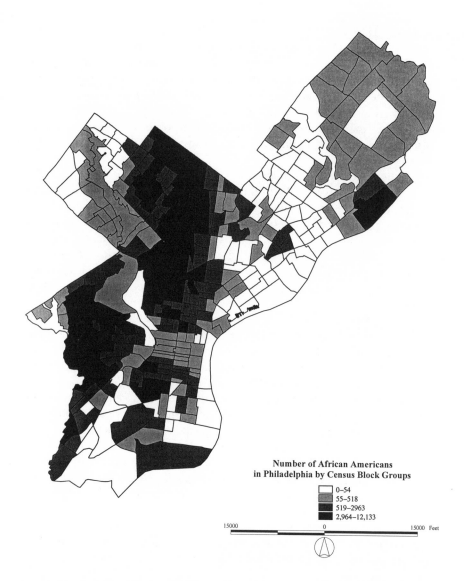

**Number of African Americans
in Philadelphia by Census Block Groups**

- 0–54
- 55–518
- 519–2963
- 2,964–12,133

15000   0   15000   Feet

Figure 11. Distribution of African American population, Philadelphia, 1990: number of African Americans by Census Block Groups. Source: U.S. Bureau of the Census, public use microdata sample for 1990.

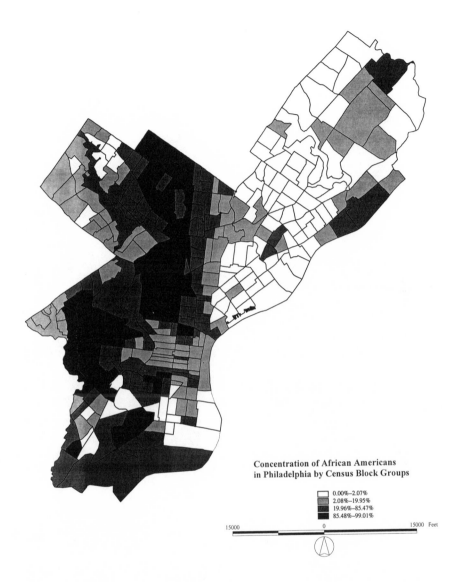

Concentration of African Americans
in Philadelphia by Census Block Groups

☐ 0.00%–2.07%
▨ 2.08%–19.95%
▨ 19.96%–85.47%
■ 85.48%–99.01%

15000   0   15000 Feet

Figure 12. Distribution of African American population, Philadelphia, 1990: concentration of African Americans by Census Block Groups. Source: U.S. Bureau of the Census, public use microdata sample for 1990.

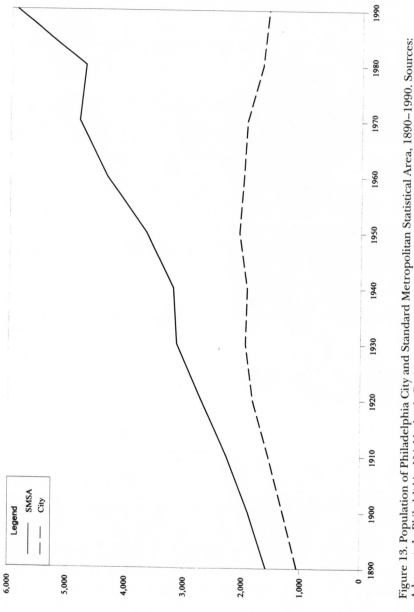

Figure 13. Population of Philadelphia City and Standard Metropolitan Statistical Area, 1890–1990. Sources: Adams et al., *Philadelphia: Neighborhoods, Division, and Conflict* (note 11), p. 9; U.S. Bureau of the Census, *Census of Population and Housing, Philadelphia (1960–1990)*.

aries, as far as the Schuylkill River. By 1990, several historic buildings important to the African American experience remained in the old Seventh Ward; however the African American population had dispersed to several segregated areas throughout the city and suburbs.

The balance of the population between the suburbs and the city began shifting toward the suburbs around the turn of the century. Figure 13 graphically presents this shifting balance. Following World War II, the city's population dominance in the region was seriously challenged by suburban growth. By 1960, the suburban population was almost twice that of the city. This shift reflected a massive exodus of people from the central city that accompanied the postwar movement of industry and the construction of suburban houses and highways. The movement was so abrupt that as early as the 1950s, the city actually lost population. In 1950, the city accounted for more than half the population of the Philadelphia SMSA (Standard Metropolitan Statistical Area); by 1960 much of the basic shift had taken place, and the city of Philadelphia accounted for less than 40 percent of the metropolitan population. That percentage has continued to decline into the 1990s.

The flight to the suburbs was predominantly white, and it left behind a city that was increasingly African American, and, more recently, Hispanic and Asian as well. Of Philadelphia's current population, about 40 percent is African American; a little over 5 percent is Asian and Hispanic. Employment opportunities followed the suburban exodus. Hence, racial minorities have been left in the city to suffer the current patterns of urban decline, joblessness, and poverty.

African American Philadelphians have had to confront those patterns under conditions of extreme segregation in housing and, consequently, education — segregation that has only increased through this century, as the data in Table 1 suggest. Table 1 presents the index of dissimilarity, a measure of residential segregation, for the city of Philadelphia for 1850 to 1990. The index of dissimilarity measures the percentage of one group that would have to change residences from areas where it is overrepresented in order to produce an even distribution.

The African American population is the most residentially segregated in the city. In 1990, it had a dissimilarity index of 83 — that is, 83 percent of Philadelphia's African American residents would have had to change their place of residence in order to match the residential distribution of the rest of the city's population. The 1970 index for African Americans stood at 75, while the comparable rates of segregation that year among populations of European origin were relatively mild. The relative difference of these indexes reflects the persistent and unique exclusion which the African American population has continued to experience in the city of Philadelphia.

DuBois did not present any statistical evidence of racial segregation; however, *The Philadelphia Negro* does present the problems of race as a unique

TABLE 1. Segregation of the African American and European Immigrant
Populations of Philadelphia*

Year	Africa	Great Britain	Germany	Ireland	Italy	Poland	Russia
1850	53	—	37	35	—	—	—
1880	61	—	32	28	—	—	—
1910	46	21	25	20	61	—	58
1920	45	21	27	20	53	52	50
1930	61	24	32	28	59	54	56
1940	68	23	35	32	60	57	57
1950	71	22	31	29	54	54	54
1960	77	21	25	24	47	32	50
1970	75	22	26	28	48	35	52
1980	83	—	—	—	—	—	—
1990	83	—	—	—	—	—	—

Sources: Hershberg et al., " A Tale of Three Cities" (note 9), Table 2, p. 468; Adams et al., *Philadelphia Neighborhoods* (note 11); Massey and Denton, *American Apartheid* (note 10), Table 3.3. * See text for explanation of index of dissimilarity.

case of structural and historical dislocation, in a language that both impressed segments of the Eurocentric academy and served the purpose of re-addressing the particularity of the problem of racism. For DuBois the African American population suffered from a legacy of structural impediments.

Here is a large group of people — perhaps forty-five thousand, a city within a city — who do not form an integral part of the larger social group. This in itself is not altogether unusual; there are other unassimilated groups: Jews, Italians, even Americans; and yet in the case of the Negroes the segregation is more conspicuous, more patent to the eye, and so intertwined with a long historic evolution, with peculiarly pressing social problems of poverty, ignorance, crime and labor, that the Negro problem far surpasses in scientific interest and social gravity most of the other race or class questions. (p. 5)

The experience of immigrants from Europe differed dramatically from that of the African American population.[9] Western European immigrants were, by 1930 if not before, experiencing relatively low levels of residential segregation from native-born whites, with dissimilarity indices hovering between 21 percent and 32 percent. Successful descendants of these immigrants were, by 1930, holding white-collar or highly skilled blue-collar jobs and living in streetcar suburbs, within the city limits but away from the city center. The immigrants from southern and eastern Europe who came to Philadelphia in appreciable numbers after 1900 were considerably more segregated from native whites; Italian immigrants, in fact, with a dissimilarity index of 59 percent in 1930, approached the level of segregation experienced that year by African Americans, who had an index of 61 percent. Yet the condition of these "New Immigrants" differed from that of African Americans in at least two key respects: their residential segregation waned significantly over time, and they were able to obtain industrial jobs when such jobs were still to be had. Philadelphians of African origin, as we have seen, became significantly more segregated with time; from the era of industrialization in the nineteenth century through the Second World War, their employment in the industrial sector was limited.[10] When the systematic job discrimination that DuBois documented began to abate in the postwar period, the industrial jobs themselves started to move out of Philadelphia, and out of the geographic reach of the African American working class.[11] In the 1960s and 1970s, the United States economy was deindustrializing in ways that had disproportionate impact on the African American population.[12] By 1970, 30 percent of the city's African American workforce was employed in manufacturing, a distinct improvement over the 1930 figure of 13 percent, and a proportion that, in fact, slightly exceeded that for whites, 28 percent of whom held manufacturing jobs.[13] Yet this 30 percent share represented a stake in a declining sector of the city's economy. European American Philadelphians in 1970 still far outdistanced African Americans in white-collar work, including clerical employment, and a startling 23 percent of the African American workforce remained in the traditional, low-paying category of "domestic and personal service." Philadelphia's European immigrants bequeathed to their descendants a legacy of economic advantage built in part on the luck of arriving in a still-industrializing city and the exclusion of African American competitors from industrial work. City residents of African origin, whose families came to Philadelphia in their greatest numbers after 1945, have inherited, in contrast, a segregated metropolis of dwindling economic opportunity.[14]

By comparing the percentage of the African American population in Philadelphia and the country at large, DuBois made two interesting observations: the rate of increase in the numbers of African Americans in the city of Philadelphia compared with that in the country overall; and the changes in the proportion of African American inhabitants in the city compared with those in the United States. I have extended DuBois's comparison to 1990 in Figure 14. The percentages of African Americans in Philadelphia and in the United States show how, in DuBois's time, African Americans resided primarily outside the city. Following World War II, the African American population was no longer a country population and had become concentrated in large urban centers. This observation is even more striking if we remember that Philadelphia has consistently ranked highly in the absolute and relative number of African Americans in its population.

Sources of Change in the African American Population

It is frequently assumed that the African American population of Philadelphia, or of any city for that matter, is "one homogenous mass" reared in the slums in which its members are observed. DuBois was of the opinion that

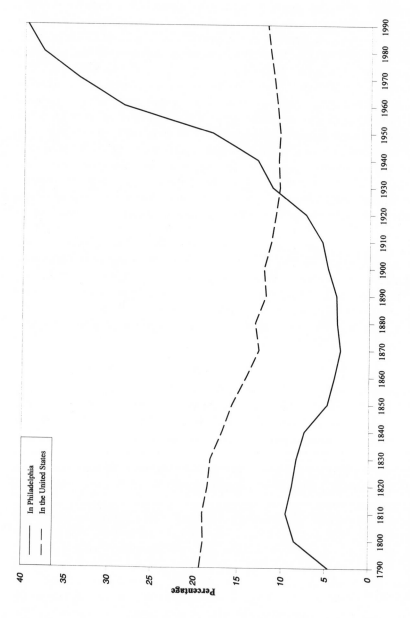

Figure 14. African-origin population of the United States and Philadelphia, 1790–1990. Sources: DuBois, *The Philadelphia Negro*; U.S. Bureau of the Census, *Census of Population and Housing: Philadelphia (1890–1990)*.

such an assumption was misleading for the period of his observations. He felt that the recent immigration from the southern part of the country was a distinguishing factor. From his perspective, the study of the African American population of Philadelphia "would properly begin in Virginia or Maryland." DuBois based that conclusion on his finding that less than a third of the African American population living in the Seventh Ward had been born in Philadelphia, and over one-half had been born in the south (pp. 73, 74, 75) (see Figure 15).

The passing of a century has produced a dramatic change in this pattern. Of today's Philadelphians of African origin, fewer than 30 percent were born outside the city. Moreover, most of those born elsewhere were born in another urban area. Unlike the subjects of DuBois's study, the contemporary "Philadelphia Negro" is a city person born.

A significant percentage, about 24 percent, of European American Philadelphians at the turn of the century, like their African American counterparts, had been born mostly outside of Philadelphia. However, unlike the African American population, the European American in migrants were foreign born. The proportion of European Philadelphians born elsewhere, however, has recently increased, while the proportion of African Americans, Latinos, and Asians with birthplaces outside the city has declined, as Figure 14 demonstrates. (The numbers for "Other" in Figure 14 illustrate the recent immigrant status of Asians and Latinos).

Health

In chapter ten, DuBois sought to understand the absolute as well as the relative health conditions of the population. He focused on mortality, arguing that the variations in mortality statistics would allow an intelligent interpretation of "Negro health." He cautioned: "On the whole, then, we must remember that reliable statistics as to Negro health are but recent in date and that as yet no important conclusions can be arrived at as to historic changes or tendencies" (pp. 147–48).

DuBois provided estimates of mortality in 1890 and for the 1884–90 period (see Table 2). He gave period estimates of 31.25 deaths (including stillbirths) and 29.52 deaths (excluding stillbirths) per 1000 African Americans for 1884–90. For 1890, he gave an estimate of 32.42 deaths, including stillbirths, per 1000. He concluded that the death rate among African American populations was "not extraordinarily" high in comparison to patterns observed in Europe. However, African American mortality was high relative to that of European Americans. As combined causes of the "high Negro death rate," DuBois emphasized environmental factors such as poor housing, bad food, and bad sanitary surroundings, and behavioral factors such as neglect of infants, "poor heredity," and ignorance (pp. 149, 150, 152, 150, 160).

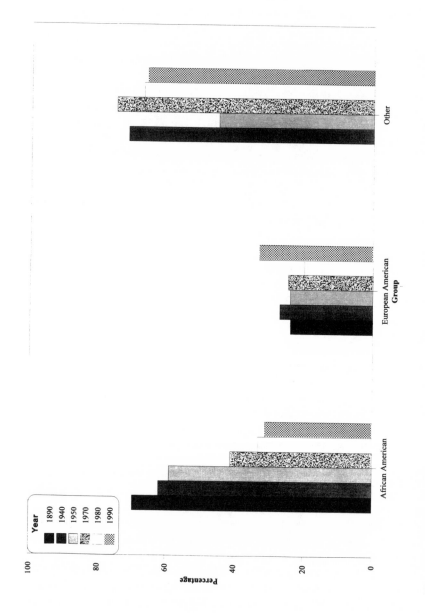

Figure 15. Racial distribution of Philadelphia in-migrants, 1890, 1940–1980. Sources: DuBois, *The Philadelphia Negro*; Hershberg et al., "A Tale of Three Cities" (note 9), Table 1; U.S. Bureau of the Census, various public use samples.

TABLE 2. Age and Sex Standardized Death Rates for African Americans and
European Americans, ca. 1890

Age	British standard*	African Americans Male	African Americans Female	European Americans Male	European Americans Female
0–14	78.23	75.81	63.12	39.37	34.25
15–20	20.66	15.01	12.66	6.34	6.07
20–24	18.70	19.75	10.46	9.65	7.7
25–34	31.50	14.12	16.24	10.95	10.55
35–44	23.97	20.52	13.55	13.73	11.43
45–54	19.39	33.67	25.48	19.44	16.35
55–64	13.09	47.7	34.57	34.04	25.82
65+	94.30	155.26	96.47	98.66	82.78
Total	21.50				
Standardized by sex					
CDR	22.48	36.02	29.23	23.85	20.79
% different from Britain (1871)		60.19	29.99	6.06	−7.53
Standardized for British age structure					
CDR	22.48	47.85	37.61	27.06	23.21
% different from Britain (1871)		112.81	67.29	20.35	3.23

Sources: DuBois, *The Philadelphia Negro*, p. 158; Wrigley and Schofield, *Population History* (note 15), Tables 7.4, A3.1. CDR, crude death rate = number of deaths in group divided by total number in group. * See note 15 for explanation.

Why was African Americans mortality so much higher than European American mortality? Why was African American health so much worse than European American health? DuBois's answer suggested a need to examine both structural and behavioral factors.

Primarily it is because the Negroes are as a mass ignorant of the laws of health. One has but to visit a Seventh Ward church on Sunday night and see an audience of 1500 sit two and three hours in the foul atmosphere of a closely shut auditorium to realize that long formed habits of life explain much Negro consumption and pneumonia; again the Negroes live in unsanitary dwellings, partly by their own fault, partly on account of the difficulty of securing decent houses by reason of race prejudice. (p. 160)

The crude death rate gives only a very general indication of the level of mortality and it changes over time. It is necessary to describe specific components of the death rate in order to understand differences among different populations. DuBois was aware of this issue and presented death rates by age and gender. In fact, he observed that "the age classification of city Negroes with its excess of females and of young people of twenty to thirty-five years of age, must serve to keep the death rate lower than its rate would be under normal circumstances" (p. 150). True to his reputation for careful scholarship, DuBois demonstrated the importance of age and sex in under-standing and comparing death rates. He did not standardize by both age and sex; however, he did suggest how the level of an observed death rate is affected by the demographic composition of the population. For com-parison of death rates over time or for different populations (i.e., racial groups), it has become standard practice since DuBois's time to determine what the difference between the rates would be if there were no differences in the age, race, or sexual composition of the population. This is especially true in attempting to compare health conditions that vary greatly by age, sex, and race.

Crude death rates, like those used by DuBois, are particularly misleading in population comparisons. A population's crude death rate may be rela-tively high because the population has a large proportion of older people, in a range of years where death rates are higher than at younger ages; or, it may be relatively low because the population has a large proportion of children and young adults, at ages where death rates are lower. DuBois presented a graph of the age-specific death rates and a table presenting age-specific death rates by sex. The crude death rate of a population may rise even though death rates at each age remain stationary, if the population as a whole ages. In Table 2 above, I have standardized DuBois's estimates by age.[15] In my standardization, I have used the population of England in 1871 as the standard for comparison. This allows us to make a relative comparison between African American and European American Philadelphians and the population of England.

The crude death rate in England, 22.48 per 1,000 population, falls below all the sex-standardized death rates in Philadelphia with the exception of that of European American women. However, the difference is greatest for African American men and women: their rates are, respectively, 60.19 per-cent higher and 29.99 percent higher than the English rate. The adjustment of the sex-specific death rates raises them significantly, reflecting the fact that the age composition of Philadelphia's population was more favorable for low crude death rates than was that of England. Standardizing the death rates amounts to equating the age distributions of all three populations. The equating of the age distributions raises the relative excess deaths of the Philadelphia populations to more than twice that of the unstandardized rates presented in Table 3. The extraordinarily high death rates of the African American population, compared to the European American popu-lation, are seen in the standardized rates, and DuBois's interpretation and comparison in *The Philadelphia Negro* becomes less tenable.

In order to measure the impact of "infant mortality," DuBois presented an average annual death rate for children under five. Table 3 presents various measures of mortality for African and European Americans for three years over the last century: 1890, 1940, and 1990. DuBois presented "the large infant mortality" by presenting "the average annual rate of

TABLE 3. Vital Rates of Philadelphia African Americans and European Americans
1890, 1940, 1990 (per 1,000 persons)

African Americans

	1890	1940	1990
CDR	32.42	14.8	11.4
IMR			
Males	231.6 ⎱	59.1	23.3
Females	191.2 ⎰		
CMR	171.44	19.08	9.12

European Americans

	1890	1940	1990
CDR	22.69	12.2	14.9
IMR			
Males	166.2 ⎱	36.9	8.6
Females	136.9 ⎰		
CMR	94.00	10.46	9.6

Sources: DuBois, *The Philadelphia Negro*, p. 69; U.S. Bureau of the Census, public use microdata samples for 1940, 1990; IMR from Condran, "Ethnic Differences in Mortality" (note 16). IMR, infant mortality rate = number of infant deaths per 1000 live births. CMR, child mortality rate = number of deaths of children under five per 1000 children under five.

171.44 (including still-births), for children under five years of age." Actually, DuBois does not calculate an infant mortality rate (IMR) as currently understood. His rate is, rather, a child mortality rate (CMR); that is, his rate reflects not only the deaths and births of infants — as does the traditional infant mortality rate (IMR) — but also the deaths and births of all other children under the age of five. In Table 3 I have used DuBois's procedure to calculate a comparable child mortality rate for 1940 and 1990. I have estimated and presented estimates of "true" infant mortality rates for the city in 1890, 1940, and 1990. Here, CDR refers to the crude death rate.

As Table 3 shows, infant and child mortality rates declined for both the African and European American populations.[16] The decline was dramatic for both populations, and the decline in child mortality was mostly due to the fall in the rate of death of infants specifically. The overall mortality rates of both the African and non-African populations declined as well. Between 1890 and 1990, the crude death rates (CDR) dropped from 32.42 per 1000 persons to 11.4 per 1000 persons for African Americans, and from 22.69 per 1000 persons to 14.9 per 1000 persons for European Americans. However, the rate of decline has been substantially greater among the European American population. This is not immediately apparent in the crude rates — that is, in the CDR and CMR. Those rates for 1990 appear to suggest that the African American mortality profile was better than that of European Americans. Here, however, the crude rates are misleading, precisely because they are not standardized for age. The main reason why African

Americans in 1990 appeared to have crude death rates and child mortality rates slightly lower than those for European Americans is that the African American population was younger overall, and thus produced lower crude rates of death. However, once we control for population composition — as the infant mortality rate does — it becomes clear that African American mortality exceeded European American mortality in 1990. African American infants, in fact, suffered a mortality rate nearly three times that of European American infants. Here one can see one of the statistical bases for the conclusion of many observers that today, the African American population is still in a health crisis.

Conjugal Condition and Family Life

To DuBois, family life was an important indicator of community development, and his study of the Seventh Ward found the African American family wanting.

On the whole, the Negro has few family festivals; birthdays are not often noticed, Christmas is a time of church and general entertainments, Thanksgiving is coming to be widely celebrated, but here again in churches as much as in homes. The home was destroyed by slavery, struggled up after emancipation, and is again not exactly threatened, but neglected in the life of city Negroes. Herein lies food for thought. (p. 196)

Particularly troubling, in DuBois's eyes, was the ward's "large number of homes without husbands," a reflection of a high incidence of widowhood, separation, desertion, and unmarried motherhood. The abundance of widows and separated persons — 22.4 percent of the ward's adult female African American population fell into that category — indicated both "widespread and early breaking up of family life" and "grave physical, economic, and moral disorder." DuBois traced the familial instability he saw evidenced in female-headed households to slavery, which had prevented the formation of independent African American families, to the disruptive impact of migration to the city, and to the economic stresses of urban life, including the low wages of African American men. Despite these factors, however, DuBois ultimately saw the mass of African American families as moving toward what he termed "the stable marriage state," or, perhaps more tellingly, "the monogamic ideal." Likewise, he asserted, among the middle laboring class, "the spirit of home life is steadily growing" (pp. 66–72, 193–94, 71–72, 195).

DuBois was one of the first scholars to connect social and economic position to family structure. Like E. Franklin Frazier after him, DuBois was convinced that given time, the African American population would settle down and accommodate its behavior to the prevailing — that is, European American — model of family life. He did not have the vision to imagine the future that free urban life would produce. When he saw signs of this future,

TABLE 4. Conjugal Condition of African Americans, Philadelphia, 1896, 1940, 1990 (percentages)

Year	Conjugal condition	20–29	30–39	40–60	60+
Men					
1896	Single	61.8	29.0	13.7	5.1
	Married	37.4	66.0	73.9	62.0
	Widowed/Separated	0.8	5.0	12.4	32.9
1940	Single	63.54	21.21	15.3	8.1
	Married	35.96	77.44	74.7	64.0
	Widowed/Separated	.50	13.6	8.7	26.7
1990	Single	77.84	42.51	14.1	7.1
	Married	20.53	50.74	58.9	60.6
	Widowed/Separated*	1.63	8.48	27.10	32.24
Women					
1896	Single	40.9	20.8	10.5	4.9
	Married	54.5	59.2	46.0	15.0
	Widowed/Separated	5.1	20.0	43.5	80.1
1940	Single	46.2	17.57	9.8	4.2
	Married	52.42	78.68	65.1	25.8
	Widowed/Separated	1.37	3.76	23.7	70.0
1990	Single	72.68	38.63	14.0	6.9
	Married	25.27	47.63	43.8	28.9
	Widowed/Separated*	3.05	13.74	37.13	64.28

Sources: DuBois, *The Philadelphia Negro*, p. 69; U.S. Bureau of the Census public use microdata samples, 1940, 1990. * Includes "divorced."

such as female-headed households and bad health, he attributed them to the legacy of plantation culture and the stresses accompanying city ward migration. Time has shown him to be wrong, on two counts. The recent trend in African American family life in Philadelphia has been away from the model of a household headed by a married couple; this trend has come about despite the fact that most Philadelphians of African origin are at least a generation distant from the migration experience and almost all were born in an urban setting.

The trend away from marriage as such is evident in the data presented in Table 4, which provides DuBois's estimates of the conjugal condition of the African American population in 1896 and my estimates for 1940 and 1990 using census data. These data illustrate the dramatic transformation in conjugal patterns that has taken place among African Americans during the past century. The number of single men and women has increased substantially for the two youngest age groups (20–29 and 30–39), while the previously large numbers married in these two groups has declined as dramatically. While the number widowed has declined, especially among women,

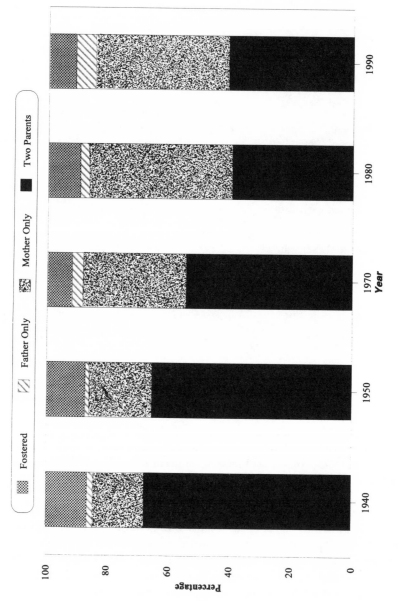

Figure 16. Living arrangements of African American children under 18 years, Philadelphia, 1940–1990. Source: U.S. Bureau of the Census, various public use samples.

the number divorced has risen sharply. These patterns are mirrored among the older population (40–60 and 60+). The major change in the older generation is the decline in widowhood and the more recent increase in divorce.

As marriage rates have dropped, so too has the proportion of African American children in two-parent families, as Figure 16 illustrates. In 1940, a majority — 67 percent — of African American children in Philadelphia lived with two parents. By 1990, only 40 percent of African American children lived in such families. Most African American children now live with only one parent, usually the mother. Moreover, the general trend toward single-parent families cuts across economic lines, as Figures 17 and 18 suggest. These figures present the living arrangements of children by their parents' poverty status (as measured by income) and home ownership status.[17] Family structure has continued to differ greatly depending on economic position. Between 1940 and 1990, strikingly larger proportions of children in poverty lived in single-parent families, compared to the number of children above the poverty line. Since 1970, greater proportions of the children of home owners have lived in two-parent families, compared to the children of non-homeowners. Yet despite these differences, the overall trend among children living in poverty and above it, living with home owners or not, has been away from living with two parents and toward living with one.

The Family, Race, Class, and Culture

In *The Philadelphia Negro*, DuBois noted, "There is always a strong tendency on the part of the community to consider the Negroes as composing one practically homogeneous mass" (p. 309). Although African Americans share a common history and the burden of racism, they differ greatly in their wealth, income, and family structure. In DuBois's analysis, one could understand the African population only by recognizing its diversity. Yet here, as in other aspects of *The Philadelphia Negro*, DuBois's great insight was muted by his Victorian prudishness. In his recognition of class as a factor, his sympathy lay with the "better class." "Nothing more exasperates the better class of Negroes than this tendency to ignore utterly their existence" (p. 310), DuBois declared. He set about to remedy this misperception among "most Philadelphians" by describing and examining the different social classes of the Seventh Ward, using two distinct class classification schemes. The first scheme, presented in chapter 11, was almost entirely according to income. It outlined six different classes: the *very poor*, the *poor*, the *fair*, the *comfortable*, those living in *good circumstances*, and the *well-to-do*. These divisions depended on his estimation of living standards. In a more definitive discussion, in chapter 15, DuBois collapsed his earlier classification into four different classes: the *aristocracy*, or the elite class, marked out by its high standing in education, wealth and "general social efficiency"; the

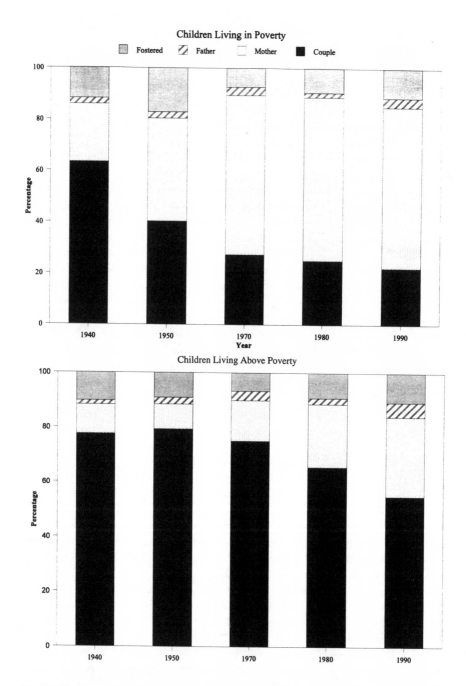

Figure 17. Child poverty status by family structure, Philadelphia, 1940–1990. Source: U.S. Bureau of the Census, various public use samples.

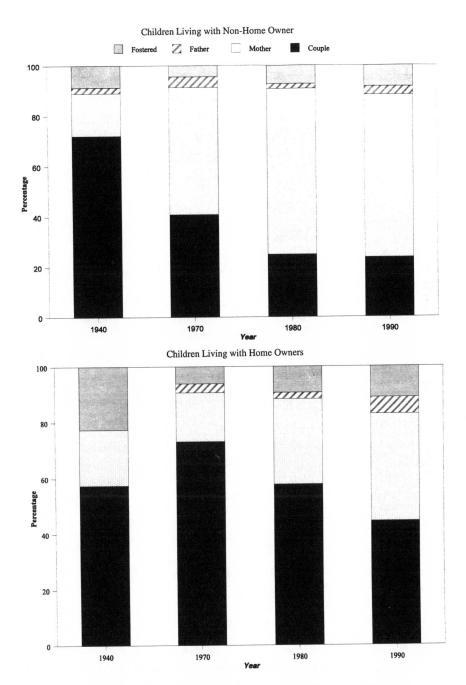

Figure 18. Homeownership by family structure, Philadelphia, 1940–1990. Source: U.S. Bureau of the Census, various public use samples.

TABLE 5. Percentage of African American Social Class Positions, Philadelphia 1896, 1940, 1990.

Year	Indicators	Poor	Working class	Aristocracy
1896	Income	66.3	25.5	8.2
	Social class	36.3	56.0	11.5
1940	Income*	53.5	38.5	8.0
1990	Income*	51.6	43.0	5.4

Sources: DuBois, *The Philadelphia Negro*, p. 171, 315–16; U.S. Bureau of the Census public use microdata samples, 1940, 1990. * See note 17 for calculation of income status.

respectable *working class*, who lived in comfortable circumstances and sent their younger children to school; the *poor*, who did not earn enough to keep them always above want (and who included the poor and the very poor mentioned in chapter 11); and the *submerged tenth*, who were criminals, prostitutes, and loafers (pp. 170–78, 316, 310–11).[18]

In Table 5 I compare DuBois's descriptive statistics of class for the Seventh Ward in 1896 with those for Philadelphia in 1940 and 1990. Table 5 suggests a decline in both the aristocracy and poor class of African Americans over the past century, while the numbers of the working class have increased. Clearly, one can speak here of the African American working class's advance. Signs of such advance are even more striking in Table 6, which demonstrates a stunning increase in African American home ownership. In 1896, only 3.6 percent of the Africans in the Seventh Ward owned the home in which they lived. Citywide in 1940, the proportion of African Americans owning homes stood at a modest 11.9 percent. By the century's end, however, this percentage has more than quadrupled: in 1990, an astonishing 52.6 percent of the African American population lived in homes that their families owned (that is, household-head homeowners versus household-head renters).

Demography, Poverty, and Progress

The demographer who attempts to assess the changes that have come over Philadelphia's African American community since DuBois walked the streets of the Seventh Ward faces a paradox. African Americans remain at a social disadvantage, one reflected in the persistence of poverty, inadequate housing, and greater health risks. This disadvantage likewise is perpetuated by forces analogous, if not identical, to those African Americans faced in the 1890s—that is, by de facto discrimination and a new kind of economic marginalization. Yet, despite these very real problems, Philadelphia's African Americans have made undeniable economic progress. The ranks of the working class have swelled, while those of the poor have, in fact, declined.

TABLE 6. Percentage of African American Homeownership, Philadelphia 1896, 1940, 1990.

Year	Homeowner	Renter
1896	3.6	96.6
1940	11.9	85.3
1990	52.6	46.3

Sources: DuBois, *The Philadelphia Negro*, p. 288; U.S. Bureau of the Census public use microdata samples, 1940, 1990.

More telling yet is the remarkable rise in home ownership. The fact that today, a majority of the city's African Americans live in homes owned by their families cannot help but indicate a measure of success in accumulating capital and gaining access to credit—and this in the face of ever more uncertain employment prospects. The question becomes why this side of African American life has received so little attention.

Part of the answer lies in the difficulties involved in comparing the African American community of Philadelphia today with that of DuBois's time. For all of its barriers, the Philadelphia of the 1890s represented a relative promised land, both for immigrants from an impoverished South and for the native-born "aristocracy" who had managed to maintain a certain level of prosperity. A century later, however, the central city stands as the home of the least well-off among the region's African Americans. The equivalent of DuBois's "aristocracy" and some portion of the working class today live not in the neglected neighborhoods of North Philadelphia, but in such middle-class sections as Mount Airy, or across the city line entirely, in the surrounding suburban counties.[19] The fall of the elite from their position as 8 percent of the city's African Americans in 1940 to 5.4 percent in 1990 reflects, in part, this movement to the suburbs. A focus on the city alone will necessarily miss a good deal of the economic success attained by African Americans in the greater metropolitan area.

But contemporary researchers also have defined their topics in such a way as to render African American economic progress less visible. Their focus remains, for the most part, on poverty, jail, and the appearance of disorganized family life. In particular, many have defined the single-parent household as itself proof of family disorganization and as a factor contributing to the plight of urban African Americans. Yet, as we have seen, such households may be one expression of a cultural predisposition toward an extended family structure and may represent a response to poverty rather than be a cause of it. Here, defining one-parent families, rather than the context of poverty in which many such families find themselves, as the "problem" has obscured the fact that a significant number of African American single parents own their own homes and live above the poverty line.

Class and Family Through a Moral Lens

DuBois, like all empirical researchers, worked both at the level of investigation and at that of interpretation. He, more than most sociologists, recognized that "moral conviction" could influence one's interpretation of empirical findings. Despite this self-awareness, he may not have realized the extent to which his own cultural preoccupations shaped his interpretation of African American Philadelphia. DuBois accepted European American behavior, and in particular the Victorian norms of family life promoted by the European American middle class, as general standards by which to gauge African American behavior. This cultural stance was explicitly assimilationist: the DuBois of *The Philadelphia Negro* urged, in effect, that African Americans assimilate culturally to European America; he did not call for a fundamental transformation of the socioeconomic system that European Americans had created, a system that relegated African Americans to the margins. The evidence of this stance surfaces in DuBois's constant moralizing, which took as its targets both the different classes of African Americans and, especially, their varying patterns of family life. The price of such a stance was that it caused DuBois to overlook much of the cultural distinctiveness of African American life, even as he recorded it.

DuBois's moralism came out strongly in his description of the class structure of African American Philadelphia. His frequent references to moral and immoral behavior among certain classes of African Americans revealed a tendency to conceptualize class and race in cultural terms—that is, to judge such behavior by European American cultural standards. Culture is not only transient behavior and values; it is also part of group social conditions and group history. In this sense, both culture and class are racialized concepts. Most social research during DuBois's sociological period (1896–1910) unequivocally argued for the superiority of Europeans and the inferiority of all African-origin peoples.[20] DuBois did not accept this belief, but he did believe in the superiority of the "aristocracy of the Negro," as he revealed in drawing attention to that class's existence: "In many respects it is right and proper to judge a people by its best classes rather than by its worst classes or middle ranks. The highest class of any group represents its possibilities rather than its exceptions, as is so often assumed in regard to the Negro" (p. 316). Moreover, he linked that superiority to the aristocracy's adoption of elite European American culture. That elite culture served as DuBois's model of "American culture," and he suggested not only that African Americans needed to assimilate to it, but that the "aristocracy of the Negro" had in fact done so. "This class," he observed, "is itself an answer to the question of the ability of the Negro to assimilate American culture" (p. 318).

The elitism inherent in DuBois's view of African America's "highest class" becomes more apparent when we examine his view of the classes lower down, for even he was not content to "judge" the African American population on the basis of its "best classes." *The Philadelphia Negro* is full of references to the "ignorance" of the poor African American as the cause of bad health and "disorganized" family and community life. While DuBois showed why moral explanations failed to account for the continued poverty of poor African Americans, he nonetheless moralized as much as those he criticized. His derogatory attitude toward lower-class Africans, like his admiration of the aristocracy's cultural assimilation, is evident throughout *The Philadelphia Negro*. This kind of moralism made it difficult, at best, for DuBois to discern the advances of the African American working class, a failing that, we have seen, he shares with many contemporary researchers.

DuBois's assimilationist cultural stance hindered his understanding of the African American experience most clearly when he turned to the topic of the family. He argued that the racial oppression begun on the slave ships and continued with the plantation regime damaged African American family life. In DuBois's mind, the slave trade and slavery left the African "low in the scale of civilization" (p. 66). He viewed family "disorganization" among the African American population as a reflection of moral decline.

The great weakness of the Negro family is still lack of respect for the marriage bond, inconsiderate entrance into it, and bad household economy and family government. Sexual looseness then arises as a secondary consequence, bringing adultery and prostitution in its train. And these results come largely from the postponement of marriage among the young. Such are the fruits of sudden social revolution. (p. 72)

DuBois openly accepted European middle-class family structure as a social norm for emulation by African Americans, as he demonstrated when describing a "better class" composed of nuclear families of "undoubted respectability," where the wife worked at home (pp. 310–11). Mothers working for wages, in fact, themselves posed a problem for home life. DuBois said as much when he observed that low wages formed a hindrance to the effort among "the great mass of the Negro population . . . to establish homes." He continued:

The low wages of men make it necessary for mothers to work and in numbers of cases to work away from home several days in the week. This leaves the children without guidance or restraint for the better part of the day—a thing disastrous to manners and morals. (pp. 193–94)

Yet in making the pattern of a nuclear family with a stay-at-home mother the norm, DuBois missed how the power relations of racial oppression undermined the possibility of such family behavior among African Americans. The racial oppression of African American women places them in a unique position relative to male power within the household. There is no indication that the power relationships among African American men and women have ever followed the European American normative pattern.[21] It has never been unusual, for example, for African American women to work outside the home; they worked in Africa prior to their enslavement, they worked while enslaved, and they undertook outside work for wages following emancipation. This long history of women making a monetary contribution to the household is illustrated in the "Special Report on Negro Domestic Service in the Seventh Ward of Philadelphia," written by Isabel Eaton, a fellow of the College Settlement Association and published in *The Philadelphia Negro*. As Eaton's study documents, the history of African American mothers in Philadelphia is a history of women going out to work for wages. The same cannot be said for most European American mothers, even in Philadelphia, a city noted for its unusually high proportion of women in an industrial workforce that was overwhelmingly European American. Polish and Italian immigrant women, for example, worked in Philadelphia textile and garment factories — but generally only until they married or had their first child (although married Polish women did work as domestics).[22] African American mothers' long-standing experience as workers outside the home made them unique, but DuBois did not integrate this illustration of their uniqueness into his analysis of African American family behavior. His moralism thus worked to prevent him from seeing the tension between European family patterns and the history and circumstances of African Americans.

DuBois's moralism influenced his view of the African American family. His interpretation of the facts was consistent with the "code of morals" then prevalent within American society and among most intellectuals. He did not criticize family structure in the context of a racialized society or explore the impact of enslavement on family structure and power relations.

The Philadelphia Negro set the pattern for the interpretation of African American family life in many subsequent studies, especially those by African American scholars. Since E. Franklin Frazier's classic book *The Negro Family in Chicago*, the assimilationist perspective has dominated research on family formation. Yet DuBois's legacy includes not simply the assimilationist approach, but also its tendency to let moral judgments cloud interpretation of empirical findings, particularly as they relate to racial differences. In the assimilationist tradition, culture and social environment are discussed in the context of presenting the aberrant cultural behavior of African Americans. *The Philadelphia Negro*, for example, represents the "problems" of the African American family as stemming from its aberrant behavior, such as "lack of respect for the marriage bond" and a resulting "sexual looseness." This pronouncement is consistent with a perspective that does not consider the meaning of the family itself. Only recently have scholars begun to investigate that meaning and to challenge the moral assumptions underlying research on African American families.[23] In this new research, single-parent families are not in themselves harmful; it is the social context, such as poverty, in which single-parent families find themselves that is disruptive and detrimental. In seeking to reach beyond the assimilationist tradition, these scholars recognize that studying the family as a stabilizer of society does not suffice to answer larger questions about the changing status and desires of men and women racially oppressed and marginalized.

Another Final Word

By questioning the views of the researcher, we reintroduce the investigator into his research. By focusing on how DuBois interpreted his results, we place his writing within a social context and discourse. DuBois's legacy to subsequent African American scholars extended beyond the difficulties he encountered reconciling his cultural preoccupations with his empirical results. He confronted related dilemmas as he faced his findings, dilemmas having to do with the place and mission of an African American scholar in a Eurocentric academy.[24] DuBois bequeathed these dilemmas, best described as ones of racial ambivalence, to the African American scholars who followed him, putting many in an extremely creative intellectual position. Focusing on these intellectuals' battle with racial ambivalence and placing them in the center of analysis reveals aspects of their empirical research obscured by a simple reflection on empirical results.[25]

Unfortunately, DuBois's model of investigation was not appreciated by scholars in the field of sociology, particularly those at the University of Chicago who, as the "Chicago School," came to dominate urban sociology. *The Philadelphia Negro* received glowing reviews in the popular press and from liberal historians, but it was ignored by academic sociologists. The prestigious *American Journal of Sociology* did not even bother to review the book. Furthermore, DuBois was never offered a professorial appointment in a major "mainstream" university department, including the sociology department at the University of Pennsylvania, which had grudgingly extended him the title of "assistant in sociology" for the duration of his study of the Seventh Ward.[26]

Decades before the Chicago School of sociology rose to prominence, DuBois had shown the uniqueness of the African experience in the United States generally and in the urban setting in particular. He described the illogical nature and historic impact of racism, and argued in an eloquent voice that it was a mistake to consider the problems of the African American population as parallel to those of European immigrants. However, these insights were in large part ignored by European American sociologists. In the tradition of the Chicago School and its early, pre-1940s research on urban conditions in the United States, most scholars confounded race, in the sense of distinctions of color, with ethnicity, in the sense of immigrant status.[27] They interpreted—and many continue to interpret—the urban plight of African Americans as comparable to the challenge European immigrants faced in adjusting to American life. For European newcomers, the problem—and, in a sense, the solution—could be summed up in the word "assimilation." But assimilation was a solution to something quite different from the problems posed to a formerly enslaved population held in contempt and pity by Americans of European origin.

For DuBois, ethnic and racial differences were distinct processes of social differentiation. In *The Philadelphia Negro*, he used social history as a counterpoint to the social Darwinism then popular in explanations of why African Americans had not succeeded in American society as had other immigrant groups.[28] In fact, DuBois argued that it was the immigration of Europeans followed by the immigration of the formerly enslaved that prevented the early advancement of the African American population in Philadelphia. Because of racial stratification, DuBois observed, "No differences of social condition allowed any Negro to escape from the group, although such escape was continually the rule among Irish, Germans, and other whites" (p. 11). European immigrants could assimilate through economic advance, but the African American remained racially marginalized and segregated regardless of economic standing. This situation prevailed well into the 1940s, as St. Clair Drake and Horace R. Cayton observe: "[U]pper-class Negroes do experience discrimination and race prejudice in the form of inconveniences, annoyances, and psychic wounding. There are exclusive shops and restaurants that discourage or refuse their patronage. They cannot buy homes in most of the better residential neighborhoods, and in others they can do so only after protest, violence, and court fights."[29]

DuBois's *The Philadelphia Negro* sought a balance between exploring the problems of a racially stratified society and explaining the oftentimes unproductive behavior of the victims of this stratification. Though he saw structural and behavioral problems as related, DuBois was often apologetic in his appreciation of the cultural and historical distinctiveness of the African American population. He shrouded his discussion of African American oppression with admonitions and moralizing to African American people about their behavior.

It is here that we can begin to see the particular scholarly bind in which DuBois found himself. The moralistic tone of *The Philadelphia Negro*, especially toward the behavior of working-class and lower-class African Americans, served to legitimate European American moral criteria. In so doing, it may have helped DuBois get the ear of some European American scholars. But whether or not DuBois consciously intended his moralizing as a tactic to gain such a hearing, that move came at a double cost. The first cost, as we have seen in his discussion of family life, was the stunting of his ability to interpret his empirical results. The second cost was estrangement from his "self" and his "people," whom he ended up objectifying. *The Philadelphia Negro* provides a powerful structural argument about the causes of African American marginalization and exclusion; however, DuBois interpreted his empirical results on the basis of his subjective preferences and his personal beliefs.

DuBois's dilemma is familiar to African American scholars today.[30] As a pioneer social scientist, he may have been among the first to discover that for African American intellectuals, participation in the academy restricts one's voice. African American intellectuals, like DuBois, conduct their research within an academy that marginalizes them and what they write and say. They are in some respects part of the larger academy, yet remain separate and marginalized within it. This condition influences their intellectual production. Seeking to articulate a message that will help change the condition of African Americans, most African American intellectuals write to an audience that is viewed as primarily composed of the "white world." The audience, demanding a certain type of language and viewing the world from a distinct Eurocentric position, becomes an obstacle to expression; for while African Americans and European Americans share space, time, and many aspects of culture, they share these things in a contested context, a context they describe in different voices. And African American intellectuals are caught in the dilemma of needing to talk to two audiences — their own "people" and the Eurocentric academy — in these different voices at the same time.

Above all, to talk in the voice that is comfortable for the Eurocentric academy, African American intellectuals must speak of themselves as an Other. They must study their "people" through the eyes of an Other and in the voice of this Other. African American social scientists, like DuBois in *The Philadelphia Negro*, speak in ways that demonstrate the dilemma of conducting empirical research on race. The African American intellectual spends most of her time talking to her European American colleagues. It is, after all, these colleagues who can offer legitimacy. But to become immersed in this academic world and to accept it as the status quo may blunt the impulse toward fundamental social change. Carter G. Woodson described the dynamic in his classic book *The Mis-Education of the Negro*:

No systematic effort toward change has been possible, for, taught the same economics, history, philosophy, literature and religion which have established the present code of morals, the Negro's mind has been brought under the control of his oppressor. The problem of holding the Negro down, therefore, is easily solved. When you control a man's thinking you do not have to worry about his actions. You do not have to tell him not to stand here or go yonder. He will find his "proper place" and will stay in it.[31]

For Woodson, the crisis of Eurocentrism biased African American scholars and forced them to assume a moral position that could not foster a change in the condition of the African American population.[32] From Woodson's perspective, the contempt and pity expressed by the European American academy influenced the research of African American scholars who shared their European colleagues' "code of morals." African American scholars sought to find their, and their subjects', "proper place" within the social structure as it existed. In this context the empirical sociology of DuBois was limited by the voice in which it was articulated. DuBois discussed his empirical findings through the Victorian morality of his day.

It may seem unusual to describe DuBois in such terms; he did go on to become one of the premier African American activists of this century and an eloquent advocate of radical social change.[33] An African American savant, DuBois confronted the paradox that the historical and social factors that racially oppressed his people were a twice-told tale that was growing old with his European American audience and patrons. Yet, he was intellectually committed to presenting this tale to them in a language that they understood. Even in that language, the book must have startled these readers, given the extent to which it broke with the racial and intellectual orthodoxies of its day. *The Philadelphia Negro* showed DuBois as one of the first scholars to pursue issues of race, class, and social structure in the analysis of African American life. Because most scholars at the time accepted the tenets of white supremacy, DuBois's antiracist assumptions contrasted strongly with mainstream sociological research and the views of the general European American public. In rejecting biological and other essentialist explanations of African American poverty and political powerlessness, the book emphasized the importance of historical, structural, and cultural factors. In its conclusion, DuBois argued that protesting the impact of racism was essential to the African American's future, "but he must never forget that he protests because those things hinder his own efforts, and that those efforts are the key to his future" (p. 390).[34] DuBois's analysis provided a systematic exposition of African American political exclusion and economic marginalization.

It is, however, how DuBois handled the issue of culture that makes his historical and structural interpretations problematic. Culture is not separate from everyday life or economic activity. On the contrary, culture is about these things. Culture comprises the imaginary world of what is seen as possible and the way in which we organize our social space and the social relationships that dominate our everyday lives. Yet DuBois judged African American cultural behavior in moral terms, and in Eurocentric moral terms at that. This is not to suggest that he should have glorified crime among the poor. However, we might have learned more if he had presented African American responses to racial oppression and capitalist society from a perspective sensitive to the oppressed, by contextualizing those responses. Instead, DuBois viewed African American behavior from the lens of the oppressor class. In particular, he advocated the cultural behaviors of those African Americans who had most embraced the cultural values of the European "aristocracy." He revealed much about his expectations for this class in recording his dismay at its ambivalence toward the mass of African Americans:

They teach the masses to a small extent, mingle with them but little, do not largely hire their labor. Instead then of social classes held together by strong ties of mutual interest we have in the case of the Negroes, classes who have much to keep them apart, and only community of blood and color prejudice to bind them together. If the Negroes were by themselves either a strong aristocratic system or a dictatorship would for the present prevail. With, however, democracy thus prematurely thrust upon them, the first impulse of the best, the wisest and richest is to segregate themselves from the mass. (p. 317)

What is it that DuBois would have the elite Negroes of Philadelphia "teach the masses"? DuBois assumed that the elite served the essential role of "buffering" the impact of living in a racially stratified society. He suggest that this class could provide an example to keep alive the perception of African American assimilation of European American family and employment norms. In his view, the elite's steady employment and family stability could serve as a norm for lower-class behavior. Yet the African American elite failed to play the role of responsible leadership; in fact, it viewed the African American masses with the same contempt expressed by the European American population.

DuBois's view of the elite as a buffer to racial stratification has been a consistent theme among major sociologists, from E. Franklin Frazier to William Julius Wilson. Both of these scholars echo DuBois in looking to the African American middle class to provide guidance for the less well-off; they also echo his disappointment at that class's limitations in its appointed task. In his classic study *Black Bourgeoisie: The Rise of a New Middle Class in the United States*, Frazier argued:

Because of its struggle to gain acceptance by whites, the black bourgeoisie has failed to play the role of a responsible elite in the Negro community. *Many individuals among the first generation of educated Negroes, who were the products of missionary education, had a sense of responsibility toward the Negro masses and identified themselves with the struggles of the masses to overcome the handicaps of ignorance and poverty.* Their influence over the masses was limited, to be sure — not, however, because of any lack of devotion on their part, but because of the control exercised by the white community. Nevertheless, they occupied a dignified position within the Negro community and were respected.[35]

In this passage, Frazier maintained that African Americans had suffered a loss of the bonds that once held the community together. Wilson expresses a similar sense of loss regarding the "modern" African American middle class:

Whereas today's black middle-class professionals no longer tend to live in ghetto neighborhoods and have moved increasingly into mainstream occupations outside the black community, the black middle-class professionals of the 1940s and 1950s (doctors, teachers, lawyers, social workers, ministers) lived in higher income neighborhoods of the ghetto and serviced the black community.[36]

The irony here is important. DuBois, Frazier, and Wilson alike view the disorder within the African American community as a breakdown in its moral order. Critical to their arguments is the notion of the moral decay of the poor, whose numbers are always rising, and the potential role of the African American middle class as a savior class. All three look back nostalgically to a golden age when this middle class is presumed to have played that role, maintaining the social ties that held the African American inner city together (for such nostalgia on DuBois's part, see pp. 31–36). Yet Frazier holds up as an example the very generation DuBois scolded for failure to "teach the masses," and Wilson, in turn, praises the postwar middle class that Frazier found so wanting. The reader may be forgiven for wondering at the continuing pursuit of this elusive golden age of the African American middle class, particularly when one scholar's golden age is another's disappointing present. That in turn may lead one to question the assignment DuBois, Frazier, and Wilson seem to have handed that middle class: namely, that it save the African American community from itself.

DuBois's recipe for change in *The Philadelphia Negro* rested on a misguided hope. In the "Final Word" that concludes the book, he advocated inclusion for African Americans, an inclusion led by their middle class: "in their efforts for uplifting of the Negro the people of Philadelphia must recognize the existence of the better class of Negroes and must gain their active aid and co-operation by generous and polite conduct" (p. 396). He did not, however, envision the need for a social transformation — for inclusion is not transformation. Surprisingly, like Booker T. Washington, DuBois here offered a solution to the race problem that suggested that African Americans accept the behavioral norms and necessities of the status quo. Like Washington, DuBois called on African Americans to change themselves into an acceptable group within the confines of the normative structures that dominated American elite bourgeois culture. As subsequent history has shown, however, inclusion in that culture has not transformed its racist nature nor forestalled its legacy of racial conflict and capitalistic exploitation. In fact, African American elites, like those described in *The Philadelphia Negro*, have tended to hold the African American "masses" in contempt. Inclusion turned out to be an escape for the "aristocracy of the Negro," an escape that resulted not in acceptance, but in a kind of invisibility. DuBois's words of the 1890s still resonate today: "The colored people are seldom judged by their best classes, and often the very existence of classes among them is ignored" (p. 316).

Ultimately, the DuBois of *The Philadelphia Negro* analyzed the structural and behavioral aspects of African American oppression from a Eurocentric perspective, arguing for an end to white racism within a cultural context where African Americans would become more "white." He held that white racism denied African Americans access to resources, political power, and acculturation. DuBois did not critique the "dominant morals and assumptions" of American society as such. Rather, he challenged the white racism that prevented full African American participation within the context of the existing social relations. He suggested that acculturation would improve African American social status. In the final analysis, *The Philadelphia Negro* sought no more than to remove the barriers to acculturation while maintaining the socioeconomic status quo.

We may disagree with DuBois's ideas about how to solve the "Philadelphia Negro problem." DuBois's conclusions include a critique of racism; however, he does not adequately critique class relations in American society, a social order that, a century after he began his study of the Seventh Ward, remains rooted in distinctions of race and class.[37] Yet none can deny his intellectual vitality despite his position on the margins of the academy, nor can we ignore his intellectual relevance within society. DuBois not only suggested a course of research; he demanded that this research lead to social action. His cultural orientation may have been prudish and conservative. But his insurgent intellectual activities still challenge us to make our social science relevant to social transformation.

I would like to thank Sena M. Browner-Hubler, Jenifer Bratter, and Thomas Pederson for assistance in the data processing for this paper. I would like to thank Michael B. Katz, Elijah Anderson, and Thomas J. Sugrue for their comments and suggestions. An earlier version of this paper was presented at the DuBois Centenary Conference, held May 5 and 6, 1995, at the University of Pennsylvania.

Notes

1. W.E.B. DuBois, *The Autobiography of W.E.B. DuBois: A Soliloquy on Viewing My Life from the Last Decade of Its First Century* (New York: International Publishers, 1968) pp. 205–6; Dan S. Green and Edwin D. Driver, "W.E.B. DuBois: A Case in the Sociology of Sociological Negation," *Phylon* 37, 4(1976): 308–33.

2. Earlier "empirical" studies were found in Benjamin C. Bacon, *Statistics of the Colored People of Philadelphia* (Philadelphia, 1856); *The Present State and Condition of the Free People of Colour of the City of Philadelphia and Adjoining Districts, as Exhibited by the Report of a Committee of the Pennsylvania Society Promoting the Abolition of Slavery, etc . . .* (Philadelphia: the Society, 1838); *A Statistical Inquiry into the Condition of the People of Color of the City and Districts of Philadelphia* (Philadelphia: Kite and Walton, 1849); Edward Needles, *Ten Years' Progress; or, A Comparison of the State and Condition of the Colored People in the City and County of Philadelphia from 1837 to 1847* (Philadelphia: Merrihew and Thompson, 1849). None of these studies were comparable to the breadth and depth of DuBois's study.

3. W.E.B. DuBois, "The Study of the Negro Problems," *Annals of the American Academy of Political and Social Science* 16 (1898): 1–23.

4. Green and Driver, "A Case in the Sociology of Sociological Negation"; Francis L. Broderick, "German Influence on the Scholarship of W.E.B. DuBois," *Phylon* 19 (1958): 367–71.

5. David Levering Lewis, *W.E.B. DuBois: Biography of a Race, 1868–1919* (New York: Henry Holt, 1993) pp. 179–89.

6. DuBois, p. 198.

7. DuBois, *Autobiography*, pp. 198–99.

8. Russell Thornton, *American Indian Holocaust and Survival: A Population History since 1492* (Norman: University of Oklahoma Press, 1987), p. 70. C. Matthew Snipp, *American Indians: The First of This Land* (New York: Russell Sage Foundation, 1989), pp. 1–25. For an interesting collection of recent research, see John W. Verano and Douglas H. Ubelaker, eds., *Disease and Demography in the Americas* (Washington, D.C.: Smithsonian Institution Press, 1992).

9. Historians have debated whether nineteenth-century European immigrants — primarily Irish, German, and English newcomers — congregated in the city more on the basis of their occupations or their ethnic background. See Russell A. Kazal, "Revisiting Assimilation: The Rise, Fall, and Reappraisal of a Concept in American Ethnic History," *American Historical Review* 100 (1995): 437–71. For the view that industry more than ethnicity determined the residential patterns of nineteenth-century Philadelphia, at least where European Americans were concerned see Theodore Hershberg, Stephanie W. Greenberg, Alan N. Burstein, William L. Yancey, and Eugene P. Erickson, "A Tale of Three Cities: Blacks, Immigrants, and Opportunity in Philadelphia, 1850–1880, 1930, 1970," *Philadelphia: Work, Space, Family, and Group Experience in the Nineteenth Century* ed. Theodore Hershberg (New York: Oxford University Press, 1981) pp. 461–91.

10. Hershberg et al., "Tale of Three Cities," pp. 471–78, tables 4, 5, 6, and 7; Douglas S. Massey and Nancy A. Denton, *American Apartheid: Segregation and the Making of the Underclass* (Cambridge, Mass.: Harvard University Press, 1993).

11. Carolyn Adams, David Bartelt, David Elesh, Ira Goldstein, Nancy Kleniewski, and William Yancey, *Philadelphia: Neighborhoods, Division and Conflict in a Postindustrial City* (Philadelphia: Temple University Press, 1991), pp. 30–55.

12. Also see William Julius Wilson, *The Truly Disadvantaged: The Inner City, the Underclass, and Public Policy* (Chicago: University of Chicago Press, 1987), pp. 134–35.

13. Hershberg et al., "Tale of Three Cities," pp. 477, 475 table 5, 481 table 9. Note that the percentages for 1930 and 1970 are only roughly comparable, in that the former are for males and females over the age of 9, while the latter are for males and females over the age of 15.

14. Hershberg et al., "Tale of Three Cities," pp. 481 table 9, 464.

15. In order to standardize the population, I have recorded the population in each age group for the English population and the age-specific death rates for both the European and African American populations. Next, I computed the cumulative product of the English population and the age-specific death rates. Finally, I divided the resulting product by the total English population for both the European and African American populations. The result is the age-standardized rate. E. A. Wrigley and R. S. Schofield, *The Population History of England, 1541–1871* (Cambridge: Cambridge University Press, 1981).

16. Gretchen A. Condran, "Ethnic Differences in Mortality in the Nineteenth Century: A Case Study of Philadelphia, 1880–1881" (paper presented at the Annual Meeting of the Population Association of America, Pittsburgh, 1983).

17. In my calculations, income status is defined as poor, middle class, and upper class. A family's membership in one of these three categories depends on its family income relative to other family incomes of that census year in the city of Phila-

delphia. A family is poor if its income is less than half the mean income of that year. An upper-class family is one whose income is twice the mean or higher. All other families are counted as middle class.

18. In a footnote, DuBois stated that "It will be noted that this classification differs materially from the economic division in Chapter XI. In that case grade four and a part of three appear as the "poor;" grade two and the rest of grade three, as the "fair to comfortable;" and a few of grade two and grade one as the well-to-do. The basis of division there was almost entirely according to income; this division brings in moral considerations and questions of expenditure, and consequently reflects more largely the personal judgement of the investigator" (p. 311).

19. Adams et al., *Philadelphia*, pp. 66–99.

20. Green and Driver, "A Case in the Sociology of Sociological Negation," 308–33.

21. See Joyce A. Ladner, *Tomorrow's Tomorrow: The Black Woman* (Lincoln: University of Nebraska Press, 1971); Herbert G. Gutman, *The Black Family in Slavery and Freedom, 1750–1925* (New York: Vintage, 1976); Jacqueline Jones, *Labor of Love, Labor of Sorrow: Black Women, Work, and the Family from Slavery to the Present* (New York: Basic Books, 1985); Antonio McDaniel, "The Power of Culture: A Review of the Idea of Africa's Influence on Family Structure in Antebellum America," *Journal of Family History* 15, 2 (1990): 225–38.

22. On Philadelphia's female workforce, see Bruce Laurie and Mark Schmitz, "Manufacture and Productivity: The Making of an Industrial Base, Philadelphia, 1850–1880," in Hershberg, *Philadelphia*, pp. 46–47; and Claudia Goldin, "Family Strategies and the Family Economy in the Late Nineteenth Century: The Role of Secondary Workers," in Hershberg, *Philadelphia*, pp. 46–47, 296–304.

23. For examples of some of this research see: Gutman, *Black Family in Slavery and Freedom*; "The Search for Applicable Theories of Black Family Life," *Journal of Marriage and the Family* 40 (1978): 117–29; McDaniel, "The Power of Culture"; Antonio McDaniel, "Historical Racial Differences in Living Arrangements of Children," *Journal of Family History* 19, 1 (1994): 57–77.

24. "Eurocentric" refers to the tradition of assuming that Europe and European peoples should be the point of departure for understanding social behavior. The Eurocentric perspective that has dominated the American and European academy views Europe as the exclusive birthplace of "high civilization." The remainder of humanity is judged on the basis of their closeness to the European model of behavior and achievements.

25. John Brown Childs writes about the history of this idea in his essay "Afro-American Intellectuals and the People's Culture," *Theory and Society* 13 (1984): 69–90. The idea that the African American scholar had a unique role to play in social development and in the enrichment of social discourse dates back to DuBois's Talented Tenth and Alain Locke's New Negro, and to A. Philip Randolph's "vanguard." Patricia Hill Collins elaborates on this idea in her essay "Learning from the Outsider Within: The Sociological Significance of Black Feminist Thought," *Social Problems* 33, no. 6 (1986): 514–31.

26. Lewis, *DuBois*, pp. 206–7, 179–80.

27. DuBois's classic effort was not replicated by mainstream sociology. Early-twentieth-century sociology was dominated by the Chicago School tradition of using the city as a laboratory for studying immigrant assimilation, and racial isolation became a special case of the problems of assimilation. For some classic examples of the Chicago School tradition see: Robert E. Park and Ernest W. Burgess, *The City* (Chicago: University of Chicago Press, 1925); Louis Wirth, *The Ghetto* (Chicago: University of Chicago Press, 1928); E. Franklin Frazier, *The Negro Family in Chicago* (Chicago: University of Chicago Press, 1932).

28. The Darwinian emphasis on the importance of heredity restricted the possibilities of social reform by stressing the limitations of human capacity. The idea that nature was continually selecting for fitness also suggested that humanitarian attempts to promote equality were of little avail. Two strains in Social Darwinist thought helped further the cause of racism: (1) that whether or not pure races had ever existed in the past, they would exist in the future because natural selection would lead to the emergence of specialized interbreeding populations; and (2) that racism had an evolutionary function. Racism caused members of one group to hate those of another and identify with their own; it accelerated the process of race purification. In the earlier conceptualization, race was a concept in comparative morphology, but the Social Darwinists conceptualized racial modification and racial purification as a process. Social Darwinism was an influential train of thought that contributed an important element to the ideology of racism in the late nineteenth and early twentieth century. This line of thought was applied most readily to social relations in the writings of Herbert Spencer, Lester Ward, and Charles Ellwood in the English speaking intellectual circles.

29. This citation comes from the classic study by St. Clair Drake and Horace R. Cayton, *Black Metropolis: A Study of Negro Life in a Northern City* (1945; reprint, Chicago: University Chicago Press, 1993), p. 551. However, as I mentioned, the Chicago School dominated early pre-1940 research on race relations. The main model of racial and ethnic stratification in the early-twentieth century used the city of Chicago as the laboratory for the scientific investigation of racial and immigrant assimilation. Both Robert E. Park and Ernest W. Burgess, the fathers of the Chicago School of urban sociology, viewed the problems of immigrant slums as a problem of temporary conditions that would be resolved by accommodation and assimilation. The African American immigrants from the North were represented as a group of migrants in the process of assimilation.

In the 1940s, *The Yankee City* series edited by W. Lloyd Warner presented evidence of how many members of ethnic groups had climbed up the class ladder and "assimilated." The social stigma of belonging to the ethnic group rapidly disappeared, freeing upper-class members of the group to try to move to higher levels; however, when this research was extended to issues of race in the South it became apparent that alongside class stratification was racial stratification. In *Deep South: A Social Anthropological Study of Caste and Class* (Chicago: University of Chicago Press, 1941), Allison Davis, Burleigh B. Garner, and Mary R. Gardner argued that the social system organized the lives of African Americans into a subordinate level and the lives of European Americans into a superordinate level. In 1945, Drake and Cayton's *Black Metropolis* returned to the DuBoisian model of the race problem. Like DuBois, Drake and Cayton emphasized the social relations of race and class positions within the society. Thus, class and culture included position in the racial hierarchy, family, clique, church, voluntary association, school, and job, rather than the arbitrary approach of defining classes by looking at statistical distributions of income or rent. Like DuBois in certain sections of *The Philadelphia Negro*, Drake and Cayton viewed the racial composition of Chicago as the product of racially prejudicial and calculating practices and decisions.

30. For more extensive discussion of the mechanisms of this marginalization and otherness see Collins, "Learning from the Outsider Within"; Harold Cruse, *The Crisis of the Negro Intellectual: A Historical Analysis of the Failure of Black Leadership* (New York: Quill, 1967); Cornel West, *Keeping Faith: Philosophy and Race in America* (New York: Routledge, 1993), chap. 5.

31. Carter G. Woodson, *The Mis-Education of the Negro* (Washington, D.C.: Associated Publishers, 1933), p. xiii.

32. Woodson's book is the classic statement of this position; however Arthur A. Schomburg actually articulated the same concern several years earlier in his essay "Racial Integrity: A Plea for the Establishment of a Chair of Negro History in Our Schools and Colleges, etc.," *Negro Society for Historical Research Occasional Papers* 3 (1913). On the differences among various African American intellectuals regarding this issue see John Brown Childs, "Afro-American Intellectuals and the People's Culture," *Theory and Society* 13 (1984): 69–90; Cruse, *Crisis of the Negro Intellectual.* More recently Cornel West has observed that African American intellectuals have often found "success" only by capitulating "often uncritically, to the prevailing paradigms and research programs of the white bourgeois academy." *Keeping Faith,* p. 72.

33. After all it was DuBois who wrote:

Keep not thou silent, O God!
   Sit not longer blind, Lord God, deaf to our prayer and dumb to our dumb suffering. Surely Thou, too art not white, O Lord, a pale, bloodless, heartless thing!
   Ah! Christ of all the Pities!
   Forgive the thought! Forgive these wild, blasphemous words! Thou art still God or our black fathers and in thy Soul's Soul sit some soft darkening of the evening, some shadowing of the velvet night.
   But whisper — speak — call, Great God, for the silence is white terror to our hearts! The way, O God, show us the way and point us the path! *Darkwater: Voices from Within the Veil* (New York: Brace and Howe, 1920), p. 27.

34. "Nevertheless the Negro problems are not more hopelessly complex than many others have been. Their elements despite their bewildering complication can be kept clearly in view: they are after all the same difficulties over which the world has grown gray: the question as to how far human intelligence can be trusted and trained; as to whether we must always have the poor with us; as to whether it is possible for the mass of men to attain righteousness on earth; and then to this is added that question of questions: after all who are Men? Is every featherless biped to be counted a man and brother? Are all races and types to be joint heirs of the new earth that men have striven to raise in thirty centuries and more? Shall we not swamp civilization in barbarism and drown genius in indulgence if we seek a mythical Humanity which shall shadow all men?" (pp. 385–86).

35. E. Franklin Frazier, *Black Bourgeoisie: The Rise of a New Middle Class in the United States* (New York: Collier, 1957), pp. 193–94.

36. Wilson, *Truly Disadvantaged,* p. 7.

37. He noted himself that at this point in his intellectual development his research agenda "was weak on its economic side." He argued that "the program ought to have been . . . the Economic Development of the American Negro Slave; on this central thread all the other subjects would have been strung." DuBois, *Autobiography,* p. 217. For some examples of the development of DuBois's thinking on class see *Black Reconstruction* (New York: Harcourt, Brace, 1935); his 1936 unpublished essay "The Negro and Social Reconstruction," in *Against Racism: Unpublished Essays, Papers, Addresses, 1887–1961,* ed. Herbert Aptheker (Amherst: University of Massachusetts Press, 1985), pp. 103–58; and *The World and Africa: An Inquiry into the Part Which Africa has Played in World History* (New York: Viking Press, 1946).

Figure 19. Wharton Settlement officials publicized the activities of "Operation Street Corner" through before-and-after photographs such as "Street Corner Hangout" and "Gang Boys Reformed," 1949. Courtesy of Temple University, Urban Archives.

Chapter 7

Operation Street Corner
*The Wharton Centre and the Juvenile Gang Problem
in Philadelphia, 1945–1958*

V. P. Franklin

> It is right and proper that Negro boys and girls should desire to rise as
> high in the world as their ability and just desert entitle them. They
> should be ever encouraged and urged to do so, although they should be
> taught also that idleness and crime are beneath and not above the
> lowest work. . . . Further, some rational means of amusement should be
> furnished the young folks. Prayer meetings and church socials have
> their place, but they cannot compete in attractiveness with the dance
> halls and gambling dens of the city. There is a legitimate demand for
> amusement on the part of the young which may be made a means of
> education, improvement, and recreation.
> —W.E.B. DuBois, *The Philadelphia Negro*

In "The Final Word," the last chapter of the now-classic work *The Philadelphia Negro: A Social Study*, the young social scientist W.E.B. DuBois tried to
make clear "the meaning of all this," especially regarding "the duty of the
whites" and "the duty of the Negroes." White Philadelphians, he argued
forcefully, must end their blatantly discriminatory treatment of their black
fellow citizens. "Such discrimination is morally wrong, politically dangerous, industrially wasteful, and socially silly. It is the duty of the whites to stop
it, and to do so primarily for their own sakes. Industrial freedom of opportunity has by long experience proven to be generally best for all" (p. 394).

At the same time, he contended that black Philadelphians have a duty to
take up all the advantages of "civilized society." "Simply because the ancestors of the present white inhabitants of America went out of their way barba-
rously to mistreat and enslave the ancestors of the present black inhabitants
gives those blacks no right to ask that the civilization and morality of the

land be seriously menaced for their benefit" (p. 389). DuBois advocated black self-determination and called on the Negro to "bend his energy to the solving of his own social problems — contributing to his poor, paying his share of the taxes and supporting the schools and public administration." Although black Philadelphians should seek the assistance of others in bringing about "self-development. . . . the bulk of the work of raising the Negro must be done by the Negro himself, and the greatest help for him will be not to hinder and curtail and discourage his efforts" (pp. 389–90).

Black Philadelphians had a long history of self-help activities stemming back to the late eighteenth century. DuBois described these in *The Philadelphia Negro*. In addition to the efforts of the black churches, insurance societies, educational and welfare institutions, and fraternal organizations, Philadelphia has a long-standing tradition of interracial cooperation, led by members of the Society of Friends, in providing social welfare and educational services for black Philadelphians. Philadelphia Quakers practiced a distinct brand of philanthropy: they often provided financial support for social services for black Philadelphians, to be carried out and administered by black professionals.[1]

One of the most noteworthy examples of this "Quaker beneficence and black control" was Philadelphia's Institute for Colored Youth, opened in 1848 through the philanthropic efforts of Quaker goldsmith Richard Humphries. From its inception, the Institute, unlike many of its nineteenth-century counterparts, had an all-black staff. Trustees of educational institutions sponsored by mainstream, white Protestant denominations, such as the American Baptists, Presbyterians, and Congregationalists, rarely hired African Americans as teachers and administrators. Although the Institute's Quaker board of directors made all the financial decisions and hired the teachers and administrators, principal Fannie Jackson Coppin and the black staff provided all the school's instructional and educational services and made sure that the Institute was an important element in the social advancement of black Philadelphians. By 1896, when DuBois came to the city, the Institute was considered one of the finest academic high schools in the city, famous for having trained some of Philadelphia's most prominent black leaders (pp. 87, 95).[2]

The hiring of the young Dr. W.E.B. DuBois to conduct a study of blacks in the Seventh Ward, like the creation of the Institute for Colored Youth, grew out of Quaker-led efforts to improve the social circumstances of blacks in Philadelphia. The city's distinctive pattern of interracial cooperation continued in the twentieth century, most notably with the founding of the Susan Parrish Wharton Memorial Settlement House, or Wharton Centre, in North Philadelphia in 1931. Although the Wharton Centre was funded largely by Quakers and other white philanthropists, both blacks and whites served on its board of directors, and African American professionals developed and administered the social programs aimed particularly at improving the conditions of black youth.

Susan Parrish Wharton and Black Social Welfare in Philadelphia

The Wharton Centre grew out of the prodigious social welfare activities of a leading Philadelphia Quaker philanthropist and DuBois's primary funder and supporter, Susan Parrish Wharton. Having come from a family that had long been active in social and moral reform movements, Wharton not surprisingly became a social activist. Her maternal grandfather, Dr. Joseph Parrish, was known for his opposition to capital punishment, for support of improved treatment for the mentally ill, and especially for his work in the antislavery movement. Susan's mother, Susanna Parrish Wharton, was active in philanthropic groups devoted to the treatment of alcoholics and the problems of American Indians. In addition, Susanna Wharton was one of the founders of Philadelphia's Children's Aid Society and encouraged her daughter to help needy children in any way she could.[3]

Wharton was closely tied to a series of ventures to improve the housing and living conditions of Philadelphia's Fifth Ward, an area with some of the city's most dilapidated housing and poorest families. In 1880 philanthropist Theodore Starr purchased a lot on Saint Mary Street in South Philadelphia and built the first of several homes he rented at low cost to black residents of the area. When Susan Parrish Wharton graduated from Vassar College in 1884, she opened Saint Mary Street Library, near the Starr homes, for poor black children. Wharton was joined at the library by her cousin Helen Parrish; together they worked closely to found a branch of the Octavia Hill Association in Philadelphia in 1888, a housing reform group that purchased and renovated dilapidated housing in the city to rent and sell to poor and working-class families. Wharton also continued her activities at Saint Mary Street, opening a cooking school in 1890, offering penny lunches to poor children in 1894, and sponsoring a kindergarten in 1901. In 1892, Susan P. Wharton, drawing from a network of female college graduates interested in social reform, invited the College Settlement Association to establish a branch in Philadelphia in one of the houses originally built by Theodore Starr, which Wharton had acquired in 1890. The Saint Mary Street Library and Neighborhood House merged with the College Settlement Association in 1892.[4]

Susan Wharton played a crucial role in the invitation of DuBois to Philadelphia. At her home in fall 1895, she convinced University of Pennsylvania provost Charles Harrison to bring the young Harvard- and Berlin-trained scholar, W.E.B. DuBois, to the city to carry out research on the black population in the Seventh Ward. When DuBois and his wife Nina arrived in the city in August 1896, they lived at the Philadelphia Settlement at 700 Lombard

Street until the summer of 1897, when they moved to 2325 Saint Albans Street.[5]

In 1893, even before she invited DuBois to the city to conduct his monumental study, Susan Wharton and a number of social reformers had founded the Whittier Centre for the Study and Practical Solution of Negro City Problems. Its purpose was to organize and coordinate philanthropic programs in South Philadelphia aimed at poor black migrants. By the 1890s, Philadelphia (unlike other northern cities that did not attract migrants until the World War I era) was drawing a steady flow of African Americans from Virginia, North and South Carolina, Georgia, and other southeastern states. Pushed out of their homes by the disastrous consequences of the crop lien and sharecropping systems, many sought better economic opportunities in the North. The depressed economic situation for southern sharecroppers was only one of the reasons for the northern black migration. The lack of educational opportunities in the South, the failure to allow blacks to participate in politics or even vote in southern elections, as well as official segregation and unofficial threats, intimidation, and violence associated with campaigns for "white supremacy," all served as important factors in pushing African Americans out of the South.[6]

At the same time, a number of important economic factors pulled southern blacks to these northern cities. Philadelphia, for example, was one of the largest industrial centers on the East Coast. It also had a large and deeply rooted resident black community. Migrants to the city in the 1890s or early 1900s were often able to find employment, not in the factories, but in various service areas. Because of pervasive employment discrimination in Philadelphia's white-owned businesses, blacks were normally considered only for what had already been designated as "Negro jobs." But in the expanding urban economy at the turn of the century, even these Negro jobs were a vast improvement over those available at home.[7]

Upon arriving in Philadelphia, southern migrants faced the problem of finding adequate and affordable housing. In *The Philadelphia Negro* DuBois reported that newcomers who settled in the Seventh Ward found high rents, overcrowding, and unsanitary health conditions, and that "over 20 per cent and possibly 30 per cent of the Negro families of this ward lack some of the very elementary accommodations necessary to health and decency." Apartments were divided by landlords, and "back tenements" were opened in alleys for new arrivals. "Most of these houses have to get their water at the hydrant in the alley, and must store their fuel in the house." DuBois concluded that "these tenement abominations of Philadelphia are perhaps better than the vast tenements of New York, but they are bad enough, and cry for reform" (pp. 293–94).

The influx of southern black migrants increased in the early 1900s. In April 1913 the Whittier Centre, in cooperation with the Philadelphia Housing Association, sponsored a survey of housing and living conditions in the

Seventh Ward. The staff of the Whittier Centre visited 1,075 black families and reported that except for the exorbitant rents, "the housing problem for the race differs in no wise from that of any other race. All alike suffer from laxity of the city, the lack of a definite program for sanitary improvements, the burden of a reactionary city council that knows no energy save to defeat or delay that which is good for the people." In the fifteen years since DuBois had lived in the Seventh Ward, housing conditions there had improved little.[8]

In an attempt to deal with these conditions, the Whittier Centre Housing Company was incorporated in May 1916 to provide "good sanitary homes" for black Philadelphians. Susan Parrish Wharton was instrumental in forming the Company and served as its vice president. By the end of 1916, the Housing Company used the money raised through the sale of stocks at $50.00 per share to purchase property for the construction of seventy two-family homes in a black neighborhood at Dickerson and Opal Streets in South Philadelphia. The new homes were then rented or sold to black families at very low rates of interest.[9]

Throughout the 1920s the Whittier Centre's philanthropic activities aimed at the improvement of the social conditions for the large black population in South Philadelphia. The Centre's mix of interventionist philanthropy and self-help would not have been unfamiliar in the Philadelphia of the young DuBois, a few decades earlier. The Centre sponsored Thrift Clubs, Coal Clubs, and Rainy Day Societies to encourage working-class blacks to save some of their money in case of a family emergency. In 1920 the tuberculosis rate among blacks was twice that of whites in the city, and the Whittier Centre paid the salaries for visiting nurses to work with black families with tubercular patients. The Centre also paid the salary of the black nurses who worked directly with black tuberculosis victims at nearby Phipps Institute. By October 1924 "at the Phipps Institute the colored staff consist of six graduate nurses, one student nurse, and three physicians; of these, three nurses are supplied by the Whittier Centre, three nurses and three physicians by the Philadelphia Health Council; at the Jefferson Hospital (Department for Diseases of the Chest) one colored physician and one colored nurse are supplied by the Philadelphia Health Council." The Centre encouraged the hiring of black hospital staff to service the health needs of the black population. This was considered "the logical method" for dealing with black health problems.[10]

Hiring black hospital staff represented an important policy shift in Quaker-funded social welfare activities aimed at Philadelphia's African American community. From the 1880s through the 1920s, white social work professionals had provided services to black Philadelphians. The social welfare workers who supported DuBois were all white. One reason for this was the lack of black social welfare professionals available to the College Settlement, the Whittier Centre, and other agencies. However, by the early 1920s, more and more college trained black professionals became available, as scholars like DuBois introduced the social sciences into black college curricula and to schools like Atlanta University, Fisk, and Howard. Beginning with the black nurses, Susan P. Wharton advocated the hiring of black professionals to provide health and social services for the black population.[11]

Black Migration to North Philadelphia

The migration of southern blacks to Philadelphia continued throughout the 1920s. According to census data, the city's black population increased from 134,224 in 1920 to 219,599 in 1930, a 63.5 percent increase in one decade. The greater part of this increase was the result of the increasing migration of southern blacks to the city. However, unlike earlier newcomers who often were confined to the densely settled back alleys of the Seventh and Thirtieth Wards in South Philadelphia, African Americans were beginning to move by the early 1920s into the less desirable sections of north-central Philadelphia. Although some upper-status blacks, the so-called Old Philadelphians, were able to afford housing in middle-class neighborhoods, especially those located near Fairmount Park, the southern migrants were forced into the older houses found east and west of Broad Street between Ridge and Huntington Avenues.[12]

The staff of the Whittier Centre had been aware of this movement from the mid-1920s. For example, it sponsored the opening in March 1923 of a tuberculosis clinic specifically geared to the treatment of black patients in North Philadelphia at Twentieth Street and Ridge Avenue. The Whittier Centre furnished one, then later two nurses during the decade.[13] By the end of the 1920s numerous social agencies from both North Philadelphia and other parts of the city began to meet and discuss the problems that the new black residents faced. At a meeting of the North Philadelphia Advisory Committee of the Philadelphia Welfare Federation held at the Reynolds Public School in November 1927, the representative from the Philadelphia Board of Public Education, Albert Whitaker, pointed out that in the North Philadelphia district (no. 5), the school census revealed a dramatic increase in black pupils. "Ten years ago, in 1917, — 5.4% of the school population was colored, today 14.5% is colored." Whitaker also discussed the social problems the investigation disclosed. For example, "it was found that many mothers in the district worked every day and left their little children at home without a mother's care. . . . In connection with the annual school census, a survey of the Children of Working Mothers was made. It was discovered that from Thompson to Diamond Street and from 15th to 26th Street there were 3,760 families who have school children. Of that number 868 were working mothers. 22% of the children were uncared for." Whitaker found "in viewing the needs of the community, I would place first the need of the Day Nursery to care for the children under school age." But there were other pressing needs. He mentioned the lack of free employment agencies in the area. At private employment agencies, "parents pay as high as $15.00 for an ordinary job." Housing was both overpriced and overcrowded. Investigators discovered that "houses which were originally built for one family are now occupied by 4 and 6 families. . . . Many of these families are paying $6 or $7 [a week] for the one room, in which they live."[14]

Lena Trent Gordon, one of the first African Americans to be employed by the city's Department of Public Welfare as a "special investigator," reported on another set of problems. "I find that in the [Public Employment] Intelligence Offices on Arch Street the positions formerly requiring colored people are now held by white people," declared Gordon. "This week not one colored person's name appeared on the bulletin boards. Factories have closed, turning out as many as 6,000 white people at a time. I certainly hope that we can establish a Free Employment Department where people who cannot afford to pay extortionate prices for positions may obtain them free of charge." She called for the formation of a "Volunteer Committee of Colored Women" to assist the increasing numbers of working mothers in North Philadelphia.[15]

Many of the white philanthropists present, however, sidestepped the serious problems of unemployment and women's work that Gordon had highlighted. Instead, they retreated to conventional philanthropy and social work. Susan Parrish Wharton, who attended the November 1927 meeting representing the Whittier Centre, emphasized those areas where the Centre had previously been active in South Philadelphia—supplying "penny lunches" to schoolchildren, organizing savings banks, and opening playgrounds—and mentioned that she was "sure that this [meeting] is the beginning of a great event in North Philadelphia." And Gordon H. Simpson, executive secretary of the Whittier Centre, revealed that a "plan of a community center in North Philadelphia has the strongest backing of a Special Committee of the Educational Department of the Council of Social Agencies of the Welfare Federation."[16]

Wharton and her colleagues held out the hope, rooted in Progressive era social welfare philosophy and theories of racial uplift, that recreational activities would materially improve the lives of poor children. Subsequently, the board of directors of the Whittier Centre commissioned a "Study Regarding Recreation for Colored People in North Philadelphia." Completed by Emily C. P. Longstreth in March 1929 and supported fully by Susan Wharton, the survey was based on interviews with over twenty agency representatives as well as black and white residents of the section. Longstreth reported that "in talking to people in the district I try to get from them the kind of recreation the people really want. Playgrounds for all ages of boys and girls with gymnasium and swimming pools seem very necessary. Also the Community Center or Neighborhood House having a Boys' Club, Girls' Club, Mothers' Club, etc. for recreational and cultural activities." Longstreth, however, rejected the model of white-dominated social work that had prevailed earlier in the century and emphasized that "most, if not all, of the staff should be Negroes."[17]

Although Susan Parrish Wharton died in July 1929, the board of directors of the Whittier Centre voted to move ahead on the plan to open a community center in North Philadelphia for African Americans and to pursue the activity as a memorial to Wharton. Fund-raising campaigns were carried out in 1929 and 1930; by the middle of 1931 over $30,000 had been secured for the purchase of two buildings and a large movie house on Twenty-second Street near Ridge Avenue. The Susan Parrish Wharton Memorial Settlement House, or Wharton Centre, was officially dedicated and opened in October 1931, and the annual reports described a wide range of activities and programs. Following in the tradition of youth activities that Wharton herself had pioneered at her Saint Mary Street settlement, the Wharton Centre's buildings were used for various clubs—the Cooking Club, Home Makers Club, Boys Handicraft Club, and Mothers Club—as well as for Boy and Girl Scout units. A movie theater on the site was converted to a gymnasium that housed "the various teams of the Settlement": boys' and girls' basketball, baseball, football, and others. During the summer, trips to the park, hikes, plays, and picnics as well as handicraft classes and outdoor showers were offered. The Centre's first annual report also noted that "all members of the staff are Negroes, carefully chosen for their ability and experience. The Board of Directors realizes that the great success of the undertaking is largely due to the skill and tact of these workers."[18]

DuBoisian Social Welfare Program for Black Youth

In his section "The Duty of the Negroes," DuBois emphasized that black Philadelphians had a responsibility to the young people in their community to provide constructive recreational activities; otherwise, the youth would be lost "to crime, disease, and death." DuBois urged the expansion of employment opportunities in the trades, commerce, and industry, as well as healthful recreation in homes, churches, and schools, particularly for the girls, as an alternative to the "gambling dens . . . saloons and clubs and bawdy houses." "Day-nurseries and sewing-schools, mothers meetings, the parks and airing places, all these things are little known or appreciated among the masses of Negroes, and their attention should be directed to them." DuBois believed that "the vast amount of preventive and rescue work" aimed at black youth must be carried out "by the Negroes themselves" (pp. 391–92).

From its opening in 1931, the staff of the Wharton Settlement actively pursued a program that was consistent with DuBois's recommendations. Throughout its history, most of the administrators and staff at the Wharton Centre were African American and, for the most part, could be considered members of the group DuBois referred to as the "Talented Tenth." According to DuBois, the "College-Bred Negro" represented "an aristocracy of talent and character" within the African American population whose knowledge and expertise should be used to uplift the black masses. "The Talented Tenth of the race," he declared in his famous 1903 essay, "must be made leaders of thought and missionaries of culture to their people. No others can do this work and the Negro colleges must train men for it. The Negro race, like all other races, is going to saved by its exceptional men."[19]

In the case of the Wharton Settlement, from the beginning its programs were planned and administered by college-bred Negro men and women. When it began operation in October 1931, the Board of Directors appointed John Caswell Smith as director and headworker and Claudia Grant became the girls headworker. Although neither had previous social work training, both were educators who had worked for the Young Men's and Young Women's Christian Association (YMCA and YWCA). John Caswell Smith was a graduate of Springfield College (Massachusetts), where he majored in physical education. There he worked for the YMCA before becoming an instructor of physical education at Virginia State College in Petersburg, Virginia. Claudia Grant, who became the director in 1937 and who remained in that position until her retirement in June 1965, was a graduate of Howard University. Before coming to the Wharton Centre she had taught elementary school in Phoenix, Arizona, and had worked with the YWCA in Pittsburgh.[20]

Journalist G. James Fleming interviewed Claudia Grant shortly after she became the director of the Centre for an October 1940 article that appeared in the *Philadelphia Tribune*, the most important black newspaper in the city.[21] Grant explained how the Centre's program had evolved over the previous nine years from an emphasis on recreation to one on individual development:

As the early years passed by, the workers and directors of the Wharton Settlement realized that merely providing recreation for masses of people was not doing particularly much good for anyone. Because of this realization, in recent years more time has been spent attempting to bring out in individuals certain undiscovered abilities which no one knew they had, as well as providing education and recreation.[22]

Nine years after it opened, the Wharton Settlement broke from the narrow emphasis on recreation that had motivated its founders. It not only provided sports programs, a glee club, art and dance classes, handicrafts, and musical training, it also sponsored groups devoted to worker education, parent-teacher relations, and public health issues. The Wharton Centre's offerings also reflected the "black vision" of social welfare. Historian Linda Gordon has noted that in contrast with many whites in the social welfare movement, black reformers advocated and provided programs to assist working mothers, especially through employment bureaus and day nurseries. Many black social welfare reformers upheld the idea that mothers should be supported by their husbands and remain at home with the children, but they acknowledged the fact that in the black community many single or married mothers had to work to support themselves and their families. Thus the Centre provided a day nursery and prenatal care for expectant women.[23]

With regard to the teenagers, the Wharton Centre's staff emphasized "preventive work" in the form of guidance and counseling to keep the young people from getting into trouble. "In the new emphasis," Claudia Grant noted, "those who share in the Wharton program are made more valuable to themselves" and their community. Journalist G. James Fleming also interviewed several youthful clients at the Wharton Centre for his 1940 *Philadelphia Tribune* article.

While waiting in the lobby of the Settlement, the writer asked a few of the boys and girls entering what the Settlement means to them.

"Wharton Settlement pulled me out of the dumps," Leo Strothers replied.

"It allows boys and girls to develop their talents and athletics," answered James Edwards. "It helps bring out the best characteristics that different boys have and shows what they are really made of."

"One reason I like the center is because it takes you out of the street and when you have no place to go, you can come here and do any activity you like, so that later in life you can better take care of yourself" is the way Lee James put it.[24]

The advent of U.S. participation in World War II brought new problems for black youth in North Philadelphia, according to the staff at the Wharton Centre. Responding to the dramatic increase in the area's juvenile gang problem, the Wharton Centre started an innovative new program called Operation Street Corner. In a February 1943 report, director Claudia Grant estimated that "approximately 150 of our boys over 18 are already serving in the armed forces, and 48 or 50 others are waiting their scheduled date of leaving. Several of our families have as many as 3 and 4 boys from the same family in the services." The young men over eighteen and not in the armed services were largely employed in the "defense plants . . . working on the round the clock shifts with long hours and little time for recreational activities."[25] In the annual report for 1944, however, the staff expressed some alarm at the conditions. "The teen age story at present, like that of many other settlements all over the country, is of course one which gives us great concern." They found that despite the new opportunities available as a result of the war, "many of the same problems of rendering an effective group work service to these young people during the years of mass unemployment are prevalent at the present time." Wharton staff noted the disruptive effects of war:

Life for these young people as for all people in a state of flux. . . . The future holds promise but in a great degree it holds fear and frustration. In an effort to live in so much confusion, values are lost and standards are lowered. Life is no longer sacred and secure. Youth seems imbued with a "live today and live dangerously attitude." In addition, education and long time planning has been replaced by immediate jobs and unheard of wages.

Despite the absence of several members of the Wharton staff who had been drafted into the armed services, the report called for "greater cooperation and coordination of public, private, and national organizations to cope with the complex problems of youth. We must bring to this work not only our knowledge and experience of the past, but current developments, skills and new insight in the present."[26]

Beginning in 1944 and continuing into 1945, the Centre's staff conducted an extensive survey of the social needs for youth in the area and developed a "neighborhood plan" for dealing with the problem of teenage gangs. "The Plan" called for the hiring of several social workers to "make contact with neighborhood boys, gain their confidence and help them plan programs of activity." The Centre's staff wanted "to learn more about work with boys" and "to learn how to develop constructive group activity — group realization and individual realization."[27]

The Gang Problem in Philadelphia

Beginning in the 1920s, Philadelphians reported problems with juvenile gangs in numerous sections of the city. Often groups of youth turned to criminal activities on a grand scale and became a bane to their working-class neighbors. The notorious Forty Thieves was one gang in North Philadelphia that attracted particular attention in the early 1930s. The *Philadelphia Tribune* presented running accounts of the group's misadventures over several years and was happy to report in February 1933 that several members of the "40 Thieves [had been] imprisoned as Robbers." Two gangs in West Philadelphia, The Tops and The Bottoms, also terrorized local residents in the 1930s and 1940s; local newspapers regularly condemned their constant warfare.[28]

In the late 1930s and 1940s Samuel Evans, a community organizer and president of the North Philadelphia Youth Movement, had focused a great deal of local and national attention on what could be done to help stem the growing juvenile gang violence. Formed in January 1937, the North Philadelphia Youth Movement organized teenagers to work for community improvement. Through Evans's efforts, "Youth City" was created in the North Philadelphia area east of Broad Street, and gang-related incidents diminished greatly as the teenagers shifted their activities to patrolling and guaranteeing the safety and security of the residents of the neighborhood. Local churches also took up collections to support the teenagers' efforts through "Youth City Sunday" activities.[29]

West of Broad Street, in the neighborhood surrounding the Wharton

Settlement, numerous teenage gangs thrived, untouched by Evans and his youth movement. A survey carried out by the Wharton Centre staff in 1945 and 1946 revealed that there were at least twenty gangs in the area and "eight in the immediate vicinity of the settlement." "The Warders," for example, was really "a collection of gangs, rather than one particular gang." There were five known groups. "They take in the area from 19th St. on the East to 22nd St. on the West and Diamond St. on the South to Dauphin St. on the North." "The Village" consisted of three gangs in the area between Twenty-fourth and Twenty-eighth, York and Dauphin Streets. The ones closest to the Centre in 1946 were the Twentieth and Norris Streets Gang and the Seventeenth and Norris Streets Gang. W. Miller Barbour, a student at Temple University, conducted the survey and became one of the earliest gang workers. He pointed out that "all along Norris St. are a number of different gang[s] that occasionally will fight among themselves, but always unite against outsiders." The other gangs surveyed included the North Coasters, Twentieth and Montgomery Avenue; the Vogueteers, who "hung out" at the Vogue Theater; the Swans, Twenty-third and Montgomery Avenue; the Mohawks, Ringgold and Taylor Streets; the Tophatters, Twenty-first and Columbia Avenue; and the Master Street Gang, Twenty-third and Master. Although each of the gangs had up to thirty members, in his comments Balbour made it clear that "these do not by any means include all of the teen-age gangs in the neighborhood served by the Settlement House or adjacent to the Settlement House area."[30]

Barbour began working closely with the gangs in the neighborhood around the Wharton Centre during the summer of 1945. He knew that fistfights between the Ward gangs and Villagers were quite common, but he also knew that the Villagers generally lost and that by the fall of 1945 there had been a deadly escalation in "gang warfare." The Wharton Centre served as a magnet for neighborhood teenagers with its Wednesday and Friday night dances. Unfortunately, these social gatherings also attracted outsiders into "the Ward" territory. "On Friday October 18th [1945] during the time that the Settlement was having its Friday night dance . . . the Villagers decided to come into the area." Earlier that week there had been an incident in which I.H., "who went around with the older Mohawks," was allegedly beaten by a group of Village boys. And on Friday the Villagers showed up at the dance "looking for boys" from the Ward.

At first they were unable to find any one because the dance being confined to the younger group none of the boys in which they were interested were in the Gym. Nevertheless they hung around Crosby Street and sure enough in time some of the boys did come. There was no apparent argument, but the shooting then began. The two boys who were shot at that we know were D. P. . . . and J. M. . . . At this time approximately 9 or 10 shots were fired. Several by-standers were narrowly missed and the whole neighborhood adjacent to Crosby Street was thrown into an uproar. The boys from the Village, however, escaped in an automobile and no one was able to get the license because the light had been put out.

On Saturday night (October 19, 1945) members of the Mohawks "went to a pool room in the Village located at 28th and Gordon. There they proceeded to break up the pool room." Sunday evening, October 20, nine to eleven Villagers invaded the Ward and surrounded the pool room at Twenty-first Street and Columbia Avenue. They were armed. "As soon as they saw the boys they thought they were looking for, the shooting began and as a result a thirteen year old girl, A. L. 2112 Columbia Avenue, was struck through the abdomen and at the time of this recording [Monday, October 21, 1945] is still very critically ill with a 50-50 chance of surviving. Two other by-standers O. B. . . . and R. T. . . . were slightly injured."

Several boys from the Ward contacted W. Miller Barbour the next evening. "Mr. Barbour, something would have to be done and done immediately," shouted one boy. The Wharton Centre's gang worker made it clear to the Warders that if they wanted help, they would have to go to the police and "give the names of the boys involved, identify them and also prosecute them." The boys agreed, and Barbour accompanied them to the police station at Nineteenth and Oxford Streets, where they offered their versions of the shootings. When the police captain asked them why they had not been to the police before, "the leader of the boys quickly pointed out that they had come to the police and that they had also gone to various agencies in an effort to solve this problem. They were there to get protection from the police or else they would have to proceed to protect themselves." When the Warders went to the second floor of the police station, they recognized three members of the rival Villagers gang who were being questioned about the Sunday evening shootings. These boys were immediately arrested, and three others involved in the incident were caught and held for a hearing. The six boys were allowed bail and held over for trial by Juvenile Court.[31] In the aftermath of the shooting and arrests, Wharton Centre workers redoubled their efforts to curb violence among North Philadelphia's black youth.

Operation Street Corner

Gang warfare was a deadly pastime, and the staff of the Wharton Centre wanted to do all they could to end it. The workers who staffed Operation Street Corner sought out local teenagers on their own turf, "even if they were organized in gangs which terrorize the neighborhood, even if they are suspicious of organized assistance, as they usually are." Their goal was to reach out to alienated youth and motivate them to turn away from violence. Workers hoped that they could organize activities that would provide an alternative to gangs. As one wrote:

The Man from Wharton Centre must be a catalyst, stimulating character potential wherever he finds it. He must be alert and sensitive to the first flicker of constructive interest and fan the interest into action by suggestion, always leaving it to the boys to carry out their own projects. The spark of constructive interest ignited in one boy, in one club spreads to inspire other boys. . . . Older brothers bring in younger ones or help them form clubs of their own. Sisters and girl friends also organize and parties and projects are often shared.

Most important, the gang worker served as a liaison between the teenage groups and the social agencies in the larger community and as an advocate for the club members in times of trouble. "[W]hen some boy tangles with the law," an Operation Street Corner "worker can stand by and help the youngster learn and not grow bitter from the experience." A promotional pamphlet recounted that:

When six club members were arrested for holding up two boys, the three members who had actually committed the misdemeanor confessed and kept the others clear. The man from Wharton stood by. He told the judge that he believed these boys and that they'd learned a lesson. The result was probation instead of three months in jail with the boys reporting regularly to the man from Wharton. There were no repeat performances.

The Centre's objective was to channel neighborhood gangs' destructive behavior into more constructive activities. They believed that membership in self-governing, quasi-governmental institutions would turn troubled youths into responsible citizens and law-abiding adults. "The gang, instead of being a chaotic group, must be helped to become an organized club. The boys carry the ball while the man from Wharton merely referees. . . . They elect their own officers, appoint their own committees, act as their own policemen, collect dues of 5c to 15c per week, purchase their own club jackets through the club treasury, vote members in or out." By 1953 Operation Street Corner included 350 former gang members, organized into fourteen clubs by two Wharton Centre staff men and one part-time student worker.[32]

Working with gangs was risky but often rewarding. In March 1953, when members of the Junior Stars informed Temple University student and gang worker James Hightower of the threats from the Eighteenth Street boys, he found them "frustrated and fearful. Some of them had secured weapons from friends for protection." But he immediately attempted to calm their fears and also "promised them that I would contact the boys from 18th Street and have a talk with them." Hightower got in touch with B. B., the leader of the boys from Eighteenth Street, but he was not interested in these appeals. B. B. claimed that "one of the Jr. Stars had hit him over the head with a Monkey Wrench and he was sorry, but he had to get even." The man from Operation Street Corner, however, did not give up. He told B. B. the violence would lead to jail. "He was indifferent and stated that he had been to jail before and did not worry about going again." The debate continued and B. B. finally agreed "to drop the hatchet" when Hightower informed him that several parents of the Junior Stars had already been to the police and alerted him of "what a couple of fathers said they would do should he or any of his friends molest their boys." Hightower continued working with both groups and even took them to the state employment office at Broad Street and Susquehanna Avenue to get job counseling. "Follow up has revealed that the boys have not gone to work as yet. However, my original purpose of encouraging the halt in plans for malicious and destructive behavior between the two groups was accomplished."[33]

When the Wharton Centre began publicizing Operation Street Corner's successes, they were flooded with requests for materials from all over the country and Canada. During an era of national concern about an alleged epidemic of juvenile delinquency, the North Philadelphia antigang efforts attracted much media attention.[34] In April 1954, group worker David Bernstein and Robert Rosenbaum, then president of the board of directors of the Wharton Centre, testified before U.S. Senate Subcommittee on Juvenile Delinquency and provided detailed information on Philadelphia's Operation Street Corner. Bernstein emphasized the Centre's reaching out to gang members on their own turf. Gang workers, he testified, were interested in "getting out to the street corner, meeting with the groups on their home ground, not asking them to come to our home ground, getting their trust, not having them come to us and have to meet our standards, whatever they might be, but we have to meet their standards in many respects."[35]

Nonetheless, not all observers considered Operation Street Corner's methods a success. In July 1953, social worker Virginia Musselman, who worked for the executive director of the National Recreation Association, requested information on Operation Street Corner. In her letter Musselman mentioned that when she was working with the Children's Bureau in New York City, she had been told "that the work done in N.Y. with street gangs somewhat on the method used at your Center had not been too successful. . . . I realize that results of this sort of work are very difficult to measure or evaluate," she wrote, but "I wonder if you have been able to set up some method of such evaluations. Your report was so optimistic that I judged that you had found some sort of measuring rod to make you feel that the work of the street corner staff had been really proved worthwhile."[36]

The letter from Musselman raised some very important questions about programs for teenagers such as Operation Street Corner. How does one measure the results of the interventions by the staff of the Centre or project? Was it worth the time and expense to organize the teenagers into clubs where Roberts Rules of Order applied, when there were no significant changes in the social conditions in the neighborhood that greeted the youngsters when they left the Centre to return home? In answering Musselman's letter, Wharton Centre executive director Claudia Grant equivocated, dodging some of the most difficult issues. She admitted that "our results have not been clearly or conclusively evaluated," but emphasized that their optimism reflected "our belief, substantiated by full and consistent process [of] recording, that we had proven that street corner work is basically no different than group work in more orthodox settings." Working with teenage gangs in the streets of North Philadelphia was merely another group activity for the Centre's staff. "[W]e can only say that the group work method can be applied as effectively on the street corner as it can in an organized building-centered program, based on our experiences."[37]

By the mid-1950s there were many other "experimental projects" aimed at ending juvenile delinquency and gang violence. Although group workers were often very optimistic about their work with teenagers, some of these projects cost the public a great deal of money and yielded few positive results. Virginia Musselman mentioned one of the projects sponsored by the New York Youth Board that cost $163,298 but claimed to have had only a minimal impact on the lives of the teenagers. "I realize that results of this sort cannot be measured in terms of money," she remarked, "but how many communities could afford to run experiments of this sort, particularly if the results do not seem — to the general lay person — to be sufficiently effective to make this type of a service part of the public program . . . ?"[38]

The staff of the Wharton Centre could point to police statistics that recorded a drop in the number of cases involving juveniles from their neighborhood. There were definitely fewer gang incidents. The staff was fond of recounting the story of the neighborhood druggist who had been terrorized by a teenage gang before the Wharton Centre's workers intervened, changing the activities and objectives of the gang members. A few months later, when the group wanted to organize a sports team, the druggist was eager to supply uniforms, and even hired one of the boys in his store. And this was not an isolated incident. The staff reported numerous comments from parents, business people, and law enforcement officers about the improvements in the behavior of teenagers in the neighborhood.[39]

Whatever its results, Operation Street Corner ended in 1958. Robert Rosenbaum, the president of the board of directors of the Wharton Centre, in a May 1962 letter to N. S. Winnet, the head of the Philadelphia Crime Prevention Association, explained the reasons why the project was abandoned:

Wharton withdrew from the type of work performed by "Operation Street Corner" for two reasons: (1) Wharton's Board and Staff were firmly convinced that working with youth groups alone would only return them into the midst of the same surroundings and environmental conditions from which we had taken them and, in order to exercise true prevention, it would be necessary to work with families, friends and neighbors to build neighborhood conditions which would tend to reduce anti-social behavior by the youngsters and which would bring about an acceptance of a greater measure of responsibility by the adults; (2) Insufficient funds were available for the continuance of employment of specialized staff.[40]

When the Wharton Centre's board and staff decided in 1958 that "a more effective use of our limited resources might be made by working intensively with adult neighborhood and community groups," they knew that they had developed an innovative program for dealing with the juvenile gang problem; they simply could not continue it without financial support for gang workers. In proposal after proposal to public and private agencies, the Centre's staff asked for funding of "street corner workers," but the money was not forthcoming. The social problems and neighborhood conditions that led to the creation of Operation Street Corner in the 1940s — unemployment, crime, family instability — still existed in the 1960s, and to some extent they had worsened.[41]

When the United Fund proposed to allocate $100,000 for work on juvenile delinquency in 1958, "the Wharton Centre went on record . . . as not favoring the giving of a few thousand dollars to each of a multiplicity of agencies, since we were convinced that this would be a waste of the funds. We stated that we would prefer to bow out in favor of a concentrated attack upon the problem in a given area as a demonstration project." As a result, the funds went to a new project, Operation Poplar, in another section of North Philadelphia. The Wharton Centre believed that its program had mitigated the gang problem in the area of North Philadelphia west of Broad Street. However, in the early 1960s, "open gang warfare" broke out again in the area. When public funds became available through the Neighborhood Youth Corps in 1965 and 1966, the Centre resumed work with teenagers at levels comparable to those in the early 1950s.[42]

The gang program at the Wharton Centre had been developed and carried out by African American professionals for its African American clientele as part of the "racial uplift" emphasis associated with black social welfare programs. As was the case with the Institute for Colored Youth in the nineteenth century, the Wharton Centre's board of directors hired qualified black professionals to run the entire program. Although both blacks and whites served on the board of directors, and in the 1950s white college students worked at the Settlement, the Centre's entire program was planned and carried out by the black staff members who knew and understood the particular circumstances in the neighborhood, possessed the training and specialized knowledge needed to deliver the social services, and were willing to be held accountable for the success or failure of the programs they offered.[43]

These black professionals were members of W.E.B. DuBois's Talented Tenth, whose role in the community was to use their training and expertise to advance the entire group. In 1899 DuBois outlined the duties and responsibilities of black community leaders in the last chapter of *The Philadelphia Negro*. "Above all, the better classes of the Negroes should recognize their duty toward the masses. They should not forget that the spirit of the twentieth century is to be the turning of the high toward the lowly, the bending of Humanity to all that is human; the recognition that in the slums of modern society lie the answers to most of our puzzling problems of organization and life, and that only as we solve those problems is our culture assured and our progress certain" (p. 392). The forces leveled against this progress were formidable, and at times it was necessary to retreat, regroup, and try another approach.

Although Operation Street Corner was suspended in 1958, new federal funds from the War on Poverty and the Neighborhood Youth Corps permitted the staff to build on its earlier activities by implementing several new programs. These activities were aimed at providing viable alternatives for black youths to the gangs and social disorder found in their neighborhoods and in the city at large. Operation Street Corner and other early programs of the Wharton Centre offered precedents for the newer interventions. Together they represented one legacy of the racial uplift philosophy eloquently articulated by W.E.B. DuBois in *The Philadelphia Negro*.

Notes

1. Black self-help activities in Philadelphia are also described in V. P. Franklin, *The Education of Black Philadelphia: The Social and Educational History of a Minority Community, 1900–1950* (Philadelphia: University of Pennsylvania Press, 1979), pp. 7–32. For examinations of Quaker benevolent activities, see Sydney V. James, *A People Among Peoples: Quaker Benevolence in Eighteenth-Century America* (Cambridge, Mass.: Harvard University Press, 1963); and Philip Benjamin, *The Philadelphia Quakers in the Industrial Age, 1865–1920* (Philadelphia: Temple University Press, 1976).

2. Linda M. Perkins, "Quaker Beneficence and Black Control: The Institute for Colored Youth, 1852–1903," in *New Perspectives on Black Educational History*, ed. V. P. Franklin and James D. Anderson (Boston: G. K. Hall and Co., 1978), pp. 19–44; and Linda M. Perkins, *Fannie Jackson Coppin and the Institute for Colored Youth, 1865–1902* (New York: Garland Publishing, 1987). Indeed, the struggles to gain the appointment of black faculty at many black colleges and secondary schools in the early decades of the twentieth century generated widespread campus protests by students and alumni. This was not the case at the Institute for Colored Youth, which had an all-black staff from its inception. See Raymond Wolters, *The New Negro on Campus: Black Campus Rebellions of the 1920s* (Princeton, N.J.: Princeton University Press, 1975).

3. Allen F. Davis and John F. Sutherland, "Reform and Uplift among Philadelphia Negroes: The Diary of Helen Parrish, 1888," *Pennsylvania Magazine of History and Biography* 94 (October 1970): 496–99; John F. Sutherland, "The Origins of Philadelphia's Octavia Hill Association: Social Reform in a 'Contented' City," *Pennsylvania Magazine of History and Biography* 99 (January 1975): 24–27; Emily C. P. Longstreth, "Susan Parrish Wharton," July 6, 1929, Wharton Centre Papers, Urban Archives, Temple University (WCP), box 1, file 1A.

4. Robert A. Woods and Albert J. Kennedy, eds., *Handbook of Settlements* (1911; reprint New York: Arno Press, 1970), pp. 262–65, 271–75; Allen F. Davis, *Spearheads for Reform: The Social Settlements and the Progressive Movement, 1890–1914* (New York: Oxford University Press, 1967), pp. 11–12, 23–24, 62, 95–96, 151.

5. David Levering Lewis, *W.E.B. DuBois: The Biography of a Race, 1868–1919* (New York: Henry Holt, 1993), pp. 185–92, 201–2.

6. The causes of the migration of southern blacks to Philadelphia and other northern cities are detailed in Franklin, *Education of Black Philadelphia*, pp. 15–28; Franklin, *Black Self-Determination: A Cultural History of African-American Resistance* (Westport, Conn.: Lawrence Hill, 1992), pp. 126–46, 194–205; and Robert Gregg, *Sparks from the Anvil of Oppression: Philadelphia's African Methodists and Southern Migrants, 1890–1940* (Philadelphia: Temple University Press, 1993). See also George M. Fredrickson, *White Supremacy: A Comparative History in American and South African History* (New York: Oxford University Press, 1981), pp. 221–38.

7. See Jones, this volume; Sadie T. Mossell, "The Standard of Living of 100 Negro Migrant Families to Philadelphia," *Annals* 98 (November 1921): 177–79; Department of Welfare, Commonwealth of Pennsylvania, *Negro Survey of Pennsylvania* (Harrisburg, 1928), pp. 34–37.

8. Bernard J. Newman, *Housing the City Negro* (pamphlet, Philadelphia: Whittier Centre, n.d.) p. 8. The pamphlet was very likely published in 1915.

9. Whittier Centre, *Annual Report, 1916* (Philadelphia, 1916), n.p., in WCP, box 1, file 1.

10. Whittier Centre, *Annual Report, 1920* (Philadelphia, 1920), p. 11; *Annual Report, 1924* (Philadelphia, 1924), p. 10; WCP, box 1, file 1.

11. For information on the training of black women in nursing in Philadelphia during this period, see Darlene Clark Hine, *Black Women in White: Racial Conflict and Cooperation in the Nursing Profession, 1890–1950* (Bloomington: Indiana University Press, 1989), pp. 34–41.

12. For discussion of the patterns of distribution of the black population in the 1920s, see Franklin, *Education of Black Philadelphia*, pp. 60–67.

13. The Whittier Centre, *Annual Report, 1924*, p. 13; WCP, box 1, file 1.

14. "Minutes of the Meeting of the North Philadelphia Advisory Committee, 28 November 1927," WCP, box 3, file 45.

15. "Minutes," pp. 3–4.

16. "Minutes," pp. 1–2. For a discussion of differing racial visions of welfare, see Linda Gordon, "Black and White Visions of Welfare: Women's Welfare Activism, 1890–1945," in *"We Specialize in the Wholly Impossible": A Reader in Black Women's History*, ed. Darlene Clark Hine, Wilma King, and Linda Reed (Brooklyn, N.Y.: Carlson Publishing, 1995), pp. 467–69.

17. Emily C. P. Longstreth, "Study Regarding Recreation for Colored People in North Philadelphia, March 28, 1929," manuscript, p. 5, in WCP, box 3, file 45.

18. The Susan Parrish Wharton Memorial Settlement House (Wharton Centre), *First Annual Report, 1931–1932* (Philadelphia, 1932), pp. 5–10, in WCP, box 1 file 1A.

19. W.E.B. DuBois, "The Talented Tenth" (1903) reprint, in *The Seventh Son: The Thought and Writings of W.E.B. DuBois*, ed. Julius Lester, (New York: Vintage Books, 1971), 1:402–3. For a discussion of DuBois's relationship to uplift ideology, see Franklin, *Black Self-Determination*, pp. 11–25.

20. *Philadelphia Tribune*, September 10, and October 29, 1931, June 17, 1937.

21. For information on the *Philadelphia Tribune*, the oldest continuously circulating black newspaper in the United States, see V. P. Franklin, " 'Voice of the Black Community': The *Philadelphia Tribune*, 1912–1941," *Pennsylvania History* 51 (October 1984): 261–84.

22. G. James Fleming, "Wharton Settlement Like Oasis in Desert in North Philadelphia," *Philadelphia Tribune*, October 24, 1940.

23. Gordon, "Black and White Visions of Welfare," pp. 467–69.

24. Gordon, "Black and White Visions of Welfare," pp. 467–69. For information

on vocational programs for black youth sponsored by the Wharton Centre at this time, see *Philadelphia Tribune*, November 7, 1940.

25. Claudia Grant, "Headworkers' Report—February 9, 1943," p. 1, WCP, box 1, file 8.

26. Wharton Centre, *Annual Report, 1944* (Philadelphia, 1944), pp. 3–4, WCP, box 1, file 1A.

27. "Wharton Settlement Neighborhood Plan, 1945," WCP, box 48, file 194.

28. *Philadelphia Tribune*, February 9, 1933, p. 1. There were numerous accounts in the *Tribune* of juvenile gang problems during this period; see, for example, February 2, 1933, January 14, 1937, December 21, 1939, April 25, 1940, April 24, 1943, and January 22, 1944.

29. For a detailed examination of "Youth City" in North Philadelphia, see Franklin, *Education of Black Philadelphia*, pp. 179–81.

30. W. M. Balbour, "Gangs and Their Locations, September, 1946," pp. 1–2; WCP, box 48, file 148; for another survey of the gangs in the vicinity of the Centre, see W. M. Miller, "Analysis of Gang Groups, June 1945—January 1947," pp. 1–2, WCP, box 49, file 201.

31. M. W. Balbour, "The Shooting of 13 Year Old A. L., October 1945," manuscript, WCP, box 49, file 202.

32. Wharton Centre, *Operation Street Corner* (pamphlet, Philadelphia, 1953) WCP, box 32, file 255. The Centre's attempt to create youth organizations was similar to anti-delinquency efforts in schools and social programs in other cities. See, for example, William Graebner, *Coming of Age in Buffalo: Youth and Authority in the Postwar Era* (Philadelphia: Temple University Press, 1990), pp. 87–117.

33. James Hightower, "Group Progress Report—March 25, 1953," WCP, box 48, file 185.

34. Over one hundred letters requesting information on Operation Street Corner may be found in WCP, box 48. See also "Center's Street Corner Project Helps Reduce Juvenile Crime," *Philadelphia Inquirer*, October 26, 1953, p. 19; and Elizabeth Lasch-Quinn, *Black Neighbors: Race and the Limits of Reform in the American Settlement House Movement, 1890–1945* (Chapel Hill: University of North Carolina Press, 1993), pp. 33–38. On the fear of juvenile delinquency generally, see James Gilbert, *A Cycle of Outrage: America's Reaction to the Juvenile Delinquent of the 1950s* (New York: Oxford University Press, 1985).

35. U.S. Senate, Committee of the Judiciary, Eighty-Third Congress, *Hearings Before the Subcommittee to Investigate Juvenile Delinquency, April 14 and 15, 1954* (Washington, D.C.: U.S. Government Printing Office, 1954), p. 52. The various congressional committees that investigated juvenile delinquency in the 1950s are discussed in Gilbert, *Cycle of Outrage*, pp. 143–61.

36. Virginia Musselman to Tanner G. Duckrey, chairman, Street Corner Advisory Committee, July 24, 1953, New York, N.Y., WCP, box 48, file 183.

37. Grant to Musselman, Philadelphia, July 27, 1953, WCP, box 48, file 183.

38. Musselman to Grant, New York, N.Y., July 30, 1953, WCP, box 48, file 183.

39. In WCP, boxes 48 and 49, there are several letters from local shopkeepers praising the positive impact of Operation Street Corner on the teenagers in the neighborhood. In July 1995 informal discussions were conducted by the author with former participants in the anti-delinquency program. Several individuals commented on the positive effects the Wharton Centre's antigang programs had on their lives.

40. Richard Rosenbaum to N. S. Winnet, May 2, 1962, in WCP, box 48, file 183. For requests by Wharton Centre staff for funding of the street gang workers in the late

1950s and early 1960s, see WCP, boxes 48 and 49. Letters were sent to the Crime Prevention Association of Philadelphia, Department of Public Recreation, the Philadelphia Youth Services Board, and other state and local agencies.

41. Rosenbaum to Winnet, May 2, 1962.

42. Correspondence between the staff of the Wharton Centre and the officials of the Neighborhood Youth Corps may be found in WCP, box 32, file 255.

43. Wharton Centre, *Operation Street Corner.*

Figure 20. Vacant lots in Philadelphia, 1992. In the shadow of the gleaming office towers of Center City Philadelphia stand abandoned buildings and rubble-strewn lots. Courtesy of Temple University Libraries, Urban Archives.

Chapter 8
The Global Inner City
Toward a Historical Analysis

Carl Husemoller Nightingale

A Global Context for U.S. Inner Cities

Throughout the evolution of his long intellectual life, W.E.B. DuBois held as an axiom that the oppression of African A.nericans was a global phenomenon with a global history. To understand the American color line — and to understand the African American urban poor — was to appreciate them both in comparison with their manifestations worldwide or as a cause or consequence of world-historical change. In *The Philadelphia Negro* DuBois reinforced his earlier contention that the slave trade was central to his international historical analysis. Earlier, in his Harvard dissertation, he had argued that the international trade in human beings had birthed "modern world commerce, modern imperialism, the modern factory system and the modern labor problem."[1] In Philadelphia, both the memory of the slave trade and the "social revolution" against it were central to the "strange social environment" of racism and despair DuBois encountered among what he called the "submerged tenth" of the urban black community. His historical analysis of the Seventh Ward also notes the international growth of industry, world migrations, and even international cultural trends (pp. 283, 284, 311).[2]

DuBois later elaborated on these germs of internationalist analysis. Post-Civil War racial injustice in America, such as Jim Crow, replicated patterns of white supremacy and exploitation inherent in the age of world imperialism. Color bars in U.S. industry epitomized the broader tendency of Western organized labor to be "cajoled and flattered into imperialistic schemes to enslave and debauch black and brown and yellow labor, until with fatal retribution they are themselves bound and gagged and rendered impotent by the resulting monopoly of the world's raw material in the hands of a dominant, cruel, and irresponsible few."[3] As a Pan-Africanist, DuBois equated the social structure of colonies with that of slums, and African Americans with "colonial folk." In his last years, as formal empires began to crumble, he castigated "the British and American shareholders in corporations, the rich cartel owners who form the aristocracy of France and Germany, and the well-paid leaders of labor unions," holding them primarily responsible for "the poverty of the majority of human beings," particularly those of color.[4] And, as the civil rights movement dawned, he warned that "the whole colored world" was looking on, "asking whether the United States is a democracy or the last center of 'white supremacy' and colonial imperialism."[5]

Since DuBois's death, scholars have tended to ignore the relationship between changes in global history and the experience of African Americans, particularly the experience of poor urban black people. That relationship has presumably changed, but we do not understand how fundamental it has been to inner-city life.

Scholarly work most clearly influenced by DuBois dates from the late 1960s and early 1970s, when radical thinkers such as William K. Tabb, Wilfred David, Ron Bailey, and Guy C. Z. Mhone wove together elements of Black Power theory with Marxist dependency theory to portray "black ghettos" as "colonies" of a "super-exploitative" white world. Ghettos served American capitalists as a reserve army of labor and the rest of American society as a source of people to do its least desirable work. The relationship was *exploitative* because what ghetto dwellers received in wages did not offset what their employers gained in profits and what white merchants outside gained from consumer goods they sold in the inner city. As a result, little capital ever accumulated in the archipelago of black urban America, and impoverishment, unemployment, and dependency on white society were the norm. The whole system was enforced by racist policies that kept black people in low-paying, low-skill jobs, and by a "native elite" of politicians, police, and social service workers who effectively served to control unrest in the colony.[6]

Though this portrait was based on a model of global imperialism and colonial dependency, and intended to foster international solidarity between U.S. blacks and other peoples of color, it actually depended little on analysis of the links between the world economy as a whole and poor urban black America, or on any sustained comparative analysis. Nor did it specify how changes in the world economy had affected the colonial relationship. Indeed, when the "ghetto as colony" theorists were confronted with the debatable criticism that the black ghetto could not be a colony in the conventional sense, because unlike other colonies it had no separate political existence and could not eventually declare its independence from world capitalism, they agreed that in fact the ghetto was a unique creation, an "internal colony," subject to "domestic colonialism."[7]

Whatever the extent of its global analysis, the colonial metaphor, along with its central notion of exploitation — like other scholarship on poor African America with ties to Black Power militancy — has essentially disappeared from academic debate. When scholars revived their interest in African American inner cities during the 1980s they told a different story, one much more focused on national trends.

This story was about the rise of a so-called underclass. Definitions of this concept have varied considerably. In the formulation most widely employed in the social sciences, and increasingly in history as well, it refers to the disastrous impact on black communities of the disappearance of America's urban industrial markets. The best-known narrator of this story, William Julius Wilson, focuses on the incentives that led American manufacturers to relocate their urban factories, first right after World War II, then increasingly during the 1970s and 1980s. The factories were moved to the less heavily taxed, less physically encumbered suburbs, where cheaper land allowed manufacturers to erect vast horizontally oriented production lines and pave over large stretches of real estate as parking lots for their employees. Later, manufacturers moved to the South and West, where they found few labor unions and workforces accustomed to lower wages. Combined with large black migration into urban areas, the deindustrialization of cities created formidable "spatial" barriers for inner-city residents, who could not afford to commute to city suburbs, let alone move farther afield. These geographic obstacles only made poor urban black people's search for work and upward social mobility — already hampered by factory automation, increasing skill requirements, a growing service job market with a highly polarized wage structure — all the more difficult.[8]

"Underclass" theorists have disagreed about the role of race in this story. Wilson originally intended to demonstrate that class inequities had become more important obstacles than racial ones to well-being for blacks in the inner city. After the civil rights movement, he pointed out, job discrimination became illegal, and the low-wage jobs were not worth fighting other groups of workers for, so color bars diminished in importance. But other researchers have since disputed his claims. Not only does racism still animate hiring decisions in urban job markets, they argue, but residential segregation by race has remained more important than the actual physical separation between the city and the suburbs as a barrier to inner-city employment.[9]

Whatever the reasons, the result for the inner cities was an experience occasionally described as "Third World": persistent poverty and violence similar to that of the favelas of Rio de Janeiro and the townships of South African cities, homelessness that made wintertime New York subway stations resemble the streets of Calcutta, or life-expectancy rates among black men in Harlem that fell below those of Bangladesh.[10] More recently, scholars have also noted the deeper global connections of the "underclass." In this respect, the concept has begun to take on some of the trappings of DuBois's notion of the "submerged tenth." Globalization of the industrial process, not domestic pressures alone, motivated the flight of manufacturing jobs from U.S. cities. Revolutionary developments in communication technology and the erection of global financial networks permitted manufacturers to organize production on an international scale. Government policies facilitated this trend, from narrow ones that allowed products assembled in "maquiladora" (assembly) plants in northern Mexico to be shipped back to U.S. markets without trade duties, to more expansive trade liberalization treaties like the North American Free Trade Agreement (NAFTA) and the General Agreement on Tariffs and Trade (GATT). American manufacturers now move their facilities more easily to Latin American and Southeast Asian sites, where governments eager for foreign investment set up "export processing zones" with access to an extremely inexpensive workforce (mostly young women migrating from the countryside), with organized labor virtually nonexistent or violently repressed, and with irresistible tax incentives. For American inner cities, this global transformation has underlain or aggravated the tragic drama of vanishing industrial employment created by domestic conditions.[11]

Scholars who put deindustrialization at center stage in the debate on poverty have focused less on the injustice of low-wage jobs than did the ghetto-as-colony scholars and more on the agony of chronic joblessness; less on structural exploitation and more on structural barriers to blue-collar industrial work; less on colonial dependency upon white America (except for a reputedly increasing "dependence" on government welfare checks) and more on the inner cities' nearly complete economic exclusion from the wider society.

The global connections of American inner cities go beyond the "underclass" story, however, as investigations by theorists of urban planning, economists, political scientists, and urban sociologists make clear. Taking off from the "world systems" theory of Immanuel Wallerstein, they view recent changes in urban economic functions, labor markets, populations, and spatial arrangements in terms of cities' rapidly evolving "transnational linkages." Although not specifically concerned with U.S.-born black people or persistent urban poverty and joblessness, they analyze changes in the global capitalist economy—the actions of multinational firms, national governments, and "supranational" government agencies like the World Bank, the International Monetary Fund, and more recently the World Trade Organization—and the response of communities and households to those changes. These changes are of such magnitude that it is clear that their impact on inner cities needs further investigation.[12]

Other analysts of the "global" functions of cities look beyond deindustrialization to explain recent changes in the U.S. urban job market. World-wide "dispersion" of financial and industrial activity, Saskia Sassen argues, has "concentrated" the control of vast corporate empires in a relatively few "global cities," in part because the complex computerized telecommunication facilities needed for managing these empires—such as New York City's Clearinghouse Interbank Paying System (CHIPS), called "the heart of global capitalism"—are extremely expensive and also immobile. The few cities that have such facilities can more easily attract the headquarters of multinational firms,[13] and those firms' managers, moreover, prefer to cluster their control centers near subcontractors of the financial and legal services that are the lifeblood of the world economy. Sassen focused on New York, London, and Tokyo, cities that play particularly critical roles in global finance. However, the trend of centralizing corporate management brought postmodern skyscrapers to the downtown areas of many other cities across the United States, from Philadelphia to Houston to Hartford.[14] It has also brought armies of high-salaried workers who have refurbished older housing stock and "gentrified" many poorer sections of the city.

Concentration of corporate control changes the social structure of cities because it requires a vast expansion of the low-wage labor force—to service the giant buildings; to staff the innumerable new hotels and restaurants; to punch reams of information into data banks; to rebuild and repaint the old houses and provide them with furniture and an array of consumer items; and to provide the daily amenities of life for those in the fast lane—from nannies and other domestic workers to fancy laundries, flower shops, dog-walking services, and outlets for foodstuffs provided by the global gourmet supermarket.[15] Work in these businesses offers low earnings, unstable or seasonal employment, and few opportunities for advancement. It is rarely unionized; and much of it falls outside government regulation of wages, taxation, safety, and immigrant documentation. Advanced capitalism has thus helped to spawn the kind of "informal economy" at its "core" that is usually associated with the cities of "peripheral," or developing, societies.[16]

Expansion of the "global assembly line" may have also encouraged what world-systems theorists call "downgraded" manufacturing to some U.S. cities—another low-wage labor market that straddles the boundary between the formal and informal economies. In industries like garments, shoes, and furniture making, manufacturers in New York's Chinatown, Chicago, Los Angeles's Alameda Avenue industrial corridor, San Diego, and Miami have responded to the challenge of competitors who rely on low-wage labor in Latin America and Asia by expanding or reintroducing sweatshop labor and homework. In 1989, according to one estimate, 50,000 workers, including numerous children, worked in 4,500 sweatshops manufacturing apparel in New York City alone. Wages have declined markedly in those industries, and factories often ignore federal work-safety regulations and local zoning laws.[17] In Miami, Cuban women gather to assemble shirts on a piecework basis in the screen-enclosed "Florida rooms" in the front of their houses; and in New York, where many apparel workers earned between $2.00 and $2.50 an hour in 1989, whole informal industrial parks, producing not only clothing but furniture, glass, and confectionery, have sprouted up in residential areas like West Astoria and Williamsburg.[18] Electronics firms have organized vast assembly plants that rely on low-wage labor in formal facilities in California's Silicon Valley, or have subcontracted assembly work to New York City's informal "basement shops" and "garage fronts."[19] The service sector of the international economy, often seen as supplanting manufacturing, has actually created its own version of factories in the form of huge data-entry complexes. These, too, count upon predominantly low-wage operators and sometimes involve informal networks of homeworkers as well.[20]

Arising from changes in the global economy, these emerging sectors of the U.S. economy also depend on global movements of people to supply their labor needs. A world-systems analysis of U.S. cities cannot ignore the "fourth wave of immigration" of the 1970s and especially the 1980s. New York, Miami, and to some extent Washington, D.C., became major ports of entry for growing groups of migrants from the Dominican Republic, Haiti, the English-speaking West Indies, Cuba, Nicaragua, and El Salvador. Los Angeles, Houston, and Chicago similarly became the principal gateways for a growing influx of Mexicans. In New York, Los Angeles, San Francisco, and Seattle, communities rapidly grew of people born in Vietnam, Laos, Cambodia, the Philippines, China, Korea, and India. Many of these fourth-wave immigrants found work in the service occupations of American global cities or in the burgeoning low-wage industrial plants. Immigrant workers from the Caribbean and Central and South America often fill informal positions in "back of the truck" construction firms and in hotels and restaurants. Cuban and Mexican workers dominate the garment sweatshops of South Florida and southern California, and recent Chinese immigrants dominate those in New York City. One New York hotel discovered that its employees spoke a total of forty-seven languages. Some electronics assembly facilities in Silicon Valley have staffs that are 80 percent women of Third World descent, principally from Asia.[21] World migrants not directly involved in either of these two low-wage service or industrial "growth sectors" of global cities have created yet another urban job market in the United States: one offering services to the immigrant communities themselves — as gypsy cab drivers, odd-job carpenters, and the like — or to consumers in the broader community, as operators of gas stations, as convenience-store franchises, and as small-grocery store owners.[22]

Movements of capital and people, and the changing role of cities in enabling those movements, are not the only starting points from which to analyze inner cities on global terms. Another, more widely-encompassing set of explanatory tools comes from the work of international economists such as Gerald Epstein, James Crotty, and David Gordon, who are above all concerned with the institutional and political underpinnings of the world economy. Though they pay little specific attention to either cities or inner cities in their work, they do suggest the outlines of a multi-causal world-historical analysis of U.S. urban poverty — one that may also help crystallize the broadest contexts of what is often called the "new" poverty of the late twentieth century. Indeed, this analysis focuses on transformations that began during the late 1960s and early 1970s and consolidated during the 1980s. Thus they closely paralleled the slowly rising poverty rates, declining U.S. real wages, and increasing income inequality that characterized those years.

This story is about the waning of what its authors probably too nostalgically call the "Golden Age" of postwar world capitalism and the advent of what they more accurately call the late-century "neo-liberal regime." Read from the perspective of a world historian, this story has economic, cultural, and political components. The United States has been at the forefront of promoting these developments, and in many cases Americans have felt their consequences most severely.[23]

A central political economic theme in the story is the deregulation of the global financial system, epitomized by the 1973 collapse of the Bretton Woods system of controls on international currency exchanges and subsequent reductions on banking regulations across the western world. These developments sent the world of moneychanging and moneylending into a widening spiral of instability, one which nevertheless eventually allowed financiers worldwide (aided by government central banks) to reestablish the high level of control over the global economy and the practices of both governments and corporations they had enjoyed in the early part of this century. The most important accomplishment of this "rentier's regime" was to hike the price of capital (as measured in terms of real interest rates) to levels not seen since the late nineteenth-century Gilded Age. Both the increase in power of financial tycoons and the price hike were justified as necessary measures to combat inflation. The effect was to abandon other macroeconomic priorities, especially full employment, living wages, greater equality, and the eradication of poverty.

In the meantime, financial markets gained remarkably effective veto power over the monetary and fiscal policies of national governments. The rentiers came down especially hard on the distribution goals of welfare states, which they deemed too inflationary.[24] Here a development in global political culture was also critical: the resurgence of classical laissez-faire liberalism. This doctrine's "free market" slogans had guided the deregulation of financial markets; in turn, those markets provided a political backbone for a variety of conservative movements worldwide, resulting in policies collectively known as "austerity." This term is somewhat misleading, for late century neo-liberals themselves had many often contradictory priorities. While most did call on governments to scale down welfare and regulatory agencies designed to protect poor people, workers, and the middle class, some also often simultaneously countenanced large buildups of the military, all sorts of tax shelters and extremely expensive government bailouts for banks and corporations, and government public works programs that, in the U.S. especially, focused heavily on prison building. Indeed, the resulting mix of policies might described more accurately as a politics of *polarity*.

Meanwhile, other changes affected the public and private political economy of the world's workplaces and communities. Though governments became more generous with subsidies to large corporations, corporate leaders also contended with new costs in the neo-liberal world. The deregulation of finance imposed higher costs on borrowing money, and gyrating exchange rates made overseas trade more perilous. Also, in the late 1960s U.S. corporations ceded their postwar hegemony over world production and contended with reawakened rivals in Europe and East Asia. All western multinational corporations also faced a kind of "revenge of the third world" when oil-producing countries suddenly increased the price of crude petroleum during the 1970s, ending the long era of relatively cheap raw materials.

To meet these new challenges, corporate leaders focused above all on cutting labor costs. One way to accomplish this was to invest overseas, or to threaten a move as a way of weakening workers' demands. The mobility of capital investment has more often reflected the desire to capture affluent markets and avoid fluctuating currency rates than a global search for low wages and pliant workforces. More important, however, even when investment overseas was motivated by efforts to cut labor costs, it was only one of a much broader range of strategies designed to disempower workers. In the United States and elsewhere, employers led a political and economic assault on unions, labor regulations, and minimum wage laws. They cut benefits and expanded involuntary overtime for full-time workers, and also expanded low-wage, part-time, "casual," and temporary work without benefits. They targeted unionized workplaces for systems of automation, and increased draconian supervision of shop floors. Campaigns to move factories abroad had parallels within countries, as corporations in the U.S. "whipsawed" state and local governments against each other — and city governments against suburban ones — to extract greater subsidies and tax benefits. Some of these strategies exacerbated the deindustrialization of cities. But more crucially, as a whole, they broke worker strength across the economy, including sectors that were less mobile geographically, such as hotels, hospitals, and other services, as well as transportation and construction. On top of this, as neo-liberal policies eroded social programs, they also threatened once-reliable jobs in local government.[25]

What relationships do poor African Americans and their inner-city communities have with this emerging world system? Are colonial metaphors appropriate? How does "underclass" theory hold up when we examine growing sectors of the urban economy instead of vanishing ones, and when we consider the declining level of workers' and communities' power, rather than the growth or disappearance of any particular sector of work, to be a crucial factor in their well-being? Is it useful to speak of a "global inner city"?

To answer these questions historians can take a number of possible paths of research. An expansion of efforts to study urban poverty, social policy, and racial segregation in international comparative context will be critical.[26] Our understandings of the origins of urban segregation also need to take into account the international contexts of western urban growth, migration, and U.S. white supremacy, especially in the first two-thirds of the century.[27] The role of cities in the global economy needs to be traced back in time: as W.E.B. DuBois well knew, the concentration of corporate control began long before the current fancy for "going global." Already in the 1890s, giant merger waves linked to the global economy produced a profusion of new skyscrapers, hotels, service jobs, fancy downtown middle-class homes, and sweatshops.[28]

This paper examines four other related research possibilities in greater detail: a history of urban African Americans and low-paid, disempowered work; a look at the impact of global migrations on those kinds of labor markets; a look at other global cultural trends and life in the inner city; and some concluding thoughts about political responses of inner city residents to the emerging world system.

A History of African Americans and Marginal Work

> Are you crazy? Whoever heard of integration between a mop and a banker?
> — "Man, Age about 38," interviewed by staff of Harlem Youth Opportunities Unlimited, 1963

Social historians interested in looking at inner cities from a global perspective will invariably need to investigate a history that, as Kenneth Kusmer notes, has largely yet to be written: that of African Americans' participation in low-wage job markets since World War II.[29] Even the few bits and pieces of evidence we already have suggest the tentative outlines of that complex story. Two analytic distinctions are useful for unraveling it. In terms of structural constraints, we need to know to what extent urban black people were *relegated* to low-wage work and to what extent they were *excluded* from it. And we need to know how black people as a group (or more likely, as a subset of a group) responded to those constraints, how much they *relied* on poorly paying jobs, and how much they critiqued, resisted, or *rejected* them as a suitable source of livelihood.

The relegation of black workers to low-paying jobs in the service and manufacturing economies of American cities is the best-known piece of the story. As Jacqueline Jones points out in this volume, DuBois himself acutely observed the vicious effects of urban color bars as he conducted the re-search for *The Philadelphia Negro* during the 1890s, a period when unions and employers were highly successful at excluding black workers from manufac-turing employment. DuBois found that in the Seventh Ward, 61.5 percent of black men and 88.5 percent of black women earned their living in the most demeaning sector of the urban economy: domestic and personal service (p. 109). Stanley Lieberson has tabulated similar figures for other cities.[30] The expanded labor needs of manufacturers during two world wars began breaking the barriers to black employment in factories, but even then black workers ended up in the least well paid, least dependable, dirtiest, hottest, most backbreaking, and most dangerous jobs. They made up a last-hired, first-fired reserve army of labor often called upon to break strikes, and they were systematically excluded from unions. Indeed, many organized white workers despised blacks as a "scab race." By the 1940s, though, blacks did make important inroads into unionized workplaces that offered more social mobility and greater economic comfort.[31]

Then, just as World War II raised the hopes of urban blacks — hopes bolstered by the federal government's initial attempts to crack down on discrimination in employment — urban industries began their long and dev-astating period of decline. Barriers of space, skill, residential segregation, and racial discrimination relegated black workers to the growing urban service economy. That fate was not bad for all residents of the inner city. As more serious assaults on discriminatory hiring got underway in the 1960s, including programs of preferential hiring on the basis of race and gender, some more comfortable, if limited, sectors of the service job market were opened to African Americans. These changes not only boosted the member-ship of the black professional and corporate class, they also opened up what might be called the narrow middle segment of the service economy as well. Many African Americans found jobs in the administration of social service programs, education, telecommunications, other utilities, and municipal services, jobs often unionized and relatively well remunerated, if vulnerable to government downsizing.[32]

Many more black workers, however, remained in the much less well paid, nonunionized work that has characterized the broad bottom of the service sector. General clerical work outside the government, data entry positions, lower-rung private-sector health-care jobs like nurses' assistants, restaurant work, domestic service, and institutional services like laundering and custo-dial work — all often paid poverty wages. Below-minimum wages and hellish working conditions are documented for yet another emerging sector of the urban economy: food processing. Poultry and fish processors have set up plants in small southern cities and towns that pay pittances to black workers from regions devastated by the mechanization of agriculture, such as the Mississippi and Arkansas Deltas, the Florida Panhandle, Tidewater North Carolina, and the Eastern Shore of Maryland.[33]

Black people's responses to these shifting structural forces have varied. African Americans and their families have a long history of reliance on miserly wages for survival; it dates from emancipation and the subsequent advent of the sharecropping system in southern agriculture. As Jacqueline Jones has shown, black men and women in the rural South often organized their lives around the search for low-wage work, traversing huge distances to keep pace with demands for seasonal labor, whether in the cotton, rice, and sugar fields or in smaller industries like turpentine plants and sawmills.[34] To get jobs as waiters and porters in southern and northern cities, black men often kept on the move and sacrificed home life, as did women entering domestic service.[35] In fact, as Kenneth Kusmer has also suggested, African Americans' search for low-wage work challenges the "spatial mismatch" notion of "underclass" theorists.[36]

These patterns persist well into the late twentieth century. Black people living in rural areas of Louisiana, for example, make extended trips, sometimes even crossing state lines, to work long days in catfish and chicken plants.[37] Though U.S.-born black women domestic workers are now a disappearing group, in Philadelphia many still take the forty-five-minute ride on the 44-G bus line (named after the wealthy Main Line town of Gladwyne) that takes them to the elaborate homes of their suburban employers. One family I knew from my years in the city organized a carpool that transported male relatives to work at a series of car washes, body shops, and detail shops in the suburbs; and the women of another family coordinated work hours, child care, and public transportation for a thirty-mile round-trip commute across the city to a private retirement home where they had found work as nurses' aides.[38]

Even increased government welfare payments and health benefits for the poor since the mid-1960s have not undercut poor black families' reliance on low-wage work. Two separate surveys conducted by the Institute for Women's Policy Research found that 40 percent of all women receiving Aid to Families with Dependent Children (AFDC) payments depend on work in the private sector to make ends meet. Kathryn Edin found similar patterns in her study of Chicago welfare recipients. Women persist in their job searches despite AFDC regulations and, as Katherine S. Newman has argued, despite extremely competitive conditions in some low-wage markets.[39] This pattern persists in survival strategies of many black Philadelphia women I know, who combine welfare with a whole variety of part-time work — in a local industrial laundry; at a catering company; at a newsstand; at a school as a recess monitor; at a Maryland chicken-processing plant; and for a few women, in illegal pursuits such as selling sex or drugs.

These traditions of reliance and complicated survival strategies are not the whole story: black workers have also sustained time-honored "patterns of resistance" to degradation at the workplace. According to Lawrence Levine, much African American folklore originated in the songs and jokes that slaves used to undercut the legitimacy of the brutal authority that ran southern plantations. More recently, black service and industrial workers — and white factory workers — have resorted to petty theft, sabotage, or deliberate slowing of the production process as a way of gaining some control over their dependent condition, much as slaves did.[40] The protest tactics of black domestic workers in the early twentieth century are especially well documented. In this volume, Tera W. Hunter has found that domestics in southern cities agreed upon codes of acceptable treatment at the workplace and led boycotts or strikes against offending employers.[41]

Perhaps the strongest expression of opposition was to quit and move on.[42] Indeed, African American migration may be more important as a sign of resistance than of dependence. When blacks left rural areas for southern cities, and then left the South altogether in the huge tides of migration to northern cities that peaked during the 1910s and again in the 1940s, their actions represented, at least in part, a rejection of the oppressive exploitation, fraud, and debt peonage of the sharecropping system.

The promise of higher wages in urban industry that lured migrants to cities proved, of course, in large part hollow. How African Americans protested systematic relegation to low-wage employment in postwar cities still awaits full investigation. Urban ethnographers from the 1960s found that earlier traditions of resistance to unsustaining employment persist there. After spending several years with a group of black men in Washington, D.C., Elliot Liebow concluded that "society (whatever its ideals regarding the dignity of labor) holds the job of the dishwasher or janitor or unskilled laborer in low esteem if not outright contempt. So does the streetcorner man. He cannot do otherwise. He cannot draw from a job those social values which other people do not put into it."[43] Liebow implies that mainstream values as well as independent traditions of protest can undergird workers' opposition to low-wage work. Like their peers across U.S. culture, the teenagers I knew in Philadelphia put a premium on finding work that teaches a marketable skill.[44]

The civil rights movement and the rise of Black Power and other movements of racial liberation in the 1960s may have emboldened traditions of everyday resistance to employers and "blind-alley jobs."[45] In 1963 volunteers from Harlem Youth Opportunities Unlimited (HARYOU), interviewed men and women from their community for the documentary *Cries from the Ghetto*. Outrage against racial oppression and the search for a sense of racial self-worth inform resentments against "Whitey" or "Charley" and the "slave" jobs he offered. Both men and women also found menial work to be a threat to their sense of gender identity. As several ethnographers have documented, inner-city men often deride low-end jobs as "working for chump change" and resentfully tag employers as "the Man."[46] Women in low-paying factory and service work also face painful slights, which can go beyond employers' insistence on calling their servants "girl" to sexual harassment or even assault at work. As Bonnie Thornton Dill has shown, domestic workers often quit their jobs in response.[47] The expansion of a culture of conspicuous consumption makes work that does not pay enough even for subsistence, let alone discretionary spending, look even more miserable, and not only to poor black workers alone.

For all their potential sources of legitimacy, these ideas and actions of resistance against low-wage work have been vulnerable. Jones notes that sharecroppers who "shifted" or "hit the grit" in search of more favorable employment when their contract year was up were often disparaged as lazy, "shiftless," and careless. Whites linked these characteristics to race and saw them as inherent characteristics of blacks.[48] Domestic workers who refused demeaning tasks suffered similar accusations of laziness, and pointed, public complaints about the quality of "the help." In the 1950s, and as I found again in the 1980s, poor African Americans in Philadelphia were as likely to voice dominant ideologies about employment and the work ethic as to critique poor working conditions and low wages. Those who rejected a demeaning job in the name of gender or racial pride could find their personal adequacy questioned once unemployed. Conflict between different ideologies about what constitutes manhood—whether resistance to low-wage work or success as the principal breadwinner (both attitudes legitimated within poor black communities and in the mainstream)—is thoroughly documented, as are its serious consequences for marriage and analogous relationships in poor communities.[49] Such conflicts can be internalized, as I have found for Philadelphia teenagers with limited credentials who experience or at least suspect racial discrimination. In them the sense that a certain job is beneath contempt often alternates with a sense of inadequacy or a gnawing fear of failure in the job market, which in turn leads to a less prideful and empowered rejection of low-wage work.

Rejection of jobs as worthy of contempt nevertheless has important legacies. That sentiment, seconded by increased opportunities in clerical and government work, probably fueled the silent emancipation of black women from domestic work, particularly live-in domestic work, from about 1950, when 41 percent of black women gainfully employed outside agriculture were domestics, to 1980, when the percentage dropped to 7 percent.[50] The sentiment may explain why African American migrants to the North no longer seek work on perishable crops in the near hinterlands of places like Philadelphia, New York, or Oakland.[51] Because of its conflict with other values tied to employment and the work ethic, its link with explosive feelings of disempowerment, and its charged racial and gender character, rejection of demeaning work doubtless fueled the urban rebellions that engulfed American cities in the late 1960s and again in the 1980s and 1990s.[52] It helps explain why young African Americans, particularly young men, increasingly opt out of the workforce altogether—or seek work in illegal enterprises that pay more.[53]

This preliminary sketch suggests that a history of the effects of global economic transformations on poor urban African American neighborhoods cannot ignore earlier forces that relegated most of their inhabitants to low-paying work, nor black workers' tensely counterpoised traditions of reliance and resistance to that work, nor the persistence of these long-standing patterns of relegation and exclusion, which limit poor African Americans' access to new kinds of jobs.

Ethnicity, Gender, and Race at the Bottom of the Global Job Market

> Her hands are small and she works fast with extreme care. Who, therefore, could be better qualified by nature and inheritance to contribute to the efficiency of a bench assembly production line than the oriental girl?
>
> — *Malaysia: The Solid State for Electronics*, an investment brochure developed by the Federal Industrial Development Authority, Kuala Lumpur, 1975

> Rosa Martinez produces apparel for U.S. Markets on her sewing machine in El Salvador. *You* can hire her for 57 cents an hour. . . . Rosa is more than just colorful. . . . She and her co-workers are known for their industriousness, reliability and quick learning.
>
> — Advertisement in *Bobbin*, the trade magazine for the U.S. Apparel Industry, paid for by the Salvadoran Foundation for Social and Economic Development, November 1990

Our principal sources for the historical effects of world migrations and expanded low-wage labor markets on poor urban black communities are studies of the impact of renewed immigration on job opportunities for U.S. citizens in general. Do immigrants take on roles in the economy that complement (or even expand) those of the U.S.-born poor? Or does the flood of foreign-born low-wage workers actually take away already-scarce jobs from American inner-city residents?

Scholars have taken different positions in this debate. "World-systems" urban theorists, with some exceptions, "answer" the question by largely ignoring the U.S.-born poor, implying that internationally linked low-wage job markets and the workers they attract are distinct from their domestic counterparts.[54] Another "complementarity" argument uses poor Americans' rejection of low-wage work to claim that immigrants take only jobs the U.S.-born do not want.[55] Clearly these arguments need emending: the changes in the global economy described by world-systems theorists have on the whole extended existing industries, such as hotels, construction, and textile sweatshops, not invented new ones. Also, many U.S.-born poor people do rely on low-wage jobs, even if they find some unsuitable.

Economists have devised a number of models to help resolve some of these questions. Most agree that, of all American workers, young U.S.-born black and Latino men are most vulnerable to competition from immigrants and to decreased wages. But clearly the "negative effects" of immigration are relatively weak when compared to those of the deindustrialization of the United States or the overall decrease in wages brought on by globalized production.[56] However, Randall K. Filer found grimmer evidence that in cities with particularly high rates of immigration, low-skilled white natives tend to leave for areas with less congested labor markets, while low-skilled U.S.-born blacks tend to remain. Filer speculates that this might relate to racially determined residential barriers, an idea that would fit Douglas Massey and Nancy Denton's conclusions about the key role of residential segregation by race.[57]

Sociologists examining ethnicity and labor markets have suggested more complex social historical approaches to these questions. Roger Waldinger found that relationships between "new" immigrants and African Americans in New York City job markets have varied considerably by industry and over time. In needle trades African Americans, both men and women, made up a small but growing part of the industry from about 1920 to the mid 1950s. But the discriminatory practices of both employers and the Jewish- and Italian-dominated International Ladies' Garment Workers Union (ILGWU) kept blacks in the least well paying jobs and out of union training programs that led to advancement. The civil rights movement emboldened workers to fight efforts by both union and management to keep wages low (as a strategy to keep shaky firms afloat) and racial barriers high — a conflict that left many African Americans embittered. By 1970, black employment in the New York apparel industry was half of its 1950 level. Using problematic union and management sources, Waldinger argues that blacks began to reject the jobs. A combination of frustration with past discrimination, increased racial awareness, and growing opportunities in the municipal sector might well have led many black people to abandon apparel work. Since whites' participation in the industry also fell precipitously at the same time, broader mainstream attitudes about this kind of work seem to have also played a role. Whatever the reasons, employers reported labor shortages in the late 1960s and 1970s (which some of them attributed to the lure of welfare for blacks) that were only alleviated by the arrival of immigrants from the Far East in the 1970s and 1980s.[58]

In hotels a different pattern held. Some African Americans, who had historically been largely relegated to "back of the house" work did advance into better-paying, more prestigious jobs during the 1980s, but they lost out in less-skilled positions even as wages and the number of jobs were actually rising throughout the industry, primarily to black Caribbeans and Africans and Latin American immigrants. Here, Waldinger's evidence suggests that immigrants "won" in large part because of employers' discriminatory practices, rather than because black citizens rejected hotel jobs (though the employers Waldinger interviewed claimed that blacks reject hotel jobs as "too servile"). Although African American employment in hotels decreased during the 1960s, the declines were never as abrupt as in textiles, and the rate of employment stabilized in the 1970s. It was during the 1980s, when immigration increased most rapidly, that black employment rates in hotels plunged.[59]

The formal sector of the construction industry has instead sustained historically notorious patterns of racial exclusion. During the 1970s and 1980s, building trades unions and contractors largely barred African Americans from the union-based training programs that could get them into positions of authority from which to recruit fellow blacks. Despite federal, state, and municipal efforts to dismantle these racial barriers, including set-aside programs favoring black and Latino firms, and despite grass-roots efforts to disrupt construction sites and demand jobs by rival worker-crews organized to assert their civil rights, those barriers have kept rates of black employment in the industry low. The massive expansion in construction work of the last two decades, the result of corporate consolidation and the gentrification of global cities, has thus offered little to poor African Americans.[60]

Immigration and globalization of industry may exclude African Americans from labor markets in less obvious ways. Sweatshops, low-wage assembly plants, and informal industrial areas tend to be located in immigrant communities; warehouses and electronics shops, in suburban industrial parks like those of North Jersey and Silicon Valley. Residents of the inner city may have trouble reaching new jobs, or may never even hear of them. According to the journalist Jane H. Lii, the inconspicuous garment sweatshop where she worked for a week in New York's Chinatown advertised for employees discreetly, with signs in Chinese.[61] The actual spatial barriers may be less important than lack of contacts within immigrant communities. Recruitment for "downgraded industrial" work and for informal construction depends heavily on the social networks immigrants first form in order to facilitate their voyage to the United States, which employers and unions later foster to ensure a steady labor supply. Similar collective arrangements have long existed in African American communities, contrary to what some informal-economy theorists assume.[62] In the neighborhood where I lived in black Philadelphia, access to all kinds of licit but informal entrepreneurial activity depended on familiarity with the community. News spread by word of mouth about jobs available in house painting and refurbishing, car repair, hair salons, moving services, landscaping, and junking and recycling. Yet U.S.-born blacks may indeed not learn of jobs created by recent changes in the world economy that are situated outside black communities. One area worth looking at is the way racial barriers operate in the contracting of under-the-table construction firms, on which many African Americans and immigrants rely for entry into the formal sector. Here both racial attitudes of homeowners and contractors and residential segregation may play a part in privileging immigrant firms.

Obstacles based on skill may further complicate the complex dynamics that govern the creation of occupational niches for any given ethnic group. True, Waldinger argues persuasively that African Americans' skill levels cannot explain their exclusion from textiles, hotels, and construction, since the immigrants hired in those industries tend to have less education than U.S.-born blacks, and since the industries usually provide on-the-job training at entry level. But as Suzanne Model suggests, the niche most clearly dominated by U.S.-born blacks in many cities — municipal government work — has provided fewer opportunities for unskilled blacks in the late twentieth century than, say, it did for the Irish in the late nineteenth century. Increasing educational qualifications in those sectors of the service economy otherwise most welcoming to African American workers may have stunted informal recruitment networks in poor black communities, helping to explain some of the tragedy of long-term unemployment. Another factor affecting intraracial job recruitment — the movement of middle- and working-class African Americans out of many inner-city neighborhoods (especially in northeastern and midwestern cities) — needs examination: it has been central to "underclass" analysis.[63]

How far has the current globally linked expansion of low-wage work given new life to the racially exclusive practices documented in many industries? In a survey of 185 Chicago employers, some of whom sought low-wage service workers, Joleen Kirschenman and Kathryn Neckerman found that black applicants for jobs were often rejected on the basis of stereotypes that conflated race, place of residence, class, and ability to work. Owners of restaurants said that they did not hire black waitresses because their customers preferred whites, and warehousers claimed that black employees were more likely to steal merchandise.[64] Waldinger reports that some hotel personnel managers justify hiring an immigrant workforce by maintaining that blacks have been "spoiled by the welfare system."[65]

Although these stereotypes manifestly exemplify homegrown traditions of American racism, the new global economy seems to have brought its own racial "logic" back to U.S. shores. Corporate managers seeking to go global encounter all sorts of investment promotion literature, such as that quoted at the beginning of this section, which advertises foreign workers in terms that conflate race, ethnicity, gender, productivity, and willingness to work for low wages. This kind of thinking closely resembles the ideas personnel managers of U.S. firms use in their hiring decisions. Karen J. Hossfeld reports that personnel managers of electronics assembly plants in Silicon Valley use a "simple formula." "Just three things," replied one production manager when asked how he chose his employees: "small, foreign, and female." Central to this logic, Hossfeld argues, is a "model minority theory" that links notions about the manual dexterity ("small detail work . . . would drive a large person . . . crazy") and productivity of Filipina, Vietnamese, and Chinese women to glorification of their willingness to work for low wages. An assistant personnel manager found Asian women "resourceful";

the owner of a disk-drive manufacturing facility praised their "good pov-erty management skills." By contrast employers thought U.S.-born black workers were "too cocky" and "troublemakers," and thus unproductive, prone to join unions, and too likely to file discrimination suits and workers' compensation claims. When one company administrator was asked why he preferred to recruit across the Pacific when he could hire workers from nearby pools of low-wage labor such as black East Palo Alto or Oakland, he responded that he did not hire African Americans because "they don't like Whites and they don't like authority — and I'm both."[66] This grim form of "ethnic transition" bears more historical examination: in employers' eyes the black "scab race" that white workers reviled at the turn of the century for their willingness to undermine organized labor is now a militant van-guard that needs to be undercut by workers deemed more "pliant" as a group.[67]

Globally linked racial logics do not affect all poor blacks equally. Elec-tronic firms in North Carolina's Research Triangle, for one example, do hire large numbers of black women, and, according to Carole Cohen, Puerto Ricans, not African Americans, play the role of last-hired, first-fired in at least one declining Philadelphia manufacturing plant.[68] But the invidious agenda of the global racial logic has a more uniform impact. Like all racial thinking, it validates the idea that individuals can be judged according to generalized claims about their race, immigrant status, and gender. More specifically, it ignores the context of immigrants' own reasons for participat-ing in low-wage work in the United States — whether the severe exploitation and poverty in their own country, or the need to conceal their undocu-mented status, or, as for Fujianese restaurant workers in New York, the need to pay off ruthless immigrant smuggling operations. Once decontextual-ized, immigrants' "willingness to work for low wages" becomes the sign of a desirable cultural background and, by extension, of racial superiority. The racial logic of world-market factory hiring practices thus helps employers justify the contrast between the low wages they pay and the high profit margins they reap; it also rhetorically negates the moral force of traditions of resistance, including African Americans', to exploitation in the labor mar-kets, discounts the links between those traditions and mainstream values, and recasts them as undesirable cultural qualities. Ignoring similarities be-tween U.S.-born whites' and blacks' reasons for rejecting low-wage work, it casts often putative group acts of job rejection by African Americans as a sign of racial inferiority. This kind of racism transforms struggling inner-city African Americans into a class of poor people who are excluded from the global market in part because they have taken on ideas with resonances in the broader stream of American (and Western) progressive attitudes toward low-status work.

Logic like this has also sadly animated much of the public and intellectual debate over the effects of immigration on domestic labor markets, and particularly those open to African Americans.[69] Racial distinctions framed in the language of the productivity of the low-wage workforce have also been fueled by, and have helped fuel, distinctions framed in the language of entrepreneurial ability.[70] At worst, such spiteful comparisons between immigrants and African Americans have increased racial tensions—between blacks and Korean merchants for example, or blacks and Latinos—in the politics of many U.S. cities.[71]

Finally, by pitting poor people against each other, these comparisons divert attention from the global corporate decisions most responsible for declining job prospects and low wages in American cities. Indeed, just as they have helped animate decisions about hiring, these renewed racial ideologies have surely also helped undergird far more important decisions about where to locate corporate investment. One of the most significant—and difficult—tasks facing historians of the global inner city is to uncover in full the racial calculus underlying the collapse of urban U.S. industry, and along with it the severe erosion of efforts to organize labor forces, stanch the outflow of opportunity, and control the widening of economic inequality.

The Inner City in the Global Village

> We'll sing in one voice
> And we'll sing one song
> Our separate lands
> Are one from now on
> We are all Asians
> And we'll sing with one song.
> —Singapore-born rapper Dick Lee

Ocean-hopping movements of investment capital, workplaces, and people (and a jagged, evolving color line) have profoundly complicated and entrenched the experience of poverty in urban African American communities. But two other quickening global movements have also crucially affected U.S. inner cities: the movement of consumer goods through expanding channels of world trade, and the movement of information, values, imagery, and rhetorical expression through expanding channels of world communication. At stake here are not only inner-city communities' economic prospects, but also many aspects of their social and cultural lives and, to some degree, the political possibilities open to their residents. The historical dynamic at work involves both the decisions of transnational corporate managers who exercise broad control over commercial and media networks, and the ways inner-city residents themselves, particularly young people, have acted to influence the character of those networks. This relationship involves U.S. inner-cities' most prominent roles in the world economy—in essence, what truly defines their status as "global inner cities" during the late twentieth century. The first of these roles is inner-city residents' importance as consumers of the fruits of global production. The second is their prominence as suppliers of some of the most valuable cultural raw material for global trade and advertising.

Corporate interests in the inner city are indeed not monolithic: The contempt that multinationals demonstrate for African Americans as workers — whether by not hiring them or by countering their critiques of low-wage work — does not extend to them as consumers. Here the impulse is to include, not exclude — and also sometimes to extol resistive culture, not quash it. Multinationals like McDonald's, Nike, the Big Six recording companies, television broadcasters, Hollywood movie moguls, the NCAA and the NBA, the financial arms of automakers and appliance manufacturers, the tobacco giants, the major distillers, and the makers of firearms — even in their own way the South American cocaine cartels — all have implemented the advice that black business associations and scholars of consumer behavior have offered since the 1930s: they have spent often huge amounts of money launching inner-city advertising campaigns.

Rejecting the long-standing premise that the "Negro market" was either too poor or not discriminating enough to deserve attention, corporate marketers have in recent decades perfected such market research tools as focus groups and "psychographic" mapping to learn all they can about inner-city life in order to cultivate new customers. The promotional strategies they devised combine targeted use of television ads with media specifically aimed at inner-city audiences, such as teen magazines, black-owned radio stations, neighborhood billboards, corner stores, check-cashing outlets, discount stores, local playgrounds, high school assemblies, basketball gyms, and — if the category of corporate marketer is extended to the drug lords who developed crack cocaine — narcotics shooting galleries. Their messages have been aimed at specific segments of the African American market, including the poor and the young, with increasing degrees of accuracy. Nike and Reebok have waged the most elaborate of these campaigns since the 1980s by giving free sneakers to coaches of summer basketball leagues and high school teams as a means to recruit talented players. This insured that the right brand of shoes would end up on the feet of the most popular athletes in inner-city parks. (It also increased the chances that the same players would be available later in their careers to endorse the same brand of shoes on television).[72]

The resulting ad campaigns have been very successful at deepening inner-city residents' participation in consumer culture. The dynamic cannot, however, be portrayed, as it sometimes is, solely as an act of naked brainwashing or absolute corporate "hegemony." As my experiences in Philadelphia suggest, the process has to some extent occurred on inner-city residents' own terms. Young people in particular have used status items, from basketball sneakers to gold jewelry to team jackets to expensive clothes and automobiles, in their own strategies to cope with the deeply seated memories of frustration and humiliation that are central to their experiences with poverty and racial exclusion. Though their tastes often run to items most heavily promoted in inner-city ads, they have also created dynamic and expressive practices of consumerism that are distinctly their own, culminating in the playful and rebellious symbolism of hip-hop fashion.

However, as was also clear to me in Philadelphia, poor urban communities pay a high price for their often heavy reliance on such strategies, a price that corporate advertisers have certainly not diminished. Just as the ghetto-as-colony theorists would argue, the high markups companies charge for their goods certainly ensure that more money leaves poor neighborhoods than stays and circulates within them—and the high-priced loans sharked by consumer-credit subsidiaries of many multinational corporations as a means to make their expensive goods available to poor people do not help.[73] The price is not only monetary, though: inclusion in consumer culture also too often comes at the expense of the physical, social, and psychic life of poor people. Sometimes the products themselves exact those kinds of costs: highly promoted fast food, alcohol, cigarettes, narcotics, and guns are each central to one or another of the many public health crises in poor urban America. Also, no matter how creatively low-income consumers reinvent consumerism, the resulting personal strategies only help to mask humiliations derived from poverty and racism; they do not help young people understand those feelings or come to terms with their origins in systems of exploitation. And, if poverty creates the need for those strategies of self-worth based on high-priced status commodities in the first place, poverty also makes it difficult for young inner-city residents to consistently afford them. In my Philadelphia neighborhood, such exacerbated frustrations strained a number of crucial relationships: those between young people and parents who could not fund their children's desires; those between young people and their peers who put often overwhelming pressure on each other to appear in public well dressed; and those between young men and women, whose courtships and romances were sometimes made or broken on the basis of the ability to provide expensive gifts and look "decent." These tensions also helped local drug pirates recruit workers, since the positions they offered were often the quickest source of funds for expensive purchases in the neighborhood. Indeed, there is some evidence that particularly unscrupulous corporate salesmen have both used and augmented drug dealers' prestige by offering them advanced copies of soon-to-be-released blockbuster basketball shoes. At their worst, rampant efforts to fan consumer desires also help motivate sometimes homicidal robberies of sneakers, team jackets, and expensive jewelry. These acts increased dramatically during the late 1980s in many inner-city neighborhoods—just when corporations aimed their most ingeniously engineered ad campaign at those communities.[74]

Whatever its effects on inner-city life, importation of globally produced goods is not the only role inner cities play in world trade. They also export valuable raw materials, though again, ultimately on unequal terms, and with, at best, ambiguous benefits. As W.E.B. DuBois first argued in the *Souls of Black Folk*, African Americans have a long history of providing the United States and the world with some of its most creative artistic innovations — spirituals, gospel music, blues, jazz, and rhythm and blues being only the best-known historic examples.[75] Poor urban neighborhoods have played critical roles in most of these great bursts of creativity, which assembled aesthetic forms from Africa and the Atlantic world and in turn inspired changes in popular music across the planet. In the 1970s, the "black metropolises" of the United States were the source of a new set of cultural explosions, collectively known as hip-hop: rap emerged from outdoor parties in the South Bronx, break dancing from the disco clubs of upper Manhattan; elaborate graffiti murals spread from the sides of New York City subway cars and abandoned buildings in many other cities; and a profusion of youthful fashion statements developed across inner-city America which matched these new art-forms. Like all cultural innovators, hip-hop artists derived their new genre from a wide variety of sources, from African griot storytelling to Jamaican and U.S. traditions of verbal jousting to the segments of old rock-and-roll or rhythm-and-blues records rappers would string together for their rhythm tracks. Commodities from global production lines have also proven especially important to the foundations of hip-hop: electronic equipment of all kinds, old 45 rpm records, Adidas sneakers, gold jewelry, and cans of spray paint, to name some of the best known. Indeed, young inner-city residents' own, self-fashioned consumer practices make up a critical piece of the overall fabric of hip-hop.[76]

At the same time, the aesthetic of hip-hop, what critic Arthur Jafa calls its "flow, layering, and rupture" — the edgy, seductively unpredictable beat of rap and break dance, the exuberant color and jagged lines of graffiti and hip-hop fashion, the defiant challenges of rap lyrics — have become a valuable commodity themselves.[77] In fact, global corporations have related to inner-city youth culture as if it were a kind of post-modern mining colony, replete with rich veins of aesthetic expression that are not only marketable themselves (as staggering worldwide sales of rap albums suggest), but also serve as fuel to fire one of the most important motors of world trade, advertising. Corporations' vast control over the manufacture and distribution of recordings and their ownership of the world's airwaves have for the most part overwhelmed the inner city's control over its own most important exports. The Big Six recording companies have swallowed up many independent, inner-city based recording studios, acquiring distribution rights to many others, and in the process they have probably been mostly responsible for the disproportionate marketing of "gangsta" rap over other voices within hip-hop.[78] More generally, multinational corporations of all stripes have exploited inner-city cultural forms, wrapping their own products in their own rendition of inner-city youth culture's defiant edge. A number of companies target what marketers call "the global teenager" by mining inner-city folklore, artistry, and resistive traditions for the cultural vibrancy they need to enliven their advertising. In this process, marketers glamorize and exoticize racial stereotypes of black athleticism, hypersexuality, and danger, adapting inner-city fashions and music to the tastes of a larger white middle-class "psychographic segment," especially its core of "wanna-bes" or "wiggers," who constitute the bulk of the market for hip-hop music and fashions in the United States. The resulting consumer crazes, refashioned as the latest from America, are sold to teens in Europe, Asia, and elsewhere.[79] The compelling rhythmic and lyric innovations of rap, for example, have proved invaluable in soundtracks for advertisements for, among many other things, "French crackers, English building societies, African soft drinks and . . . American jeans," according to *Billboard* magazine.[80]

Of course, hip-hop, inner-city culture as a whole, and its relation to broader global culture are by no means solely driven by consumerism. Examples from inner-city youth culture also help make this point clearly. Historians of hip-hop like George Lipsitz, Tricia Rose, Ernest Allen, and Robin D. G. Kelley have rightly called on scholars to recognize voices in hip-hop that often transcend the consumerism, misogyny, and glorification of violence of the most widely marketed manifestations of rap, and instead call for intentional resistance to structural oppression. Some rap artists have eloquently contested mainstream America's erasure and contempt by airing more complex and positive representations of African American identity. Their efforts, though still somewhat fragile, both reflect and influence other "world musicians' " portrayals of the "complex and plural" experiences of people living in postcolonial nations and subject to renewed worldwide migration, articulating a variety of transnational or national identities intended to soothe ethnic wounds and counter oppressive governments and racist ideologies.[81] Women musicians challenge hip-hop's misogynistic strain; other musicians criticize and suggest alternatives to the violence of inner-city life, not only that fomented by the drug trade but also, more pointedly, that of the police; some have even offered a critique of capitalism, albeit an ambivalent one.[82]

Since rap has been such a desired commodity itself, global trade and mass communication have allowed these more promising political messages to spread worldwide. In the process, inner-city culture's resistive qualities seem to have found a number of echoes, as millions of copies of rap recordings and eagerly sought pirated renditions saturated markets across the world, and hip-hop videos and sound tracks reached the estimated 203 million households connected to MTV's global cable and satellite networks (not counting the untold millions added when MTV Asia was inaugurated in 1991). Inspired by the nationalist message of groups like Public Enemy, pan-Asianist rappers have sprung up in Taipei, Seoul, Hong Kong, Bombay, and

Tokyo. The tapes of American rappers may have also inspired their Italian, French, German, and Japanese counterparts to illuminate working-class subcultures in places like Palermo, Frankfurt, the gritty suburbs of Paris, and "backstreet" Tokyo.[83] Rap artists' exposure of routinized police brutality in American inner cities may also have inspired other musicians' responses to state-sponsored injustice in France, the United Kingdom, Nigeria, Haiti, and many other places in the world.

But if inner-city voices have found something of a forum in global culture, and inner-city cultural exports have to a great extent quickened the pulse of the planet, this limited access to world trade and media has not guaranteed the integrity of urban poor people's most thoughtful political sentiments. If hip-hop can sell fine biscuits to Parisians, we should not be surprised when the Republic of Singapore deploys rap jingles, derived from an art form whose voice is central to resistance against police brutality, to remind teenagers of that country's authoritarian social codes and of the infamous punishments, such as canings, that come with them.[84] Television newscasters routinely broadcast footage of poor people dressed in fancy clothes and gold trimmed BMWs in ways that portray what might have been desperate and fleeting searches for status instead as evidence of profligacy and undeservingness. In countries particularly concerned about the survival of local cultures in the face of U.S. consumerism, inner cities pay another bitterly ironic price for their especially prominent role as providers of material for corporate advertising: there the United States' most sorely oppressed and plundered urban communities themselves sometimes face the charge of "cultural imperialism."

There is much insight in the idea that the cultural relationship between the corporate "global village" and the inner city is inherently "dialogic" — or, to use another metaphor, a "two-way street." But we must recognize that the cultural "street" built by corporations into poor urban America is a vast expressway filled with reckless traffic — and that most promising aspects of inner-city political culture still travel in great part against that flow.[85] The inner city thus imports not only glorified consumerism and various mass-cultural subversions of its own resistive politics but also, for example, efforts by McDonald's to counter critiques of low-wage labor by advertisements filled with happy young black workers that artfully hide the company's low wages, erratic shifts, and discriminatory hiring practices; portray low-wage work as clean and fun ("McDonald's is a happy place"); and promote its promise of upward mobility through individual effort (that is, into McDonald's vaunted managerships).[86] Through mass media and through recruiting networks that dig deep into inner-city nightclubs and playgrounds, multinational recording studios and the NBA and NCAA meanwhile transmit other illusory work values based on the glamorous and meteoric success stories of their stars.[87] On the streets meanwhile, employers from the drug cartels gut the moral authority of kids who refuse low wages by celebrating their murderous work through all-too-plausible references to American entrepreneurial ingenuity.[88]

Also ubiquitous on the small and large screens of inner-city homes and neighborhood theaters is the same vast wash of sanitized, masculinist, glorified violence that is everywhere so central to the American corporate cultural imagination. As I have argued elsewhere, the values inherent in this kind of imagery can only have aggravated the crises of social life in inner cities.[89]

Ultimately, of course, inner-city consumption of global corporate culture only helps to fund multinational capital's sizable responsibility for excluding poor urban America from the nation's economic and social life. The capacity of sneakers and gold chains to express personal power and status was orchestrated by advertising agencies subcontracting for giant companies that symbolically removed those objects from their material origins in structures that contribute to inner-city oppression. Follow a flashy Air Ndestrukt basketball shoe back through boardrooms and "concept sessions" at ad agencies (where it got both its quasi-Afrocentric moniker and its evocation of invulnerability and violence), and you end up in a sneaker factory in Indonesia run by Korean manufacturers contracting to Nike, who perpetuate the flight of manufacturing work that devastated inner cities by finding cheap labor in yet another country.[90] Follow the gold filaments that are woven into the inner-city's herringbone chains, and you end up three miles deep in a South African mine run on a migrant labor system that, with its reserves and townships and hostels, was once the model for "grand" apartheid, history's "highest stage" of institutionalized white supremacy.[91] Using these examples may be to dwell unfairly on over-hyped consumer practices of inner-city youth. However, they do suggest that the most effective political possibilities available to the inner-city dwellers as residents of the global village may not come from further access to its high-tech "marketplace" and "town square" but from intentional and targeted withdrawal from it. Here the powerful legacies of consumer boycotts led by African Americans — not only Jesse Jackson's recent actions against Coca-Cola and Nike, but the civil rights movement itself — could serve as compelling inspiration.

The story of inner cities and global villages also contains bigger lessons for world historians interested in the cultural and political life of poor urban American communities. For too long, inner-city culture has been studied either solely as a central force in creating urban social problems, or else as a badly understood and badly measured "variable" in quantitative analyses of poverty. As such, scholars often assume that inner-city life exists apart, isolated, and autonomous from broader cultural changes. The most extreme of these notions is embodied in "culture of poverty" theory, which sees the families and neighborhoods of the poor as the only means of inner-city cultural transmission — and alien, "upside-down" values as the only inner-city cultural product. Looking at young inner-city residents' participation in global corporate consumer culture is only one way to grasp the dimensions of a much more complex reality. In my reading, the urban poor live in what would be better described as a globally-linked *culture of richness and ambiguity.*[92]

Unequal "dialogues" between corporations and youthful artists from the inner-city are not the only dynamic shaping this complex culture or its interactions with other cultures. The ideas of governments, political leaders, religious institutions, and mass political, social and cultural movements, to name the most powerful, also resonate in the thinking of urban poor people of all ages, and inner-city residents alter those ideas, assemble pieces of them into new patterns of thought, and give them new meanings for different contexts. As with global corporate culture in the inner city the process involves not only consumerism, but most of the world's historic secular and spiritual ideologies. The history of this rich cultural mixing in global inner cities remains mostly unwritten. The hints we have about inner-city critiques of low-wage work suggest inner-city connections with the broader world history of reform liberalism or social democracy—just as informal entrepreneurs' evocation of Reaganesque platitudes suggest an inner-city version of laissez faire. Nationalism has a more manifest career in inner-city life; Marxism, at least at first glance, a much spottier one. Global militarism, sadly, has its inner-city variants, as do various ideologies of male supremacy. Commentary on the ideas and imagery of white supremacy has a complex, sometimes ambiguous, and widespread presence as well, most notably in rap's inversions of black male stereotypes. Liberal and radical languages of freedom, rights, and anti-racism also have manifest presences in global inner cities, as do a smattering of various forms of feminism. These, in turn, are often cloaked in liberatory messages derived from evangelical Christianity and Islam. Finally, inner-city political culture is also laced with more obscure spiritual faiths and folkways with worldwide origins, from Haitian Vodun to European Masonry to the numerological musings of Middle Eastern secret societies.[93] Indeed, global inner cities contain their own fabulously complex internal dialogues, and their tenacious ambiguity defies analyses that see poor people's culture as solely "resistive" just as definitively as they defy other labels like culture-of-poverty theory's "tangle of pathology."[94]

Ultimately, though, the impact of the global politics of inner-city culture, the possibilities of resistive aspects of inner-city cultural politics, and the effectiveness of inner-city political culture as a whole must be measured in terms of the ways they increase inner-city residents' power within the late twentieth century's rapidly changing global political economy. Assessing how U.S. inner cities have fared at the gates of global power is the principle reason for world-historical analyses of urban poverty. The question opens up still other fields of inquiry.

Conclusion: Inner Cities and Global Power

> In this age, when the ends of the world are being brought so near
> together, the millions of black men in Africa, America, and the Islands
> of the Sea, not to speak of the brown and yellow myriads elsewhere, are
> bound to have great influence upon the world in the future.
> —W.E.B. DuBois, "To the Nations of the World" July, 1900

Understanding the experience of poverty among urban African Americans
in the context of world history requires substantial overhauling of current
judgments — especially traditional notions of colonialism and such unfortunately named concepts as "underclass." No analysis should omit the economic deprivation caused to urban African Americans by exclusion from
well-paid, unionized, empowered work; by relegation to domestic low-wage
labor markets and their analogues; by conflicted relationships with and
racial and ethnic exclusion from "global city" service and low-wage manufacturing; by the inner city's place dead last on the list of locations for
"world market" factories; by continuing residential "hypersegregation" by
race and the consequent removal of poor urban African Americans from
the pushes and pulls that animate the world migration system; and by the
political economic arrangements of a neo-liberal world order that underpin
global policies of austerity and polarity. The history of inner-city residents'
responses to the constraints of changing job markets, marked by patterns of
dependency and rejection and influenced by critiques of exploitation and
conflicting hegemonic discourses about the work ethic and consumerism,
cannot be ignored. Culturally, American inner cities have been attractive to
multinational corporations and also vulnerable to various forms of cultural
exploitation; and though inclusion in global culture allows some inner-city
residents to at least transmit their voices and feelings to substantial international audiences, the urban poor still have little power to assure the integrity
or the political effectiveness of those messages.

These various, evolving relationships also help define the central political
imperative facing inner city communities — one that W.E.B. DuBois recognized a century ago and championed for the rest of his lifetime: whatever
hope the American urban poor harbor for greater self-determination depends, more vitally than ever before, on their capacity to build bonds across
borders and across continents.

Recent world-historical transformations of government put the severity of
this imperative into clear contextual perspective. If federal, state, and local
governments in the United States have found it easy to ignore the voices of
the poor in the past, their recent tendency to refer decisions about movements of capital, trade, and cultural property to much less accountable
transnational institutions has only diminished the ability of inner-city residents to make themselves heard. As the world rids itself of customs barriers,

there has been much talk of the need for labor and environmental regulations to supplement global trade agreements, but there has been little or no concern about the international roots of persistent poverty in American cities. Nor have vaunted side agreements to international trade treaties adequately addressed the declining wages, deteriorating conditions, gender inequities, or racial discrimination that pervade the job markets that seem destined to be poor urban African Americans' only viable source of sustenance for a long time to come. In turn, the head-over-heels rush to entice American and other Western corporations to remain on their native shores has undermined national governments' will to sustain their social safety nets and provide the health care, child care, and living wages that global capitalism should be paying for but is not. At the same time, the yoke of state repression has increased, particularly in the form of police brutality and massive expansion of the social death of incarceration.[95]

If "free trade" is ever to become a halfway equitable means of building sustainable wealth worldwide, the global institutions in charge of it and the national governments increasingly subject to it will have to hear much more from poor urban African Americans and their allies. As workplaces disappear, or as employers retrench — confident of labor surpluses or perfectly happy to close up and move in the event of resistance — struggles over work values will make sense only on an international stage. Any political activity in the cultural realm will ultimately need strongly organized constituencies to sustain the integrity and political effectiveness of its critical message no matter how broadly it is disseminated by global mass media.

The imperative of international mobilization should also prompt historians of global inner cities to examine whether the experiences of poor urban communities throughout the world have tended to converge or become more disparate as their fates have been tied up in global historical change, and whether those changes have structurally increased or decreased the possibility of international solidarity of poor people. Although structural relationships of American inner cities with the emerging world order are not exactly like those elsewhere or those of the past, the urban African American poor do share many characteristics with the urban poor of other parts of the world. Ethnographic and sociological works on the poor in France's notorious suburban *cités* and England's urban neighborhoods of color use American inner cities as a yardstick when seeking to understand their own postindustrial urban crises. Not surprisingly, many similar themes have emerged: industrial flight, racial segregation and hatred, rising rates of crime among young men, the erosion of welfare states, and the expansion of domestic security states. Scholars have also nervously noted the similarities between the "long hot summers" of the United States and the Bonfire Nights of Chapeltown (Leeds) in 1973–75, Notting Hill's Carnival Riots in 1976, the Brixton riots of 1983, the 1981 antipolice "rodeos" of Venissieux in the outskirts of Lyon, and Paris's 1990 suburban *émeutes* (uprisings) in Argenteuil, Sartrouville, and Mantes-la-Jolie. The prospect of the "Americanization" of European cities has, predictably, played a huge part in the "moral panic" that has greeted these events. But the comparison need not be sensationalized to affirm that the distinct histories of urban life in America and Europe may be converging as their cities endure common experiences with world change.[96]

Those comparisons should be drawn further, to encompass the urban poor of the world's Eastern and Southern Hemispheres. How do the experiences of poor people suffering the drain of industrial opportunity compare to those being asked to accept "downgraded" versions of it, whether within the United States or the West as a whole or more widely, in Asia and Latin America? Looking at world migration patterns since 1950 in a comparative framework might yield useful historical insights. How has African American migration from the South fit into the dynamics of global movements of people, and how do we make sense of the apparent sudden end of migration among poor urban African Americans just when movement elsewhere has picked up dramatically? Comparing the history of plans in the United States to create "enterprise zones" in several major American inner cities with that of their intellectual forebears, the "export processing zones" of Asia and Latin America, could provide useful lessons on the effects of industrial movement, migration, and the suspect wisdom of relying upon tax incentives, wage supports, and racially inspired government boosterism of workforces in the context of the global "race to the bottom." Comparisons with the South African townships would also be useful on the issues of hypersegregation and of ethnic politics in the workplace, as would comparisons between U.S. urban blacks and the experience of Puerto Rican Americans.[97]

Comparisons of poor people's multifarious responses to global change should go beyond comparisons of riots, though broadening comparisons of collective violence to include the "IMF riots" protesting austerity policies in Lima, Kingston, Kinshasa, Alexandria, Ankara, and dozens of other cities and towns across the world would be a fruitful enterprise.[98] Transnational historical comparisons of successful models of community development and resistance in the workplace — in South Asia, Latin America, and Africa, as well as in the West — that address their political and intellectual connections could restore balance to the story.[99] Has collapsing union strength in the West served to warn off organizers in Asia and the Southern Hemisphere? What inspiration, conversely, have American locals received from international organizing efforts originating south of the border?[100] Players of globally disseminated cultural politics as well as more traditional organizers and historians could benefit from broader studies of "everyday" forms of shop-floor and community resistance as well, from the often-hidden, often-subverted African American inner-city critique of low-wage labor, to Malaysian women working in export processing zones who are "periodically seized by spirit possession on the shop floor of modern factories," to the Vietnamese immigrant women in Silicon Valley who "play the China doll" to extract concessions from their employers, to the eloquent media "communiqués" of the Zapatista leaders of southern Mexico.[101]

A final assessment of whether the historically determined structures of inner-city poverty contain within themselves the seeds of sustained international opposition will probably not be written for a while. However, as well as keeping our eyes out for the germination of those seeds, historians should probably also be sensitive to signs of growth in other kinds of alliances. Late-twentieth-century global restructuring has not only injured the inhabitants of inner cities, but severely limited the opportunities and the wages in broader segments of American and Western societies. If a critical analysis of the new global laissez-faire and its troubling political economy can reverse current trends toward the political polarization between the poor on the one hand and the working and middle classes on the other, it will provide its ultimate test as a theory of inner-city history and world history.

In *The Philadelphia Negro*, W.E.B. DuBois set out on his own academic and activist journey animated by the hopes offered by that kind of critical theory. A hundred years later, as historians of inner cities continue our work, we need to sustain our own time's fragile but reviving guardianship of those hopes — for they are by far the best we have.

Notes

1. W.E.B. DuBois, "The Negro's Fatherland," *Survey* 39 (November 10, 1917): 141, quoted in David Levering Lewis, *W.E.B. DuBois: A Reader* (New York: Henry Holt, 1995), p. 653.

2. For his elaboration of the "peculiar history and condition of the American Negro," see pp. 282–84. For a broader discussion of slavery and the black population of Philadelphia, see pp. 10–45; on immigration, 25–32; and for a brief mention of international cultural trends on black entrepreneurs, see p. 120.

3. W.E.B. DuBois, "A Second Journey to Pan-Africa," *New Republic* 29 (December 7, 1921): 39–42, quoted in Lewis, *Reader*, p. 666.

4. "Colonial folk" and longer quote from W.E.B. DuBois, "Whites in Africa after Negro Autonomy," from *In Albert Schweitzer's Realm: A Symposium*, ed. A. A. Roback (Cambridge, Mass.: Sci-Art Publishers, 1962), pp. 243–55, quoted in Lewis, *A Reader*, p. 688; W.E.B. DuBois, "The Disfranchised Colonies," from *Color and Democracy: Colonies and Peace* (1945), in Lewis, *A Reader*, pp. 676–82.

5. W.E.B. DuBois, "What Is the Meaning of 'All Deliberate Speed'?" *National Guardian*, November 4, 1957, in Lewis, *A Reader*, p. 423.

6. William K. Tabb, *The Political Economy of the Black Ghetto* (New York: Norton, 1970), pp. 21–34; Wilfred L. David, "Black America in Development Perspective, Part I" and "Part II," *Review of Black Political Economy* 3, 2 (Winter 1973): 89–104; 3, 4 (Summer 1973): 79–112; Ron Bailey, "Economic Aspects of the Black Internal Colony," *Review of Black Political Economy* 3, 4 (Summer 1973): 43–72; Guy C. A. Mhone, "Structural Oppression and the Persistence of Black Poverty," *Journal of Afro-*

American Issues 3 (1975): 406; Robert Blauner, *Racial Oppression in America* (New York: Harper and Row, 1972), chap. 3. For a useful discussion of the "ghetto as colony" school, see Michael Katz, *The Undeserving Poor: From the War on Poverty to the War on Welfare* (New York: Pantheon, 1989), pp. 52–65.

7. For these critiques of the "ghetto as colony" theory, see Donald Harris, "The Black Ghetto as Colony: A Theoretical Critique and Alternative Formulation," *Review of Black Political Economy* 2, 4 (Summer 1972): 3–33; Joseph Seward, "Developmental Economics and Black America: A Reply to Professor David," *Review of Black Political Economy* 5, 2 (Winter 1975): 185–201. For one response to the critiques, see William K. Tabb, "Marxian Exploitation and Domestic Colonialism: A Reply to Donald J. Harris," *Review of Black Political Economy* 4, 4 (Summer 1974): 69–87.

8. William Julius Wilson, *The Declining Significance of Race: Blacks and Changing American Institutions* (Chicago: University of Chicago Press, 1978), pp. 81–121; Wilson, *The Truly Disadvantaged: The Inner City, the Underclass, and Public Policy* (Chicago: University of Chicago Press, 1987), pp. 3–109. Much of the groundwork for this thesis was laid earlier by other scholars. See Charles Killingsworth, "The Continuing Labor Market Twist," *Monthly Labor Review* 91 (September 1968): 12–17; Killingsworth, "Negroes in a Changing Labor Market," in *Employment, Race, and Poverty*, ed. Arthur Ross and Herbert Hill (New York: Harcourt, Brace 1967), pp. 49–70; John Kasarda, "Urban Change and Minority Opportunities," in *The New Urban Reality*, ed. Paul Peterson (Washington, D.C.: Brookings Institution, 1985), pp. 33–68; Carolyn Adams, David Bartelt, David Elesh, Ira Goldstein, Nancy Kleniewski, and William Yancey, *Philadelphia: Neighborhood, Division, and Conflict in a Postindustrial City* (Philadelphia: Temple University Press, 1991), pp. 22–43.

The best historical analysis of this story is Thomas J. Sugrue, *The Origins of the Urban Crisis: Race and Inequality in Postwar Detroit* (Princeton, N.J.: Princeton University Press, 1996); and Sugrue, "The Structures of Urban Poverty: The Reorganization of Space and Work in Three Periods of American History," in *The "Underclass" Debate: Views from History*, ed. Michael Katz (Princeton, N.J.: Princeton University Press, 1993), pp. 85–117. See also Kenneth L. Kusmer, "African Americans in the City Since World War II: From the Industrial to the Post-Industrial Era," *Journal of Urban History* 21 (March 1995): pp. 458–505.

9. See Joleen Kirschenmann and Kathryn Neckerman, "We'd Love to Hire Them, But, . . ." in *The Urban Underclass* ed. Christopher Jencks and Paul Peterson (Washington, D.C.: Brookings Institution, 1991) pp. 203–34; Sugrue, "Structures of Urban Poverty," pp. 106–7, 110–14; Douglas S. Massey and Nancy A. Denton, *American Apartheid: Segregation and the Making of the Underclass* (Cambridge, Mass: Harvard University Press, 1993).

10. See Colin McCord and Harold P. Freeman, "Excess Mortality in Harlem," *New England Journal of Medicine* 322, 3 (January 18, 1990): 173–77; Richard B. Freeman and Harry J. Holzer, "The Black Youth Employment Crisis: Summary of Findings," in *The Black Youth Employment Crisis*, ed. Freeman and Holzer (Chicago: University of Chicago Press, 1986), p. 3.

11. In fact, scholars studying different aspects of poverty in urban African American communities have only recently made it a standard part of their analyses to include changes in global economic structures. See, for example, William Julius Wilson, *When Work Disappears: The World of The New Urban Poor* (New York: Knopf, 1996), pp. 28–29, 152–55; Sugrue, "Structures of Urban Poverty," pp. 102–4; Mike Davis, "Chinatown Revisited? The 'Internationalization' of Downtown Los Angeles," and "The Empty Quarter," in *Sex, Death, and God in L.A.*, ed. David Reid (New York: Random House, 1992), pp. 19–53, 54–74; Tricia Rose, *Black Noise: Rap Music and Black Culture in Contemporary America* (Hanover, N.H.: Wesleyan University Press/

University Press of New England, 1994), pp. 27–29; Philippe Bourgois, "In Search of Horatio Alger: Culture and Ideology in the Crack Economy" *Contemporary Drug Problems* 16, 4 (winter 1989): 627. Jacqueline Jones has added a new "Epilogue" to her *Labor of Love, Labor of Sorrow: Black Women, Work, and the Family, from Slavery to the Present* (New York: Vintage, 1985) that discusses how global changes have affected women. "A New Epilogue to the Vintage Edition," page proofs distributed at the 109th Annual Meeting of the American Historical Association, January 1995, p. 326.

On the link between the global economy and plant closings, see also Barry Bluestone and Bennett Harrison, *The Deindustrialization of America: Plant Closings, Community Abandonment, and the Dismantling of Basic Industry* (New York: Basic Books, 1982), chap. 2; David C. Perry, "The Politics of Dependency in Deindustrializing America: The Case of Buffalo, New York," in *The Capitalist City: Global Restructuring and Community Politics*, ed. Michael Peter Smith and Joe Feagin (Oxford: Basil Blackwell, 1987), pp. 113–37; Richard Child Hill and Joe R. Feagin, "Detroit and Houston: Two Cities in Global Perspective," in Smith and Feagin, *Capitalist City*, pp. 155–77; Edward Soja, "Economic Restructuring and the Internationalization of the Los Angeles Region," in Smith and Feagin, *Capitalist City*, pp. 178–98. For the impact of global restructuring on Appalachia see, John Gaventa, "From the Mountains to the Maquiladoras: A Case Study of Capital Flight and Its Impact on Workers," in *Appalachia in an International Context*, ed. Philip J. Obermiller and William W. Philliber (Westport, Conn.: Praeger, 1994), pp. 165–76.

On the relation between global production networks and declining wages and increasing inequality, see Walter R. Mead, *The Low-Wage Challenge to Global Growth: The Labor Cost-Productivity Imbalance in Newly Industrialized Countries* (Washington, D.C.: Economic Policy Institute, 1990); Richard Barnet and John Cavanagh, *Global Dreams: Imperial Corporations and the New World Order* (New York: Simon and Schuster, 1994), pp. 257–358; James H. Johnson, Jr., Melvin L. Oliver, and Lawrence Bobo, "Understanding the Contours of Deepening Urban Inequality: Theoretical Underpinnings and Research Design of a Multi-City Study" *Urban Geography* 15 (1994): 77–89.

12. For some of the theoretical underpinnings of this work, see Immanuel Wallerstein, *The Modern World System*, Vol. 1: *Capitalist Agriculture and the Origins of the European World-Economy in the Sixteenth Century* (New York: Academic Press, 1974); Vol. 2, *Mercantilism and the Consolidation of the European World-Economy, 1600–1750* (New York: Academic Press, 1980); Vol. 3, *The Second Era of Great Expansion of the Capitalist World-Economy, 1730–1840s* (New York: Academic Press, 1989); *The Capitalist World-Economy: Essays* (New York: Cambridge University Press, 1979); Manuel Castells, *The Informational City: Information Technology, Economic Restructuring, and the Urban-Regional Process* (New York: Basil Blackwell, 1989); John Friedman, "The World City Hypothesis," *Development and Change* 17, 1 (January 1986): 69–83; Michael Timberlake, "World-System Theory and the Study of Comparative Urbanization," in Smith and Feagin, *Capitalist City*, pp. 37–65; Norman J. Glickman, "Cities and the International Division of Labor," in Smith and Feagin, *Capitalist City*, pp. 66–86; Michael Peter Smith and Richard Tardanico, "Urban Theory Reconsidered: Production, Reproduction, and Collective Action," in Smith and Feagin, *Capitalist City*, pp. 87–112; Kathryn Ward, *Women in the World-System: Impact on Status and Fertility* (New York: Praeger, 1984); Joseph Grunwald and Kenneth Flam, *The Global Factory: Foreign Assembly in International Trade* (Washington, D.C.: Brookings Institution, 1985); Anthony D. King, *Urbanism, Colonialism and the World Economy* (London: Routledge, 1990); *Global Cities: Post-Imperialism and the Internationalization of London* (London: Routledge, 1990); Saskia Sassen, *The Global City: New York, London, Tokyo* (Princeton, N.J.: Princeton University Press, 1991); and Martin Shefter, ed., *Capital of the*

American Century: The National and International Influence of New York City (New York: Russell Sage Foundation, 1993). For a view that is in some respects critical, see Thomas Muller, *Immigrants and the American City* (New York: New York University Press, 1993), esp. chap. 4.

13. Sassen, *Global City*, p. 19. On CHIPS, see Barnet and Cavanagh, *Global Dreams*, pp. 387–89.

14. Joe R. Feagin and Michael Peter Smith, "Cities and the New International Division of Labor: An Overview," in *Capitalist City*, pp. 6–9; Judith Goode, "Polishing the Rustbelt: Immigrants Enter a Restructuring Philadelphia," in *Newcomers in the Workplace: Immigrants and the Restructuring of the U.S. Economy*, ed. Louise Lamphere, Alex Stepick, and Guillermo Grenier (Philadelphia: Temple University Press, 1994), pp. 199–230; Hill and Feagin, "Detroit and Houston," pp. 138–54; Soja, "Economic Restructuring," pp. 178–98.

15. Sassen, *Global City*, p. 291; Sassen-Koob, "New York City's Informal Economy," in *The Informal Economy*, ed. Alejandro Portes, Manuel Castells, and Lauren A. Benton (Baltimore: Johns Hopkins University Press, 1989), pp. 71–72.

16. Patricia Fernandez-Kelly and Anna M. Garcia, "Informalization at the Core: Hispanic Women, Homework, and the Advanced Capitalist State," in Portes, Castells, and Benton, *Informal Economy*, pp. 247–64; Sassen, *Global City*, p. 10.

17. The legal minimum wage in 1989 was $3.35. U.S. General Accounting Office, Human Resources Division (GAO, HRD), *"Sweatshops" in New York City: A Local Example of a Nationwide Problem* (Washington, D.C.: General Accounting Office, 1989), pp. 8, 21. See also GAO, HRD, *"Sweatshops" in the U.S.: Opinions on Their Extent and Possible Enforcement Options* (Washington, D.C.: General Accounting Office, 1988); and Jane H. Lii, "Week in Sweatshop Reveals Grim Conspiracy of the Poor," *New York Times*, March 12, 1995, pp. 1, 40. The use of sweatshops in New York's garment industry also reflects the special needs of the local "spot" market and the need to meet capricious surges in demand for certain styles of clothing. See Roger Waldinger, *Through the Eye of the Needle: Immigrants and Enterprise in New York's Garment Trades* (New York: New York University Press, 1986); and Local 23–25 International Ladies Garment Workers Union and the New York Skirt and Sportswear Association, *The Chinatown Garment Industry Study* (study by Abeles, Schwartz, Haeckel and Silverblatt, Inc., June 1983). On violations of child labor laws, see Brian Dumaine, "Illegal Child Labor Comes Back," *Fortune*, April 5, 1993, p. 86. See also Peter Kwong, *The New Chinatown* (New York: Hill and Wang, 1987); and Min Zhou, *Chinatown: The Socioeconomic Potential of an Urban Enclave* (Philadelphia: Temple University Press, 1992).

18. Sassen-Koob, "New York City's Informal Economy," pp. 60–77; Sassen, *Global City*, 290; Patricia Fernandez-Kelly and Anna Garcia, "Informalization at the Core: Hispanic Women, Homework, and the Advanced Capitalist State," in Portes, Castells, and Benton, *The Informal Economy*, pp. 247–64; Edna Bonacich, "Asians in the Los Angeles Garment Industry," in *The New Asian Immigration in Los Angeles and Global Restructuring*, ed. Paul Ong, Edna Bonacich and Lucie Cheng (Philadelphia: Temple University Press, 1994), pp. 137–63; Alejandro Portes and Alex Stepick, *City on the Edge: The Transformation of Miami* (Berkeley and Los Angeles: University of California Press, 1993), pp. 40–41, 154.

19. Karen Hossfeld, "Hiring Immigrant Women: Silicon Valley's 'Simple Formula,'" in *Women of Color in U.S. Society*, ed. Maxine Baca Zinn and Bonnie Thornton Dill (Philadelphia: Temple University Press, 1994), pp. 65–94; Ruth Taplin, "Women in World Market Factories: East and West," *Ethnic and Racial Studies* 9, 2 (April 1986): 168–95. On New York, see Sassen-Koob, "New York's Informal Economy," pp. 67–68.

20. U.S. workers in these industries also face increased competition from lower-wage workforces abroad. See John Yearwood, "A Ticket to Pride: A Barbados Unit of AMR Excels at Data Entry," *Dallas Morning News*, p. 1-H.

21. Louise Lamphere, Alex Stepick, and Guillermo Grenier, *Newcomers in the Workplace: Immigrants and the Restructuring of the U.S. Economy* (Philadelphia: Temple University Press, 1994); Portes and Stepick, *City on the Edge*, pp. 40–41, 127–28, 133–34, 154; Guillermo J. Grenier, "The Cuban-American Labor Movement in Dade County: An Emerging Immigrant Working Class," in *Miami Now! Immigration, Ethnicity, and Social Change*, ed. Guillermo (Gainesville: University of Florida Press, 1992), Grenier and Alex Stepick III, p. 144; Fernandez-Kelly and Garcia, "Informalization at the Core," p. 257; Hossfeld, "Hiring Immigrant Women," p. 72; on immigrants in New York City hotels see Roger Waldinger, "Who Gets the Lousy Jobs? in *Still the Promised City? African Americans and New Immigrants in New York, 1940–1990*, chap. 5 (Cambridge, Mass.: Harvard University Press, 1996), pp. 137–73.

22. Sassen, *Global City*, pp. 290–91.

23. The argument I present here combines portions of arguments put forward by a number of scholars. See James Crotty, Gerald Epstein, and Patricia Kelly, "Multinational Corporations and Technological Change: Global Stagnation, Inequality, and Unemployment" (paper prepared for the Economic Policy Institute Conference on "Globalization and Progressive Economic Policy: What Are the Real Constraints? What Are the Real Options," Washington, D.C., June 21–23, 1996); James Crotty, "The Rise and Fall of the Keynesian Revolution in the Age of the Global Marketplace," in *Creating a New World Economy: Forces of Change and Plans for Action*, ed. Gerald Epstein, Julie Graham, and Jessica Nembhard for the Center for Popular Economics (Philadelphia: Temple University Press, 1993), pp. 163–82; Gerald Epstein, "Power, Profits, and Corporations in the Global Economy," in Epstein, Graham, and Nembhard, *Creating a New World Economy*, pp. 19–46; James Crotty and Gerald Epstein, "In Defense of Capital Controls," Working Paper 1996-1 (University of Massachusetts Department of Economics, 1996); David M. Gordon, "The Global Economy: New Edifice or Crumbling Foundations?" *New Left Review* 168 (March–April 1988): 24–65. For a popular account that makes a similar argument, see William Greider, *One World, Ready or Not: The Manic Logic of Global Capitalism* (New York: Simon and Schuster, 1997).

24. Crotty, "The Rise and Fall of the Keynesian Revolution"; Crotty and Epstein, "In Defense of Capital Controls"; Howard M. Wachtel, *Money Mandarins: The Making of a New Supranational Economic Order* (New York: Pantheon, 1986). On the era of financial instability, see Fred L. Block, *The Origins of International Economic Disorder: A Study of United States International Monetary Policy from World War II to the Present* (Berkeley and Los Angeles: University of California Press, 1977); Gerald Epstein, "Financial Instability and the Structure of the International Monetary System," in *Instability and Change in the World Economy*, ed. Arthur MacEwan and William K. Tabb (New York: Monthly Review Press, 1989), pp. 101–20. On the role of Paul Volcker and the Federal Reserve in austerity, see William Greider, *Secrets of the Temple: How the Federal Reserve Runs the Country* (New York: Simon and Schuster, 1987). On cultural aspects of the neo-liberal revival, see Jane Kelsey, *Economic Fundamentalism* (London: Pluto Press, 1995).

25. Crotty, "The Rise and Fall of the Keynesian Revolution"; Bennett Harrison and Barry Bluestone, *The Great U-Turn: Corporate Restructuring and the Polarizing of America* (New York: Basic Books, 1988); Samuel Bowles, David M. Gordon, and Thomas E. Weiskopf, *After the Wasteland: A Democratic Economics for the Year 2000* (Armonk, N.Y.: M.E. Sharpe, 1990), chap. 5; Richard B. Freeman, "How Labor Fares in Advanced Economies," in *Working Under Different Rules*, ed. Freeman (New York: Russell Sage

Foundation, 1994), pp. 1–28; David M. Gordon, *Fat and Mean: The Corporate Squeeze of Working Americans and the Myth of Managerial "Downsizing"* (New York: Free Press, 1996).

26. The work of pioneers in this effort can be found in Else Oyen, S. M. Miller and Syed Abdus Samad, eds., *Poverty: A Global Review* (Oslo: Scandinavian University Press, 1996); Katherine McFate, Roger Lawson, and William Julius Wilson, eds., *Poverty, Inequality and the Future of Social Policy: Western States in the New World Order* (New York: Russell Sage Foundation, 1985); Enzo Mingione, ed., *Urban Poverty and the Underclass: A Reader* (London: Blackwell, 1996); Timothy Smeeding and Lee Rainwater, *Income Distribution in OECD Countries: Evidence from the Luxembourg Income Study* (Washington D.C.: OECD Publications and Information Center, 1995).

27. Carl Nightingale, " 'Chocolate Cities' in a World of Poverty," unpublished paper.

28. See David Bunting, *The Rise of Large American Corporations, 1889–1919* (New York: Garland, 1986); Naomi Lamoreaux, *The Great Merger Movement in American Business, 1895–1904* (Cambridge: Cambridge University Press, 1985); Olivier Zunz, *Making America Corporate, 1870–1920* (Chicago: University of Chicago Press, 1990), pp. 1–36, 103–24. On the downtown office boom of the 1950s, see Jon C. Teaford, *The Rough Road to Renaissance: Urban Revitalization in America, 1940–1985* (Baltimore: Johns Hopkins University Press, 1990), pp. 131–35.

29. Kusmer, "African Americans in the City," p. 486.

30. See Jacqueline Jones, this volume; Stanley Lieberson, *A Piece of the Pie: Blacks and Whites Since 1880* (Berkeley: University of California Press, 1980), pp. 292–362.

31. See James Grossman, "The White Man's Union: The Great Migration and the Resonance of Race and Class in Chicago, 1916–1922," in *The Great Migration in Historical Perspective*, ed. Joe Trotter (Bloomington: Indiana University Press, 1991), pp. 83–105; Consumers' League of New York City, *A New Day for the Colored Woman Worker: A Study of Colored Women in Industry* (New York: [n.p.], 1919).

32. Steven P. Erie, "Rainbow's End: From the Old to the New Urban Ethnic Politics," in *Urban Ethnicity in the United States*, ed. Lionel Maldonaldo and Joan Moore (Beverly Hills, Calif.: Sage, 1994), pp. 249–75; Waldinger, in *Still the Promised City?* chap. 7.

33. Tony Horwitz, "9 to Nowhere: These Six Growth Jobs Are Dull, Dead-End, Sometimes Dangerous," *Wall Street Journal*, December 1, 1994, pp. A1, A8–9; for a more detailed discussion of Gulf Coast fisheries and poultry processing, see David Griffith, *Jones's Minimal: Low-Wage Labor in the United States* (Albany: State University of New York Press, 1993).

34. Jacqueline Jones, "Southern Diaspora: Origins of the Northern 'Underclass,' " in Katz, *The "Underclass" Debate*, pp. 27–54.

35. Elizabeth H. Pleck, *Black Migration and Poverty: Boston, 1865–1900* (New York: Academic Press, 1979), pp. 134–37.

36. Kusmer, "African Americans in the City," pp. 29–30; David T. Ellwood, "The Spatial Mismatch Hypothesis: Are There Teenage Jobs Missing in the Inner City?" in *The Black Youth Employment Crisis*, ed. Richard B. Freeman and Harry J. Holzer (Chicago: University of Chicago Press, 1986), pp. 147–90.

37. Carrie Teegardin, "Growing Up Southern: American Big-City Refugee Finds Safe Haven," *Atlanta Constitution*, June 9, 1993, p. A-1. See also Griffith, *Jones's Minimal*.

38. See also Elliot Liebow's description of transportation to construction jobs. *Tally's Corner: A Study of Negro Streetcorner Men* (Boston: Little, Brown, 1967), pp. 43–44.

39. Institute for Women's Policy Research (IWPR), *Combining Work and Welfare: An*

Alternative Poverty Strategy (Washington, D.C.: IWPR, 1992), pp. 9–33; and IWPR, *Welfare That Works: The Working Lives of AFDC Recipients* (Washington, D.C.: IWPR, 1995), pp. 15–52; Kathryn Eden's data are included in Christopher Jencks, *Rethinking Social Policy: Race, Poverty, and the Underclass* (Cambridge, Mass.: Harvard University Press, 1992), chap. 6; Katherine S. Newman, "What Inner-City Jobs for Welfare Moms?" *New York Times*, May 20, 1995, p. 23; Newman, "Finding Work in the Inner City: How Hard Is It Now? How Hard is it for AFDC Recipients?" (paper).

40. Lawrence Levine, *Black Culture and Black Consciousness: Afro-American Folk Thought from Slavery to Freedom* (Oxford: Oxford University Press, 1977), pp. 81–135, 300–319, 370–85; Liebow, *Tally's Corner*, pp. 37–39; Robin D. G. Kelley, *Race Rebels: Culture, Politics, and the Black Working Class* (New York: Free Press, 1994), pp. 17–25.

41. See Tera W. Hunter's essay in this volume. Also, see Hunter, "Domination and Resistance: The Politics of Wage Household Labor in New South Atlanta," *Labor History* 34 (spring-summer 1993), pp. 205–20; Jones, *Labor of Love*, pp. 257–58; Diane Van Raaphorst, *Union Maids Not Wanted: Organizing Domestic Workers, 1870–1940* (New York: Praeger, 1988); Brenda Clegg Gray, *Black Female Domestic Servants During the Depression in New York City, 1930–1940* (New York: Garland, 1993); Judith Rollins, *Between Women: Domestics and Their Employers* (Philadelphia: Temple University Press, 1985); David M. Katzman, *Seven Days a Week: Women and Domestic Service in Industrializing America* (New York, Oxford University Press, 1978).

42. Kelley, *Race Rebels*, p. 25; Jones, "Southern Diaspora," p. 39.

43. Liebow, *Tally's Corner*, pp. 58–59. Using statistical evidence from a National Bureau of Economic Research project on black and white teenagers that dates from 1979 and 1980, Harry J. Holzer concluded that "young blacks have modeled their expectations and aspirations after those of the white society around them" ("Black Youth Nonemployment: Duration and Job Search," in Freeman and Holzer, *The Black Youth Employment Crisis*, p. 65).

44. See also Jay McLeod, *Ain't No Making It: Levelled Aspirations in a Low-Income Neighborhood* (Boulder, Colo.: Westview Press, 1987), pp. 60–81.

45. HARYOU, Inc., *Youth in the Ghetto*, pp. 313–50. Robin D. G. Kelley argues that race or "a sense of 'blackness' " plays a central role in work-related as well as other aspects of what he calls African Americans' "infrapolitics." See *Race Rebels*, pp. 5, 26–27. Philippe Bourgois adds that "the 'personal failure' of those who survive on the street is articulated in the idiom of race." See "In Search of Horatio Alger," p. 628.

46. See Liebow, *Tally's Corner*, pp. 62–63: HARYOU, *Youth in the Ghetto*, pp. 332–33; Lee Rainwater, *Behind Ghetto Walls: Black Families in a Federal Slum* (Chicago: Aldine, 1970), pp. 155–87, 316–60; Elijah Anderson, *A Place on the Corner* (Chicago: University of Chicago Press, 1976), pp. 66; Bourgois, "In Search of Horatio Alger," pp. 627–31.

47. Bonnie Thornton Dill, *Across the Boundaries of Race and Class: An Exploration of Work and Family Among Black Female Domestic Servants* (New York: Garland, 1994), pp. 90–106.

48. Jacqueline Jones, *The Dispossessed: America's Underclasses from the Civil War to the Present* (New York: Basic Books, 1992), pp. 104–26.

49. Carl H. Nightingale, *On the Edge: A History of Poor Black Children and Their American Dreams* (New York: Basic Books, 1993), pp. 59–62; Liebow, *Tally's Corner*, pp. 72–160, 208–31; Rainwater, *Behind Ghetto Walls*, pp. 157–87, 316–97; Elijah Anderson, *Streetwise: Race, Class, and Change in an Urban Community* (Chicago: University of Chicago Press, 1990), pp. 112–37.

50. Forty-one percent of gainfully employed black women in nonagricultural work were domestics in 1950, according to Jacqueline Jones (*Labor of Love*, p. 257); in 1960, according to Ken Kusmer, the figure was 35 percent and in 1980 it was 7

percent ("African Americans in the City," p. 42). See also Julianne Malveaux, "From Domestic Worker to Household Technician: Black Women in a Changing Occupation," in Phyllis A. Wallace, *Black Women in the Labor Force* (Cambridge: Cambridge University Press, 1980), pp. 85–98.

51. John McPhee wrote about the blue "Farm Labor" trucks that were owned and driven by blacks who picked up black workers off the streets of Philadelphia and transported them to the blueberry fields of New Jersey during the late 1960s. At seven cents a pint, good pickers could make $18 during the day. *The Pine Barrens* (New York: Farrar, Strauss Giroux, 1967), pp. 89–95. More recently, I have been told by a Laotian friend that the blueberry farmers rely more heavily on Laotians and Vietnamese from Philadelphia, as well as on immigrant Mexicans who live and work on neighboring tomato and eggplant farms. For blacks' rejection of the slavery-like conditions of sugar harvesting in 1940s South Florida, see Alec Wilkinson, *Big Sugar: Seasons in the Cane Fields of Florida* (New York: Knopf, 1989), pp. 122–43.

52. According to the Kerner Commission, after all, the average rioter in the 1960s was "almost invariably underemployed or employed at a menial job" and "proud of his race." National Commission on Civil Disorders, *Report of the National Advisory Commission on Civil Disorders* (New York: E. P. Dutton, 1968), p. 111.

53. Mercer Sullivan, *Getting Paid: Youth, Crime, and Work in the Inner City* (Ithaca, N.Y.: Cornell University Press, 1989); Philippe Bourgois, *In Search of Respect: Selling Crack in El Barrio* (Cambridge: Cambridge University Press, 1995); W. Kip Viscusi, "Market Incentives for Criminal Behavior," in Freeman and Holzer, *The Black Youth Employment Crisis*, pp. 301–52.

54. The indexes of Smith and Feagin's *Capitalist City* and Saskia Sassen's *Global City*, for example, contain no references to "blacks" or "African Americans," and citations to categories like "race" and "minority workers" (their preferred terms) tend to focus on immigrants.

55. See, for example, Muller, *Immigrants and the American City*, pp. 167–85.

56. Joseph G. Altonji and David Card found "a modest degree of competition between immigrants and less-skilled natives," though they agree with Muller that there is "little evidence that inflows of immigrants are associated with large or systematic effects on the employment or unemployment rates of less-skilled natives." "Immigration and Labor Market Outcomes," in *Immigration, Trade, and the Labor Market*, ed. John M. Abowd and Richard B. Freeman (Chicago: Chicago University Press, 1991), p. 226. See also Paul Ong and Abel Valenzuela "Job Competition Between Immigrants and African Americans," *Poverty and Race* (newsletter of the Poverty and Race Research Action Council) 4, 2 (March–April 1995): 9–12; Ong and Valenzuela, "The Political Economy of Job Competition Between Immigrants and African Americans," in *Ethnic Los Angeles*, ed. Roger Waldinger and Mehdi Bozorgmehr (New York: Russell Sage Foundation Press, forthcoming).

On wages, see George J. Borjas, Richard B. Freeman, and Lawrence F. Katz, "Labor Market Effects of Immigration and Trade," in *Immigration and the Work Force: Economic Consequences for the United States and Source Areas*, ed. George J. Borjas and Richard B. Freeman (Chicago: University of Chicago Press, 1992), p. 243; Joseph G. Altonji and David Card, "The Effects of Immigration on the Labor Market Outcomes of Less-Skilled Natives," in Abowd and Freeman, *Immigration, Trade, and the Labor Market*, pp. 201–34; and Peter Kuhn and Ian Wooton, "Immigration, International Trade, and the Wages of Native Workers," in Abowd and Freeman, *Immigration, Trade, and the Labor Market*, pp. 285–304.

57. Randall K. Filer, "Immigrant Arrivals and the Migratory Patterns of Native Workers," in Borjas and Freeman, *Immigration and the Work Force*, pp. 267–68. See Massey and Denton, *American Apartheid*, pp. 118–42, 160–62.

58. Waldinger, *Still the Promised City?* pp. 137–73.

59. Ibid.

60. Roger Waldinger and Thomas Bailey, "The Continuing Significance of Race: Racial Conflict and Racial Discrimination in Construction," *Politics and Society* 19 (1991): 291–323. On this topic in general, see also Suzanne Model, "The Ethnic Niche and the Structure of Opportunity: Immigrants and Minorities in New York City," in Katz, *"Underclass" Debate*, pp. 161–93; Roger Waldinger, "Changing Ladders and Musical Chairs: Ethnicity and Opportunity in Post-Industrial New York," *Politics and Society* 15 (1986–87): 369–402; Alex Stepick, Guillermo Grenier, with Hafidh A. Hafidh, Sue Chafee, and Debbie Draznin, "The View from the Back of the House: Restaurants and Hotels in Miami," in Lamphere, Stepick, and Grenier, *Newcomers in the Workplace*, pp. 181–98; Goode, "Polishing the Rustbelt," pp. 199–230.

61. Lii, "Week in Sweatshop," p. 40.

62. Saskia Sassen claims that informal "neighborhood subeconomies have been a rather common development in immigrant communities, but rare in native minority neighborhoods." "New York's Informal Economy," pp. 74–75). Her statement may be more accurate for informal industrial plants.

63. Model, "Ethnic Niche," pp. 181–86, 191–93; Waldinger, *Still the Promised City?* pp. 206–53; Stephen Erie, "Rainbow's End," pp. 265–71.

64. Kirschenman and Neckerman, "We'd Like to Hire Them, But," pp. 209–17, see also Philip Moss and Chris Tilly, "Raised Hurdles for Black Men: Evidence from the Interviews with Employers" (paper, Department of Policy Planning, University of Massachusetts — Lowell).

65. Waldinger, *Still the Promised City?*, pp. 137–73.

66. Hossfeld, "Hiring Immigrant Women," pp. 65, 75–76, 80–81; for more evidence about the roots of this logic in corporate practices in Southeast Asia, see Ruth Taplin, "Women in World Market Factories: East and West," *Ethnic and Racial Studies* 9, 2 (April 1986): 168–95.

67. Edna Bonacich makes a similar point in "Advanced Capitalism and Black/White Relations in the United States: A Split Labor Market Analysis," *American Sociological Review* 41, no. 1 (February, 1976): 48.

68. Hossfeld, "Hiring Immigrant Women," p. 80. Carole Cohen, "Facing Job Loss: Changing Relationships in a Multicultural Urban Factory," in Lamphere, Stepick, and Grenier, *Newcomers in the Workplace*, pp. 231–50.

69. Thomas Sowell has made the most elaborate case for the validity of distinctions between groups based on evaluations of their productivity. See *Race and Culture: A World View* (New York, Basic Books, 1994), chap. 5. Lawrence Mead has provided probably the most sweeping denunciations of inner-city work values in his *The New Politics of Poverty: The Nonworking Poor in America* (New York: Basic Books, 1992). In his advocacy of immigration, Thomas Muller reduces all young black teenagers' complicated views on low-wage jobs to a matter of "motivation," and cites with black approval Los Angeles community leader George Givens: "young blacks today don't want to stay at the bottom. After the Civil Rights Movement there was a false message that you didn't have to work yourself up." *Immigration and the American City*, p. 176.

70. See Joe Davidson, "Shoplifting Black Dollars," *Emerge*, March 1995, pp. 26–30.

71. See Judith Goode and Jo Anne Schneider, *Reshaping Ethnic and Racial Relations in Philadelphia: Immigrants in a Divided City* (Philadelphia: Temple University Press, 1994), esp. pp. 61–98; Paul Ong, Kye Young Park, and Yasmin Tong, "The Korean-Black Conflict and the State," in Ong, Bonacich, and Cheng, *New Asian Immigration in Los Angeles*, pp. 264–94; and Regina Freer, "Black-Korean Conflict," in *The Los Angeles Riots: Lessons for the Urban Future*, ed. Mark Baldassare (Boulder, Colo.: West-

view Press, 1994), pp. 175–204; Sumi K. Cho, "Korean Americans vs. African Americans: Conflict and Construction," in *Reading Rodney King, Reading Urban Uprising*, ed. Robert Gooding-Williams (New York: Routledge, 1993), pp. 196–214. On black-Hispanic tensions see Jack Miles, "Blacks vs. Browns: African Americans and Latinos," *Atlantic*, October 1992, p. 41; and Portes and Stepick, *City on the Edge*, pp. 12–16, 140–41, 176–77, 182–84, 196–202.

72. Nightingale, *On the Edge*, pp. 135–42; "The Making of a Homicidal Consumerism: Structures of Cultural Exploitation and Inner-City Community Life, 1930–1990" (paper presented at the 109th Annual Meeting of the American Historical Association, Chicago, January 1995). On psychographic mapping and focus groups see Peter Childers, "Colors on the Map: Narrative, Geography, and the Multicultural Work of Target Marketing" (paper presented at the Conference on New Economic Criticism, Cleveland, Ohio, October 1994). Also see Theodore Levitt, "The Globalization of Markets," *Harvard Business Review* 61 (May–June 1983): 99–102; Teresa Domzal and Jerome B. Kernan, "Mirror, Mirror: Some Postmodern Reflections on Global Advertising," *Journal of Advertising* 22, 1 (December 1993): 1–25.

On basketball recruitment, see Alexander Wolff and Armen Keteyian, *Raw Recruits: The High Stakes Game Colleges Play to Get Their Basketball Stars — And What It Costs to Win* (New York: Pocket Books, 1991), pp. 73–96.

73. See Michael Hudson, *Merchants of Misery: How America Profits from Poverty* (Monroe, Maine: Common Courage Press, 1996); John P. Cashey, *Fringe Banking: Check Cashing Outlets, Pawnshops, and the Poor* (New York: Russell Sage Foundation, 1994).

74. Nightingale, "The Making of a Homicidal Consumerism," pp. 15–21; *On the Edge*, pp. 142–65; and "How Consumerism Affects Young People Coping with Poverty" (paper delivered at the Judge Baker Children's Center, Boslin, April 1996).

75. W.E.B. DuBois, *The Souls of Black Folk* (Millwood, N.Y.: Kraus-Thompson, 1973).

76. Rose, *Black Noise*, pp. 1–96.

77. Jafa's ideas are discussed in Rose, *Black Noise*, 38–40.

78. Kelly, *Race Rebels*, pp. 224–26; David Solomon, "The Real Face of Rap," *New Republic*, November 11, 1991, pp. 24–29, 75.

79. On the invention of "wiggers" as a "psychographic group" among advertisers, see Bernice Kanner, "An Extremely Hard Sell: Black Ads Go Mainstream," *New York Magazine*, April 11, 1994, p. 12. Also see Shawn Tully, "Teens: The Most Global Market of All," *Fortune*, May 16, 1994, p. 93.

80. Sinclair, "Rapping the World: As Its Influence Spreads, French, Russian, African & Chinese Posses Bust Rhymes on the 'Global Bush Telegraph of the Street,'" *Billboard*, November 28, 1992, p. R-16.

81. George Lipsitz, *Dangerous Crossroads: Popular Music, Postmodernism and the Poetics of Place* (London: Verso, 1994), pp. 64, 23–135.

82. Rose, *Black Noise*, pp. 99–183; Kelley, *Race Rebels*, pp. 183–227; on gangsta rap and capitalism, see pp. 195–96, 200–201; Lipsitz, *Dangerous Crossroads*, pp. 1–23, 95–156; Ernest Allen, "Making the Strong Survive: The Contours and Contradictions of Message Rap," in *Droppin' Science: Critical Essays on Rap Music and Hip-Hop Culture*, ed. William Eric Perkins (Philadelphia: Temple University Press, 1996), pp. 159–91.

83. David Sinclair, "Rapping the World" Watanabe, "In the East,"; "Pop Audience Gets Icon of Its Own," *Los Angeles Times*, May 19, 1992, p. H-2; John Huey and Tricia Welsh, "America's Hottest Export: Pop Culture," *Fortune*, December 31, 1990, p. 50.

84. Geraldine Heng, "Singapore: An Eastern Fashion-Driven Society," *Straits Times*, May 2, 1992.

85. For the outlines of this metaphor I am indebted to comments made by Loic

J. D. Wacquant on a portion of this paper when it was delivered at the International Symposium on Social Exclusion and the "New Urban Underclass," Berlin, Germany, June 1996.

86. John Gabriel's portrayal of McDonald's global strategies helped me in this section, as have the perceptions of a number of Philadelphia African American kids I have known. Gabriel, *Racism, Culture, Markets* (London: Routledge, 1994), pp. 98–128. See also Robin Kelley's description of work and infrapolitics at McDonalds in his *Race Rebels*, pp. 1–3; and George Ritzer, *The McDonaldization of Society* (London: Pine Forge, 1993). On discriminatory hiring practices in one fast food restaurant in New York City, see Newman, "Finding Work in the Inner City."

87. Wolff and Keteyian, *Raw Recruits*; Darcy Frey, *The Last Shot: City Streets, Basketball Dreams* (New York: Houghton Mifflin, 1994); and the movie *Hoop Dreams*. On the work attitudes of prominent recording stars toward their careers, and individualistic notions of "juice" and the "power move," see "Juice: Who's Got the Power," in *Vibe*, 13, no. 7 (September 1995): 77–121.

88. Bourgois, *In Search of Respect*; "In Search of Horatio Alger"; Ansley Hamid, "The Political Economy of Crack-Related Violence," *Contemporary Drug Problems* 17 (1990): 31–78; Terry Williams, *The Cocaine Kids: The Inside Story of a Teenage Drug Ring* (Reading, Mass.: Addison-Wesley, 1989); William Finnegan, "Out There," *New Yorker*, September 10, 1990, pp. 51–86, and September 17, 1990, pp. 60–90.

89. Nightingale, *On the Edge*, pp. 166–85.

90. Nina Baker, "The Hidden Hands of Nike," *Portland Oregonian*, August 9, 1992; and "Successful Marketer of Shoes Has a Simple Goal: To Be No. 1," *Oregonian*, August 10, 1992; Cynthia Enloe, "The Globetrotting Sneaker," *Ms.*, March–April 1995: 10–15; ABC News, *Prime Time Live*, segment on Nike, transcript no. 353, June 9, 1994; Donald Katz, "Triumph of the Swoosh," *Sports Illustrated*, August 16, 1993, p. 53; *Just Do It: The Nike Spirit in the Corporate World* (New York: Random House, 1994), pp. 160–206.

91. See Peter Fuhrman, "Italy's Gold Standard," *Forbes*, June 21, 1993, p. 92.

92. Some recent articulations of culture of poverty theory include Glenn Loury, "Crisis in Black America," *American Family* 9 (May 1986), pp. 1–5; and Lawrence Mead, *Beyond Entitlement: The Social Obligations of Citizenship* (New York: Free Press, 1986).

93. On the origins of the teachings of the Nation of Islam in the teachings of European and Middle Eastern secret societies, see Ernest Allen, Jr., "Religious Heterodoxy and Nationalist Tradition: The Continuing Evolution of the Nation of Islam," *Black Scholar* 26, 3–4 (1995): 6–8.

94. On African American culture and resistance, see Kelley, *Race Rebels*, pp. 8–10; Lipsitz, *Dangerous Crossroads*, 23–48, 135–56. An even more textured analysis is in Jeff Ferrell, *Crimes of Style: Urban Graffiti and the Politics of Criminality* (Boston: Northeastern University Press, 1996), pp. 186–208.

95. See, among others, Katherine McFate, Roger Lawson, and William Julius Wilson, eds., *Poverty, Inequality, and the Future of Social Policy: Western States in the New World Order* (New York: Russell Sage Foundation, 1995). On imprisonment see Michael Tonry, *Malign Neglect: Race, Crime, and Punishment in America* (Oxford: Oxford University Press, 1995); Jerome G. Miller, *Search and Destroy: African American Males in the Criminal Justice System* (Cambridge: Cambridge University Press, 1996).

96. See Adil Jazouli, *Les annes banlieues* (Paris: Editions du seuil, 1993), pp. 19–22, 150–57; Jazouli, *Une saison en banlieue: Courants et prospectives dans les quartiers populaires* (Paris: Plon, 1995); François Dubet, *La galère: Jeunes en survie* (Paris: Fayard, 1987); Dubet and Didier Lapeyronnie, *Les quartiers d'exil* (Paris: Editions due Seuil, 1992); Paul Gilroy, *There Ain't No Black in the Union Jack: The Cultural Politics of Race and*

Nation (Chicago: University of Chicago Press, 1987), pp. 92–99, 176–78, 236–40; Chris Mullard, *Race, Power, and Resistance* (London: Routledge, 1985); John Salomos, *Black Youth, Racism, and the State: The Politics of Ideology and Policy* (Cambridge: Cambridge University Press, 1988). German *gastarbeiter* neighborhoods and northern Italy's vast poor suburban communities, many containing large numbers of immigrants, might also profitably be brought into this analysis. See Hartmut Haeussermann, Andreas Kapphan, and Rainer Muenz, *Berlin: Immigration, Social Problems, Political Approaches* (unpublished English edition, Berlin, 1995); Maria Immacolata Macioti and Enrico Pugliese, *Gli immigrati in Italia* (Bari: Editori Laterza, 1991).

97. See Joan Moore and Racquel Pinderhughes, eds., *In the Barrios: Latinos and the Underclass Debate* (New York: Russell Sage Foundation, 1993); Vilma Ortiz, "Latinos and Industrial Change in New York and Los Angeles," in *Hispanics in the Labor Force*, ed. Edwin Melendez, Clara Rodriguez, and Janis Barry Figueroa (New York: Plenum, 1991): 119–32.

98. John Walton, "Urban Protest and the Global Political Economy. The IMF Riots," in Smith and Feagin, *Capitalist City*, pp. 364–86; Jeremy Brecher and Tim Costello, *Global Village or Global Pillage: Economic Reconstruction from the Bottom Up* (Boston: South End Press, 1994), pp. 85–94, 173–78. Ruth Wilson Gilmore draws attention to the connections between austerity rioting in "debtor nations" and the South Central Los Angeles uprising of 1992 in her "Terror Austerity Race Gender Excess Theater," in Gooding-Williams, *Reading Rodney King*, pp. 27–28.

99. On neighborhood organizing in the United States, see Robert Halpern, *Rebuilding the Inner City: A History of Neighborhood Initiatives to Address Poverty in the United States* (New York: Columbia University Press, 1995); Peter Medoff and Holly Sklar, *Streets of Hope: The Fall and Rise of an Urban Neighborhood* (Boston: South End Press, 1994); Janet Abu-Lughod, ed., *From Urban Village to East Village: The Battle for New York's Lower East Side* (Oxford: Basil Blackwell, 1994); Pierre Clavel and Wim Wiewel, eds., *Harold Washington and the Neighborhoods: Progressive City Government in Chicago, 1983–1987* (New Brunswick, N.J.: Rutgers University Press, 1991); Jim Rooney, *Organizing the South Bronx* (Albany: State University of New York Press, 1995); Ira Katznelson, *City Trenches: Urban Politics and the Patterning of Class in the United States* (Chicago: University of Chicago Press, 1981). On comparisons between the United Kingdom and the United States see Jacobs, *Fractured Cities*, pp. 151–94; and on the United States of America, Canada, and Israel, see Shlomo Hassan and David Ley, eds., *Neighborhood Organizations and the Welfare State* (Toronto: University of Toronto Press, 1994). On France, see Adil Jazouli, *Une saison en banlieue*. On Bangladesh see N. W. Wahid, ed., *The Grameen Bank: Poverty Relief in Bangladesh* (Boulder, Colo.: Westview Press, 1993); and Susan Holcombe, *Managing to Empower: The Grameen Bank's Experience of Poverty Alleviation* (Atlantic Highlands, N.J.: Zed Books, 1995). For international connections between these kinds of efforts, see Michael Shuman, *Towards a Global Village: International Community Development Initiatives* (London: Pluto Press in association with Towns and Development and Institute for Policy Studies, 1994).

100. See Brecher and Costello, *Global Village or Global Pillage*, pp. 138–37 and 154–57, and the acknowledgments of Lipsitz's *Dangerous Crossroads*, pp. vi–vii. On Asian and Latin American organizing efforts across the world and in the United States, see, among many others, *Economic Growth and Poverty: Report of the Regional Dialogue Held in Hanoi, Vietnam 14th–23rd October, 1990*, ed. Rita Raj-Hashim and Noeleen Heyzer (Kuala Lumpur: Asian and Pacific Development Centre, 1991); Rohana Ariffin, "Malaysian Women's Participation in Trade Unions," *Daughters in Industry*, ed. Noeleen Heyzer (Kuala Lumpur: Asian and Pacific Development Centre, 1988), pp. 239–66; Soma Jayakody and Hema Goonatilake, "Industrial Action by Women

Workers in Sri Lanka: The Polytex Garment Workers," in Heyzer, *Daughters of Industry*, pp. 292–307; Rosalinda Pineda-Ofroneo and Rosario del Rosario, "Filipino Women Workers in Strike Actions," in Heyzer, *Daughters of Industry*, 308–27; Enloe, "Global Sneaker," pp. 15; Leland T. Saito and John Horton, "The New Chinese Immigration and the Rise of Asian American Politics in Monterey Park, California," in Ong, Bonacich, and Cheng, *New Asian Immigration*, pp. 233–63; Yen Espiritu and Paul Ong, "Class Constraints on Racial Solidarity among Asian Americans," in Ong, Bonacich, and Cheng, *New Asian Immigration*, pp. 295–322; Guillermo J. Grenier, "The Cuban-American Labor Movement in Dade County," in Grenier and Stepick, *Miami Now!* pp. 133–59.

101. Aihwa Ong, *Spirits of Resistance and Capitalist Discipline: Factory Women in Malaysia* (Albany: State University Press of New York, 1987, p. xiii; Karen J. Hossfeld, " 'Their Logic Against Them': Contradictions in Sex, Race, and Class in Silicon Valley," in *Women Workers and Global Restructuring* ed. Kathryn Ward, pp. 175–76; Frank Bardacke, Leslie Lopez, and the Watsonville, California, Human Rights Committee, trans., *Shadows of Tender Fury: The Letters and Communiques of Subcommandante Marcos and the Zapatista Army of National Liberation* (New York: Monthly Review Press, 1995). On "everyday" forms of political resistance, see James C. Scott, *Weapons of the Weak: Everyday Forms of Peasant Resistance* (New Haven, Conn.: Yale University Press, 1985); *Domination and the Arts of Resistance: Hidden Transcripts* (New Haven, Conn.: Yale University Press, 1990).

Chapter 9
Drugs and Violence in the Inner City

Elijah Anderson

In 1899, W.E.B. DuBois published *The Philadelphia Negro*, which was a major contribution to our understanding of the social situation of African Americans in cities. Although this fact was not appreciated at the time, the book has become a classic of urban studies. Like so much significant ethnography, this description of social life in the period has become part of the wider historical record. DuBois was concerned with the reasons black Americans were poorly integrated into the mainstream system in the wake of their great migration from the rural South to the urban North after the abolition of slavery. The situation he discovered was one of race prejudice, ethnic competition, and consequent black exclusion and inability to participate in mainstream society, all in the social context of white supremacy. This pattern of exclusion resulted in deep and debilitating social pathologies in the black community, the legacy of which persists to this day.

In making sense of the social organization of the black community, DuBois developed a typology made up of four classes. The first were the well-to-do; the second the hardworking, decent laborers who were getting by fairly well; the third the "worthy poor," those who were working or trying to work but barely making ends meet; and the fourth the "submerged tenth," those who were in effect beneath the surface of socioeconomic viability. DuBois portrayed the submerged tenth as largely characterized by irresponsibility, drinking, violence, robbery, thievery, and alienation. But the situation of the submerged tenth was not a prominent theme in his study as a whole. Today, the counterpart of this class, the so-called ghetto underclass, appears much more entrenched and its pathologies more prevalent, but the outlines DuBois provided in *The Philadelphia Negro* can be clearly traced in the contemporary picture.

The growth and transformation of this underclass is in large part a result

Figure 21. Graffiti memorial to casualties of drug wars in Philadelphia in the 1990s. Copyright *The Philadelphia Inquirer*/Bonnie Weller.

of the profound economic changes that the country—in particular, urban areas like Philadelphia—has undergone in the past twenty to thirty years. Deindustrialization and the growth of the global economy have led to a steady loss of the unskilled and semiskilled manufacturing jobs that, with mixed results, had sustained the urban working class since the start of the industrial revolution.[1] At the same time, a sustained political attack on welfare programs has led to a much weakened social safety net.[2] For the most desperate people, many of whom are not making an effective adjustment to these changes—elements of today's submerged tenth—the underground economy of drugs and crime often emerges to pick up the slack.[3] To be sure, the active participants in this economy are at serious risk of violence, death, and incarceration. But equally important, those living near drug dealers and other hustlers are often victimized. At times, decent and law-abiding people become victims of random violence or are otherwise ensnared in the schemes of the underground economy's participants. Sometimes even those from decent families, particularly the young, become seduced by the ways of the street.

In today's ghetto there appears to be much more crime and higher levels of violence and homicide than in the earlier period. In addition, an ideology of alienation supporting an oppositional culture has developed, which can be seen with particular clarity in the rap music that encourages its young listeners to kill cops, to rape, and the like. Nowhere is this situation better highlighted than in the connection between drugs and violence, as young men involved in the drug trade often apply the ideology glorified in rap music to the problem of making a living and survival in what has become an oppositional if not an outlaw culture.[4]

In *The Philadelphia Negro*, DuBois pointed to the problems that kept young African American men from finding jobs: the lack of education, connections, social skills, and white skin color, as well as the adoption of a certain outlook, an unwillingness to work, and a lack of hope for the future. Today it is clear what that persistent state of affairs has led to.

The severe problem of racial discrimination DuBois uncovered certainly persists in Philadelphia and other cities, but, as discussed below, it has been transformed and at times has taken on a more practical form. More conventional people often seek to place much social distance between themselves and anonymous black people they encounter in public. And many young blacks sometimes in direct response find it difficult to take white people or even conventional black people seriously, and actively live their lives in opposition to them and everything they are taken to represent. Lacking trust in mainstream institutions, many turn to "hustling" in the underground economy. This has implications for middle-class blacks, many of whom have remained in Philadelphia and often work hard to defend themselves and their loved ones from those espousing the oppositional culture but also from the criminal element.

In many working-class and impoverished black communities today, particularly as faith in the criminal justice system erodes, social behavior in public is organized around a "code of the streets."[5] Feeling that they cannot depend on the police and other civil authorities to protect them from danger, residents often take personal responsibility for their security. They may yield, but often they are prepared to let others know in no uncertain terms that there will be dire consequences if they are violated. And they tend to teach their children to stand up for themselves physically, or to meet violence with violence. Growing up in such environments, young people are sometimes lured into the way of the street or become its prey. For too many of these youths, the drug trade seems to be a ready niche, a viable way to "get by" or to enhance their wealth even if they are not full-time participants.

Because the drug trade is organized around a code of conduct approximating the code of the streets and employing violence as the basis for social control, the drug culture contributes significantly to the violence of inner-city neighborhoods. Furthermore, many inner-city boys admire drug dealers and emulate their style, making it difficult for outsiders to distinguish a dealer from a law-abiding teenager. Part of this style is to project a violent image, and boys who are only "playing tough" may find themselves challenged and honor bound to fight. In addition, the trappings of drug dealers (the Timberland boots, the gold chains) are expensive, encouraging those without drug profits or other financial resources simply to steal.

The Cultural Economic Connection

As indicated above, anyone who wants to understand the widespread social dislocation in the inner-city poor community must approach these problems — along with other urban ills — from a structural as well as a cultural standpoint.[6] Both liberals and conservatives today tend to stress values like individual responsibility when considering issues like drugs, violence, teen pregnancy, family formation, and the work ethic. Some commentators readily blame "welfare" for poverty and find it hard to see how anyone — even the poor — would deliberately deviate from the norms of the mainstream culture. But the profound changes our society is presently undergoing in the way it organizes work have enormous cultural implications for the ability of the populations most severely affected by these developments to function in accordance with mainstream norms.

The United States has for some time been moving from a manufacturing to a service and high-tech economy in which the well-being of workers, particularly those of low skills and limited education, is subjugated to the bottom line. In cities like Philadelphia, certain neighborhoods have been devastated by the effects of deindustrialization. Many jobs have become automated, been transferred to developing countries, or have moved to nearby satellite cities like King of Prussia. For those who cannot afford a car, travel requires two hours on public transportation from the old city neighborhoods where concentrations of black people, Hispanics, and working-class whites live.[7]

With widespread joblessness, many inner-city people become stressed and their communities become distressed. Poor people adapt to these circumstances in the ways they know, meeting the exigencies of their situation as best they can. The kinds of problems that trigger moral outrage begin to emerge: teen pregnancy, welfare dependency, and the underground economy. Its cottage industries of drugs, prostitution, welfare scams, and other rackets is there to pick up the economic slack. Quasi-legal hustling is part of it; people do odd jobs under the table and teach young people to follow their lead. Some people have a regular second or third job entirely off the books.

The drug trade is certainly illegal, but it is the most lucrative and most accessible element of the underground economy and has become a way of life in many of these inner-city communities. Many youngsters dream of leading the drug dealer's life, or at least their highly glamorized conceptions of this life. Of course drugs have been around for a long time, but they have become deeply rooted in the inner-city black community, a situation largely tolerated by civic authorities and the police. As law-abiding residents witness this situation, they become ever more cynical and alienated.

Here it is important to underscore the connections between jobs, drugs, and alienation. Many of the young blacks who have difficulty obtaining a job feel victimized by prejudice and discrimination. Such feelings of victimization lead to greater understanding if not tolerance for those who resort to dealing drugs to "survive." In these circumstances, the drug trade, so dangerous and problematic for local communities and for society, becomes normal happenstance. As one young drug dealer I profiled asked me, "Eli, why is it so hard for me to get a job but so easy for me to sell drugs?"[8] In destitute inner-city communities, it is in fact becoming increasingly difficult to distinguish poverty from drug involvement. For example, many welfare mothers have become intimately connected with the drug trade, either as users or as what might be called support personnel, by allowing drug-dealing boyfriends or male relatives to use their homes as crackhouses or drug depots in exchange for money or favors.

In addition, the young man who sells drugs is often encouraged and motivated to create new markets, sometimes enlisting his own family members into the drug culture, thus at times leading to their drug dependency. Why? Because he has come to covet the material things he sees dangled before him, things that become important not simply as practical items but as status symbols among his peers. A particular brand of eyeglasses or shoes or pants can indicate a person's social standing, allowing him a certain amount of self-esteem. Timberland boots, for example, which support a roughneck or macho image, are now being worn by many drug dealers and have come to be considered hip. So the owner of such items, through his exhibitions and displays, is able to gain deference from and status among his peers. Media images—television, movies, the consumer mentality—fuel these desires as well. And when the regular economy cannot provide the means for satisfying these desires, some of the most desperate people turn to the underground economy.

But the despair, the alienation, and the distress are still there, and this condition encourages the development and spread of an oppositional culture. For those living according to the rules of that culture, it becomes important to be tough, to act as though one is beyond the reach of lawful authority—to "go for bad." In this scenario, anything associated with conventional white society is seen as square; the hip things are at odds with it. The untied sneakers, the pants worn well below the waist, the hat turned backward—all have become a style. These unconventional symbols have been taken over by people who have made them into status symbols, but they are status symbols *to the extent that* they go against what is conventional.

Exacerbating the antagonism toward the conventional is the way residents of the ghetto become personally victimized by all this. Not only does their community get a bad reputation, but the people themselves, particularly black males, become demonized. They are stereotyped; everyone from that community who dresses and who looks that way is a priori seen as being at odds with conventional society. The anonymous law-abiding black male is often taken as a threat to conventional society. Yet many ghetto males are caught in a bind because they are espousing their particular ways of dressing and acting simply to be self-respecting among their neighborhood peers. A boy may be completely decent, but to the extent that he takes on the *presentation* of "badness" to enhance his local public image, even as a form of self-defense, he further alienates himself in the eyes of the wider society, which has denounced people "like him," as inclined to violate its norms, values, rules, and conventions, to threaten it.

Such cultural displays in turn make such young people even less employable. Armed with negative stereotypes, employers sometimes discriminate against whole census tracts or zip codes where impoverished people live. The decent people are strongly associated with the indecent people, and the employers often do not worry about making distinctions. They just want to avoid the whole troublesome situation, selecting whites over blacks. Kirschenman and Neckerman conducted a study in Chicago[9] to discover the extent to which employers discriminated against young black people. They found that discrimination was rife: many of the employers much preferred white women and immigrants to young black people.

Similarly, in Philadelphia, a great many black boys and girls, especially the boys, are feared by employers. Even when they do get work, there is often a racial division of labor in the workplace. Inner-city black boys and girls tend to get stuck in entry-level jobs and are rarely promoted. One very clear example of this in present-day Philadelphia is the restaurant business, in which an obvious division of labor exists. In upscale and moderately priced restaurants, blacks are conspicuously absent from the waitstaff but over-represented among the kitchen help. In addition, if there is a problem with stealing or some other trouble on the job, they are prime suspects and are sometimes summarily dismissed.[10] Such experiences and the reports of such experiences contribute to their working conception of the world. Their resulting bitterness and alienation then nurture the oppositional culture. To be self-respecting, many young men and women must exhibit a certain contempt for a system that they are sure has contempt for them. When such factors are added to the consequences of deindustrialization, the result is an incendiary situation, as DuBois appreciated.[11]

The attraction of the violence-prone drug trade thus results from a combination of inadequate opportunity in the regular economy, on the one hand, and the imperatives of street life, on the other. The interplay between these two factors is powerfully at work in the social organization of the underground economy in inner-city neighborhoods.

Clocking: The Drug Trade as a Living

The transition from the regular to the underground economy, particularly the drug trade, is not simple. Some young people are able to dabble in it for a while and then return to the regular economy, or they operate simultaneously in both. But the drug trade and the wages it pays sometimes become overwhelming and downright addictive. People may manage to quit when a better opportunity appears or when they confront death or jail (for themselves or for loved ones or friends) and begin to have second thoughts. More likely, however, working in the drug trade becomes a regular occupation for the most desperate, and then they are said to be "clocking."

The introduction of crack has exacerbated the problem. Because it is cheap and readily available, it can support many dealers. And boys can acquire the skills required — "street knowledge" and the ability to enact it — just by growing up in the impoverished inner-city neighborhood. Whatever a boy's home life is like, growing up in the 'hood means learning to some degree the code of the streets, the prescriptions and proscriptions of public behavior. He must be able to handle himself in public, and his parents, no matter how decent they are, may strongly encourage him to learn the rules. And because of various barriers he can often parlay that experience into a place in the drug trade much more easily than into a reasonable job. The relative ease of that transition speaks volumes about the life circumstances of inner-city adolescents.

For so many impoverished young black men of the inner city, the opportunity for dealing drugs is literally just outside the door. By selling drugs they have a chance for more money in their pockets than they could get by legal means, and they can present themselves to peers as hip, in sharp contrast to the square image of those who work in places like McDonald's and wear "silly" uniforms. In fact, the oppositional culture has dubbed opting to sell drugs "getting legal." One decent, law-abiding young man was often accosted by his drug-dealing peers as he stepped outside his door and headed for his regular job with the remark, "Hey, Martin. When you gon' get legal?" He would simply reply, "Later for that. Later for that."[12] When one needs money, which is always, this way of making it can seem like a godsend, and other boys encourage him to sell.

A common way of getting into the drug trade is to be part of a neighborhood peer group that begins to sell. A boy's social group can be easily transformed from a play group or a group that hangs around the corner listening to rap music or playing basketball — relatively innocuous things — to a drug gang. The change requires a drug organizer to approach the group and consult the leader or "main man." The leader then begins to distribute opportunities to deal drugs — which is a kind of power — to various friends, his "boys." In time the small neighborhood group becomes a force to be reckoned with in the community, while taking an ever sharper interest in issues of turf and territory. The group then works to confuse concerns having to do with money and with protecting turf. The leader can paint an enticing picture for these boys, and he has incentive to do so because the deed enhances his power. With "top dogs," "middle dogs," and "low dogs," the system resembles a pyramid scheme.[13]

Youths who have strong family grounding — very decent folks, churchgoing families with a nuclear or quasi-nuclear structure and with love and concern for the younger people — are often the most resistant. But those who are drawn by the group, who get caught up with the responsibilities of breadwinning, with little opportunity to do so in the regular economy, sometimes resolve the tension by joining the drug trade. In turn, as they become serious dealers, these boys often will sell drugs to anybody who will buy them, including their own relatives; money and group loyalty become paramount issues. In this connection, they may develop not only an excuse but a whole rap, a way of cajoling people to try crack just to get them hooked, because they know how quickly one can become addicted. For instance, they may approach someone as a friend and invite him or her to share some of their own supply, saying things like, "It's not going to hurt you, it's not bad, you can handle it."

Strikingly, they may even become customers themselves — it is easy enough to become hooked by trying it once. Through the posturing required to prevail in the street life, many young people come to feel invincible, or they develop a profound need to show others they feel this way. And the power that accrues to dealers compounds the sense that they can control anything, even a crack cocaine high. In these circumstances, they become "the man." Sometimes such a dealer does manage on crack off and on for a couple of years. Getting high now and then, he feels he is handling it, but, as the wiser dealers say, there is a fine line between handling it and having it handle you. At some inopportune moment he may be suddenly overcome with an insatiable need for the drug. Such a person is said to be "jonesing" for it; he is filled with such an intense desire for a high that he loses control of his actions. The predator becomes the prey—a common occurrence.

As in any marketing enterprise, the drug trade requires production and distribution networks.[14] Another requirement is social control. Among drug dealers, that requirement is satisfied by the use and threat of violence. Violence is not always intended, but it occurs easily as a result of both the intense competition for customers and the general disorganization that marks the lives of so many young dealers. Misunderstandings easily arise, such as "messing up" somebody's money—not paying for drugs that one has been advanced, thus squandering the dealer's investment. The older and established dealers are obligated to "do in" the people who have messed up their money because otherwise they would lose credibility and status on the streets. Attempted takeovers of the business of rival dealers are also common. Although there is room in the system for more people now than there was before crack, competition remains fierce, especially as the belief that anyone can get rich dealing drugs becomes increasingly prevalent. The push to get in on the drug trade can in this sense be likened to the gold rush.

It is understood on the streets that the drug trade itself is unforgiving. To make a misstep is to risk getting roughed up, shot, or killed. When a seemingly senseless killing occurs, people in the community immediately assume it is drug-related. Those who get into the trade realize they are playing with fire, but given the presumed financial stakes may feel that they have no choice or that they are up to the challenge. Often the people who get hurt "deserved it" in terms of the code of the drug trade: they "crossed somebody big" or they "thought they were slick." People in the community understand this rationale, and it seems that the police acknowledge it too. Once a crime is labeled drug-related, there often seems to be little interest and accountability in bringing the people who perpetrated it to justice.

Arguments over "business" are frequently settled on the spot, often on the basis of arbitrary considerations, unfounded assumptions, or outright lies. There is also an ongoing fight for turf because of the large number of dealers, some connected with an organization, others freelancing. When a gang is set up in a particular area, its members know the streets and control the turf. As the trade becomes profitable, however, would-be dealers from outside the gang may want to do business in the same area or even take it over. But a person who tries to muscle in is threatening not just the current dealer's economic well-being but that part of the community as well. The connections of many of these boys go deep in the community through extended families, who may rely on the money. If a dealer is pushed out, he and a portion of the community can face financial disaster. As a result, some dealers are ready to fight to keep their turf, and people often get wounded or killed in the process.

There are major and minor turf wars. In fact, a major turf war often spawns smaller ones. In a major fight — whether the weapons are words, fists, or guns, but especially if they are guns — the dispute gets settled, at least for the time being. But everyone has an interpretation of what happened. The interpretations are exchanged in the various neighborhood institutions, including barbershops, taverns, and streetcorners, where people gather and talk, and an understanding of the original fight is negotiated. Since at least some of the people involved know the principal participants personally, they may take sides, becoming emotionally invested in having their version of the event prevail, and the discussions themselves can become heated and lead to violence.

Some boys simply want the status associated with being a dealer. They want to wear a beeper, to be seen to be "clocking," to be connected with something worthwhile, even though it is an underground enterprise. Drug dealers are living the fast life; they are living on the edge. Older people will give young dealers advice, telling them that they are "living too fast." But everyone knows that once a person gets into that world, it is very hard to get out. The dealer can get hooked on the money and the material things it can buy, just as someone can get hooked on the drug; the adventure, the thrill of danger, and the respect people give him are also addictive. Furthermore, his associates in the trade may not let him out because he knows too much and might pass information on to the wrong people, or they may want to make him an example. Much of his ability to maneuver depends on his identity and connections (his cousins, brothers, uncles, his other associates in the trade, his gang members, his boys) and on his status. Often, the higher his status, the more leeway and independence he has, the more "juice" he has. The truly independent people, those who have achieved a high level of respect, may be able to get out in ways other people cannot, because they have established that they can be trusted. But often the only sure way of getting out is to get out of town.

Violent Fallout

Drug users also engage in violence. Many users start out as victims — when family members, boyfriends or girlfriends who deal drugs actively get them hooked in order to expand their markets — but they then become victimizers, robbing others to support their habits. Although some of the violence is focused and some is not, the result is a constant sense of uncertainty, the belief that anything can happen at any time. The successful dealer must be ever vigilant, but this vigilance makes him jittery and prone to react violently to the slightest perceived provocation. Furthermore, under the influence of drugs people's behavior may become unpredictable or truly dangerous. In these situations, innocent bystanders, sometimes small children, can be shot or killed. Since drug trafficking permeates so much of the inner-city community, all its residents, whether they are involved with drugs or not, are at risk of finding themselves the unintended victim of a stray bullet. The awareness of this constant danger fosters anxiety and skittishness even among the decent people, who therefore become more likely themselves to overreact in an uncertain encounter; these people, if possible, may move.

Also fueling the violence that attends the drug trade is the proliferation of guns, which have become for many easily accessible. There were guns in the community in the past, but they were mostly in the hands of adults. Today kids fourteen and younger have guns, or they know how and where to get them. In the inner-city community, one can often hear gunshots in the distance but no sirens afterward. The likelihood is that the shots are being fired by young boys playing with guns, at times just shooting them off for the fun of it, usually in the middle of the night. Guns can have personalities and status attached to them; they even have records. The price of a used gun indicates its history. A gun that "has a body on it" (it was used to kill someone) is cheap because the person who is ultimately caught with it might be held responsible for murder. Moreover, in a society where so much economic inequality exists, for the severely alienated and desperate a gun can become like a bank card—an equalizer. Such a boy—or, increasingly, a girl—who desperately needs money may use one to stick somebody up without a second thought. In a peculiar way, however, the prevalence of and ready access to guns may keep certain strangers honest and more careful in how they approach others. In these circumstances, a kind of Wild West mentality obtains in some of the more dangerous neighborhoods, in which the fear of getting shot can constrain people from violating others.

As a result of the general atmosphere of danger, even people with a nonviolent orientation buy guns for protection. In Philadelphia not long ago, a black minister and resident of an inner-city community shot and killed an intruder. The incident sparked a good deal of discussion, but the general reaction of his black neighbors was, "Well, he did what he had to do." In fact, such incidents do not occur just in the inner city. In the gentrified neighborhood adjacent to the minister's, a white doctor going to bed one night he heard a rumbling downstairs. He came down with his gun and in the darkness announced, "I have a gun." The rumbling continued, so he fired, killing an intruder in his kitchen with a bullet to the back of the head. He and his wife went to the police station to report the incident, returned home at two in the morning, and cleaned up the blood. It turned out that the intruder was apparently trying to steal the small kitchen television set to sell on the street, which could have brought a few dollars for crack. But this white doctor was so disturbed at having killed a young black man in those circumstances that he immediately moved out of his house and left the community. Thus the casualties of violence include people who simply get caught up in it, not just those who get shot but sometimes those who perpetrate the violence as well.

The Crack Culture: Rationale and Consequences

It must be continually underscored that much of this violence and drug activity is a reflection of the dislocations brought about by economic transformations, shifts that are occurring in the context of the new global economy. As indicated above, where the wider economy is not receptive to these dislocated people, the underground economy is. That does not mean that anyone without a job is suddenly going to become a drug dealer; the process is not that simple. But the facts of race relations, unemployment, dislocation, and destitution encourage alienation, and alienation allows for a certain receptivity to overtures made by people seeking youthful new recruits for the drug trade.

Numerous inner-city black people continue to be locked out of many working-class occupations. Lack of education and training are often at issue, but, as DuBois noted, so is the problem of employers' racial preferences and social connections with prospective coworkers. For example, the building trades — plumbing, carpentry, roofing, and so forth — are organized around family connections: fathers and uncles bring in sons and nephews. To get a certificate to work in these trades, a young man requires a mentor, who not only teaches him skills but legitimizes him as a member of the trade. So the system perpetuates the dominance of ethnic groups who have been organized a long time. Now the inner-city drug trade is composed of uncles and nephews too. From this perspective, working-class Italians and Irish and others have their niche, and many alienated and desperate young blacks, at least those who are enterprising, can be said to have their niche too — in the drug trade. As DuBois would have appreciated, such behavior, while not to be condoned, is understandable as a manifestation of racism and persistent poverty.

In the inner-city community drug dealing thus becomes recognized as work, though it is an occupation that overwhelming numbers of residents surely despise. Yet there are Robin Hood types among the drug dealers, who distribute some of their profits in the community, buying things for people, financially helping out their friends and relatives, as well as complete strangers. One drug dealer told me how bad he felt when he found out that a woman who had bought crack from one of his underlings had kids and had used all her welfare money for the drugs. He sought the woman out and gave her half her money back. His rationale was that business is business but the kids shouldn't go hungry.

Crack's addictive quality has led to the rapid establishment of a crack culture and makes it easy to maintain a clientele. The belief in the community is that crack addiction is immediate and permanent. Once you try crack, it is said, you're always "chasing the ghost" — the high that you get the first time is so intense that you can never achieve it again, but the desire to do so is so strong that you keep pursuing it. One drug dealer told me that he has never seen anybody walk away from crack permanently; even if a user gets off it for two years, he said, the right drug dealer can easily hook him again by talking to him in the right way. I said to this dealer, "Knowing this, why do you sell crack? Isn't this like killing people, annihilating your own people?" He replied nonchalantly, "Well, if I wasn't doing it, somebody else would." To many inner-city residents, crack has become a seemingly permanent fixture of life, and dealing is a way to earn a living, even to become rich, though very few reach such a status.

Conclusion

For those who have read *The Philadelphia Negro* this description will have a familiar ring. Criminal activity and its social consequences were much less entrenched in the black community of the 1890s, but the attraction of the nonconventional world as a driving force behind the social pathologies of the day remains unchanged. DuBois's typically unsparing assessment of its influence sounds strikingly contemporary:

> The size of the more desperate class of criminals and their shrewd abettors is of course comparatively small, but it is large enough to characterize the slum districts. Around this central body lies a large crowd of satellites and feeders: young idlers attracted by excitement, shiftless and lazy ne'er-do-wells, who have sunk from better things, and a rough crowd of pleasure seekers and libertines. These are the fellows who figure in the police courts for larceny and fighting, and drift thus into graver crime or shrewder dissoluteness. . . . Their environment in this city makes it easier for them to live by crime or the results of crime than by work, and being without ambition — or perhaps having lost ambition and grown bitter with the world — they drift with the stream. (pp. 312–13)

In any so-called underclass community, there are people who are decent and people who are of the street.[15] "Decent" and "street" are labels that people themselves use. Most people in these communities are decent, law-abiding, ethical people who treat others with consideration, go to church, and strive to have their own versions of intact families. In many ways, these people are quite conservative socially (it is often not fully appreciated how much these decent people have in common with the Religious Right). Their outlook is to shaped by a generally higher degree of education and sense of connection to the outside world. They have a kind of savoir faire, are able to get along with people inside and outside the community, and are more capable of working within the system. They can be said to have a certain degree of human capital. But what is human capital in a situation in which the economy is unraveling and the jobs are not there?

The people who make up the hard-core street element, in contrast, tend to be in many ways bereft of the human capital that would allow them to negotiate the wider system at all: the education, the savoir faire, the sense of connection to the outside world tend to be missing for them. They are sometimes proudly unconventional, sometimes just plain unconventional. They tend to be more than ready to settle any kind of dispute with violence. It is for such people that the code of the streets is a way of life, not a put-on. A hundred years ago, DuBois uncovered the social seeds that have today grown into this destabilizing group of street-oriented people. He noted that the forces that influence the African American man to engage in criminal behavior include

the immense influence of his peculiar environment on the black Philadelphian; the influence of homes badly situated and badly managed, with parents untrained for their responsibilities; the influence of social surroundings which by poor laws and inefficient administration leave the bad to be made worse; the influence of economic exclusion which admits Negroes only to those parts of the economic world where it is hardest to maintain ambition and self-respect; and finally that indefinable but real and mighty moral influence that causes men to have a real sense of manhood or leads them to lose aspiration and self-respect. (pp. 285–86)

In contrast, for many of the decent people, comporting themselves in accordance with the code of the streets results from code-switching, the movement from a code of decency to the code of the streets. People code-switch for defensive purposes. In part because of the changes in city government since the 1980s and the unavailability of resources, some city agencies today operate on a skeleton employee force. Thus code enforcement is nil. The police are known to respond to inner-city calls often only in dire emergencies. Moreover, a black man might call the police for assistance, but before the police are done, the caller himself might wind up going to jail. For people who believe that the police are not there for them, that the police have abdicated their responsibility to the community, public safety and defense become matters of personal responsibility.

No matter how decent they are, many inner-city residents have come to assume the posture of the street in order to let people know that "if you violate me, there could be serious consequences for you." The decent people sometimes call this behavior "getting ignorant" — getting on the level of the street-oriented people, meeting violence with violence, meeting talk with talk, and "going for bad" when necessary. The "sho' nuff" street people, however, do not have to put the posture on. They have internalized it; it is second nature to them. For instance, a decent kid simply walks down the aisle on a crowded bus and inadvertently bumps into a "sho' nuff street boy." The street boy stands back, opens his coat to show his piece (gun), and, looking the decent boy dead in the face, says, "I'm letting you live. I'm just *letting* you live." That is not a put-on; that is a way of life. The decent kid, despite his precautions, is not as good at enacting this role and has failed to forestall a confrontation with a street-oriented individual.

As indicated above, not every street-oriented person is a drug dealer, but drug dealing abides by the code of the streets. Therefore, in the drug-infested neighborhood the street code sets the standard in public. In private — in their homes and on the job — the majority of residents are trying to live decent lives in accordance with mainstream values. Most people succeed. However, the streets and other public areas become the domain of the street-oriented drug dealers, which are subject to their laws and where the consequences of such a system of social control reign supreme. The need to learn to function in public may thus work to undermine the lessons of decency parents are trying to instill in their children. The result, as DuBois observed, is that "The children of this class [the 'worthy poor'] are the feeders of the criminal classes [the 'submerged tenth']. Often in the same family one can find respectable and striving parents weighed down by idle, impudent sons and wayward daughters" (p. 315).

When the drug trade is rampant in a community, it creates violence, fear, danger, and outright hatred. The environment of the neighborhood becomes dangerous and engenders anxiety throughout the inner-city black community. Children grow up fearful. The sense of community, even of communion, is undermined. People do not easily trust one another; some lose the ability to trust anyone at all. Young black males are subject to particular scrutiny. A fashionably dressed young black male immediately raises suspicions that he is involved in the drug trade, so people both in and outside the community may be predisposed not to be civil to him. But the worst part of it is that one can never be sure who is who, and this uncertainty takes its toll on people's psychic well-being. The sense of peace and comity as the normal state of affairs has been lost. Peace comes to be seen as the space between episodes of violence.

Moreover, the constant suspicion encourages the cycle of violence. People arm themselves to be ready to meet violence with violence, and the proliferation of firearms serves to escalate the use of deadly force. It is easy to believe that any young person one passes on the street is likely to have a gun. When people are on edge, they are more likely to pull the trigger with little provocation. And if it turns out that their responses are unwarranted, it is likely to provoke retaliation. A split-second misjudgment can and often does result in death or permanent injury.

In addition, therefore, to the direct violence that results in physical casualties, there is social fallout. An important connection between drugs and violence is the lifestyle of the dealer himself. The dealer is seen as a cool or hip person. He has a lot of money and he has to show it. He wears the latest styles and expensive jewelry, drives a certain kind of car, and carries a certain kind of gun. Other young people, law-abiding or not, seek to emulate these drug-dealer role models by acquiring these adornments for themselves. It is not easy to acquire these things if one does not have much money. Decent parents may work two or three jobs to provide clothes and jewelry for their son through legal means to keep him from going wrong. A crisis in priorities is occurring. People sometimes appease their children to keep them out of the fast life. The outlaw oppositional culture has become so strong that even law-abiding and decent youths will imitate aspects of the fast life in order to get respect from peers, who may also be law-abiding but are likewise mimicking the street style so as get respect on the streets. Young people therefore pretend to have money, pretend to have freedom and independence, and pretend to be violent, even if none of this is true. The employers and other law-abiding people, including white people and black middle-class people who live in adjacent communities, may be easily confused about who is a drug dealer and who is not. Out of a perceived need for protection, they try to avoid all the people who look this way. That, in turn, further alienates inner-city young people.

A complicating factor is that many decent young people want to create this confusion because it may be protective, thrilling, and to some extent self-aggrandizing. In a street-oriented culture filled with pretense, posturing, and the need to emulate the dealers, it is important even for the decent people to sometimes "go for bad." A certain amount of respect accrues to those who can do so successfully, and this helps them negotiate the inner-city streets. But situations that involve a large amount of posturing about violence can quickly turn into the real thing.

It is worth noting that the tendency to imitate the fast life is not peculiar to black inner-city teenagers. White middle-class teenagers also emulate this style, although perhaps in a less effective way. The things that happen in the inner-city subculture, which is so driven by the drug trade and drug culture, are subject to cultural diffusion through the system into the middle class, both white and black. But the middle-class versions are not usually as deadly in their consequences as the versions worked out by so many of the inner-city young people. Middle-class youths have more money and many more ways of expressing themselves. When it comes to violence, they are much more willing to back down than to get into a fight to the death.

Many people in the depressed underclass community understand the economic need for the drug trade. Some believe that the boys who deal drugs are not necessarily bad boys but simply doing what they need to do to make money. So they may not totally condemn the dealing but accept it in a way, becoming inured to it because it is so common in the neighborhood. The Robin Hood phenomenon mentioned above helps the justification process.

Hence a common adaptation is to "see but don't see," a tendency to see but ignore drug transactions — and those involved. Many law-abiding people are simply afraid to get involved. They do not even want people to notice that they have witnessed what is going on. They are concerned for their own safety. In particular, after a shooting or a gang war people tend to clam up out of fear of retribution, observing a code of silence. If a bust occurs, anyone who was considered to be paying too much attention to that drug activity might be suspected of having told the police about it, and then may hear from certain dealers of the neighborhood. The way people deal with this fear and the need to protect themselves is by seeing but not seeing.

Many impoverished parents "see but don't see" for another reason: they realize that their own son is probably involved in the trade. They disapprove of this participation, but they may also benefit from it. A mother may receive money, even large sums of money, from her son, but she does not ask too many questions about its source. She just accepts that the money is there somehow. Since it is sorely needed, there is a strong incentive not to interrupt its flow, her own decency notwithstanding. Some people are so torn over what they are tolerating that they pray and ask forgiveness from the Lord for their de facto approbation. Yet they cannot bring themselves to intervene and put a stop to the drug dealing. Again, it comes back to the problem of poverty — the way the economy is unraveling in so many such communities, putting people up against the wall and encouraging them to do immoral things that they otherwise might be reluctant to do. Some people tolerate this situation almost against their will.

Since the street code of conduct is founded on violence and the threat of violence, the more inner-city youths choose this route in life, the more normative the code of the streets — and violence — becomes in these neighborhoods. Neighbors are forced to choose between an abstract code of justice and a practical code geared toward survival in the public spaces of their community. Increasingly, inner-city residents are opting for the code of the streets, either as a conscious decision to protect themselves and their self-esteem or as a gut reaction to a sudden dangerous situation. Children growing up in these circumstances learn early in life that this is the way things are, and the lessons of those who might teach them otherwise become less and less relevant. Surrounded by the violence and what many view as municipal indifference to innocent victims of drug dealers and users, the decent people are finding it increasingly difficult to maintain a sense of community.

The ramifications of this state of affairs reach far beyond inner-city communities themselves. A startling study by the Sentencing Project recently revealed that 33 percent of young black men in their twenties are under the supervision of the criminal justice system — in jail, in prison, on probation, or on parole. This is an astounding figure and must be considered partially responsible for the widespread perception of young black men as dangerous and not to be trusted. This kind of demonization affects all young blacks, those of the middle class and the dwindling working class as well as well as those of the street.

The question might be asked, What can account for the disproportionate percentage of blacks among the adjudicated? Already in DuBois's day, African Americans were overrepresented in the prison population, but the jump in their numbers over the past generation has been exponential. Part of the answer would have to be crack cocaine. The prison terms for crack cocaine are stiffer than those for powder cocaine, which is more prevalent in the middle class and more expensive. Another issue is that proportionately more blacks are dealers, and that fact speaks to the overall inability of young black men to get into the workforce. The quasi-glamorous hipness of dealing, certifying one as firmly in the oppositional culture, is also a factor.

This one statistic is perhaps the most eloquent testament to the social consequences of ignoring the economic transformation the country is experiencing, probably the most important transformation since the Industrial Revolution — the movement from manufacturing to service and high-tech in the context of an increasingly global economy. Corporations are sending large numbers of jobs to foreign lands where labor costs a fraction of what it costs in the United States. Workers here must thus compete with those of third world countries, a situation that drives their standard of living downward. Indeed, the workers have become less and less important as the stockholders have become more important. CEOs who do not show a profit in the first quarter have their own jobs on the line, so they are encouraged to make short-term decisions. In this scenario, they become largely indifferent to what happens in inner-city Philadelphia and other cities. They appear to be mainly concerned with the bottom line. But when they take jobs out of the city and leave its people poor and highly concentrated, they make it possible for the drug economy to become a way of life, an unforgiving way of life organized around violence and predatory activity. Only by reestablishing a viable mainstream economy in the inner city, particularly one that provides access to jobs for young inner-city men, can we hope to undermine this drug economy that fosters so much violence.

Notes

1. See Loïc Wacquant and William Julius Wilson, "The Cost of Racial and Class Exclusion in the Inner City," in *The Ghetto Underclass: Social Science Perspectives*, ed. William Julius Wilson (Newbury Park, Calif.: Sage, 1989), pp. 8–25, and William Julius Wilson, *The Truly Disadvantaged: The Inner City, the Underclass, and Public Policy* (Chicago: University of Chicago Press, 1987).

2. See Michael B. Katz, *The Undeserving Poor: From the War on Poverty to the War on Welfare* (New York: Pantheon, 1989), and Fred Block et al., *The Mean Season: The Attack on the Welfare State* (New York: Pantheon, 1987).

3. See Elijah Anderson, *Streetwise: Race, Class, and Change in an Urban Community* (Chicago: University of Chicago Press, 1990).

4. Elijah Anderson, "The Story of John Turner," *Public Interest* 108 (Summer 1992).

5. Elijah Anderson, "Code of the Streets," *Atlantic Monthly* (May 1994).

6. See Charles Valentine, *Culture and Poverty: Critique and Counter-Proposals* (Chicago: University of Chicago Press, 1968); Barry Bluestone and Bennett Harrison, *The Deindustrialization of America: Plant Closings, Community Abandonment, and the Dismantling of Basic Industry* (New York: Basic Books, 1982); and William Julius Wilson, *The Truly Disadvantaged: The Inner City, the Underclass, and Public Policy* (Chicago: University of Chicago Press, 1987).

7. Judith Goode and Jo Anne Schneider, *Reshaping Ethnic and Social Relations in Philadelphia: Immigrants in a Divided City* (Philadelphia: Temple University Press, 1994).

8. Anderson, "Story of John Turner."

9. Jolene Kirschenman and Kathryn Neckerman, " 'We'd Like to Hire Them, But . . .': Race in the Minds of Employers," in *The Urban Underclass*, ed. Christopher Jencks and Paul E. Peterson (Washington, D.C.: Brookings Institution, 1991), pp. 203–32.

10. Elijah Anderson, "Some Observations on Black Youth Employment," in *Youth Employment and Public Policy*, ed. Bernard Anderson and Isabel Sawhill (Englewood Cliffs, N.J.: Prentice-Hall, 1980), pp. 64–87.

11. This issue, strongly related to ethnic competition in the workplace, has deep roots in Philadelphia's history. See Roger Lane, *Roots of Violence in Black Philadelphia, 1860–1900* (Cambridge, Mass.: Harvard University Press, 1986).

12. Personal interview.

13. See Anderson, *Streetwise*.

14. Terry Williams, *The Cocaine Kids: The Inside Story of a Teenage Drug Ring* (Reading, Mass.: Addison-Wesley, 1990).

15. Anderson, "Code of the Streets."

Contributors

MICHAEL B. KATZ is Sheldon and Lucy Hackney Professor of History at the University of Pennsylvania. He is author or editor of fourteen books on the history of poverty, social policy, and education, including *In the Shadow of the Poorhouse: A Social History of Welfare in America* (second edition, 1996).

THOMAS J. SUGRUE is Associate Professor of History at the University of Pennsylvania and is author of the prize-winning book, *The Origins of the Urban Crisis: Race and Inequality in Postward Detroit* (1996). He is currently writing a history of racial integration and its critics in twentieth-century America.

ELIJAH ANDERSON is Charles and William Day Professor of the Social Sciences and Professor of Sociology at the University of Pennsylvania. A leading ethnographer and urban sociologist, he is author of *Streetwise: Race, Class, and Change in an Urban Community* (1991) and *A Place on the Corner* (1978).

MIA BAY is Assistant Professor of History at Rutgers University, New Brunswick and co-director of the research project on the Black Atlantic at the Rutgers Center for Historical Analysis. She is author of the forthcoming book: *The White Image in the Black Mind: African American Ideas About White People, 1830–1925*.

V. P. FRANKLIN is Professor of History at Drexel University. He is the co-editor of *New Perspectives on Black Educational History* (1978), and the author of *The Education of Black Philadelphia* (1979); *Black Self-Determination: A Cultural History of African-American Resistance* (1992); and *Living Our Stories, Telling Our Truths: The Making of the African-American Intellectual Tradition* (1995).

ROBERT GREGG is Assistant Professor of History at the Richard Stockton College of New Jersey. He is author of *Sparks from the Anvil of Oppression: Philadelphia's African Methodists and Southern Migrants, 1890–1940* (1993) and the forthcoming book, *Inside Out, Outside In: Essays in Comparative History.*

THOMAS C. HOLT is James Westfall Thompson Professor of History at the University of Chicago. The past president of the American Historical Association, he is author of *Black over White: Negro Political Leadership in South Carolina During Reconstruction* (1977) and *The Problem of Freedom: Race, Labor, and Politics in Jamaica and Britain, 1832–1938* (1992).

TERA W. HUNTER is Associate Professor of History at Carnegie Mellon University. A specialist in African American, labor, and women's history, she is author of *To 'Joy My Freedom: Southern Black Women's Lives and Labors After the Civil War* (1997).

JACQUELINE JONES is Harry S Truman Professor of American Civilization at Brandeis University. Her most recent book is *American Work: Four Centuries of Black and White Labor* (1998). She is also author of several other books including the award-winning *Labor of Love, Labor of Sorrow: Black Women, Work, and the Family from Slavery to the Present* (1985) and *The Dispossessed: America's Underclasses from the Civil War to the Present* (1992).

ANTONIO MCDANIEL is Associate Professor of Sociology and a member of the Population Studies Center at the University of Pennsylvania. He is author of *Swing Low, Sweet Chariot: The Mortality Cost of Colonizing Liberia in the Nineteenth Century* (1995) and of numerous articles on demography, racial stratification, and social change in the United States and Africa.

CARL HUSEMOLLER NIGHTINGALE is Assistant Professor of History at the University of Massachusetts, Amherst. He is author of *On the Edge: A History of Poor Black Children and Their American Dreams* (1993) and is currently at work on a book about world historical change and American urban poverty.

Index

Adams, Henry, 80, 81, 82
Adas, Michael, 80
Addams, Jane, 16
Africa, 90
African American population: of Atlanta
    (1880–90), 129; class structure in Phila-
    delphia (DuBois), 50; conjugal condition
    in Philadelphia (1890, 1940, 1990), 172–
    75; differences in benefits (1890s, 1990s),
    30; disadvantages in Philadelphia for, 31–
    32; diversity of, 175, 178; DuBois's focus
    on health conditions, 167, 169–72; growth
    in Philadelphia (1790–1990), 157–67;
    home ownership in Philadelphia (1896,
    1940, 1990), 4, 175, 177–79; of Philadel-
    phia (1880–90), 1290–30; in Philadel-
    phia's Seventh Ward, 1–4, 8, 159; poverty
    in Philadelphia, 30, 115–16; social classes
    in Philadelphia (1896, 1940, 1990), 175,
    178; structural impediments for, 164
African American population, middle class:
    DuBois's approval of cultural behavior of,
    186–87; establishment of, 31; founding
    of NAACP and Urban League, 122; shun-
    ning poor blacks, 121, 187–88
African American population, poor: in Phila-
    delphia and Atlanta, 129–30; shunned by
    black elite, 121, 187; Urban League as ad-
    vocate for, 122
African Americans: attitude of DuBois to-
    ward lower-class, 181; in colonial Phila-
    delphia, 106; economic progress of, 178–
    79; experiences in labor market and labor
    force, 104–5; of Farmville, Virginia, 114–
    15; in marginal jobs, 225–30; prison popu-
    lation representation, 276

Agassiz, Louis, 46
Allen, Ernest, 239
American Federation of Labor (AFL), 122
Appiah, Anthony, 63, 69–70, 89
Asian population, Philadelphia, 163
Assimilation: DuBois's perspective on,
    180–82, 187; of European immigrants,
    184
Association for the Protection of Colored
    Women, 13
Atlanta: composition of population, 129;
    concentration of domestic workers in,
    135; Decatur Street, 143; economics and
    population of (1880–90), 128–29; indus-
    tries of turn-of-the-century, 129

Baby farms, 132
Bailey, Ron, 218
Baltzell, E. Digby, 83
Barbour, W. Miller, 206–7
Beard, Charles, 87
Beard, Mary, 87
Becker, Carl L., 87
Behavior, African American: antisocial, 119–
    20; DuBois's criticism of, 180, 186; factors
    influencing criminal, 272–73
Benevolent associations: benefits and ser-
    vices of, 142; class lines of African Ameri-
    can, 121
Bernstein, David, 209
Beveridge, Albert J., 80
Birth of a Nation, The, 91, 93
Black Folk: Then and Now (DuBois), 79, 93–94
Black Reconstruction in America (DuBois), 79–
    80, 91–93, 95
Blum, Gabriel, 138

Boas, Franz, 43, 56, 90
Booth, Charles, 13, 49–50, 83, 155
Brossard, James H. S., 18, 20
Brown, John, 88–89
Burgess, John William, 80, 92–93
Burk, Jesse Y., 18

Carlyle, Thomas, 87–89
Carter, E. R., 47
Cayton, Horace, 184
Channing, Edward, 80–81
Charity: for African Americans (1890s), 30;
    scientific, 28–29
Chicago School of sociology, 183
Children, African American: effect of social
    environment on, 120; influence of racial
    discrimination on, 118–19; living arrange-
    ments in Philadelphia (1940–90), 173–
    76; living in poverty, 175–76; mortality
    rates according to DuBois, 170–72
Children of Working Mothers survey, 200
Children's Aid Society, Philadelphia, 197
Churches: of blacks in Philadelphia (1890s),
    9; importance for black women, 142–43;
    social services of, 142
Cigar Makers International Union (CMIU),
    111
Cities: changing social structure of, 221; de-
    industrialization of, 224; effect of global-
    ization on inner, 220–22; effect of
    information flow and international trade
    on, 235–42; world-historical analysis of
    poverty in U.S., 223
Civic Club, 15
Code of the streets: in drug trade, 272–73;
    foundation of, 275; learning, 265; social
    behavior organized around, 262; as way of
    life, 272
Code-switching, 272
Cohen, Carole, 234
College Settlement Association: emergence
    of (1892), 197; fellowship money raised
    by, 16; organization of (1890), 6–7; Phila-
    delphia Settlement as part of, 5–6, 11; re-
    quest to DuBois, 156
College Settlement for Women (1889), 6
College Settlement News, 11
Communal life: of African American work-
    ing women, 140–41, 143; DuBois's crit-
    icism of, 144
Community, African American: DuBois's
    typology of, 259

Competition: between blacks and whites in
    labor market (1890s), 104–8; in drug
    trade, 267–68; from immigrants in labor
    market, 230–35
Congress of Industrial Organizations (CIO),
    122
Cooke, Jay, 128
Cooperation, interracial, 196
Coppin, Fannie Jackson, 15, 196
Crack cocaine, 270–76
Crime: attraction of young blacks to, 271;
    blacks in illegal occupations, 119–20;
    gang-related in Philadelphia, 205–7; in
    present-day ghetto, 261. See also Drug
    trade
Crogman, William, 46
Crotty, James, 222–23
Crummell, Alexander, 62, 79, 90
Culture: blacks' lack of (DuBois), 156–57; of
    crack cocaine and drug trade, 270–76;
    differences in (Boas), 43, 56; of drug
    trade, 263–68; DuBois's belief in Euro-
    pean American, 180–83, 186; inner-city,
    238–42; practices criticized by DuBois,
    144–45

Data: collection by DuBois of, 83–84; Du-
    Bois's appeal for, 48; of DuBois's research,
    51–54
Daughters of Bethel, 142
Daughters of Zion, 142
David, Wilfred, 218
Davis, Katherine Bement, 12, 26–27, 29
Deindustrialization: of cities, 224; effect of,
    261–63
Deprivation: effect on black psyche, 117
Dewey, Davis R., 19
Dill, Bonnie Thornton, 229
Discrimination: DuBois's perception of labor
    market, 29–30; DuBois's perception of so-
    cial, 104; effect on black psyche, 117–19;
    of employers against blacks, 264
Domestic workers: African Americans as,
    109–10, 115–16, 142; African Americans
    in Seventh Ward as, 10; African American
    women as, 106, 131–38; counteracting low
    wages, 137–38, 228–29; DuBois's criticism
    of, 136–37, 144; social networks of, 143;
    white European immigrants as, 110
Douglass, Frederick, 46
Douglass Hospital and Training School, 9
Drake, St. Clair, 184

Drug trade: attraction of, 261–68; culture of crack cocaine, 270–76; life style of dealers, 273–74; organization of conduct in, 262; production and distribution networks, 267; in underground economy, 263–68; violence in, 267–70, 273–75

DuBois, Nina (wife of W.E.B.), 1, 197

DuBois, W. E. B.: amusements approved by, 143; analysis of Philadelphia's Seventh Ward, vii, 226; Black Marxism of, 90–91; on Boas's concept of culture, 56; campaign against *Birth of a Nation*, 91, 93; consistent ideas of, 74; criticism of investigative methods of, 183; critique of Hoffman's book on race traits, 22, 45; education of, 1; historical writings, 79; influences on research methodology and conceptualization, 50–51, 83, 87; international historical analysis, 217–19; on limits on employment available to blacks, 109–13; moral standards of, 180–83; on the Negro problem, 27–28; *New York Times* articles (1901), 29–30; on reasons for poverty of blacks, 115–16; recommendations in *Philadelphia Negro*, 121–22, 202; research findings and recipe for change, 51–55, 183–89; research related to blacks in Philadelphia, 22–25, 41–51; research related to prostitution, 140; on self-determination for blacks, 196; study of Farmville, Virginia, 62, 84, 114–15; on trade-union movement, 110–12; use of Marxist terminology, 79–80

Dudley, Helena S., 7–8, 12–13, 15–16

Dunning, William A., 80, 92–93

Dusk of Dawn (DuBois), 70

Eaton, Isabel, 10, 13, 16, 108, 128, 132–36, 112–13, 128, 182

Economy, global: growth of, 261; U.S. move from manufacturing to service sector, 276

Edin, Kathryn, 227

Education: blacks attaining, 118; changes in curricula of black universities, 199–200; Institute for Colored Youth, 196; limits of availability to blacks, 109

Employers' discriminatory practices, 226, 231, 264

Employment: of black migrants to Philadelphia (1890s), 198; blacks in illegal, 119–20; of blacks in nineteenth-century Philadelphia, 3–4, 106–16; blacks' rejection of demeaning work, 228–29; of black workers in Seventh Ward, 10, 14; data and conclusions of DuBois related to blacks, 53–54; DuBois's analysis related to blacks, 25; DuBois on discrimination in, 29–30; effect of globalization on, 220. *See also* Domestic workers; Drug trade; Manufacturing sector; Services sector; Underground economy; Unemployment

Employment agencies, 132–33

Epstein, Gerald, 222–23

Ethnology: of black sociologists, 45–47; DuBois's opposition to black interpretation, 47–48; of white sociologists, 45–46

Eurocentrism, 185

Evans, Samuel, 205

Falkner, Roland, 19, 20, 22

Family, the: composition of black (1990s), 173, 175; DuBois's analysis of black family, 172–75, 181; DuBois's criticism of female-headed, 130–31, 144, 172; DuBois's social norm using European, 172, 180–82; quality of black family life, 117; single-parent, 182–83. *See also* Children, African American; Men, African American; Women, African American

Farmville, Virginia, 62, 84, 114–15

Female Cox Association, 142

Filer, Randall K., 231

Financial markets, global, 223–24

Fleming, G. James, 203–4

Fleming, Walter L., 93

Foner, Eric, 77

Fox, Hannah, 4–5, 7, 10, 11

Frazier, E. Franklin, 83, 131, 182, 187–88

Gangs in Philadelphia, 205–12

Genovese, Eugene, 82

Ghetto, the: of Black Power theory, 218; crime in present-day, 261; of underclass, 259, 261

Gilman, Sander L., 42, 47

Gilroy, Paul, 94

Girls' Home, 9

Gordon, David, 222–23

Gordon, Lena Trent, 201

Gordon, Linda, 203

Grant, Claudia, 203–4, 209–10

Great Migration, 122, 159

Guernier, Eugene, 93

Hamilton, J. G. de Roulhac, 93
Harrison, Charles C., 1, 10, 13, 18, 19–20, 83, 197
Hart, Albert Bushnell, 81–82, 87
Hayne, Joseph, 46
Hegel, G. W. F., 87, 89
Heidegger, Martin, 69–70
Hightower, James, 208–9
Hill, Octavia, 4
Himmelfarb, Gertrude, 49
Hispanic population, Philadelphia, 163
Historical analysis, international (DuBois), 217–19
Holbrook, Agnes Sinclair, 13
Home for Aged and Infirm Colored Persons, 9
Home for the Homeless, 9
Hossfeld, Karen J., 233
House of Industry, 9
Housing: of black migrants, 198–99, 201; home ownership of Philadelphia's African Americans, 4, 175, 177–79; of middle-class blacks, 200; Whittier Centre provisions of, 199
Hull House, 16
Human capital, 271–72
Humphries, Richard, 196
Hunter, Tera, 228

Immigrants: competition for job opportunities, 230–35; competition with Philadelphia's black artisans, 106–8; employment of European, 107–8; inflow of European, 157–59; in low-wage employment, 222; Philadelphia: competition with black domestics, 131–32; segregation in Philadelphia of European and black (1850–1990), 163–65; in Seventh Ward, 10–11
Immigration: DuBois's perception of European, 184; fourth wave of (1970s and 1980s), 222
Industrial Workers of the World (IWW), 122
Informal economy. See Underground economy
Information flow, 235–42
Institute for Colored Youth, Philadelphia, 9, 196
Intellectuals, African American, 185

Jafa, Arthur, 238
James, C. L. R., 80, 82

James, Edmund, 19–20
James, William, 87
Jim Crow: in Philadelphia and Atlanta, 129–30
John Brown (DuBois), 79, 87, 88–89
Johnson, Harvey, 46
Jones, Jacqueline, 225, 227, 229
Jones' School for Girls, 9

Kelley, Florence, 16
Kelley, Robin D. G., 239
Kirkbride, Eliza Butler, 7
Kirschenman, Joleen, 233, 264
Klein, A. Norman, 82
Kletzing, H. F., 46
Kusmer, Kenneth, 225, 227

Labor conflicts, World War I, 122
Labor force: blacks at onset of Civil War in, 106; blacks in postbellum, 107; black women working as domestics, 127–28; effect of discrimination on blacks, 117–19; women day-laborers, 112
Labor markets: competition between blacks and whites (1890s), 104–8; with deindustrialization, 261; DuBois's perception of discrimination in, 104; factors in exclusion of blacks from, 230–35; with globalization, 220–22; services sector, 226. See also Domestic workers; Employment
Labor movement: under New Deal legislation, 122–23; rejuvenation during and after World War I, 122
Labor unions: discrimination against blacks, 110–11, 122, 226, 231–32; integration of blacks and whites, 111; persistent racial discrimination in, 123
Lange, Werner J., 53
Lasch-Quinn, Elisabeth, 16
Legislation, New Deal, 122
Levine, Lawrence, 227
Lewis, David Levering, 50, 52, 62, 82, 87
Licht, Walter, 108–9
Lieberson, Stanley, 226
Liebow, Elliot, 228
Lii, Jane H., 232
Lindsay, Samuel McCune, 14, 17–18, 20–23, 27–28, 83
Lipsitz, George, 239
Living conditions: of black migrants, 198–99; effect of poor, 116; in Seventh Ward (1890s), 9–10

Logan, Rayford, 24, 122
Longstreth, Emily C. P., 201–2

Malcolm X, 79
Manufacturing sector: blacks employed in (1970s), 165; effect of move to service sector on, 276; factors in reduction of, 261; few blacks in turn-of-the-century, 107–8, 226; international network of, 220–21; low-wage employment in, 221–22; nineteenth-century Philadelphia, 2–4. *See also* Multinational corporations
Marx, Karl, 91
Marxism: of DuBois, 90–91, 94; post–World War I, 90
Mayhew, Henry, 83
Meier, August, 77
Men, African American: as barbers, 107; in catering business (early 1800s), 106–7; jobs as menial laborers, 106; menial labor of, 106; unemployed, 131; wages of, 117, 131. *See also* Manufacturing sector; Women, African American
Mhone, Guy C. Z., 218
Migrants, African American: flow from Southern states (1890s, early 1900s), 30–31, 198–200; slaves as, 159; women moving from South to North, 132–33
Migration, African American: DuBois's position on, 113–15, 167; Great Migration, 122, 159; influx in late nineteenth century, 141; as sign of resistance, 228
Miller, Kelly, 56
Model, Suzanne, 233
Monogenesis, Christian: as argument against black inferiority, 45–47; bypassed by DuBois, 47–48, 55
Moore, Frederick W., 19
Moral standards: of DuBois, 180–83; DuBois on discrimination, 195
Mortality rates: among black men, 130; among blacks in Philadelphia, 116, 167, 169–72
Morton, Samuel, 45
Moynihan, Daniel Patrick, 131
Multinational corporations: contempt for black workers, 236; exploitation of inner-city culture, 238–39; overseas investment, 224
Musselman, Virginia, 209
Mutual aid societies, 142

National Association for the Advancement of Colored People (NAACP): founding (1910), 122; victories of, 122
National Urban League, 122
Neckerman, Kathryn, 233, 264
Negro, The (DuBois), 79, 87, 90
Nehru, Jawarhalal, 80
New Deal legislation, 122
Newman, Katherine S., 227
Nkrumah, Kwame, 80
Nott, Josiah, 46
Novick, Peter, 77, 79, 80

Octavia Hill Association, 197

Padmore, George, 80
Pan-toting, 137–38
Parrish, Helen, 4, 197
Parrish, Joseph, 197
Patten, Simon N., 19–20
Philadelphia: composition and distribution of population, 129, 157–68; distribution of blacks in (1790–1990), 154f, 157, 159–67; DuBois's analysis of Seventh Ward, vii–viii, 6–9, 13, 22–23, 62–63, 143, 159–63, 198; economics and population of (1880–90), 128–29; growth of black population in, 157–59, 200; industries of turn-of-the-century, 128–29; nineteenth-century economy, 1–2; racial distribution (1790–1990), 158–59; Seventh and Lombard Streets, 143
Philadelphia Housing Association, 198–99
Philadelphia Negro, The (DuBois): conceptual advances in, 56; contribution of, 103; recognition of, 41–42; research methods of, 22–25, 41–51; reviews of, 26–27
Philadelphia Settlement: DuBois's home, 1; during DuBois's tenure, 11–12; founding of, 4–6, 83; institutions preceding, 9; new location (1898), 16–17; physical description, 8
Philanthropy: of Society of Friends, 196; of Whittier Centre, 198–99; 199
Phillips, Ulrich Bonnell, 93
Phipps Institute, 199
Political system: beginning of interracial cooperation in, 122–23; role of blacks in, 14–15, 122
Polygenesis argument, 45–46
Poverty: among children in Philadelphia (1940–90), 175–76; approaches of scien-

Poverty (*cont.*)
    tific charity and progressive reform, 29; of
    black population in Philadelphia, 115–16;
    Booth's research methods in study of, 49–
    50; Philadelphia (1890s), 8; world-
    historical analysis of U.S. urban, 223, 235
Progressive reform movement: approach to
    poverty, 29; DuBois as product of, 121,
    145; DuBois's contribution to, 87;
    Salmon, Eaton, and DuBois in, 128

Race: Boas's ideas about, 43; changing mean-
    ing of, 123; differences in and meaning of
    (DuBois), 48, 64–66; dilemma for black
    intellectuals related to, 185; DuBois's
    ideas about and portrayal of, 24–29, 43,
    47–48, 68–73, 87–90, 112; DuBois's solu-
    tion to problem of, 188; idea of, 63–64;
    ideas in "Conservation of Races," 63–69;
    as illusion, 73; predictions of Social Dar-
    winism, 44–45
Racial discrimination: DuBois's recognition
    of, 143–44; persistence in labor market,
    123; persistence of problem, 261; secular
    argument of DuBois against, 55; from so-
    cial conflict (DuBois), 103–4
Racial equality, DuBois's vision, vii
Racism: advocacy of overthrow (DuBois), 73;
    of DuBois's international historical anal-
    ysis, 217–19; influence of Social Darwin-
    ism on, 192n28; in underclass debate, 219.
    See also Monogenesis; Polygenesis
Rampersad, Arnold, 81
Ramsdell, Charles W., 93
Ranke, Leopold von, 80, 81
Raspberry Street Schools, 9
Reconstruction: Burgess's interpretation, 93;
    DuBois's interpretation of, 88, 91–92
Religious associations, African American, 121
Rhodes, James Ford, 80
Robinson, Cedric, 90
Rose, Tricia, 239
Rosenbaum, Robert, 209, 210
Rudwick, Elliott, 77

Saint Mary Street: description (1892), 7–8; il-
    lustration, xii; Philadelphia Settlement in,
    4–9
Saint Mary Street Colored Mission Sabbath
    School, 4
Saint Mary Street Library, 4, 197
Salmon, Lucy Maynard, 128

Sassen, Saskia, 221
Schmoller, Gustav von, 50–51, 83, 155
Scudder, Vida, 6
Secret societies, 9, 142–43
Segregation: Atlanta's residential laws
    (1922), 130; of blacks and immigrants in
    Philadelphia, 163–65
Self-help activities: of black Philadelphians,
    196; DuBois's axiom related to, 85; pro-
    moted by Whittier Centre, 199
Sentencing Project study, 275–76
Services sector: effect of move from manufac-
    turing to, 276; employment in, 221–22;
    employment of blacks in, 226
Settlement movement: residence in settle-
    ment house, 12–13, 16; spread of, 6–7
Settlements: founded by College Settlements
    Association, 7; origins of college, 6
Settlement workers: Philadelphia Settle-
    ment, 11–12; research of, 15–16
Simpson, Gordon H., 201
Sisters of Friendship, 142
Sisters of Love, 142
Slavery: in colonial Philadelphia, 106; Du-
    Bois's beliefs about influence of, 181;
    gradual abolition in Philadelphia, 106;
    John Brown's understanding of (DuBois),
    88–89; stigma of, 105
Slave trade: development of (DuBois), 72–
    73; DuBois's study of, 79, 82; effect on sub-
    merged tenth (DuBois), 217
Smith, John Caswell, 203
Social Darwinism: ideas in DuBois's research
    related to, 52–54; racism according to,
    44–45, 192n28
Social environment: effect of slave trade on
    black, 217; effect on children (DuBois),
    120
Socialism (DuBois), 73
Social services: of Society of Friends, 196; of
    Wharton Centre, 203–5; of Whittier Cen-
    tre, 198–202
Society: social classes of blacks in Phila-
    delphia (1896, 1940, 1990), 175, 178; so-
    cial control in drug trade, 262, 267, 273;
    social organizations of Philadelphia blacks
    (1890s), 9; submerged tenth of DuBois,
    50, 130–31, 140, 217, 220, 259, 261; tal-
    ented tenth of DuBois, 6, 50, 79, 203, 211
Society for Organizing Charity (SOC), Phila-
    delphia, 12; assistance from (1890s), 30;
    founding (1878), 29

Society of Friends, 196

Sociology: in "Conservation of Races," 72; criticism of DuBois's research methods, 183–84; of DuBois's first period, 79, 81; *Philadelphia Negro* in narrative of, 82; race relations analysis (1890s), 44–45

Sons and Daughters of Delaware, 142

Sons and Daughters of Moses, 142

Souls of Black Folk, The (DuBois), 79, 86, 87, 94–95, 238; "Conservation of Races" essay, 61–72; "Of the Dawn of Freedom" essay, 88

Spencer, Herbert, 44, 54

Starr, Theodore, 197

Steiner, Bernard C., 22

Stepan, Nancy Leys, 42, 47

Stillé, Charles J., 83

Submerged tenth (DuBois), 50, 130–31, 140, 217, 220, 259, 261

Suppression of the African Slave-Trade (DuBois), 79, 82, 91, 95

Tabb, William K., 218

Talented Tenth: of DuBois, 6, 50, 79, 203; work at Wharton Centre, 211

Tanner, Benjamin Tucker, 46

Taylor, Frederick Winslow, 108

Theodore Starr Park, 11, 16

Thompson, Robert Ellis, 19

Toussaint L'Ouverture, Pierre-Dominique, 82

Toynbee Hall, 6

Trade, international, 235–42

Tuberculosis, 116

Turner, Frederick Jackson, 80

Turner, Henry MacNeal, 47

Underclass, the: definitions of, 219–20; ghetto, 259, 261; human capital of, 271–72; similarity to DuBois's "submerged tenth" concept, 130–31

Underground economy: drug trade in, 261, 263–64; factors creating, 221; Philadelphia and Atlanta, 139; transition from regular to, 265–68

Unemployment: for black men, 120, 131; of inner-city people, 263

University Extension Center, 9

University of Pennsylvania: as cosponsor of DuBois's research, 4; DuBois's criticism and support of, 25–26; goals in commissioning DuBois's study, 43; relocation

(1896–97), 17, 83; Wharton School, 17–21, 156

Van Gasken, Frances C., 11

Villard, Oswald Garrison, 89

Violence in drug trade, 267–70, 273–75

Wages: of black workers, 117; for domestic work, 133; higher levels for whites, 117

Wagner, Adolf, 83, 155

Waldinger, Roger, 231, 233

Wallerstein, Immanuel, 220

Warner, Amos, 20

Washington, Booker T., 44, 85

Weber, Max, 83

Wharton, Susanna Parrish (mother of Susan), 197

Wharton, Susan Parrish, 4, 6, 10, 13, 16, 83, 197–99, 201–2

Wharton Centre: black administrators and staff, 202–12; founding of (1931), 196–97, 202; Operation Street Corner gang program, 204–5, 207–12; as sponsor of social gatherings, 206; survey of gangs, 206–7

Wharton School: affiliation of College Settlement Association with, 156; economics and statistics teaching, 19–20; instruction in sociology, 17–21

Whitaker, Albert, 200–201

White population: Atlanta (1880–90), 129; exodus from Philadelphia (1890–1990), 162–63; home ownership (1890s), 4; of Philadelphia (1880–90), 129; poor whites in Philadelphia and Atlanta, 129–30; in Seventh Ward, 10–11; working class as adversaries of blacks, 122

Whites: as domestic workers, 110; European American middle class, 180–81

Whittier Centre for the Study and Practical Solution of Negro City Problems, 198–202

Whittier Centre Housing Company, 199

Williams, Eric, 72, 80, 82

Williams, George Washington, 46

Wilson, William Julius, 187–88, 219

Wilson, Woodrow, 91

Woman's Exchange, 9

Women, African American: Atlanta: as domestic workers, 132–33, 135–37; Atlanta: employment outside domestic work, 139–40; communal labor of, 140–41, 143; as domestic workers, 106, 116–17, 131–38,

Women, African American (*cont.*)
227; employment outside domestic work,
138–39; historical work experiences of,
181–82; illegal jobs of, 139–40; limited
work opportunities for, 127–28; as majority of black population, 130; marital status (1899), 130; monetary contributions
to family, 181–82; Philadelphia: as domestic workers, 127–28, 131–33; Philadelphia: employment outside domestic
work, 138–40; as prostitutes, 139–40;
wages of, 117; work patterns and wages
of, 117, 131
Women, European American: work experiences of, 182

Women, white: Atlanta: employment opportunities, 139–40; as prostitutes, 139–40
Women as settlement workers, 12
Woods, Katherine Pearson, 16
Woodson, Carter G., 77, 185
Woolfold, Ada S., 16
Workers: black workers in low-paying jobs,
225–30; black workers in services sector,
226; effect of corporate overseas investment on, 224. *See also* Domestic workers;
Employment; Manufacturing sector
Workplace: discriminatory division of labor
in, 104, 264–65; working conditions for
blacks, 116; working conditions for domestic workers, 134–35